LIVES IN TIME AND PLACE

The Problems and Promises of Developmental Science

RICHARD A. SETTERSTEN, JR.

Jon A. Hendricks, Editor
SOCIETY AND AGING SERIES

CRC Press
Taylor & Francis Group
Boca Raton London New York

CRC Press is an imprint of the
Taylor & Francis Group, an **informa** business

CRC Press
Taylor & Francis Group
6000 Broken Sound Parkway NW, Suite 300
Boca Raton, FL 33487-2742

First issued in paperback 2018

© 1999 by Taylor & Francis Group, LLC
CRC Press is an imprint of Taylor & Francis Group, an Informa business

No claim to original U.S. Government works

ISBN-13: 978-0-89503-200-3 (hbk)
ISBN-13: 978-0-415-78421-4 (pbk)

This book contains information obtained from authentic and highly regarded sources. Reasonable efforts have been made to publish reliable data and information, but the author and publisher cannot assume responsibility for the validity of all materials or the consequences of their use. The authors and publishers have attempted to trace the copyright holders of all material reproduced in this publication and apologize to copyright holders if permission to publish in this form has not been obtained. If any copyright material has not been acknowledged please write and let us know so we may rectify in any future reprint.

Except as permitted under U.S. Copyright Law, no part of this book may be reprinted, reproduced, transmitted, or utilized in any form by any electronic, mechanical, or other means, now known or hereafter invented, including photocopying, microfilming, and recording, or in any information storage or retrieval system, without written permission from the publishers.

For permission to photocopy or use material electronically from this work, please access www.copyright.com (http://www.copyright.com/) or contact the Copyright Clearance Center, Inc. (CCC), 222 Rosewood Drive, Danvers, MA 01923, 978-750-8400. CCC is a not-for-profit organization that provides licenses and registration for a variety of users. For organizations that have been granted a photocopy license by the CCC, a separate system of payment has been arranged.

Library of Congress Catalog Number: 99-25384

Library of Congress Cataloging-in-Publication Data

Settersten, Richard A.
   Lives in time and place : the problems and promises of developmental science / Richard A. Settersten.
   p.   cm. - - (Society and aging series)
   Includes bibliographical references.
   ISBN: 0-89503-200-7 (hardcover)
   1. Developmental psychology. 2. Life cycle, Human. I. Title.
II. Series.
BF713.S48   1999   99-25384
155 - - dc21   CIP

Visit the Taylor & Francis Web site at
http://www.taylorandfrancis.com

and the CRC Press Web site at
http://www.crcpress.com

Acknowledgments

I would like to extened my gratitude to Professors Fay Lomax Cook and Tom Cook, for their unwavering confidence and guidance as mentors while I was a doctoral student of Human Development and Social Policy, and a fellow at the Institute for Policy Research, at Northwestern University (I would also like to acknowledge several traineeships provided by the National Institute on Aging and the Retirement Research Foundation, as well as a fellowship provided by the John D. and Catherine T. MacArthur Foundation); to Professor Karl Ulrich Mayer, for sponsoring a fellowship in the Department of Sociology and Social Policy at the Max Planck Institute for Human Development and Education in Berlin, Germany; and to Professors Glen Elder (University of North Carolina-Chapel Hill), Matilda Riley (National Institute on Aging), Paul Baltes (Max Planck Institute for Human Development and Education), and Robert Binstock (Case Western Reserve University) for their intellectual inspiration. Your lives and work have affected me in countless ways.

Several colleagues and students at Case Western Reserve University also deserve special recognition: Dean John Bassett, of the College of Arts and Sciences, and Professor Eva Kahana, Chair of the Department of Sociology, for their support; Professors Gary Deimling, Susan Hinze, Kyle Kercher, and Eleanor Stoller, with whom I share daily departmental life; and two former doctoral students, Ms. Joan Holup and Ms. Wendy Schoeppner, for their assistance in gathering literature and managing references. Most importantly, I wish to express my deepest appreciation to Ms. Loren Lovegreen and Ms. Lisa Dobransky, the two tireless doctoral students without whom this book would not have been possible.

I also wish to thank Professor Jon (Joe) Hendricks, of Oregon State University and Editor of the *Society and Aging* series of which this book is part, for his enthusiasm about this project and his confidence in my scholarship. Special thanks are also due to Ms. Bobbi Olszewski and other members of the Baywood staff for their hard work in bringing the manuscript to press.

Finally, I dedicate this book to Professors Gunhild Hagestad and Bernice Neugarten, of Northwestern University and the University of Chicago, respectively, for teaching me about the study of lives; and to Dan Dowhower, for teaching me how to live life. Of the many things you are, I most admire—and am most grateful for—your generosity and kindness.

To everyone who played a role in this book, thank you.

— R. A. S.

Table of Contents

INTRODUCTION 1

CHAPTER 1
The Study of Lives: Emerging Propositions and Controversies 5

Propositions from Life-Course Sociology 7
Propositions from Life-Span Developmental Psychology 25
Propositions Related to the Ecology of Human Development 33
Propositions Related to the "Triaxial" View of Human Lives 38
Emerging Debates on the Nature and Rhythm of the Life Course 39
Toward a More Flexible Life Course? Barriers and Opportunities 41

CHAPTER 2
Challenges Posed by Age and Age Structuring 65

Age Structuring and Gender 66
Age Structuring Along Other Social Dimensions 68
Age Structuring and Life Spheres 68
Age Structuring Across Cultures 69
Age Structuring and New Time Budgets for the Life Course 76
Types of Age and Time 77
Subjective Age Identification 84
Age Norms and Expectations 86
Age and Developmental Goal-Setting 96
Age-Related Images and Stereotypes 101
Life Periods 104
Age and Social Policy 106

CHAPTER 3
Challenges Posed by Generation and Cohort 109

Common Uses of the Concept of "Generation" 109
Landmarks for Contemporary Thought on Cohort: A Discussion 110
Measuring and Analyzing Cohort 117
Metaphors of Cohort Aging 134
The Problem of Historical Specificity 134

CHAPTER 4
Challenges to Understanding Lives the Long Way 137

Central Concepts and Parameters in the Study of the Life Course 137
Gathering, Organizing, and Analyzing Life-Course Data 149

CHAPTER 5
Challenges Posed by Place and Other Issues 193

Bringing Context In: Theoretical and Methodological Issues 193
Other Strategies for Analyzing Lives 211
Other Emerging Issues Related to Studying Lives 218

CHAPTER 6
An Agenda for Developmental Science 235

The Challenges Facing Developmental Science 235
Toward a New Era of Developmental Science 254

REFERENCES 257

AUTHOR INDEX 297

SUBJECT INDEX 307

ABOUT THE AUTHOR 319

The world, the race, the soul—in
space and time the universes,
All bound as is befitting each—all
surely going somewhere.

Walt Whitman, "Going Somewhere," 1867 edition of *Leaves of Grass*

Introduction

"Time," Luckmann (1991) proclaims, "is constitutive of human life in society. Of course it is also constitutive of human life in nature: *All* life is in time" (p. 151). And to paraphrase Frank (1939), time, along with place, are of the greatest significance for scientific inquiry about human lives.

As we think about the connections between lives, time, and place, we quickly become aware of the dynamic and contextual nature of our lives: As we grow up and older, some of our personality traits and characteristics, motivations, desires, aspirations, and expectations change. We move through age strata of the population, through generations within families, through schools and work organizations, through communities, and through the course of history. We accept and relinquish roles and behaviors that are expected of us across these points and in these settings. And the many settings in which our lives take place are, as we, changing, multi-dimensional, interactive, and interdependent.

As we attempt to understand the interactions between the dynamic nature of individual and group life and the dynamic nature of social settings, our scientific work becomes immensely complicated. At the same time, in contemporary and ever-changing societies, an effective analysis and explanation of lives becomes all the more pressing. This information is crucial for developing and reforming social policies, services, and interventions aimed at improving human development and welfare. One thing is certain: Matters of time and place are, and are becoming increasingly, complex and important in all areas of inquiry that relate to human lives.

The study of lives is, of necessity, an interdisciplinary and multi-method enterprise. Unfortunately, the trend in contemporary scientific research seems to be one of increased academic and methodological specialization rather than integration. As our scientific treatments become more elaborate, they become increasingly fragmented within and between academic disciplines, within and between the study of specific life periods, and across methods. Our ultimate challenge lies in moving away from this fragmentation toward a more integrated study of lives or "developmental science" (Carolina Consortium on Human Development, 1996). (I use the terms "study of lives" and "developmental science" interchangeably throughout the book. By these, I mean a synthesis of the central concepts, propositions, and methods related to human development, one that bridges scholarship in different disciplines and on different life periods.)

The many promises of developmental science depend upon whether we are able to bridge disparate disciplinary orientations and intellectual chasms, further several emerging debates, and overcome many theoretical and methodological barriers, most of which involve time or place in some form. This book is about those challenges. It explicates and critiques the central propositions and controversies in life-course sociology, life-span developmental psychology, and other disciplines; it searches for points of similarity and points of departure between them; and it discusses the emergence of developmental science as a field in its own right. While the book draws most heavily on research on adult development and aging, the challenges discussed herein are pertinent to all life periods. In fact, one of the central challenges facing developmental scientists is the significant need to extend theory and research beyond specific life periods and toward the whole of human life. Besides the challenge of studying lives *in* whole, another challenge relates to studying lives *as* wholes: As integrated systems of social, psychological, and biological functioning; and as individuals and groups with real voices and living complicated lives in a complex world. This book focuses on many of the central concepts, measures, and strategies for crafting research on age, cohort, and the life course. As such, it stands as a critique of the current state of research on the life course, and will serve as a resource for those who would like to conduct life-course research.

Chapter 1 explicates emerging propositions and controversies related to the study of lives. This first half of this chapter discusses propositions from the disciplines of life-course sociology and life-span developmental psychology, propositions related to the ecology of human development, and propositions related to the "triaxial" view of human development (the latter of which emphasizes the need to understand human experiences across three levels—those we share with all members of our species, those we share with some others, and those that are unique). The latter half of this chapter discusses several emerging debates on the nature and rhythm of the life course in modern societies. One set of debates concerns the degree to which the lives of successive cohorts have generally become "chronologized" (bound to age, and in which lifetime is of central concern), "institutionalized" (structured by social institutions and the state and its policies), and "standardized" (the degree to which their life patterns exhibit regularity, especially with respect to the timing of major life experiences). Where these debates are concerned, some scholars have argued that the life course, as a whole, has become rigidly structured and experienced; while others have argued precisely the opposite: That the life course has become, or at least has the *potential* to become, flexibly structured and experienced. Another debate concerns the degree to which pathways though specific life spheres (especially family, work, and education) have become more or less chronologized, institutionalized, and standardized. And still another debate relates to differences in the degree to which men's and women's lives are chronologized, institutionalized, and standardized. Chapter 1 closes with an exploration of some of the opportunities and barriers associated with creating more flexible lives.

Chapter 2 discusses challenges related to age and age structuring. Age structuring refers to the fact that every society has unique ways of thinking about, and organizing lives around, age. Age structuring may be *formal*, operating at the level of social structure and social institutions, or it may be *informal*, tapping the ways in which individuals and groups in a society divide the life course into meaningful segments, define the kinds of behavior considered appropriate for individuals of different ages, and designate the proper timing and sequencing of life experiences. This chapter begins by exploring some of the ways in which age and age structuring might differ by gender and along other social dimensions, across life spheres, and across cultures; and how these might be altered as a function of the dramatic change that has occurred in key demographic parameters in this century, especially longevity and mortality, fertility, and morbidity. This chapter then addresses the measurement and uses of different types of age, including chronological, biological, psychological, and social age. These are followed by a discussion of subjective age identification; age norms and expectations; and developmental goal-setting. The measurement of age-related images and stereotypes, and of life phases, are also covered. Chapter 2 closes with a brief discussion of the challenges of age and social policy, and particularly whether need- or age-based approaches to social policies should be advocated, and whether age-based policies bring the potential for age divisiveness in society.

Chapter 3 addresses the many challenges posed by generation and cohort. After a brief discussion of the common uses of the concept of "generation," this chapter returns to several classic essays that contain insights relevant to contemporary thought on cohort. It then examines issues related to measuring and analyzing cohort, including challenges associated with demonstrating cohort effects, handling the age-period-cohort problem, linking lives and history, examining cohort trajectories, and understanding the societal significance of cohort. As this chapter nears its end, it entertains metaphors of cohort aging that exist in popular culture and social science theory. It closes with a discussion of the problem of "historical specificity." That is, because most developmental research is cross-sectional, and because the longest-standing longitudinal studies are very restricted in cohort composition, much of our developmental knowledge is historically specific. Yet our theory and data are discussed as if they are valid across historical periods. The problem of historical specificity has largely been disregarded, but it is a serious problem to which we must now respond.

Chapter 4 takes up the central challenges related to understanding lives over time. This chapter opens with a discussion of the central concepts and parameters for describing the life course. The central portion of this chapter is devoted to the conceptual and methodological challenges associated with taking a long view on human lives, including the use of life-history calendars and matrices, retrospective and prospective strategies, and secondary and archival data; handling trajectories; characterizing continuity and discontinuity, and measuring change.

Chapter 5 begins by turning our attention to the central challenges associated with understanding lives in place—that is, it asks how social contexts affect human lives, and how we might better bring them into our theory and research. The chapter then explores other strategies for analyzing lives, including variable- versus person-oriented approaches; general versus differential approaches; outcome- versus process-oriented approaches; approaches the emphasize the person, the environment or the link between them; formal versus naturalistic approaches; and comparative approaches. The final section comments on several other important issues that are emerging in developmental science—questions about the relative roles of social structure and human agency in shaping lives; the documentation and explanation of heterogeneity; and what constitutes "successful" development.

To usher in what promises to be an exciting new era of developmental science, we must confront many significant challenges. Drawing largely on discussion from previous chapters, Chapter 6 highlights the most pressing of these challenges. Chapter 6 also takes up a discussion of what brings us to our subject matter, whether we can do better by it, how we might find meaning and significance in our research, and whether and how the fragmentation of disciplinary, substantive, and methodological treatments might be overcome. As such, this chapter stands as a synthesis of the book and sets an agenda for the future—as we strive to understand lives in whole and as wholes, through time and in place.

CHAPTER
1

The Study of Lives: Emerging Propositions and Controversies

This chapter explicates and discusses propositions and controversies related to the study of lives from the vantage points of different academic orientations. In this chapter and throughout the book, the disciplines of sociology and psychology are drawn upon most heavily, though select work is also included from anthropology, biology, demography, economics, history, and social policy. What are the central principles and debates that underlie and guide developmental research in these fields?[1] What are their strengths and shortcomings? At what points do these approaches to studying lives converge and diverge? The issues addressed in subsequent chapters will also relate to the propositions and controversies outlined here; they will illustrate the importance of these propositions and controversies, and inform us of what we know and need to know about them.

This first half of the chapter discusses propositions from the disciplines of life-course sociology and life-span developmental psychology, propositions related to the ecology of human development, and propositions related to the "triaxial" view of human development. The latter half of the chapter discusses several emerging debates on the nature of the life course in modern societies, including theses related to the "chronologization," "standardization," and "institutionalization" of lives, and explores some of the opportunities and barriers associated with creating greater flexibility in the life course.

Before turning to these discussions, a prefatory comment on the distinction between "life course," "life span," and "life cycle" is in order. Earlier notions of these concepts were at least in principle based on holistic conceptions of human lives (O'Rand & Krecker, 1990). The dominant theme was borrowed from biology: maturation and growth, followed by decline and regression. Only as a minor subtopic did the idea of *lifelong* development, whether actual or potential, begin to

---

[1] In covering these central propositions and controversies, I must restrict my discussion to a select but representative set of the most influential scholarship in these fields.

surface (Baltes, Lindenberger, & Staudinger, 1998). As the study of human lives has become more elaborate, its treatments have become more differentiated across disciplinary and methodological lines; even disciplinary treatments have become very specialized. While the terms "life course," "life span," and "life cycle" are often used interchangeably, most disciplines have a preference for one over the others. For example, the term "life course" is generally used by sociologists, the term "life span" by psychologists, and the term "life cycle" by biologists (and also by sociologists of the "family life cycle").[2] These terms differ in their intellectual origins and concerns. As we shall see, one of the emphases of the life-course perspective in sociology is what Nydegger (1986a) has called the "role course": age-related role transitions that are *"socially created, socially recognized,* and *shared"* (Hagestad & Neugarten, 1985, p. 35). The life-course perspective also focuses on the collective experiences of groups, and on the social forces that structure lives. In contrast, the life-span orientation in psychology emphasizes "intra-psychic" (or interior) phenomena and changes in these phenomena over the span of an individual's life. In contrast, the term "life cycle," strictly defined, refers to "maturational and generational processes driven by mechanisms of reproduction in natural populations" (O'Rand & Krecker, 1990, p. 242). That is, models of the life cycle posit movement through a fixed sequence of irreversible stages, some component of which is usually tied to the reproduction of the organism.[3] These models are *cyclical* in that they are believed to repeat themselves from one generation to the next in a given population.[4] However, as the terms "life course," "life span," and "life cycle" are commonly used, they typically do not carry strong assumptions and instead denote temporality in a general sense.

---

[2] Models of the "family life cycle" were popular among family sociologists writing in the post-war years through the early 1960s. In these models, family life was construed as moving through a fixed sequence of stages. These stages were marked by "courtship, engagement, marriage, birth of the first and last child, children's transition in school, departure of the eldest and youngest child from the home, and marital dissolution through the death of one spouse" (Elder, 1988, p. 945). These models seem wholly inappropriate in contemporary times, in which marriage and parenting are often independent of one another; family size has shrunk; a period of cohabitation often occurs before marriage; "alternative" and single-parent families are more prevalent; divorce occurs in record numbers; children return to the nest; and the joint survival time of spouses has lengthened. In addition, these early models of the family life cycle were primarily focused on the *sequencing* of these experiences rather than their *timing.*

[3] Many of the models of early "stage theorists" in the discipline of psychology were also characterized by some of these elements (e.g., Erikson, 1980; Freud, 1923/1974).

[4] These models seem deterministic and leave little or no room for deviation from the cycle (Bryman, Bytheway, Allatt, & Keil, 1987). There is little hope for such models in contemporary research: Few scholars are willing to place much value in models that are proposed as fixed and universal (transcending both time and place). As such, these models ignore the important ways in which lives are self-regulated and self-determined, and the degree to which the course they run is flexible. In addition, models that tie human development explicitly to reproduction obviously cannot be applied to the many individuals who do not, or cannot, parent. Human lives are simply not cyclical: Individuals "do not regularly return to the same points along the span of life," nor do they end life in the same state or circumstances in which they began it (Germain, 1994, p. 260). Recent scholarship, as we shall later see, has emphasized variability in human experiences and the need to understand the sources and consequences of variability.

PROPOSITIONS FROM LIFE-COURSE SOCIOLOGY

Though not often cited, the early sociological works of Eisenstadt (1956) and Cain (1964) were influential in bringing about contemporary life-course ideas. Drawing on classic writings on age status by Linton (1942), Parsons (1942), and Davis (1948) from the 1930s and 1940s, Eisenstadt and Cain both placed ideas about age status within the context of the entire life course. For example, Cain (1964, p. 272) suggested that "a social structure may be viewed as a system of statuses, and among the universal criteria in the articulation of a status system is the age of its members." From this vantage point, the life course is composed of a series of successive age-statuses that individuals are expected to hold. The age status system is "developed by a culture to give order and predictability to the course followed by individuals" as they grow older (Cain, 1964, p. 278). At about the same time, the anthropological work of Turner (1969) and, still earlier, of Benedict (1938), Fortes (1949), and van Gennep (1908/1960), was similarly instrumental in turning our attention to ways in which the passage of life time, and movement through role transitions in particular, is socially structured by rituals, ceremonies, rites and duties, and institutional procedures.

Since then, the link between social structures and human lives has been of central concern to sociologists of the life course. The work of Riley and her colleagues has been especially important in this regard (e.g., Riley, Foner, Moore, Hess, & Roth, 1968; Riley, Johnson, & Foner, 1972; Riley, Foner, & Waring, 1988). While highly critical of elements of the age-stratification framework of Riley and her colleagues, Cain himself describes their work as the "primary reason that social scientists have finally begun to recognize the significance of age and aging in ordering and directing human affairs" (Cain, 1987, p. 278).

The age-stratification framework emphasizes the movement of individuals, as they grow up and older, through various age "strata" or groups within society (see Figure 1). The horizontal axis calls attention to historical time, and the vertical axis draws attention to age. At any given point in time, represented by the vertical bars, the population is composed of various age strata. Yet an *age stratum* is a position in social structure; it is constantly replenished as old members move out of it and new members into it. This dynamic is represented by the diagonal bars, in which cohorts of individuals, born at specific points in historical time, are located in different age strata as their lives unfold.

As individuals move through these strata, they move through sequences of roles and statuses, many of which are also located in age-differentiated social and institutional settings (see Figure 2). For example, high schools and senior centers are age-homogeneous environments, with the former being largely composed of young people and with the latter being largely composed of old people. While individuals in different age strata are often found in different social and institutional contexts, some contexts are also age-heterogeneous. For example, the larger family matrix, and even the immediate family environment, is composed of individuals of many different ages. And regardless of whether specific settings are age-homogeneous or age-heterogeneous, age strata are nonetheless interdependent. What happens in one

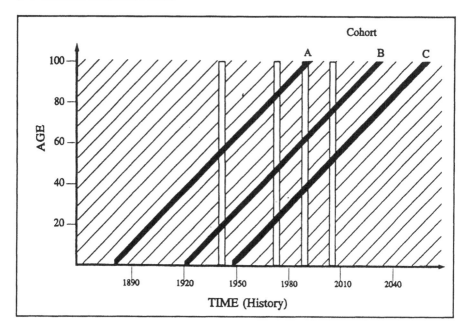

Figure 1. The age stratification system: A schematic overview.
Source: Riley, M. W., & Riley, J. W., Jr. (1994). Structural lag: Past and future. In M. W. Riley, R. L. Kahn, & A. Foner (Eds.), *Age and structural lag: Society's failure to provide meaningful opportunities in work, family, and leisure.* New York: John Wiley & Sons. p. 19.

stratum often has consequences for others, as the lives of members of different age strata are intertwined; and individuals in different age strata interact with, and are reciprocally socialized by, each other.

At the same time, chasms or conflicts may emerge between age strata. For example, shared experiences or interests within a stratum may foster its solidarity as an age-based group. Following the theoretical tradition of Max Weber and the field of social stratification in sociology, classes of successively higher ranks have increasingly greater access to valued materials or resources, greater social respect and prestige, and greater ability to control the behavior of others. Age stratification, as a specific type of stratification, therefore treats age status as a hierarchical social rank, with successive age strata affording more of the privileges just noted. (In reality, however, age may not bring these privileges, at least not in automatic and unconditional ways.) When age is linked to social rank, it brings the potential for unequal and conflicting relations between age groups in society and over the course of history. (See Chapter 2 for a discussion of the potential for age divisiveness in society.) Because population processes ultimately drive this model, factors such as cohort size and the structure of the age-sex pyramid influence the number of people in different roles in society, and therefore partially determine the amount

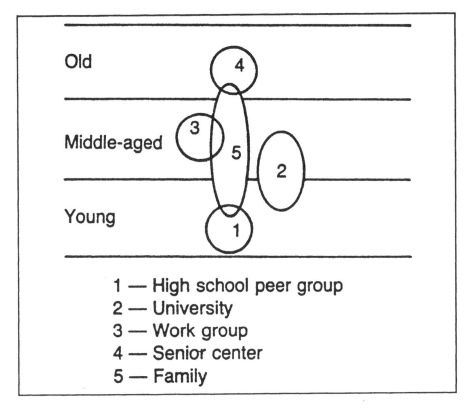

Figure 2. Relation of groups to age strata (a schematic view).
Source: Riley, M. W., Foner, A., & Waring, J. (1988). Sociology of age. In N. Smelser (Ed.), *Handbook of sociology.* Newbury Park, CA: Sage Publications. p. 246.

of competition for those roles within and between age groups (Featherman, 1986; Kertzer, 1989).

More recently, Riley's work emphasizes the "dynamic interplay" between individuals and society, both of which undergo change and influence each other. This interplay is composed of two separate but interdependent "dynamisms" (Riley, Kahn, & Foner, 1994, p. 4):

(1) People in successive cohorts (or generations) grow up and grow old in different ways because the surrounding social structures are changing. That is, the process of aging from birth to death is not entirely fixed or determined by biology, but is influenced by the changing social structures and roles in which people lead their lives.
(2) Alterations in the ways in which people grow up and grow old, in turn, press on the surrounding social structures to change them. That is, the roles available to people at particular ages are not fixed or immutable but are

reshaped by the collective actions and attitudes of the people who are continually aging, moving through the roles, and being replaced by their successors from more recent cohorts.

Therefore, human lives are shaped by, and themselves shape, social structures, and both are constantly changing.[5] While provocative, these concepts, and the dynamics between them, are difficult to handle in both theory and practice. (The challenges of measuring and analyzing change within and between individuals, as well as change in social contexts, will be addressed in Chapters 4 and 5.) How might we conceptualize and measure "structures," and *changing* structures? Which aspects of "lives," and of *changing* lives, should we study? How might we analyze the link between them and their reciprocal relations? What processes or mechanisms drive these changes and relations?

Riley also argues that while lives change rapidly (and they have, in fact, changed dramatically in this century), social structures fail to keep pace with these changes, thereby creating "structural lag." Yet many questions remain unexplored: How and why does this lag occur? Can anything be done to control it? From where do pressures for structural change come, and how do these pressures come about? What are the effects of structural lag? The asynchrony between structures and lives presumably creates strain for everyone, from individuals to the larger society. But need the effects of asynchrony be only negative, or might asynchrony also serve positive functions? For whom does lag carry negative or positive effects, and in what forms?

In one direction of the interplay, where change in social structures creates change in lives, Riley and Riley suggest that "the shifting character of work and the family, and by wars, depressions, energy shortages, and the like have significantly altered lives in the course of this century" (1994, p. 22). However, as I will argue in Chapter 3, little is actually known about *precisely how* these larger scale changes have had important effects on lives, particularly in the long term, and how these changes have taken on significant personal meanings.[6] Riley also reminds us of important intervention research that has demonstrated how changes in the environment can produce powerful developmental gains, even among individuals who are already functioning at high levels.

---

[5] Riley often uses the term "social structures" interchangeably with "age structures," though age structures would seem a subset of the larger concept of "social structures" (see also the discussion of the concept of "social structure" in Chapter 5). These ideas are also in line with writings of several classical and contemporary social theorists, especially the "structuration theory" of Anthony Giddens (1979, 1984). The theory of structuration emphasizes the "duality of structure." To understand social action (and interaction) we must understand the rules and resources of institutional structures, and vice versa. As Turner (1991, p. 523) puts it: "social structure is used by active agents; in so using the properties of structure, they transform or reproduce this structure. Thus the process of structuration requires a conceptualization of structure, of the agents who use structure, and of the ways that these are mutually implicated in each other to produce varying patterns of human organization." These ideas are therefore directly in line with the emerging emphasis in the developmental literature on the relative roles of individual agency and social structure in shaping human lives, which will be discussed in this chapter and in Chapter 5.

[6] An exception here is the work of Elder and colleagues, which will be discussed shortly.

In the other direction of the interplay, little research has explored the "radical postulate" that changes in lives can, in turn, bring about changes in structures. This reciprocity, with human beings actively shaping their environments, is a key element in ecological formulations, and is emerging as a dominant proposition in developmental science at large. (This proposition will be discussed later in this chapter.) However, relative to other work, Riley focuses much more on large-scale macro-level phenomena than on individual-level phenomena.

The age stratification framework, as a macro-level framework, draws our attention to larger, distal forces that impact human lives. Yet it is difficult to specify precisely how these phenomena affect lives, what factors and mechanisms bring about these effects, and which individuals and groups are and are not affected. (See Chapter 3 for a discussion of these challenges, especially those related to studying the effects of historical events and periods of social change within and between cohorts.) Individuals and groups are variably exposed to these phenomena, and the effects of these phenomena may be tempered by the "locational" status (e.g., gender, race, cohort) and resources (e.g., social, psychological, or economic) of an individual or group.[7]

The age stratification framework also overemphasizes the ways in which the life course is structured *for* individuals and groups rather than the ways in which the life course is actively negotiated, uniquely experienced, and subjectively interpreted *by* individuals and groups. This is true of much sociological work, which tends to take a rather deterministic approach to studying human development, assigning individuals little capacity for agency and or action (Hendricks, 1992; Marshall, 1995b). (Debates about the role of human agency versus that of social structure in shaping the life course will be discussed in Chapter 5.)

The age stratification framework may also be criticized for too closely drawing parallels between age stratification and other types of stratification (e.g., social class, race, or stratification by sex), and particularly for assuming that "age-based inequality" is hierarchical, and for neither clarifying this concept nor specifying its forms. Similarly, the age stratification framework may be criticized for its limited attention to cohort, for obscuring the distinction between an age stratum and a cohort, and for its lack of attention to the directions provided for, and constraints placed upon, people in different strata. In fact, Cain (1987) argues that "age stratification theory provides an inaccurate conceptualization of age-related social phenomena, and that it provides an intellectual rationale for undermining a commitment to fairness and equity among various age groups" (p. 291). In the end, Cain argues that the life course must instead be represented as an "horizontal progression, not as a vertical and hierarchical arrangement" (p. 291).

However, Riley's work, as well as that of Ryder (1964, 1965), has been instrumental in calling our attention to the connection between human lives and social

---

[7] Of course, locational status and resources are not mutually exclusive. Locational status at least partially (and some would argue largely) determines the resources to which an individual or group has access.

structure, as we have already seen, and especially to the age structure of the population and the dynamics of "cohort flow and replenishment," to use Waring's (1975) phrase. This led to new thought on the link between life course and social change (see Elder's principles outlined below, as well as Chapter 4). Riley's work, along with the pioneering work of Neugarten and her colleagues at the University of Chicago in the 1950s and 1960s, was also instrumental in focusing our attention on *adult* life, especially middle age and beyond, and on the meanings and uses of age for individuals and society (e.g., Neugarten, 1968a).

The most important of Riley's other propositions are her four "fallacies" of developmental research: the life-course fallacy, and the fallacies of cohort-centrism, age reification, and reifying historical time (Riley, Foner, & Waring, 1988). The *life-course fallacy* refers to the fact that developmentalists often mistake the age *differences* discovered in cross-sectional research designs for age (maturational) *changes*, which can only genuinely be documented with certain types of longitudinal designs. (These issues relate to the challenges of separating age, period, and cohort effects, and to the challenges of conducting longitudinal research, which are discussed in Chapters 3 and 4.) The *fallacy of cohort-centrism* reminds us that all cohorts do not age alike, and that we cannot assume that what is typical for one cohort applies to other cohorts. The experience of aging is bound by cohort and the ways in which social, cultural, and environmental changes have uniquely affected a cohort. (Chapter 3 is devoted to the challenges posed by generation and cohort.)

The *fallacy of age reification* calls attention to developmentalists' misuse of chronological age: Researchers often use age as a causal variable, paying little attention to why age is important, what exactly it indexes, and the mechanisms through which it plays itself out in their models. Age, in and of itself, is an "empty" variable. (Chapter 2 is devoted to the challenges of age and age structuring.) Like the fallacy of age reification, the *fallacy of reifying historical time* calls attention to the fact that historical time is also an "empty" variable. Researchers often use aspects of historical events and periods of social change as causal variables, but give little thought to why and precisely how these large-scale events and changes affect the development of individuals and cohorts or take on important personal meanings. (These challenges will be discussed in Chapter 3.)

The fallacies of cohort-centrism and of reifying historical time illustrate one of the central propositions of life-course sociology: that lives are linked to historical time. This link is what Mills (1959) called the "interplay of man and society, of biography and history, of self and world" (p. 4). In a triumphant passage from Mills' treatise on the *Sociological Imagination* (1959), Mills proclaims that "we have come to know that an individuals lives, from one generation to the next, in some society; that he lives out a biography, and that he lives it out within some historical sequence. By the fact of his living he contributes, however minutely, *to* the shaping of society and *to* the course of its history, even as he is made *by* society and *by* its historical push and shove" (p. 7, emphasis added). Similarly, Hughes (1950/1984) reminds us that "Every man is born, lives, and dies in historic time. As he runs through the [life course], each phase if it joins with events in the world . . . Such joining of a man's life with events, large and small, are his unique career, and give him many of his personal problems" (p. 124).

However, social theorists have suggested that individuals may seldom be aware of the intricate connection between the course of their own lives and the course of national or world history. But in order to fully understand human development, it is important for us to better grasp history, biography, and the relations between the two, and *changes* in these over time. (For an overview of social and psychological thought on the link between personality and social structure, see the now classic writings of Gerth & Mills, 1953; Inkeles, 1959; Parsons, 1964; and, more recently, House, 1981; House & Mortimer, 1990.)[8] These connections are so important that Riley, Kahn, and Foner (1994) recently described them as the "new challenge" for developmental scientists: the challenge of understanding how individual life paths, and the collective life trajectories of birth cohorts, are shaped by changing social structures and the course of history. This new challenge serves as a reminder that history, and the imprint it leaves on human lives, lies at the heart of one of the most central concepts with which developmental scientists must wrestle: cohort (Riley, 1973; Riley & Uhlenberg, 1996; Rosow, 1978; Ryder, 1965; Uhlenberg & Miner, 1996). (The challenges of cohort will be discussed in Chapter 3.)

Perhaps more than any other sociologist, the work of Elder and his colleagues has driven recent advances in life-course theory and research. Elder's framework sets out to examine the ways in which historical events and larger periods of social change have an effect on the subsequent life course. Elder and Caspi (1990) describe two models for studying the effects of specific historical events and larger periods of social change on the life course. However, these models are helpful in thinking about the connections between earlier and later experiences more generally. These models are presented in Figure 3. In Model A, a specific life "outcome" is our focus, and we move backward through time, building into our model past events that may be directly linked to our outcome. These experiences may be *proximal* to our outcome in time, or they may be *distal*. For example, if we are interested in understanding the timing of fatherhood as an outcome, we might link it to more proximal states, such as immediate career demands (X) or financial status (Z); and we might link it to events more distal, such as the timing of marriage (Y), which may be linked to

---

[8] Alwin (1995) notes that most developmental theories of personality either emphasize or assume that processes of socialization in social environments are "generally thought to be responsible not only for the development of regularities in behavior, but also for the medium through which individuals acquire a range of behavioral dispositions, involving language and other symbolic systems, identities, values and goal priorities, beliefs, social norms and ways of behaving, skills, and knowledge" (p. 213). Yet I would argue that most references to socialization are vague and unspecified. Socialization processes and their sources are treated as large, external, abstract forces that loom above, and impose themselves upon, individuals. While the concept of socialization is an integral part of developmental thought, little is known about the precise sources of socialization and their relative importance, how their messages are transmitted, the content of those messages, and their successes and failures. Most importantly, little is known about socialization processes as they extend *across* the life course, and particularly throughout adult life and into old age. In fact, I am aware of only a few papers on socialization beyond childhood, all of which were published two to three decades ago (e.g., Brim, 1966, 1968; Bush & Simmons, 1981; Mortimer & Simmons, 1978; Wheeler, 1966).

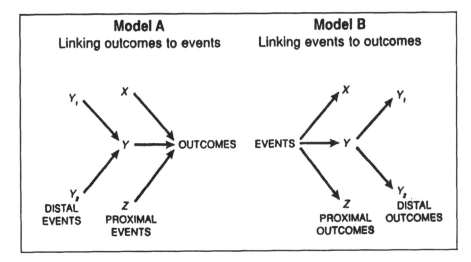

Figure 3. Studying social change in the life course: Two models.
Source: Elder, G. H., Jr., & Caspi, A. (1990). Studying lives in a changing society: Sociological and personaological explorations. In A. I. Rabin (Ed.), *Studying persons and lives: The Henry A. Murray lectures in personality.* New York: Springer. p. 212.

events still further back in time, such as the timing of school completion (Y_1) or the timing of military service (Y_2). In this case, we capture an event in which we are particularly interested, such as military service, as one of many prior experiences that ultimately affect the timing of fatherhood.

In Model B, on the other hand, a specific event earlier in life is our focal point. Here, we examine the ways in which that particular experience plays itself out over time, tracing its short- and long-term effects (both proximal and distal outcomes). For example, if we are interested in understanding the effects of military service, we begin with that experience and link it to proximal outcomes, such as a disruption to work history (X) or psycho-social adjustment (Z); and we might link it to more distal outcomes, such as a delay in marriage (Y), which may lead to late fatherhood (Y_1) or affect marital satisfaction (Y_2).

If we are interested in studying the full range of consequences brought about by an experience, and if we are interested in charting out the mechanisms through which that experience expresses itself, Model B is clearly preferable. Model A, the outcome-oriented model, slights these issues. As Elder and Caspi (1990) note, "even if some antecedents [in Model A] tap historical changes of great significance, the design does not focus on the process by which they find expression in lives. We end up with a partial assessment of a historical event . . . History thus becomes a smaller part of the picture from analysis through interpretation" (pp. 212-213). In contrast, the very intention of Model B is to seek "to understand the consequences of a type of social change for the life course, [pursuing] the implications of change wherever they may lead" (p. 214).

Elder offers five principles to help us examine the link between social change and the life course: the life-stage principle, the interdependence of lives, control cycles, situational imperatives, and the accentuation principle. The *life-stage principle* states that the impact of an historical event (such as a war or economic crisis, which is easily dated) or a larger period of historical change (such as the civil rights or women's movements, which is more difficult to date in precise terms), should generally depend on the timing of that event or period of change within an individual's life. And as a birth cohort grows up and older, its members encounter historical events and changes at approximately the same point in the life course; successive birth cohorts encounter those events and changes at different points in the life course. As a result, the impact of the event or change is likely contingent on the position of the cohort when the historical event or change occurs.

As an example of the life-stage principle, consider children's experiences during the Great Depression. Children who were in early or middle childhood at that time were completely dependent on their families; youth in their early teens were too young to leave school, but too old to be completely dependent on their families; many adolescents were expected to find employment or care for younger siblings and manage household activities while their mothers worked. We might think about the life-stage principle more generally as one of *timing*—that the nature of an individual's experience with an event or transition is dependent on when (the age at which) it occurs. (As we shall later see, timing is one of five key parameters for describing and analyzing life-course experiences and trajectories.) For Elder and others, age serves as a proxy for the general "life stage" of the individual or cohort. This strategy may become less effective as a means for approximating life stage as lives potentially become more individualized. (This debate will be outlined later in this chapter, and the challenges of cohort will be discussed in Chapter 3.)

The principle of *interdependence,* or of *linked lives,* is simply that individual lives are intimately connected to those of others, and that an individual's development is bound to, and shaped by, those ties. This basic idea, which is tied to literature on attachment, social exchange, and social roles, underlies many concepts, including "interpersonal synchrony" and dyssynchrony (Cairns, Neckerman, & Cairns, 1989), "counterpart transitions" (Riley, Foner, & Waring, 1988), "consociates" (Plath, 1980), "life-event webs" (Pruchno, Blow, & Smyer, 1984), "ripple" effects (Hagestad, 1981), "developmental reciprocities" (Klein, Jorgensen, & Miller, 1979), and "social support convoys" (Kahn & Antonucci, 1980).

While we recognize that lives, in actuality, are critically interwoven, we generally study lives as if they exist in isolation of others. We must begin to ask questions of our respondents meant to tap the interdependence of lives, capture those experiences from the vantage points of those involved, and unpack the nature, meanings, and consequences of interdependence over time. One assumption in the literature is that interdependence creates unexpected changes and circumstances. What happens in the life of one individual has implications for the life of another, and this interdependence creates the need to actively coordinate and synchronize lives as much as possible to reduce potential friction. When lives are "out of synch," or asynchronous, relationships are likely strained in significant ways. For example, couples generally plan retirement jointly; the timing of retirement for one partner is often contingent on when the other plans to retire, and vice versa.

Another assumption in the literature is that these linkages are enabling and provide important resources to individuals. For example, during times of hardship, family members serve as important sources of emotional or economic support. At the same time, these linkages may also constrain and foreclose the options open to individuals (e.g., they may lead to an unequal distribution of work and family roles and responsibilities). For example, "women in the middle" (Brody, 1981) who simultaneously care for both older parents and dependent children may do so at the expense of their careers. Much remains to be learned about both the enabling *and* constraining aspects of interdependence.

Besides interdependence between spouses or partners, and between parents and young children or young adult children, we also have much to learn about the interdependence of these relations in later periods of life, and about the impact of multi-generational linkages and dynamics on the lives of individual family members. In addition, we must develop methods that allow us to simultaneously take account of multiple lives in our analyses. We are in great need of strategies that permit us to bundle lives together and examine what Plath (1982) calls the "bumping and grinding of lives in action."

Elder's three remaining principles relate to changes in the environment and their impact on the life course. Changes in the environment upset the balance in individual or group life, threatening one's sense of control or the ability to control one's circumstances. These changes impose new demands, or *situational imperatives,* on individuals or families. This creates a *control cycle,* as individuals struggle to regain equilibrium. For example, the Great Depression created economic strain for families and forced families to respond. Households became more "labor intensive," as families had to produce more goods and services instead of buying them; teenagers played adult roles within the household, caring for their younger siblings and taking greater responsibility for domestic chores so that both parents could search for work.

Situational imperatives typically accentuate the existing characteristics of individuals and the dynamics in place in environments, whether positive or negative (hence, the *accentuation principle*). For example, fathers' tendencies toward irritability and "explosiveness" with children became magnified during the Great Depression. Generally, accentuation involves *negative* characteristics or dynamics, though this should not preclude the possibility that *positive* characteristics or dynamics might also (or instead) be accentuated. For example, the documentary *Troublesome Creek* records the efforts of an Iowa family to save their debt-ridden small farm that has been in their family for 125 years. In the film, Jeanne Jordan, the daughter of Mary Jane Jordan, notes that her mother has long been the "family optimist"; but in her struggle to save the farm, her optimism increases in an effort to raise the spirits of the other family members. An alternative meaning of the accentuation principle, though not an explicit part of Elder's framework, is that in adapting to new circumstances, people draw on the social and psychological resources that they bring to those situations. That is, they rely on and accentuate their strengths in adjusting to these impositions and in regaining control.

Several of the projects that form Elder's research program have demonstrated the power of some of these principles in the lives of children and adolescents in the Great Depression (e.g., Elder, 1974), Iowan families who experienced the farm crisis of the 1980s (e.g., Conger & Elder, 1994), and men who served in the military during World War II (e.g., Clipp & Elder, 1995; Elder, 1986, 1987; Elder, Shanahan, & Clipp, 1994).

Like Elder, Alwin (1995) emphasizes the importance of linking individual development and social structure, and suggests that there are two basic approaches to studying this link. In the first approach, we look for the origins of social experience and try to find evidence of the influence of social structures on individuals. We often examine how social structures condition or constrain individuals' opportunities, and we correlate position in social structure and the properties of individuals. As discussed later, this approach is problematic in that the characteristics of individuals are often used as proxies for their position in social structure. A second, less developed (but emerging) view takes a more dynamic view of the person and the environment. This view brings many significant theoretical and methodological challenges, which are discussed in later chapters. In the meantime, let me emphasize the five central principles that Alwin suggests characterize this second, more dynamic approach. First, similar to Riley and others, Alwin's *principle of reciprocity* states that links between individuals and their environments are reciprocal (individuals influence their environments just as they are influenced by their environments).

Second, the *principle of behavioral individuality* states that we must view each individual as unique, part of which is due to the unique experiences between the individual and her or his environments. At the same time, the third principle, that of *common experience,* stresses the fact that while each individual is unique, she or he is nonetheless similar to others, part of which is the result of common or shared experiences between individuals and their environments. There is an obvious tension between the principle of behavioral individuality and the principle of common experience. (In Chapter 3, this tension will also emerge around two of the problems related to the definition of cohort, that of "distinctive experience" and that of "differential effects.")

Fourth, the *principle of temporal heterogeneity* emphasizes the fact "human experiences change over historical time" (p. 222). However, Alwin's use of the term "heterogeneity" is different from that of others (see Chapter 5). Alwin does *not* seem to be referring to the fact that individuals become increasingly different from one another over time as a function of their unique experiences in history (though the principle of behavioral individuality, noted above, did emphasize heterogeneity with respect to the more general experiences of an individual with the environment). Instead, Alwin seems to be referring to the simple fact that history is always changing, and that the potential kinds of experiences that individuals or groups might have are also changing with it. Alwin's use of this principle therefore seems focused on general historical change (historical time) itself, without any specific concern for how individuals and groups are affected by history, or which specific aspects of history affect them. As such, the principle of temporal heterogeneity seems an integral part of Alwin's fifth principle, the *principle of life-span dynamics.* The principle of life-span dynamics emphasizes that the "link between the person and the society is not necessarily invariant over biographical time" (p. 223). That is, individual time is framed by historical time, and individual time is shaped by the nature of the societies of which they are part during that particular slice of historical time. As the two kinds of time unfold, the relationship between them is ever-changing. These principles reinforce my plea, and those of others, for developmental scientists to study lives *in time* and to take the many challenges posed by time more seriously in our theory and research.

Recent research in life-course sociology has also emphasized *variability*. That is, the life course is not uniform, but is instead the product of a multi-faceted set of social, biological, and psychological factors and experiences that interact to shape the pathways of individuals and groups in unique ways. (The challenges posed by variability will be discussed in Chapter 5.) This relates to one of the central propositions in both the psychological and sociological literature: that human lives are more malleable, or "plastic," than was once thought.

Another important proposition in both psychological and sociological literature is that development throughout adulthood, and especially in later life, need not be about decline (or at least not only about decline), but may also involve important gains. Development is now considered a *lifelong* process, beginning at birth and continuing to death, and not a process that ends in early childhood or early adulthood, as many scholars long believed. Psychological, social, and even biological gains may continue through the many decades of adult life.

In addition, the assumption that experiences early in childhood largely determine subsequent pathways through adolescence and adulthood is no longer *en vogue*. While early life-course experiences certainly set the stage for, and have an impact on, later experiences, these experiences need not be deterministic nor so constraining that individuals cannot move beyond them in some capacity. (See also the discussion of the "Mathew Effect," and of issues related to risk and resilience, in Chapter 5.) However, much remains to be learned about the bridges between earlier and later development, and especially between the first and second halves of life.

The ethos in contemporary literature is therefore dramatically different from the ethos just decades ago. For example, Ryder, writing in 1965, was highly critical of models of individual development at that time, particularly the "early crystallization" model that dominated the literature and neglected the issue of social change:

> [T]he literature on human development presents life as a movement from amorphous plasticity toward terminal rigidity. The preparatory phase, during which individuals are susceptible to influence, is distinguished from the participatory phase, during which their predetermined destiny is unfolded. [For example,] the central social-psychological postulate in the spirit of Freud is that the core of personality is laid down at the beginning of life; what may look like changes later are merely minor variants on the established theme. The popularity of this assertion is as indubitable as its irrefutability. Discussion in this vein confuses ineluctable species characteristics and culturally variable designs, and fails to cope with the phenomenon of societal change (pp. 851-852).

Models that depict human lives in these ways neglect their dynamic and variable nature. However, it is important to remember that through the first half of this century, the study of human development was largely the study of child development. It was not until the relatively recent past that developmental scientists turned their attention to *adult* development and *aging*. As developmental scientists began to turn their attention to the years beyond childhood, several important challenges emerged (Elder, 1998). This shift made it clear that the concepts and issues at stake with respect to children's development would not serve well the study of adults; it raised difficult questions about the ways in which lives remained stable or changed over time; and it called for greater attention to proximal and distal social contexts and their impact on lives. These remain some of the most important challenges facing contemporary developmental scholarship. In addition, these early models were developed under very different demographic conditions. As discussed later in this chapter, dramatic demographic change in this century alone—in longevity and mortality, morbidity, and fertility—has set new and largely unknown parameters on human life and development.

Sociological research has also emphasized the importance of understanding *lives in place;* that is, the ways in which lives are shaped by the settings in which they are lived. These settings include larger cultural and sub-cultural contexts, and the many primary contexts in which everyday life takes place: families, peer and friendship groups, schools, workplaces, and neighborhoods. (The challenges associated with understanding the effects of social contexts on lives will be discussed in Chapter 5.)

Life *events, transitions,* and *trajectories* are central concepts in sociological approaches to the life course (Elder, 1998). The concept of a life *trajectory,* or *pathway,* is similar to that of a career. A trajectory is long in scope, charting the course of an individual's experiences in specific life domains (or spheres) over time. The individual life course is composed of multiple, interdependent trajectories (for example, work, family, and educational trajectories). Trajectories are punctuated by a sequence of successive life events and transitions. Events and transitions are brief in scope, and refer to changes in an individual's state. However, an *event* is usually conceptualized as a relatively abrupt change, while a *transition* is usually conceptualized as a more gradual change, and one which is usually tied to the acquisition or relinquishment of roles. (These concepts, and other central parameters for describing lives, will be discussed in Chapter 4.)

Sociological research has also called attention to the *interlocked nature of trajectories and roles.* Family, work, and educational trajectories are intertwined, and individuals occupy many roles simultaneously. What happens along one trajectory likely has an effect on what happens along another, and roles held along each trajectory are often coordinated with roles along another. Women's labor force patterns are a good example, as work-related decisions are often a function of family demands and responsibilities. Asynchronous trajectories are likely to create strain for individuals, as when demands in one sphere are incompatible with those in another. (The challenges associated with analyzing single and multiple trajectories are discussed in Chapter 5.)

In addition to Elder's principles already described, Mayer's explication of the assumptions and tenets of life course research stands as the clearest statement of the sociological perspective, and particularly the *macro-sociological* perspective (e.g., Mayer & Tuma, 1990). Mayer confines most life-course research to multidisciplinary theory and research that emerged in the United States and Western Europe in the mid-1970s and beyond, whereas Elder (1992) traces the origin of the life-course tradition in sociology to two eras further back in time.[9]

For Mayer, the life course refers to the "social processes extending over the individual life span or over significant portions of it, especially [with regard to] the family cycle, educational and training histories, and employment and occupational careers. The life course is shaped by, among other things, cultural beliefs about the individual biography, institutionalized sequences of roles and positions, legal age restrictions, and the decisions of individual actors" (Mayer & Tuma, 1990, p. 3).

Like life-span psychologists, life-course sociologists take as their mission to *describe* and *explain* individual-level life outcomes. However, life-course sociologists pay greater attention to the micro-social and, especially, macro-social forces and experiences that shape those outcomes and the life course as a whole. *Macro-sociological* approaches focus on the ways in which social forces, including social institutions and social policies, structure the life course. These forces guide, and even dictate, the movement of individuals through social roles, positions, and statuses through time, giving the life course its shape and equipping it with a set of standard meanings, expectations, and aspirations. In addition, the macro-sociological approach focuses on the collective life patterns of birth cohorts, and on differences in life-course patterns both within and between cohorts.

However, in macro-sociological frameworks, the life course is often portrayed as being shaped exclusively by social structures and forces. As a result, subjective concerns are generally of little or no importance in these frameworks. Whether individuals are aware of larger structural influences, and how individuals evaluate, live out, and give meaning to their lives, are largely irrelevant. For example, an "institutionalized" life course (as it is structured through social institutions and policies), which will be discussed shortly, may be "pervasive" in the degree to which it generally structures experiences, but "loose" in the personal meanings and particular experiences it holds for the individual (Marshall, 1995a). The institutionalized life course is a "set of rules and preferences of a formalized but highly abstract kind. There is a great deal of slippage when it becomes translated into the actual experience of individuals, whose real life courses have more anomalies and

---

[9] Elder suggests that the first wave of research relevant to the life-course tradition was associated with the Chicago school of sociology (~1915-1935), which focused on social problems and experimented with the gathering of life histories as a research method. Here, the life-course tradition was particularly inspired by Thomas and Znaniecki's (1918-1920) *The Polish Peasant in Europe and America,* which used and advocated qualitative life histories and archival records as a method for examining the link between social change and individual and family lives. The second wave of relevant work occurred in the 1960s, with new interest in adult development and aging and in understanding variability in human experiences. These developments were especially associated with the work of Neugarten, Ryder, and Riley, noted earlier in this chapter.

THE STUDY OF LIVES / 21

unpredictabilities than the official system" (Meyer, 1986a, p. 203). So while the "official" (institutional) model of the life course structures individual expectations and self-definitions, the *precise* ways in which these expectations are fulfilled and self- definitions are created are not institutionalized (Marshall, 1995a).

In contrast, *micro-sociological* approaches take the subjective to be central phenomena of interest. These approaches focus on the subjective experiences of individual "actors," the meanings actors create and the plans they make as they move through life. In some micro-sociological approaches, individuals may even be aware of, and react to, macro-level social forces. These approaches may also contrast the ways in which individual life courses actually unfold relative to official "institutionalized" versions of the life course. However, in other micro-sociological frameworks, distal social structures and forces are neglected. While sociological approaches to the life course can be found at purely macro- or micro-sociological levels, *it is the intersection between these levels that represents the most exciting juncture for the study of lives.*

For macro-sociologists, the life course is also understood to be a *unit of social structure* and an *institution of socialization* in its own right. For example, Mayer stresses the view that the life course "is an element of social structure that is a product of both individual action, organizational processes, and institutional and historical forces" (Mayer & Tuma, 1990, p. 6). As individuals became increasingly freed from traditional forms of informal social control (e.g., status, locality, family; Kohli, 1986a), the state began to regulate individuals more formally, thereby "institutionalizing" lives.[10] As a result, individual lives have become increasingly structured by separate institutional domains and by the state's regulation of those domains (Mayer & Müller, 1986). In fact, some sociologists have conceptualized the life course as a series of "status passages" (Glaser & Strauss, 1971) that are embedded in the structure of the state (see edited volumes by Heinz, 1991a, 1991b, 1992; Weymann & Heinz, 1996). In this framework, we must better understand the social processes that move people between state-regulated positions, and the experiences people have as they do so. These scholars are particularly concerned with discontinuity, and the ways in which structural arrangements place individuals at risk for discontinuous lives. At the same time, the state and its policies are often aimed at

---

[10]The term "institutionalization" is problematic to the degree that it is a "catch-all term whose most general sense is expressed by Feibleman's (1956, p. 52) well-known saying that institutions are frozen answers to fundamental questions" (Levy, 1996, p. 91). We should therefore make our formulations more explicit. Precisely what forms does institutionalization take, and through what mechanisms does it come about? To move in this direction, we might consider two components of institutionalization: (1) the "proportion of a person's actions and relationships which take place in institutionalized interaction fields (scope of institutional coverage)," and (2) the "degree of control exerted [over the individual] within these fields (domination)" (Levy, 1996, p. 198). We might examine whether there has been an increase (or decrease) in the number of specific passages that are regulated (e.g., entries and exists from institutional fields); the degree to which those passages are regulated by time and age; the duration of participation within specific institutional "fields"; the rigidity (or flexibility) around the sequencing of an individual's participation in those fields; and the number of available options at any given entry or exit point. We might also consider both direct and indirect forms of institutionalization, and whether these forms of institutionalization unify or fragment life-course experiences.

fostering continuity by providing individuals with resources in times of need and reducing the degree to which the individual is dependent on others. This work has shown that we can no longer portray the life course as a stateless entity.

Social policies are often problematic in that they treat statuses in binary "0,1" terms; that is, they characterize an individual as being either fully in or fully out of a status (e.g., fully in or out of the labor force, or completely in or completely out of school) (Leibfried, 1998). As (or if) the life course becomes destandardized (that is, as life patterns exhibit greater variability, which will be discussed later), statuses and their categorizations become less clear. As a result, a mismatch may occur between the actual statuses of individuals (which are more complicated than simple dichotomies) and the ways in which our policies deal with these statuses and categorize individuals. This is not only an issue for the policies of the welfare state, but also for the policies of organizations. In Leibfried's terms, social policies are "rough instruments" rather than "continuous adjustors." In addition, social policies, and much life-course research for that matter, are fixated on what Leibfried calls the "2 e's"—entry and exit, particularly into and from paid work—rather than the life course as a whole. How much can we extrapolate future policies on the basis of current ones? How can we adapt social policies to respond to (and shape) new life-courses? This also reiterates the earlier point that individual life courses can only be understood within *the contexts of historical time* and the *collective life patterns of the birth cohorts* to which they belong.

Kohli's (1986a, 1986b) ideas strengthen the position that the life course, as a social institution, creates a system of rules and regulations that order key dimensions of life, and has become increasingly important over historical time. Kohli (1986a) describes an historical shift toward (a) *temporalization,* in which the life course emerges as an institution in its own right, and in which lifetime as a whole becomes a core dimension of social structure; (b) *chronologization,* in which age becomes a (if not the) basic element of social structure, and the life course becomes standardized in an age-normative fashion; (c) *individualization,* in which individuals are released from the traditional ties and mechanisms of social control associated with of "status, locality, and family"; and (d) an *emphasis on the system of labor,* in which the life course becomes increasingly organized around the occupational system within a society. In addition, Kohli notes that the "patterns of rules constituting the life course" can be considered at two different levels: at an objective *structural* level (that is, as a sequence of positions, or "careers," through which individuals move in the course of their lives); and at a subjective *biographical* level (that is, that we must consider the individual's perspective, decisions, and actions).

The emergence of an age-bound life course as an institution of socialization, and as a system of rules and regulations that order life, resulted from and solved several structural problems. These problems included the need (a) to organize public services and transfers in a rational manner (see also Neugarten, 1982), (b) for new forms of social control particularly as the process of individualization freed individuals from traditional forms of social control, (c) to find ways to allocate positions and roles in different social domains (see also Sørensen, 1986), and (d) to better integrate and synchronize aspects of family and work.

As noted earlier, sociological frameworks also emphasize that the state and its policies have come to play a greater role in structuring the life course (Mayer & Müller, 1986; Mayer & Schöpflin, 1989; Meyer, 1986a, 1986b; Thomas, Meyer, Ramirez, & Boli-Bennett, 1987). This authority evolved through the establishment of citizen rights and duties, as well as through the emergence of the welfare state. The state promotes a "higher degree of structure in the life course" by defining most of the "ports of entry and exit" through which people move as their lives unfold (Mayer & Müller, 1986). As the state has increasingly sought to act directly on individuals, age has become a central dimension with which the state is concerned. The work of sociologist Meyer (1986a, 1986b) also supports the notion that the life course has become highly institutionalized in modern societies, in which individuals have freedom only within a framework of institutional constraints.

The institutionalization of lives occurs not only through state intervention and regulation of the life course, and the opportunities and constraints created by its policies. It also occurs through "institutional careers" or pathways in secondary and higher education and in work organizations, and through the collective conditions that specific cohorts face and in which multiple cohorts interact. Institutionalization means not only that the life course is explicitly regulated and structured in these ways, but it also involves "the structuring of the *life-world perspectives* by which individuals orient themselves and plan their actions" (Kohli & Meyer, 1986, p. 147). Thus, this perspective holds that social institutions and policies create both constraints and new "potentialities" for individuals, actively organize the life course, link life stages, and enhance the development of the self (by integrating action and situations at a subjective level, and by fostering a sense of continuity for the self over time). At the same time, both Kohli and Meyer note that there is evidence that the process of institutionalization has stopped or may even have reversed itself (e.g., Held, 1986), thereby carrying the potential to *de*institutionalize lives. However, they suggest that such claims must "at least be grounded in a framework which accounts for the fact that this would mean the reversal of a secular trend" (Kohli & Meyer, 1986, p. 147).

As noted earlier, life-course research must not only cover *multiple life domains* (e.g., family, work, education), but it must *link domains* together (what happens in one domain often has implications for another). Likewise, single events (e.g., marriage, divorce) or specific life phases (e.g., adolescence, adulthood, or old age) cannot be adequately understood if they are studied in isolation. Instead, they must be examined *within the context of the prior life course* (that is, as outcomes and consequences of earlier conditions and experiences). The impact of earlier conditions and experiences may also be unintended or unforeseen. As a result, the life course becomes "an endogenous causal system."

Life-course research must also be conducted at *multiple levels of analysis,* linking, for example, "individual development, formal organizations (e.g., schools, firms), cohorts, ethnic groups, localities, and nation-states" (Mayer & Tuma, 1990, p. 7). *Time* and *timing* are essential for our understanding of the life course, and *lifetime* is both an important resource and constraint. For example, at an individual level, being "on-time" or "off-time" may affect role duration, time left over for other activities, and perceptions of success or failure. Besides examining individual time, life-course theory and research must also take into account other kinds of time, including "organizational time (e.g., age of a firm), historical eras (e.g., the 'war' years), and point-in-time events (e.g., a change in national laws)" (Mayer & Tuma, 1990, p. 7). These linkages (between multiple levels of analysis and different kinds of time) must be made both theoretically *and* methodologically. Approaches to handling these linkages are discussed in Chapters 4 and 5.)

As we will see momentarily, both life-span psychologists and life-course sociologists state the importance of *multidisciplinary research* as a central proposition of their perspectives. Yet sociological research on the life course seems broader in practice, covering the fields of demography, economics, social history, sociology of the family, the sociology of education and labor markets, social stratification and social mobility, and social psychology and socialization. However, as discussed in the final chapter, genuinely *interdisciplinary* research seldom occurs.

Mayer also puts forth a few additional propositions with which most sociologists will agree: that the life course is not synonymous with aging; that the duration of time spent in a role or position is often more important than chronological age in understanding the life course (chronological age is not a perfect indicator of position in the life course); and that patterns of age norms are secondary, and not primary, determinants of the life course. In addition, Mayer argues that psychological and biological forces operate *independently* from the socio-structural forces outlined above, and only partly condition the life course.

Finally, the framework of Clausen (1986, 1993) explicates four important "classes of influence" on an individual's development over time and her or his performance in various roles that structure the life course. These, too, are representative of the emphases of many life-course sociologists. First, we must consider the *attributes* of the person, whether these are *given or developed* (e.g., intelligence, appearance, strength, health, temperament). Second, we must consider the individual's sources of *support, guidance, and socialization* (e.g., things that initially orient individuals to the world in which they will function, and things that will assist them in coping with life circumstances and situations). Third, we must consider the *opportunities* available to the person or the *obstacles* that are encountered in the environment. These are likely to be influenced by one's social class, ethnic group, age, sex, and social network; they may be due to the effects of war, depression, and other major social changes; or they may be completely due to chance. And fourth, we must consider the *investments of effort* that individuals make on their own behalf, not only in the degree to which they are committed to specific goals, but also in the ways they mobilize resources to reach their goals.

With respect to the second class of influence—the sources of support, guidance, and socialization—it seems important to recognize that some of these influences may be negative as well as positive. The second class of influence, along with the third class—that of opportunities and obstacles, would also seem related to many social factors and contexts. For example, the opportunities and obstacles that individuals face, and the degree to which they receive positive support, guidance, and socialization, are a function of how individuals are sorted in schools and workplaces, and how they are treated in families, peer groups, neighborhoods, and society at large. These draw our attention to the importance of interactions between individuals and social contexts, and to social processes operating within those contexts. We need to understand not only the ways in which contexts, and changes in contexts, shape individuals' lives over time, but also the ways in which individuals select, are selected into, and themselves shape those contexts. (These tasks are daunting both conceptually and empirically, and are discussed more fully in Chapter 5.)

PROPOSITIONS FROM LIFE-SPAN DEVELOPMENTAL PSYCHOLOGY

The traditional concept of development in psychology proposes the general and universal movement of individuals through a fixed, linear, irreversible, age-dependent sequence of qualitatively different stages toward some ultimate end (for further discussion, see Baltes et al., 1998; Youniss, 1995). In this conception, individuals move through increasingly higher levels of functioning, incorporating at each level the capacities that were developed at earlier points. Developmental scientists gradually realized that these general, unidirectional growth models did not reflect their data, which instead often suggested non-linear and even discontinuous patterns, differences in the timing and the rates of functioning, simultaneous gains and losses, and little or no transfer between earlier and later functioning and experiences. The traditional psychological model also does not take into account the multiple and interacting social contexts in which individuals live, the degree to which these contexts constrain or promote developmental opportunities, and the ways in which contexts create individual differentiation. It overlooks the process of adaptation, especially that required of individuals in everyday life, with its many demands and tasks. And because these models are proposed as universal (and are therefore assumed to transcend time and place), they completely disregard dynamics between age, period, and cohort, and the challenges they pose for theory and research (see Chapter 3).

At the other extreme of psychological approaches to development are views of "probabilistic epigenesis," to use Gottlieb's (1970) term. In these views, development "does not follow an invariant or inevitable course, and, more specifically, that the sequence or outcome of individual behavioral development is probable rather than certain (Gottlieb, 1970, p. 123). Probabilistic ontogenesis results from "indeterminate combinations of genes and environments," and multi-level interactions between them (Scarr, 1982, p. 852). From this vantage point, development cannot be well predicted, and certainly cannot be explained by general laws. As a result, the traditional psychological view that human development is dictated by invariant and universal nomological principles is "seriously hampered by the fact that developmental trajectories observed in different biographical, cultural, and historical contexts usually exhibit a broad range of variation" (Brandtstädter, 1990, p. 83), creating what Gubrium and Holstein (1995, p. 207) have called "life-course malleability." There is therefore a growing tendency to consider as futile those efforts aimed at discovering nomological principles of human development.

However, is the conclusion that developmental scientists should only hope to form historically- and culturally-specific "quasi-laws" too premature a conclusion? Perhaps in our search for nomological principles we adhere too strictly to the "common lore" that developmental phenomena must be shown to be manifested in *precisely* the same matter across *all* social, historical, and cultural contexts (Brandtstädter, 1990). Is this a reasonable proposition, or is it too demanding? If we adhere strictly to the principle that developmental phenomena are irreversible because time itself is irreversible, do we render many methodological axioms futile and set limits on the verification of discoveries across cultures and historical periods? (For further discussion, see Valsiner [1998].)

The early work of Bühler and her collaborators, and that of Erikson, was important in setting the stage for the life-span orientation in psychology (see Valsiner & Lawrence, 1997). But perhaps more than any other life-span psychologist in the last few decades, it is the work of Baltes that has been most instrumental in shaping contemporary developmental scholarship. The fundamental premise of lifespan developmental psychology is that "ontogenesis" (individual development) is *lifelong* (Baltes et al., 1998). That is, development does not stop in adulthood, but extends across the whole of life from birth to death; in addition, no single age period is taken to be more important than any other. (Few would contest the former point, though the latter point seems questionable, as possible gains during the later years of life surely pale in comparison to gains in the early years, and as possible losses in the early years of life pale in comparison to losses in the late years.)[11] While development during any given period of life may be unique, it is experienced within the context of the past, present, and (anticipated) future. Some developmental processes are "continuous" and extend across life (Baltes calls these processes "cumulative," though this implies that these processes also grow exponentially,which need not be the case). Other processes are unique to certain periods or "discontinuous" over time (Baltes calls these "innovative," though this implies that these processes are positive, which need not be the case). (The concepts of continuity and discontinuity, and of stability and change, are discussed in Chapter 4.)

An example of the proposition of lifelong development is the anthropological research of Gutmann, who has long emphasized the possibility that the second half of life may be filled with new potentials and capacities (see Gutmann [1997] for a compilation of his research). This theme is especially salient in Gutmann's earlier research, the focus of which was the "strong face of aging," its sources, its powers, and the significant contributions that elders make to other people's lives and to

---

[11]In recent work, Baltes has stated that in late adulthood, and especially advanced old age, the balance between gains and losses in outcomes becomes less positive, if not negative (Baltes, 1997). In addition, the plasticity (or malleability) of human potential decreases with age, and the optimization of development becomes increasingly difficult, particularly as life is extended to its maximum biological limits (Baltes & Smith, 1999).

society. The aging self, in particular, has the chance to expand in later life, and does not necessarily become stagnant or fragmented.[12]

The analytic level with which life-span developmental psychologists are concerned is the individual, and the individual's "mind and behavior." As Baltes and his colleagues put it:

> [T]he objective of life-span psychology is: (1) to offer an organized account of the overall structure and sequence of development across the life span; (2) to identify the interconnections between earlier and later developmental events and processes; (3) to delineate the factors and mechanisms which are the foundation of life-span development; and (4) to specify the biological and environmental opportunities and constraints which shape life-span development of individuals. With such information, life-span developmentalists further aspire to determine the range of possible development of individuals, to empower them to live their lives as desirably (and effectively) as possible, and to help them avoid dysfunctional and undesirable behavioral outcomes (Baltes et al., 1998, p. 1030).

As I will later argue, the current state of research in life-span psychology, and in developmental science at large, has significant distance to go in meeting these objectives. A conception of "environmental opportunities and constraints," stated as part of the fourth objective, is particularly absent.

Life-span developmental theory and research is aimed at examining *regularity* in development (presumably across time and space); *individual differences* in development between people ("inter-individual" differences); and *plasticity* (malleability, modifiability) of development within individuals ("intra-individual" plasticity). It is also presumably aimed at understanding the *degree* of regularity, inter-individual differences, and intra-individual plasticity in development, and *how* and *why* each of these occur.

These emphases led Baltes and his colleagues to define the three major "adaptive tasks" or "developmental objectives" of the human organism as: (1) *growth* (behaviors directed at attaining higher levels of functioning or "adaptive capacity"), (2) *maintenance and recovery* (which together form what they label "resilience"; these behaviors are directed at maintaining one's levels of functioning when confronted with challenges, or at restoring one's prior level of functioning after a period of decline), and (3) *regulation or management of loss* (behaviors directed at maintaining adequate, though lower, levels of functioning when maintenance and resilience are not possible). To these ends, Baltes and his colleagues suggest that an individual's resources are allocated differently depending on life period. More resources are allocated toward growth during childhood, toward maintenance and recovery during adulthood, and toward the regulation of loss during old age. These

---

[12] However, Gutmann's later, more clinical, work shifted toward the "weaker face of aging," to its psychological disorders, and to the movement from being an "elder" to being "aged." This is an important break from much gerontological scholarship, which continues to stress the positive aspects of aging to the neglect of the negative aspects (see also the section on " 'Successful' Development and Aging" in Chapter 5).

scholars also take a "deficit-breeds-growth" view of development, suggesting that growth is possible even in the face of limitations or constraints. That is, when an individual faces deficits of some kind, these deficits may pose challenges that can create opportunities, or serve as catalysts, for "adaptive capacities."

In the framework of life-span psychology, individual development is *multidimensional* and *multidirectional*. Development occurs along multiple domains, and its direction may vary along, or even within, these domains. In fact, development is viewed as the simultaneous occurrence of both gains (growth) and losses (declines) within and between domains of functioning (see also Uttal and Perlmutter, 1989). In this tradition, one of the most common approaches is to define "successful" or "effective" development in terms of *maximizing* or *promoting gains* and *minimizing* or *managing losses* (Baltes, 1987; Dixon & Bäckman, 1995; Marsiske, Lang, Baltes, & Baltes, 1995). Baltes and his colleagues even go so far as to say that "there is no development without a loss, as there is no loss without a gain" (Baltes et al., 1998, p. 1046). As a result, they argue that a gain-loss conception is able to incorporate emphases on the "active or passive, conscious or subconscious, internal or external, and continuous and discontinuous" (p. 1044). This also does not preclude the possibility that the sum-total of gains and losses may be positive at an overall, systemic level, and may continue over time. The question of what constitutes "gain," "loss," and "stability" are tricky matters, concerns about which are addressed in Chapter 4. Complicating these matters further is the possibility that "what is considered a gain and what [is considered] a loss changes with age, involves objective in addition to subjective criteria, and is conditioned by predilection, cultural context, as well as historical time" (Baltes et al., 1998, p. 1030). However, definitions of gain and loss have rarely been consistent or even explicit, and psychological treatments of development have largely neglected cultural and historical contexts.

In an effort to strengthen these definitions, we might, for example, make a distinction between gains and losses that are permanent (irreversible) or impermanent (reversible), those that are more or less beneficial or devastating depending on the age or period of life at which they are experienced, or those that are biologically-based versus psychologically-based (Uttal & Perlmutter, 1989). And as we consider the relations between gains and losses, we need not assume that the two are causally related, which is typical of scholarship in this area. Along these lines, Uttal and Perlmutter (1989) introduce four interesting models for thinking about the relationship between gains and losses. Two models assume that gains and losses are causally related: the *suppression* model, which assumes that gains precede and cause losses; and the *compensation* model, which assumes that losses precede and cause gains. In contrast, two models do *not* assume that gains and losses are causally related: the *unrelated phenomenon* model, which stresses "simultaneous gains and losses that follow the occurrence of other simultaneous but independent factors; and the *spurious phenomenon* model, which stresses "simultaneous gains and losses that follow the occurrence of a single other factor" (p. 107). The challenge of determining whether and how gains and losses are related, especially within a causal framework, is very difficult, but we must take seriously the challenge of expanding our theory and research in these directions.

The role of *optimization* is also a crucial element in psychological frameworks, and particularly in Baltes' model of "selective optimization with compensation" (SOC) (Baltes & Baltes, 1990; Marsiske et al., 1995). The SOC model can be applied to either general or domain-specific conditions. The individual selects an optimal developmental pathway in which developmental gains are maximized and developmental losses are minimized. This pathway is selected from a pool of more or less constrained potentialities and the subsequent selective optimization of the entered pathways . . . As a given pathway of ontogenetic development is chosen and optimized, others are ignored or suppressed" (p. 1045). (For a related discussion, see the section on the "Cultural Canalization of Development" in Chapter 2.) When losses are experienced, and especially when those losses affect the individual's means to a developmental end, the individual finds ways to compensate for those losses by acquiring new means, whether internal or external, to that end. Therefore, the SOC model treats development as a process of *selective adaptation* within the *confines of limitations and resources* (presumably of any type, psychological, social, or otherwise).

More recently, Baltes has incorporated what Kruglanski (1996) has called "equifinality" into his framework. *Equifinality* emphasizes that the same developmental outcome may be reached through a variety of means (or some combination therein). Two kinds of equifinality may be applied to development goals. One type of equifinality is based on the *contingency principle,* in which the appropriate choices for attaining the developmental goal will depend on one's situation or circumstances. The other type of equifinality is based on the *substitutability principle,* in which, if one path to a goal is blocked, the goal can be reached via an alternative, substitutable path.

Baltes' SOC model need not be restricted to the study of later life. These models, which emphasize adaptation, are useful for thinking about development at any age (Elder, 1998). However, these models make the narrow assumption that individuals are simply (and ultimately) concerned with maximizing personal developmental gain. Instead, it would seem important to consider gain-loss dynamics within the context of larger social relationships. For example, an individual may be interested in maximizing the difference between personal gain and the gain of another person (*competitive*); an individual may be concerned more with minimizing the gain of another person rather than maximizing personal gain (*vindictive*); an individual may seek to maximize both personal gain and the gain of another person (*cooperative*); or an individual may be even more concerned with maximizing another person's gain over her or his own gain (*altruistic*). (For an interesting application of these principles, see Thorngate [1992].) These more complex dynamics might also be extended to the interaction between individuals and groups (e.g., family, community, nation). For example, an individual might accept personal loss for the benefit of a group, or an individual might seek personal gain at the expense of a group.

As noted earlier, life-span psychologists emphasize the plasticity of the human organism, and the need for developmental scientists to study individual "potentialities" and "test the limits" of human potential, its conditions, and its ranges. The emphasis on plasticity in developmental thought seems partly a counter-response to prevalent assumptions that the course of human life takes the shape of an inverted-U: significant growth during the early years, stability through the middle years, and significant decline in later life. Of course, plasticity can be a "double-edged sword" in that a system that is open to improvement is generally also open to decline (Lerner, 1985, p. 182). Along these lines, Baltes and his colleagues do note that "despite the sizable plasticity of homo sapiens, not everything is possible in ontogenetic development, and development follows principles which make universal [constant] growth impossible" (Baltes et al., 1998, p. 1048). Baltes and his colleagues now categorize the traditional conception of development (noted above) as a "special class" of phenomena within their reformulation of development as an "ongoing, changing, and interacting system of gains *and losses* in adaptive capacity" (p. 1046). Whether one views plasticity at a general or domain-specific level, the degree of plasticity may differ by age (Marsiske et al., 1995). In addition, plasticity may be examined with respect to "baseline reserve capacity" (the actual level of plasticity of an individual) or with respect to "developmental reserve capacity" (the possible level of plasticity of an individual, given the right conditions, and given an intervention to assist the individual in optimizing her or his potential) (Kliegl & Baltes, 1987).

The concept of plasticity has long existed (Baltes, 1984, p. ix). For example, it appeared as a significant entry in Baldwin and Poulton's (1902) *Dictionary of Philosophy and Psychology*, and was defined there as "that property of living substance or of an organism whereby it alters its form under changed conditions of life" (Vol. 2, p. 302). The significance and forms of plasticity examined over the decades of this century have varied, but significant interest in the concept sparked in the 1970s and 1980s and has continued steadily through today. Lerner (1984, p. ix) suggests that this interest is likely the "direct expression of some basic tensions inherent in the developmental enterprise" (Lerner, 1984, p. ix). The significant tension about which Lerner speaks is that developmental scientists (or some subset thereof) are, on the one hand, attracted to a search for universal developmental processes and mechanisms; on the other hand, many (if not most) developmental scientists question such universals, particularly as we acknowledge the need to understand the specific conditions that regulate developmental processes and mechanisms, and as we search for applications to improve developmental plasticity (or to at least improve the *potential* for plasticity).

For developmental science to progress, we must renew theory and research in line with fundamental questions about the nature and limits of human plasticity (Lerner, 1984). First, to what degree does plasticity exist at different levels of analysis (e.g., from the genetic through societal levels), and in what forms? What are its lower and upper limits? Second, how does plasticity come about, and what are its enabling functions across various levels of analysis? Third, how might answers to the prior questions vary by age? And fourth, how might answers to these questions be useful in guiding developmental modification and intervention? When do the potential gains of our action (or inaction) outweigh the potential costs? Might there also be unintended effects of action (or inaction)?

The life-span perspective in developmental psychology necessitates a long view of individual development, as does the life-course perspective in sociology. Developmental scientists claiming to take either of these perspectives must better incorporate the whole of life into their thinking. It is inadequate to focus on a specific life period without considering (theoretically or empirically) the ways in which given developmental sequelae might play themselves out over time. There is a significant need for developmentalists who concentrate on different life periods to not only work together, but especially to *integrate* existing theory and research across multiple life periods into their work. Baltes and his colleagues (1998) make a similar point, noting that ". . . for good life-span theory to evolve, it takes more than courtship and mutual recognition. It takes a new effort to serious exploration of theory that . . . has in its *primary* substantive focus the structure, sequence, and dynamics of the *entire* life course" (p. 1034, emphasis added). This also relates to another key proposition on which most developmental scientists, regardless of discipline, agree: that the study of lives is, of necessity, a *multidisciplinary* enterprise; what is more, it ought to be an *interdisciplinary* enterprise (though as we will see in Chapter 6, several barriers have largely prevented this from happening).

The Treatment of Context in Life-Span Psychology

The "nature-nurture question" has long engaged the attention of developmental psychologists (Plomin, 1994; Plomin & McClearn, 1993). How much of human development is attributable to heredity, how much to the environment, and why? These questions have most often been explained in relation to psychological traits and characteristics, and to cognitive and intellectual functioning. While gene-environment interactions are difficult to examine for any life period, these questions become increasingly difficult to explore with age. (That is, as years of experience in and with the environment cumulate, it becomes increasingly difficult to disentangle the unique contributions of heredity, the environment, and the interaction between them in producing development.)

While "historical embeddedness" and "contextualism as paradigm" are included among the family of life-span propositions, few life-span psychologists take these principles seriously in their theory or research. The proposition of *historical embeddedness* means that individual development is shaped by the unique social and cultural conditions that exist at any given point in history. And the proposition of *contextualism as paradigm* means that individual development is influenced by the interaction of three systems of developmental forces: (1) "normative age-graded," (2) "normative history-graded," and (3) "non-normative" influences (Baltes, Reese, & Lipsitt, 1980). *Age-graded* influences are age-correlated biological and social experiences that shape the development of all individuals. *History-graded* influences are those aspects of biology and of the social environment that shape (presumably all) individuals' development, but differ across historical periods. However, the principles of Elder and his colleagues and those of Riley and her colleagues, which were described earlier, suggest that historical factors are not experienced in "normative" ways by all individuals, but that their effects instead differ depending on the age (or life stage) of the individual or on other personal characteristics. *Nonnormative* influences are those biological or social experiences that are infrequent (and even idiosyncratic) but nonetheless have important effects on individual development. These three sets of influences interact over time and create both similarities and differences between people. However, these are not "contexts" in the way that other social scientists, and particularly sociologists, have conceptualized them. While recent life-span psychologists have paid more attention to the social, cultural, and historical forces that shape development, they "generally fail to apprehend *social structure* as a constituitive force in development" (Elder, 1998, p. 944, emphasis added). In the words of Kohli and Meyer (1986, p. 146), [i]t is "not sufficient to speak of 'context' or 'environment' as an aggregate of variables or factors. Instead, they have to be conceptualized as a patterned set of rules and mechanisms which regulate a key dimension of life, namely, its temporal extension. In this sense, the life course is one of the basic social institutions, systematically connected with the other elements of social structure."

Dannefer has presented the hardest-hitting critique of the approach to context in life-span psychology, arguing that it is little more than *ontogenetic reductionism*—the "practice of treating socially produced and patterned phenomena as rooted in the characteristics of the individual organism" (Dannefer, 1984, p. 847). (This critique led to counter-charges of "sociological reductionism" [Featherman & Lerner, 1985]. Just as it makes little sense to "level down" and reduce most of individual development to micro-biological and physiological processes, it also makes little sense to "level up" and attribute most of individual development to macro-sociological processes operating in more distal environments.) Ontogenetic reductionism leads to the superficial treatment of context and largely disregards the social processes that organize the life courses of individuals and cohorts. In Dannefer's words, to "state that the environment is important, to mention it often, and to include in it definitional statements [does] not together mean that research will be designed, nor findings interpreted, in a way that apprehends social structure as a constitutive force in development, and that views the social environment as more than a setting that facilitates maturational unfolding" (p. 847).

Baltes' framework, as most approaches in developmental psychology, can be criticized for considering the environment most relevant in creating differences between cohorts (as a result of historical context) and in bringing about developmental patterns that deviate from the "normative" (which they treat in a statistical sense by focusing on modal age patterns or, in most cases, average age patterns). However, in research, the "degree to which a normal or modal pattern occurs will likely depend on the degree of homogeneity of the *environments* from which the sampled individuals are drawn" (Dannefer, 1984, p. 848). In addition, while Baltes offers "socialization" as an example of normative age-graded environmental influence, we cannot assume that the content and transmission of socialization processes are uniform across a society. When we do, we disregard important individual differences among age peers, and the "differentiated and stratified every-day experiences" in social contexts that produce them; in addition, frequent and general references to "social change" in these frameworks also suggest that the environment would be less important, or perhaps might even be ignored, if it were not for this (Dannefer, 1984, p. 848). Yet the social remains critical to the study of human development, regardless of whether society is stable or undergoing change, as we will see in the next section on the ecology of human development.

Nonetheless, the early work of Baltes, Schaie, and their colleagues (e.g., Baltes, Reese, & Lipsitt, 1980; Baltes, Cornelius, & Nesselroade, 1979; Baltes, Reese, & Nesselroade, 1977; Schaie, 1965; Schaie & Baltes, 1975) on age- and history-graded influences, and the corresponding separation of age, period, and cohort effects, set the stage for many of the important methodological advances that followed. These include (a) a movement from cross-sectional, to longitudinal, and finally to cross-sequential designs; (b) new concern with describing and classifying life experiences, their correlates, and their consequences and important methodological advances brought about by event-history analysis and associated methods; (c) more use of experimental simulation in research; and (d) methods designed to "test-the-limits" of human plasticity or potential (Baltes et al., 1998).

PROPOSITIONS RELATED TO THE ECOLOGY OF HUMAN DEVELOPMENT

Life-course sociologists have taken issue with the degree to which life-span psychologists have downplayed or even neglected the role of social, cultural, and historical contexts. However, Bronfenbrenner's "bio-ecological" framework, most notably outlined in the landmark *Ecology of Human Development: Experiments by Nature and Design* (1979), is an exception in this regard. Bronfenbrenner has long emphasized principles only now being advocated seriously in contemporary developmental scholarship. In addition, the early emphasis of Riegel (1976, 1979) on the "dialectical" contradictions between individuals and external forces was instrumental in pushing forward the conception of human development as a dynamic, contextual, and transactional process. These early ecological frameworks were also facilitated by the work of field theorists in the discipline of psychology.

Bronfenbrenner builds his framework on the classic psychological work of Lewin (1931, 1935). Lewin posed the equation, $B = f(PE)$, which states that behavior (B) is a joint function of the person (P) and the environment (E). Bronfenbrenner (1988) altered this equation to $D = f(PE)$, replacing B with D, which stands for an individual's development more broadly, rather than concrete behavior. Bronfenbrenner's emphasis on the developing person, the environment, and the interaction between the two, posed a new theoretical perspective for research on human development. Development, for Bronfenbrenner, is defined as a lasting change in the way in which an individual perceives and deals with the environment.

Levels of the ecological environment are compared to a set of Russian dolls, each inside the next. At the inner-most level is the immediate setting containing the developing person, which is surrounded by successively larger or more distal settings. This conception of the environment cannot be taken too literally, because social settings are rarely perfectly nested one inside another, and there are multiple settings that may be equally near to or far from the developing person. The structures and processes in the immediate setting containing the developing person are labeled the *microsystem*. The basic unit of analysis in such a schema is the dyad, but larger interpersonal systems are also important—triads, tetrads, and beyond.

The next level, the *mesosystem*, leads us away from single immediate settings, and instead toward the connections and processes occurring between two or more immediate settings in which an individual is present. The mesosystem therefore essentially becomes a system of microsystems (for example, a child's development is shaped by the relationship between home and school, both of which are settings the child experiences directly).

As we move farther afield, we recognize that an individual's development may be significantly affected by settings in which the individual is not even present, or the *exosystem*. The exosystem consists of the connections and processes between two or more settings, at least one of which does *not* contain the developing person, but nonetheless has an important effect on the individual (for example, a child's development may be shaped by the relationship between the home, in which the child is contained, and the parent's workplace, in which the child is not contained). Finally, moving still farther afield, we recognize that all levels of the ecological environment are nested within a culture or subculture, an overarching *macrosystem*.

These systems point to the fact that it is important to consider not only the mechanisms through which features of the immediate setting affect the individual, but also the mechanisms through which features of more distal settings can influence the individual both directly and indirectly. A similar dynamic is an important element in the framework of Elder and his colleagues, described above, in which large-scale macro events, such as wars or depressions, play themselves out in individual lives, and as those effects are often filtered through, and experienced in, lower-order, more proximal settings.

Interlocking meso-level primary worlds—such as communities and neighborhoods, workplaces, families, and peer groups—would seem particularly important in filtering more distal level changes. For example, Hagestad (1990) suggests that it is through primary groups that "historical events affect resources and the adequacy of existing [coping] strategies; cultural values and norms are interpreted and mediated; societal demands are buffered; timetables are negotiated; and shared understandings are created and re-created in long chains of interaction" (p. 162). Similarly, Hareven (1994) argues that, historically, the family has been the setting in which most life-course events and transitions are experienced and given meaning. Of the many factors that shape human behavior and experience, interpersonal relationships are certainly among the most powerful and become an important force in connecting people to larger environments (Peterson, 1992). As we seek to understand various levels of the environment that affect lives, we must therefore understand the relationships between people and groups within those settings. These examples also illustrate the importance of linking micro and macro levels of analysis as we develop theory and conduct research.

Bronfenbrenner initially labeled his model a "process-person-context" (PPC) approach to studying human lives. As such, any research design in line with this model must gather data in three separate areas: the *contexts* in which development occurs; the *personal characteristics* of the individuals in those contexts; and the *processes* that bring about development. More recently, Bronfenbrenner (1995; Bronfenbrenner & Ceci, 1994; Bronfenbrenner & Morris, 1998) renamed this a "bio-ecological model," and added an additional dimension—time—resulting in a "process-person-context-*time*" (PPCT) approach. With this addition, Bronfenbrenner emphasizes the fact that processes, people, and contexts are not static, but dynamic. This is consistent with an emerging emphasis on time and change in developmental theory and research.

Full PPCT research designs and models remain rare in developmental research, though "truncated" designs and models (missing select elements related to processes, personal characteristics, contexts, or time) have become more prevalent. Most research has also focused on the proximal influences on human lives, especially Bronfenbrenner's innermost level, the "microsystem." We must examine more distal forces operating at the meso-, exo-, and macro-levels, as well as the mechanisms through which these forces affect individuals. One of the most difficult challenges facing life-course researchers is to adequately chart out the ways in which macro-level forces play themselves out in lives, and the ways in which *changes* in larger environmental contexts create *changes* in individuals. (These and related challenges are discussed in Chapter 5.)

When Bronfenbrenner's framework was introduced, what was probably its most unusual feature was its conception of development. Its emphasis was *not* on traditional psychological processes of perception, motivation, thinking, or learning, but instead on their *content:* on what was perceived, feared, thought about, or acquired, and how the nature of these "psychological materials" changed as a function of the individual's exposure to, and interaction with, the environment. Development was redefined as the individual's evolving conception of, and relation to, the ecological environment, and the individual's growing capacity to discover, sustain, or alter its properties. Also unique were Bronfenbrenner's emphases on *reciprocal activity and interaction* between the individual and the environment; and on *ecological transitions* in which an individual experiences a shift in settings, a change in roles along with a shift in settings, or a change in behavior within an existing setting (e.g., entering school, being promoted, graduating, marrying, parenting, moving). For further discussion of Bronfenbrenner's influential ideas, particularly as reflected in contemporary scholarship, see a recent volume edited in his honor (Moen, Elder, & Lüscher, 1995).

Holistic, interactionist views of individual development have gained momentum and experienced growing acceptance in recent years, particularly through the work of Ford (1987; Ford & Ford, 1987; Ford & Lerner, 1992), Lerner (1991), Magnusson (1988, 1995), Thelen (1992; Thelen & Smith, 1994), and others. For example, Magnusson (1995) conceptualizes human development within a "total person-environment system." Individuals function and develop as "total integrated organisms" (or organized wholes) and their functioning and development are ongoing reciprocal processes of continuous interaction across different levels in the person-environment system over time. Magnusson argues that the concept of "dynamic interaction" itself is built upon several interrelated principles. These include the principles of (a) *multi-determination,* in that we must consider all levels of the system, and the ways in which development is determined by those levels; (b) *interdependence,* in that factors in the system may be mutually dependent on each other without having reciprocal relations; (c) *reciprocity,* in that some factors will, in fact, influence each other reciprocally; (d) *temporality,* in that development is an ongoing, temporal process, and time must lie at the heart of any model of development; (e) *non-linearity,* in that neither the relationships between factors nor the functional form of development itself need be linear; and (f) *integration,* in that operating factors at all levels of the system must be coordinated to maximize its functioning.

Magnusson also argues that developmental science must involve the search for "lawful organization of structures" and "lawful processes of individual development." But are these independent? Individuals differ in the extent to which these structures and processes are organized and function as and within subsystems, and in the ways in which these subsystems are, in turn, organized and function. To understand individual differences, then, our task must be to unearth the patterns of operating factors in these subsystems and in the system as a whole. Yet if we take "development" only to be change, which Magnusson does,[13] and if we assume that individuals and their environments are ever-changing, to what degree should we expect "lawful organization" to exist in the first place?

We must consider changes in individual functioning across time, stated above as the principle of temporality. This means that we must examine how the entire *system* of biological, psychological, and social factors changes across time as a result of an individual's "maturation, experience, and learning" (p. 9). The important methodological implication of this principle is that we cannot study specific aspects of the person isolated from the whole. We must try to assemble and track the ways in which a total picture of structures and processes changes over time. What makes this ever more complicated is that both the *degree* of functioning and the *pace* of change likely differ across sub-systems and specific aspects of functioning. In addition, micro-level processes may operate according to shorter or finer time schedules than processes operating at higher levels in the system. The methodological implication of this point is that the appropriate research design, and particularly its appropriate time span, will depend on which aspects of functioning are being studied. From a practical standpoint, neither our theories nor our methods are able to simultaneously account for an unlimited number of multi-level factors, each of which may operate to a different degree and move at a different pace.

As noted earlier, Magnusson claims development as "lawful continuity"; that is, that "the [holistic] functioning of an individual at a certain stage of development is lawfully related to the [holistic] functioning of the individual at a previous stage"

---

[13]Magnusson argues that any conception of development must include two components. First, it must involve change in the size, shape, and/or function of the organism. Second, development must involve time (though time is not the same as development). As a result, Magnusson argues that "processes that go on without change, within existing structures, do not constitute development" (p. 20).

(p. 10). Yet it would seem that the simple *relatedness* of functioning over time, and especially over only two points, neither indicates that functioning is *continuous* nor that it is *lawful.* The term "lawful continuity" also gives the impression that functioning at one point can easily predict, or even rigidly determine, functioning at a later point. At the same time, Magnusson states that "individual development follows lawful principles, but is not necessarily predictable at all levels of the structures and processes involved" (p. 11). Shall our conception of development be one of lawfulness but unpredictability? If so, how can we hope to study it? What can be learned? What are our goals?

For Magnusson, the overarching goal of scientific research, including developmental research, is to "formulate, as laws, the basic principles that show how and why domains of the total space of phenomena function as they do at various levels of complexity" (p. 11). Is this a goal to which developmental science can (or should) ever aspire? To a great degree, Magnusson views *prediction* as the ultimate goal of empirical developmental research. Yet we must also do well in *explaining and understanding* development, identifying the factors that shape it and the mechanisms through which they do so. There have been incremental shifts toward explanation in developmental research from the 1930s through the present (see commentaries by Bronfenbrenner, 1963, and Looft, 1972). Since the 1970s, developmental scientists have more often adopted more pluralistic approaches to studying human lives, focusing on, and assembling together, multiple theories, explanations, and processes (Lerner, 1995). In addition, theoretical concerns now more often lead the collection and interpretation of data, and the two are more often evaluated in terms of each other (Lerner, 1995).

The recent momentum and acceptance of these views seems tied to new emphases in the life sciences on interactions between biological processes and their behavioral, cognitive, and social factors; discussion in the social sciences of methods and models from the natural sciences that permit the analysis of nonlinear, dynamic systems (including chaos, catastrophe, and general systems theories); and serious acknowledgment of the need to conduct longitudinal research (Bergman & Magnusson, 1997).

These and similar frameworks are excellent as broad heuristic devices, or what Winegar (1997) might call "metatheoretical frameworks" of developmental science. But because they are so global and interactive, they are nearly impossible to handle in both our theoretical and empirical work. Advocates of holistic, interactionist approaches defend themselves against such charges, saying that the intention of these models is not, and has never been, that the entire universe ought to be examined in a single study. Drawing a parallel to the natural sciences, Bergman and Magnusson (1997) remind us that "the fact that specific studies in, for example, nuclear physics or astrophysics are planned and interpreted with reference to the same general model of nature does not imply that each study includes the whole universe. A common general theoretical framework does, however, facilitate communication between different researchers and the accumulation of knowledge" (p. 291). Advocates of these approaches hope that individual scientists will plan and implement their work at a specific level of the system and on a circumscribed set of topics, but also be able to more effectively communicate with other scientists and interpret research within a common theoretical framework (Magnusson, 1995).

PROPOSITIONS RELATED TO THE "TRIAXIAL" VIEW OF HUMAN LIVES

What Gutmann (1987) calls the "triaxial" view of human lives is reflected in the statement made famous by Kluckhohn and Murray in their classic essay on the determinants of personality formation: "Every man is in certain respects (a) like all other men, (b) like some other men, (c) like no other man" (Kluckhohn & Murray, 1948/1965, p. 53).[14] Human lives can be conceptualized along these three levels. At the first level, where each man is like all other men, we must consider factors that make the human species distinct, and the characteristics that ensure its survival. As Gutmann puts it, this level "refers to the human body, to the reservoir of elemental appetites and developmental possibilities that underwrite the physical survival of the individual and, through sexual reproduction, of the species as a whole . . . [It] refers to the familiar hungers, excitements, and fears that define our human nature, and that are shared by all normally endowed men and women across the human race" (p. 11).

At the second level, where each man is like some other men, we must consider common experiences of living as part of a specific culture or subculture, or as a member of a social category or group. Here, shared languages, attitudes, and customs make some people similar and others dissimilar. At this level, Gutmann issues a warning:

> Sociologists, the students of second-level phenomena, too often ignore the effects of psychological earthquakes and attribute all shaping power to the effects of our social "weather." Studying individuals in one society, it is quite easy for them to confuse native drive with external social pressures, or to mistake the innate rhythms of intrinsic development for the pace of socially induced change . . . Such confounding of the species and social influences can easily grow out of studies restricted to single societies, pitched exclusively at [the] second level (p. 12).

Gutmann's point might be extended by noting that psychologists also too often ignore the importance of social weather in understanding psychological earthquakes, and that *all* developmental scientists, regardless of discipline, risk confounding species and social influences when they focus on a single culture.

At the third level, where each man is like no other man, we must consider that configuration of characteristics and experiences that create and preserve the uniqueness of each individual. A metaphor for this level is the fingerprint. While the

---

[14]Gutmann cites the source of this quote as Kardiner and Linton's (1945) *The psychological frontiers of society*, written a few years before Kluckhohn and Murray's (1948/1965) essay, which appeared in their edited volume (with Schneider), *Personality in nature, society, and culture*. Gutmann cites the quote in a slightly different way: "In some ways, each man is like all men; in some ways, each man is like some other men; and in some ways, each man is like no other men." However, to my knowledge, the statement was not made by Kardiner and Linton, but was instead made by Kluckhohn and Murray (and appears on page 53 of the second edition of their volume, issued in 1965).

fingerprint is unique to our species, "each of us has a fingerprint so distinct from all others that it can be used as a form of identification, unchallengeable in any court of law" (Gutmann, 1987, p. 13).

EMERGING DEBATES ON THE NATURE AND RHYTHM OF THE LIFE COURSE

Several recent scholarly and policy debates relate time and age to the nature and rhythm of the life course in modern societies (see also Settersten, 1997a). One set of debates concerns the degree to which the lives of successive cohorts have been (a) *chronologized* (bound to age, and in which *lifetime* is of central concern),[15] (b) *institutionalized* (structured by social institutions and the state and its policies),[16] and (c) *standardized* (the degree to which their life patterns exhibit regularity, especially with respect to the timing of major life experiences).[17] Where these issues are concerned, some scholars have argued that the life course, as a whole, is rigidly structured and experienced; while others have argued precisely the opposite: that the life course is, or at least has the *potential* to become, flexibly structured and experienced.

For example, there is some evidence that many life experiences, particularly those occurring early in the life course, have not only become more age-linked, but also more compressed within a shorter period of lifetime, leading to a more

---

[15] Several investigators have argued that the dimensions of time and age are now salient dimensions of social life (e.g., Chudacoff, 1989; Kohli, 1986a; Young, 1988). Borrowing a term coined by German sociologist Kohli (1986a), I refer to this as the debate about the "chronologization" of lives. Along these lines, Chudacoff (1989) argues that an important turning point occurred in the early part of this century. It was at this point in history that an increased awareness of age presumably emerged as part of a larger process of "social segmentation" in America: Organizations became more bureaucratic; landmark developments occurred in science, industry, and communication; concerns about efficiency and productivity grew; and society became more dependent on the clock and concerned about being "on time." Historian Graff (1995) also suggests that these and other large-scale developments in the first two decades of this century (e.g., major shifts in immigration and urbanization, social policies aimed at women and the young) transformed pathways to adulthood, culminating in patterns we now consider "modern." Similarly, Kohli (1986a) describes an emphasis on a new kind of time: *life* time, with age calibrating its axis. With the historical trends just noted, chronological age presumably became the basic criterion of life, and an age-bound life course resulted from, and solved, several structural problems (as described earlier in this chapter). Findings that support the chronologization thesis contradict the common assumption that we have made dramatic efforts to combat ageism in contemporary societies (Kertzer, 1989), and that achievement matters more than forms of ascription in determining life experiences (and that age, in particular, matters little) (Kohli, 1986b).

[16] Aspects of the institutionalization thesis were described earlier in this chapter. Related issues are also elaborated in Chapter 2 under "States and their Policies," "Social Policy and the Question of Age Versus Need," and "Social Policy and the Question of Age Divisiveness."

[17] There are multiple ways to think about the "standardization" of the life course. An event may be "standard" simply in that it occurs, or also with respect to *when* it occurs (its timing) (Henretta, 1992). It may also hold a standard place within an ordered sequence of experiences, have standard spacing with respect to another experience or set of experiences, or be of standard duration. However, we have not yet begun to explore standardization in these more complex ways. In addition, if life patterns have, in fact, become increasingly "standardized," this need not have been brought about by increasing "institutionalization." While such a conclusion is plausible, the institutionalization thesis remains not yet proven in the eyes of some scholars, as does the standardization thesis on which it relies.

standardized life course (Hogan, 1981; Modell, 1989; Modell, Furstenberg, & Hershberg, 1976; Modell, Furstenberg, & Strong, 1978; Winsborough, 1980). In this scenario, we might expect the importance of age to be heightened and age distinctions sharpened. In contrast, other scholars have refuted these theses, arguing instead that lives are, or have the *potential* to become, *destandardized* and *deinstitutionalized*—or at least partially so. Along these lines, Held (1986) suggests that "it is not entirely clear whether the imagery of an extremely age-graded, sequenced role structure fully captures the social reality of highly developed societies" (p. 158).

A second debate concerns the degree to which *trajectories though different life spheres* have been more or less chronologized, institutionalized, and standardized (e.g., Buchmann, 1989; Chudacoff, 1989; Held, 1986; Kohli, 1986a; Mayer & Mueller, 1986; Meyer, 1986a; Modell, 1989). Here, most scholars have suggested that work and educational trajectories are more rigidly structured and experienced than trajectories in the family domain, which instead seem to be characterized by a fair amount of flexibility. However, there is also evidence of increased flexibility in the work and educational spheres. For example, Held (1986) argues that some groups of individuals in modern societies do not "enter into an age-graded, sequenced occupational structure [or] formally retire" (p. 158). (Most of the evidence on both the standardization and institutionalization of the life course relates to occupational systems, and the degree to which occupational activity has become the central organizing principle of the life course.) Held's point is also echoed by Buchmann (1989) and others (Brose, 1989; Henretta, 1994) who also suggest that the economic sphere may now be characterized by greater flexibility, particularly as age-structured lifetime models of employment seem to be eroding.[18]

---

[18] In addition to the erosion of age-structured lifetime models of work, Buchmann (1989) also suggests a few other factors that may have created partial destandardization of the life course, with the biggest factor being an apparent dissolution of the link between social class, life chances, and life styles. The "structural and cultural individualization of the life course," Buchmann says, "has reached such a high level in advanced industrial society that the formerly tight coupling between social class and the socio-cultural milieu encompassing shared valued, action orientations, common styles of life, and collectively defined biographical prospects has greatly eroded" (p. 69). (However, many sociologists of stratification worldwide would seriously challenge this point.) In addition, future returns on educational investments are unpredictable in a market that has "decoupled" the link between education and later occupational opportunities, and in which rapid technological change outdates many positions and requires individuals to continually "retool" themselves. Another factor is the rampant ideology of individualism, which emphasizes personal growth and personal choice (though as I noted earlier, this may also be a reaction to a highly institutionalized life course). Along these lines, both Buchmann and Held suggest that when the life course becomes too institutionalized, cultural traditions and customs become less important and new "biographical options" are sought out and tested, especially in life spheres that are not, or cannot be, well regulated (such as the family sphere). Together, these factors, coupled with some evidence on increased variability in life course patterns (especially in the least institutionalized sphere, the family), suggest that the life course may now be, or become, destandardized. It is also possible that *informal* age structuring may be stronger in spheres that are not, or cannot, be *formally* regulated by the state (that is, because work and educational spheres are more heavily regulated at a formal level, there may not be as great a need for the informal regulation of these spheres; in contrast, because the family sphere cannot be well regulated at a formal level, the degree of *informal* age structuring may be stronger) (see Settersten & Hagestad, 1996b). These, too, are important areas for further exploration.

(This and other pertinent factors related to flexibility will be discussed in the section on "Opportunities for Life-Course Flexibility.") In a "post-Fordist" age, earlier models of the life course may no longer remain applicable, particularly in the economic sphere (for a discussion of "post-Fordism," see Amin, 1994).

A third debate concerns the degree to which *men's or women's lives* have been more or less chronologized, institutionalized, and standardized. Scholars have suggested that the social meanings of age and time differ for men and women, that men and women use different guidelines to measure the progress of their lives, that men and women may have different needs for predictability and order, and that their lives may run on different kinds of time (e.g., Gilligan, 1982; Hagestad & Neugarten, 1985; Hagestad, 1991; Hernes, 1987; Moen, 1996). These differences may be linked to the fact that the traditional lives of most women have been more firmly bound to the family sphere, which seems to operate on non-linear time, while the traditional lives of men have been more firmly bound to spheres outside the family, which instead seem to operate on linear time. The result is that men's lives are (or are perceived as) more rigid, while women's lives are (or are perceived as) more flexible, with the obvious exception of biological clocks around reproduction. At the same time, both men and women alike are simultaneously tied to multiple spheres and in multiple ways. Much of the inflexibility that individuals may feel as they move through the life course is likely the result of clashes between the structure and nature of family, work, and educational spheres as these spheres are negotiated over time.

Much more empirical evidence is needed to shed light on each of these debates, even at a descriptive level. To what degree are lives in contemporary societies chronologized, institutionalized, and standardized (or how dechronologized, deinstitutionalized, or destandardized, as the case may be)? Are experiences in some spheres more chronologized, institutionalized, and standardized than in other spheres? How do these patterns vary by sex, race, social class, or other characteristics of individuals and groups? How do these patterns vary across culture? How have they changed over time?

Once these patterns (or lack thereof) have been documented, what factors and processes might then be proposed to explain them? What are the consequences of these patterns for individual lives, for families and other groups, and for social, political, and economic institutions and policies? For example, at an individual level, how might these patterns affect personal meanings and experiences, life plans, and the experience and use of time? As another example, if chronologization, institutionalization, and standardization provide important frameworks for maintaining personal or social continuity (or for managing personal or social *dis*continuity), what results for individuals, social institutions, and society at large when these frameworks crumble?

TOWARD A MORE FLEXIBLE LIFE COURSE? BARRIERS AND OPPORTUNITIES[19]

Riley equates the problem of "structural lag," discussed earlier, with society's inability to provide "meaningful opportunities" in education, work, family, and leisure for people of *all* ages. This is the result of an inflexible age-constrained life course.[20] A primary challenge facing developmental scientists and policymakers is how to modify existing "age-differentiated" structures and instead build "age-integrated" structures. While the degree of age segregation and age integration varies across cultures (Keith, Fry, Glascock, Ikels, Dickerson-Putnam, Harpending, & Draper, 1994), an age-differentiated life course is common in most modern societies. In an age-differentiated life course, social roles and activities are restricted to, and allocated on the basis of, age or life stage (see Figure 4). Here, the life course is rigidly segmented into three separate periods of education, work, and leisure (this is discussed in the section below on the "Tripartition of the Life Course"). Such a structure is convenient in that it creates "orderliness" in the entry to, and exit from, social roles and activities. At the same time, it is "ageist" in that it restricts opportunities for various types of activities to specific periods of life. Instead, we might find ways to build an age-integrated life course, in which age barriers are removed, and in which opportunities for roles and activities in education, work, and leisure are open to all people, regardless of age. A more flexible life course would permit older people to have greater range of options and choices open to them; adults and especially women to feel less strain in combining work and family roles; young people to better integrate experiences in work and school; and children to become more valued members of, and be given greater responsibility in, their families, schools, and communities. (It is also important to note that little is known about how the voluntary and community sectors affect lives or structure the life course.)

The sphere of family is often de-emphasized in, or curiously absent from, these frameworks. Many of the arguments on which claims of inflexibility are based take work to be the central organizing principle of the life course, but family roles and responsibilities are also an important part of this equation. Family demands often condition participation in educational, work, and leisure activities, particularly through the middle years. However, relative to the spheres of education, work, and leisure, the family sphere seems more age-integrated in that it naturally assembles and connects individuals of varied ages. At the same time, families are nonetheless differentiated by age and generation. In addition, demographic change has altered the very structure of the extended family matrix. Increases in longevity and decreases in fertility have created "bean pole" family structures (Bengtson, Rosenthal, & Burton, 1990). More generations are alive at once, generations are

---

[19]An early version of this framework was developed in Settersten and Lovegreen (1998), which focused on educational opportunities during the middle years.

[20]However, Riley and her colleagues feel that the problem of structural lag is felt most acutely by older people because of their "protracted longevity, their increasing numbers in the population, and—save for the disadvantaged minority—their remarkably good health and effective functioning" (Riley, Foner, & Kahn, 1994, p. 18). At present, they argue, older people have "empty role structures" (p. 25).

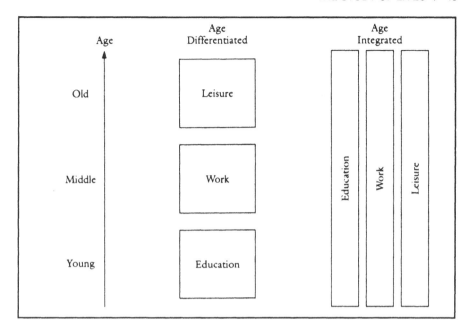

Figure 4. Ideal types of social structures.
Source: Riley, M. W., & Riley, J. W., Jr. (1994). Structural lag: Past and future. In M. W. Riley, R. L. Kahn, & A. Foner (Eds.), *Age and structural lag: Society's failure to provide meaningful opportunities in work, family, and leisure.* New York: John Wiley & Sons. p. 26.

significantly differently from one another in age, and there are fewer members within each generation.

Unlike age-differentiated structures in education, work, and leisure, the differentiation in family structures just described need not be negative. In fact, these changes may actually lead to more positive family experiences. For example, children now come to know grandparents, great-grandparents, and even great-great-grandparents; and spouses, parents and children, and siblings survive jointly for long periods of time. However, as Bengtson and his colleagues wryly note, these changes also bring the potential for "long-term lousy relationships" (Bengtson, Rosenthal, & Burton, 1996, p. 269).

In an age-integrated family scenario, Riley and her colleagues envision a "boundless network of kin and kin-*like* relationships, in which people of any age— inside or outside the traditional family or household—are free to choose (or to earn the right) to support, love, or confide in one another. Or they may choose to avoid stressful or unpleasant relationships" (Riley, Kahn, & Foner, 1994, p. 28). However, these arrangements would also seem possible in the age-differentiated structure they describe. The issue here seems to have less to do with age and generational structure than it does with creating positive, healthy, close relationships with other people who serve the functions that we associate with "family." As both kin and kin-*like*

Table 1. Barriers to Life-Course Flexibility

- The Tripartition of the Life Course
- The Male and Female Life Course
- Employer Pension and Social Security Rules
- Scholarship, Tuition, and Financial Aid Rules
- Educational and Occupational Tracking
- Age Biases Against Older Students and Workers
- Social Responses to Adult Students
- Shortened Period of Gainful Work
- The "Midlife Squeeze"
- State and Public Resistance to Flexibility

relationships become more complex, we must face difficult questions about—and hopefully enlarge—our social and legal definitions of "family": questions about which types of unions and families are "legitimate" in society and worthy of the support and protection of the state. Another important point here is that family roles and activities need not be constrained by age or to specific life periods, but might instead extend across the entire life course (though admittedly changing in form over time).

Besides age integration, other forms of integration seem equally important. As a society, we must work harder to provide meaningful opportunities in education, work, family, and leisure for both women *and* men, both non-whites *and* whites, and both the working- and lower-classes *and* the middle- and upper-classes. The "de-" sides of the chronologization, institutionalization, and standardization continua all provide new hope that the life course is now, or at least has the *potential* to become, more flexibly structured and experienced. What factors might serve as new opportunities for life-course flexibility? What factors might serve as barriers to that flexibility? Some of the factors that constrain the life course and, in particular, rigidly structure and experience much of *adult* life, will first be explored. These barriers are outlined in Table 1, and each factor will be discussed in turn.[21]

Barriers to Life-Course Flexibility

The Tripartition of the Life Course

One of the most significant barriers to the pursuit of educational experiences in adult life is inherent in the very structure of the life course itself: the "tripartition" (Kohli, 1986a), "triangularization" (Smelser & Halpern, 1978), or "3 boxes" (Best, 1980) of the life course. From this perspective, work functions as the central organizing principle of the life course, which is split into three distinct periods. The early segment is devoted to education and training for work; the middle segment is

---

[21] Admittedly, this is not an exhaustive list of factors that constrain the life course.

devoted to continuous work activity; and the final segment is devoted to leisure and the absence of work activity. In such a regime, educational, work, and leisure experiences are therefore significantly age segregated (see also Riley & Riley, 1994; Marshall, 1995b). Of course, for current cohorts of people in their later years, this "tripartition" may be more characteristic of the structure of men's lives than women's lives; however, for younger cohorts it is also likely to characterize the life structures of many women.

Despite hopes that we might move away from the rigid tripartition of the life course, there is growing enthusiasm for late-life leisure, and proposals to increase the age of "normal" retirement are unpopular among both employees and employers (Rix, 1998). Any strategies aimed at encouraging older workers to postpone retirement must confront the fact that most jobs open to older workers have low wages and few benefits (given changes in the labor market in recent years) (Rix, 1998). How can we better ensure that the older workers of tomorrow acquire and update their skills over their careers in an effort to guarantee their place in a competitive labor market later on (should this be desired)? And how might we promote options for those who are disadvantaged, do not have resources, or do not work for companies that support and provide opportunities for retraining?

Most discussion about the inflexibility of the life course centers around the centrality of work and preparation for work in the first two periods. The last period is instead presumably organized around "leisure," though the "social organization of leisure has long been neglected" (Hendricks & Cutler, 1990, p. 225). In fact, most proposals for reorganizing the life course involve the restructuring of work. The assumption is that the time gained by restructuring work will be devoted to education or family pursuits, not leisure. Yet why not also find ways to promote leisure activities throughout life? This would certainly create a more humane society. The trend toward earlier and earlier retirement suggests that individuals desire more time for non-work activities. As a result, we must explore the values of, and opportunities for, leisure within and across societies (Hendricks & Cutler, 1990).

The Male and Female Life Course

Two of the biggest barriers to building more flexible lives relate to the fact that the structure and experience of men's and women's lives continues to be different despite important gains in recent decades (Sørensen, 1991). First, women continue to shoulder the major responsibility for the care and raising of children, and these responsibilities strongly condition women's educational attainment and enrollment and their attachment to the labor market.[22] Second, the position of women in the labor market remains one of marked disadvantage relative to men, even *net* of all

---

[22]It is worth noting that while significant attention has been devoted to understanding how family roles and responsibilities have impacted worklife (particularly where women's employment is concerned), we have not paid much attention to the reverse: to the question of how work roles and responsibilities have impacted family life.

qualifications, skills, family roles, and responsibilities.[23] The two are clearly linked. To achieve more flexibility, we must therefore find ways to encourage men to take equal responsibility for the care and raising of children, and we must create high demand for, and place more value on, women's labor (Sørensen, 1991). This means that we must find ways to reduce the degree to which experiences in family, education and work are sorted as a function of gender.[24]

How might we move away from separate "male" and "female" life courses, and instead move toward a "gender neutral" life course (for lack of a better term) in which life chances and experiences are not sorted in this way? Sørensen (1991) suggests that this might take the form of one of two scenarios. One possibility is to create a course similar to that of many working mothers, in which experiences in the labor force fluctuate hand-in-hand with family demands. At certain times, their labor force attachment is strong; at other times, they reduce work time or take leaves of absence; and at still other times, they juggle both work and family demands with equal intensity. This patterning is what has led scholars to describe women's work trajectories as "discontinuous" or "disorderly" relative to those of most men (e.g., Treiman, 1985). In the new scenario, however, this course would exist for *both* men and women, which is a major and perhaps insurmountable challenge. The other possibility is to instead sponsor two different courses—one that is family-centered, and one that is work-centered. The challenges here, which may be equally insurmountable, are to make the family-centered course socially valued and attractive to men, and to give women as much chance as men to follow the work-centered course. An explication of whether and how we might achieve these possibilities is beyond the scope of this chapter, and there is no consensus on these matters in either the political or academic arenas. Nonetheless, the chasm between the male and female life course is one of the most important barriers that must be overcome if we hope to build a more flexible life course.

But is the real issue here that women's lives have not been flexible? Some might even argue that women's lives are already much more flexible than men's lives precisely because women are more likely to cycle between full- and part-time work and education in response to changing family responsibilities. Instead, the problem at hand is that, regardless of the significant changes in women's life patterns, their *educational and work patterns* have not fully converged with those of men, and probably cannot fully converge under current life-course regimes. The convergence

---

[23] Despite considerable growth in women's presence in higher education and the labor market, women also remain concentrated in areas that typically generate lower lifetime earning potential (Centre for Educational Research and Innovation, 1987). Significantly larger proportions of women than men train for, and take positions in, the fields of education, social sciences, and the liberal arts rather than the natural sciences and technological studies. Part of this difference is driven by the fact that women are socialized in these directions from very early ages (Eccles, 1994). In addition, women with occupational training and positions identical to that of men continue to receive unequal pay for the same work (Jacobs, 1995; Reskin & Padavic, 1994).

[24] As noted in Chapter 2, "sex" refers to the "reproductive and sexual characteristics that differentiate the female from the male, and "gender" refers to "all social and psychological attributes linked to the social roles of men and women" (Rossi, 1986, p. 113).

between men's and women's lives in the past couple decades is mainly the result of *women's* patterns of schooling and employment moving closer to men's; men's patterns have remained largely unchanged (Sørensen, 1991). In addition, while women's labor force activity has moved toward that of men, it does not match men's patterns, which are characterized by decades of continuous full-time employment. As noted above, women's work trajectories—at least those of married women with children—continue to be more "discontinuous" than men's work trajectories, given that women adjust their work activity in response to family demands. Unattached women, especially single or divorced women with children, cannot afford this flexibility. It is for this group of women that the lack of flexibility is a particularly problematic issue.[25]

As mentioned above, little has changed with respect to the restructuring of men's lives. This is probably the most important barrier to overcome, given that the quality of men's lives, especially their family lives, would certainly benefit from new-found flexibility. An important question therefore is not only how *men themselves* might value flexibility, but also how others might support flexibility *for* men. Many men must desire more flexibility in their work patterns, which would provide the opportunity to spend additional time with their families, return to school, or engage in leisure activities. But they may also feel that neither their responsibility to provide for their families (whether actual or expected) nor the structure of the occupational sphere afford such flexibility (e.g., loss of job security; loss of promotion opportunities; peers, superiors, and others may react negatively to them, given that adult men who work only part-time, leave careers for other pursuits, or are otherwise not fully committed to work roles are often viewed, and view themselves, as failures).

Without the lead of men, concerns about flexibility may simply be viewed as concerns of women, and of making accommodations for them. This will only perpetuate separate and unequal, or at least differently valued, roles and responsibilities (Hinrichs, Roche, & Sirianni, 1991; Krüger, 1996). What is ironic about these discussions is that it is *men* whose lives are more rigidly "boxed," who have far fewer opportunities to divert from this structure, and who may have most to gain from attempts at flexibility. In many discussions of the life course, women's lives are described as if the family sphere is most, if not exclusively, important, or that the connections between family and work are problematic for women alone; just as

---

[25]This raises another important issue: For some individuals, educational and work-related pursuits in adulthood are not a luxury but are needed to support oneself and one's family. For example, many divorced women have low earning power without a return to school. This would seem especially true of those cohorts of women now at midlife or beyond, many of whom interrupted or postponed their schooling to begin and raise their families, and many of whom had marginal attachment to the labor market over their reproductive years. For these women, education in the middle years may be viewed as a "second chance." For divorced women in particular, a return to school may also be viewed as the only solution to gaining income; that is, education is viewed as the key to job mobility, which, in turn, will create greater earning potential. At the same time, it is precisely these women who have fewest resources to manage a return to school because they must work full-time to provide for their children and are often solely responsible for the care of their children.

men's lives are described as if the work sphere is most, if not exclusively, important to them. Many women may feel that men "have it all" and may be bitter about having to compromise their work lives in the name of the family; at the same time, many men may also feel resentful of the work commitments that are expected of them, and of lost opportunities with their families and in their personal lives that result. Ideologies around gender create and support much of the inflexibility that *both* men and women feel.

As noted earlier, much discussion about the structure of the life course is focused on its organization around educational and work activities. Surprisingly, the family sphere is absent from these discussions. As Krüger (1996) points out, we must recognize that the family sphere is simultaneously interconnected to educational and work institutions, that we participate in multiple spheres simultaneously, and that our "central analytic focus" should be on "the mixture of different potential linking of loyalties, superimpositions and exclusions between institutions that simultaneously impinge" on individuals' lives and that are often asynchronous (p. 130). Educational institutions, the labor market, *and* the family should be central to and claim relevance for both men *and* women (Krüger, 1996).

Rules Related to Employer Pensions and Social Security Benefits

While later investments in education and training may now be rational, pension policies—private and public alike—often work against, and even penalize, those who take flexible pathways. Benefit eligibility and levels are intimately tied to one's work history, and especially to the amount of time spent in continuous, full-time employment. For example, in *defined benefit* plans, pension levels are generally a function of the duration of service and the last few years of earnings. Vesting rules may also result in a complete loss of benefits if the employee leaves the position before the vestment period has been completed, just as they often penalize workers who leave before retirement. In *defined contribution* plans, on the other hand, the employer makes an annual investment based on a percentage of the employee's annual income. Defined contribution plans also generally have much shorter vesting periods and are often portable. As a result, defined contribution plans do not penalize flexible pathways to the same degree as defined benefit plans. While the shift toward "contingent" models has been accompanied by a shift toward defined contribution plans, the majority of covered workers continue to have defined benefit plans (Quadagno & Hardy, 1996).

Similarly, Social Security benefits depend on an individual's monthly earnings averaged over thirty-five years of work; Social Security benefits generally increase in value with longer, more continuous work (Burkhauser & Quinn, 1994). In addition, new rules related to Social Security benefits further discourage flexibility, including rules related to delayed retirement credits, the penalty associated with earnings above the exempt amount, the age of eligibility, and the penalty for drawing on benefits early (Burkhauser & Quinn, 1994).

Finally, with prolonged education at the lower end of the life course, individuals from more recent cohorts get a comparatively late start in building their pension funds, private or public. This may also reduce the likelihood of taking work leaves or reducing work commitments for other pursuits during the middle years, given that such pursuits may ultimately reduce one's economic status in later life.

Rules Related to Scholarships, Tuition Benefits, and Financial Aid

Recent tax-reform debates in Congress have included proposals to tax tuition scholarships, including graduate-level fellowships and tuition waivers. These reforms have major implications for the likelihood of educational pursuits in adult life. For students at private universities, where annual full-time tuition charges run as much as $20,000 or more, these tax bills will be sizable and may make education, at least at those universities, unaffordable.

Worse still, most scholarships, federal grants, work-study funds, and low-interest loans are generally only awarded to full-time degree-seeking students. This dramatically decreases the pool of adult students eligible for these forms of assistance, given that most adult students are enrolled on a part-time basis. As a result, expenses for educational activity must be paid out-of-pocket, making a return to school unaffordable for many students.

Many company benefit policies provide tuition assistance, in whole or in part, *only* if the courses taken are related to the employee's job. While these policies do provide some opportunity for adults to refresh their skills in job-related areas, these policies work against flexibility in that they *reinforce already existing occupational positions or pathways* rather than allow individuals to seek training for new occupational positions or pathways or to simply enrich themselves by exploring new areas of inquiry. Many company tuition policies also require their employees to pay the tuition bill up front, and the employee is later reimbursed upon satisfactory completion of the course or reimbursed at different levels depending on the grade(s) received. These factors not only make educational pursuits difficult for many adults, but they also make them somewhat risky from the standpoint of the employee, especially those already hesitant to return to school after a long absence.

Educational and Occupational Tracking

Tracking through primary and secondary schools also has clear implications for later educational and occupational options. In many countries, educational tracks are explicit, and an individual's performance at critical junctures along the way determines the track onto which she or he is placed (Rosenbaum, 1976; Rosenbaum, Kariya, Settersten, & Maier, 1990).[26] Ultimately, each educational track also determines the range of future occupational positions to which an individual has access. Where educational tracks are explicit and strong, the individual has little or no opportunity to veer from that track once it has been assigned. In such a scenario, the likelihood of "second chances," whether to make up for past mistakes or to change

---

[26]Given that the practice of tracking goes against American ideals of equality and individualism, its existence in the United States is often denied. However, scholars have noted that educational tracking does exist, and that these tracks are often simply "hidden" from students and parents (Oakes, 1985; Rosenbaum, 1976).

earlier decisions, seems slim.[27] Interestingly, Levin and Levin (1991) suggest that, unlike many societies, the United States tolerates educational "late blooming" even though individuals express a preference for higher-educational experiences that are "on-time" in early adulthood. This tolerance may allow Americans opportunities for educational experiences in adulthood that are not possible in other societies. But it may also encourage "temporal loafing," in which students believe that poor performance early in their educational careers will not prevent later opportunities. In reality, an individual's past academic record does play an important role in determining later educational options or in determining what remedial work needs to be done before better options are available.

Similarly, promotional tracks in many organizations are explicitly structured on the basis of age and tenure in the organization, and an individual's current or future chances at promotion are dependent on her or his prior promotional record and successful movement through a series of hierarchical positions (Kerckhoff, 1993; Rosenbaum, 1984; Turner, 1960). Many professions (e.g., law, medicine, the academy) are also more generally structured by a set of "nested" or prerequisite positions or experiences, which need not be, and generally are not, restricted to a single organization. These factors make full-time continuous work histories crucial for promotional chances, leave little room for other pursuits, and make late entry into some occupations very difficult.

These issues serve as reminders of the power of a principle known as the "Matthew effect" in the sociological literature on the life course (Dannefer, 1987; Merton, 1968; O'Rand, 1996a, 1996b). This principle, which will be discussed in Chapters 4 and 5, proposes that the effects of advantage and disadvantage cumulate over the life course, a good deal of which is socially produced through mechanisms such as tracking. Where educational and occupational pathways are concerned, an individual's early successes may lead to later successes and increase her or his options, while early failures may seriously foreclose an individual's later opportunities.

Age Biases Against Older Students and Workers

Those who return to school or change occupations in their middle or later years may face or be fearful of age discrimination. The admissions process in educational institutions and programs and the hiring processes of employers may intentionally or unintentionally favor younger candidates. For example, faculty in graduate programs may be concerned that the skills of older students may not be "up to par" with those of students of traditional ages, and that these students will require them to make greater investments of time and energy to help them through their programs.

---

[27]However, recent decades have seen the increased presence of adults of "non-traditional" ages in post-secondary educational institutions, one group of which might be labeled "second-chancers." This perpetuates the image that the American system is flexible. In addition, American academic institutions were built on the idea that the university should respond to the needs of the wider community and provide a "broad, liberal, and practical education to the community at large," which is much different than most European models (for an interesting discussion of these differences, see Schütze, 1987, pp. 9-10).

Moreover, faculty may be less inclined to invest in older students if they believe that there will be few returns to those investments in the long run. For example, faculty may recognize that older students have fewer years ahead of them to carry on their traditions or those of the department, or that these students will not be as mobile as younger students with fewer work and family obligations. Similarly, employers may consider older workers more expensive to hire, more costly to insure, more costly to train (given a more limited time horizon), and less able to learn new technological skills (Downs, 1995). These factors may also lead to greater difficulty in securing a new position upon completion of a new degree or training program.

Social Responses to Adult Students

When the term "non-traditional" student is used in undergraduate settings, it generally refers to an adult student of any age. However, "non-traditional" students are a diverse group, ranging from adults who have delayed higher education by only a few years to those who return to school in later life. The term "non-traditional" is less applicable in graduate settings, in which the age composition of students in most programs is much more variable than that in undergraduate programs. Nonetheless, several experiences are likely common to the non-traditional student, regardless of the individual's age or circumstances.

From the standpoint of the traditional student, the "non-traditional" student is often viewed as either an asset or liability in the classroom. On the one hand, the traditional student may appreciate the rich life experiences that non-traditional students bring with them, and the non-traditional student may serve as a role model or mentor to younger students. On the other hand, non-traditional students are often more self-selected, self-directed, and invested than younger students (Atchley, 1994; Krain, 1995), and traditional students often seem irritated by these characteristics.

From the standpoint of faculty, these characteristics generally make non-traditional students a welcome addition to the classroom. At the same time, many faculty and administrators may feel that the skills of non-traditional students are significantly lower than those of traditional students in daytime classes, and therefore encourage them to enroll in weekend or evening courses specifically designed with the adult student in mind. Whether reality or misperception, these courses are often viewed as "watered-down" versions of the daytime curriculum. In fact, the age composition of the student body is often associated with the status and prestige of an educational institution. As Davies (1995, p. 297) points out, the "main status of institutions is linked to their reputation with young students, and an institutional profile which demonstrates a high proportion of [non-traditional students] in undergraduate programs is often associated with lower status." Because young adults are the priority for most universities, older adults may find their access to educational programs at those universities restricted.

Shortened Period of Gainful Work

The worldwide shift in retirement patterns is moving in a direction opposite to that which would presumably promote greater flexibility: Rather than delaying retirement, which might free up time earlier in life for non-work activities, individuals are retiring earlier (Guillemard & Rein, 1993; Kohli, 1994). However, there is some evidence that this decline may now have tapered off (Quinn & Burkhauser, 1994). The trend toward early retirement at the upper end of worklife, coupled with an extension of schooling at the lower end of worklife, has made the period of gainful work shorter. This may make flexible work time and the pursuit of other experiences during adulthood less desirable, at least under the current education-work-retirement regime, since there are fewer years devoted to the middle work segment. In addition, early retirement, coupled with increased longevity, has lengthened the period of retirement. This may in turn make full-time employment, and contributions to public and private pensions and savings, even more crucial during the middle years.

The Midlife "Squeeze"

Several factors would seem to promote the extension of work into the later years, thereby freeing up time at midlife for non-work activities (see later section "New Possibilities for Work in the Last Third of Life"). At the same time, the middle years may be a particularly difficult period in which to devote oneself to other activities, given constraints of both time and money. Many middle-aged adults need additional time and resources not only to manage the care of aging parents, but also to provide for young adult children, a period which has been prolonged with extensions in schooling for recent cohorts of young adults. The middle years are also important for building pensions and savings for the later years. Together, these factors may make the pursuit of non-work experiences in the middle years all the more difficult.

State and Public Resistance to Flexibility

Time, energy, and money are limited commodities for most adults. My assumption, and one that runs throughout the literature, is that regardless of how much an individual would like to pursue educational or leisure experiences during the adult years, or spend additional time with family, these experiences are only possible if resources are freed up to do so. Regardless of how much these experiences are needed or desired, they are often considered a luxury during adulthood. This is where the importance of work flexibility, in particular, comes into play: Without flexible work lives, many adults could not manage to find time to engage in these activities, let alone find the financial means to do so. Most work, educational, and family policies aimed at creating flexibility therefore have concerns about time at their core, whether they relate to freeing up time for individuals or to restructuring social institutions so that they are less rigidly organized around it (e.g., lengthening vacation time, shortening the workweek or workday, supporting leaves for educational or family reasons, offering differently-timed career tracks, changing age-related policies around retirement). Of course, freeing up time in adulthood and restructuring social institutions are major feats in and of themselves; finding ways to make non-work experiences attractive, affordable, or possible are still others.

Most importantly, regardless of how we try to achieve a greater degree of flexibility in the life course, most policies aimed at promoting flexibility will require financing through tax money and public resources. This is likely to generate substantial controversy in any society because it brings to public discourse, and heightens, the significant "tensions between market and law, economy and politics, liberty and quality" (Weymann, 1996a, p. 253). For example, Rehn and his colleagues, who began advocating the concept of "free choice" as part of radical pension reform in Sweden during the late 1950s, proposed that the state should give individuals, as a right of citizenship, an account on which to draw throughout their lives. Individuals would at any time have a "drawing right" to one-third of that account for any purpose of their choosing, whether to take a vacation, build new skills or return to school, or simply alleviate temporary economic pressures. The remaining two-thirds would be held in reserve to cover possible risks and a necessary minimum for old age insurance. Rehn reports that this idea "horrified" many people, including members of the government, most of whom were worried that people would abuse these freedoms or that individuals would be unable to make sound decisions about what was in their best interests. While this piece of their early reform proposals was never adopted, other parts were implemented over the years, along with several additional innovative policies (see Rehn, 1977, 1990). An important lesson to take away from Rehn and his colleagues' attempts at reform is that the push toward flexibility is not an easy road; it takes time for the public and politicians to get used to these ideas. Another lesson is that these proposals will be more or less attractive depending on the economic times: In an era where we may need to push people to work longer, rather than retire sooner, many of the proposals that Rehn describes may be less than ideal for the development of the country. Nonetheless, these proposals are important for the development of individuals and families. A final lesson is that the value of non-work activities will vary as a function of a state's political ideology and its conception of civil society. In particular, ideas about what basic rights come with citizenship (e.g., income, education, health insurance) will lie at the heart of these tensions. For example, is the pursuit of education, especially higher education, a universal right for each citizen, regardless of the abilities or resources? Or is it the privilege of a few? What about the pursuit of leisure?

Opportunities for Life-Course Flexibility

In the prior section, I described several barriers that create a life course that is difficult to negotiate and manage. Despite these barriers, several factors may create the potential for greater flexibility in the life course and new opportunities to simultaneously manage work, family, education, and leisure experiences, particularly through the middle decades of adult life. These new opportunities are outlined in Table 2, and each factor will be discussed in turn.[28]

---

[28] Admittedly, this is not an exhaustive list of factors that foster life-course flexibility.

Table 2. Opportunities for Life-Course Flexibility

- New Time Budgets for Adulthood
- New Possibilities for Work in the Last Third of Life
- New Routes to Retirement
- The Erosion of "Lifetime" Models of Work
- Flextime Work Policies
- Growth in Adult Enrollment in Higher Education and in Educational Programs Aimed at Adults

New "Time Budgets" for Adulthood

Historical shifts in key demographic parameters, particularly longevity and fertility, have created the potential for new "time budgets of adulthood." We now have more, and healthier, years to spend in educational, work, family, and leisure roles and activities. As a result, age may be less important in determining social roles and life experiences, and educational, work, and leisure experiences might be better allocated across the entire life course rather than restricted to specific periods. Roles and activities may be prolonged, their time schedules loosened, and their sequencing more complex (Neugarten & Neugarten, 1986; Riley, 1985; Riley & Riley, 1994). These demographic changes therefore create the potential for new opportunities in education, work, family, and leisure for individuals of all ages (for good examples, see Riley, Kahn, & Foner, 1994). As a result, new hopes for a more flexible life course have surfaced, particularly if we can manage to build age-integrated social structures (Riley & Riley, 1994) and establish more egalitarian relations between women and men in both the public and private spheres (Sørensen, 1991). These possibilities may also reflect the fact that an aging society is heavily female (given the sex differential in life expectancy), which may create a more humane and caring society (e.g., Rossi, 1986). (However, this entails the questionable assumptions that the values and concerns of women, and of older women in particular, will dominate society, and that women's values are uniform, even across cohorts.) This scenario is reminiscent of Neugarten and Hagestad's (1976) reflections about the possibility of an "age-irrelevant society," in which the importance of age might diminish as a dimension of individual and social life.

For example, consider the implication of changes in longevity for educational experiences during adulthood. With extended lifetime, we might find ways to provide educational and training experiences not only during childhood, adolescence, and young adulthood, but also throughout the middle and later years. In fact, Sørensen (1991) reminds us that human capital theory posits that individuals will pursue education and training related to occupational skills only if they think they will earn returns on those costs. While many adults may be hesitant to make late investments in education and training, middle-to-later-life investments may nonetheless be rational given the extension of lifetime.

As another example, consider the implication of changes in fertility for educational experiences in adult life. Reduced fertility, coupled with increased longevity, means that the proportion of lifetime devoted to childbearing and active childrearing has decreased; in addition, advances in birth control have created more control over the timing of birth (Sørensen, 1991). Together, these factors suggest that family constraints on labor force and educational activities may now be fewer, especially for women, and that individuals may now have a greater amount of time to spend on non-family activities throughout their adult years.

However, much of the work in this area is speculative, and we have much to learn about *precisely how* change in these demographic parameters has affected individual lives, collective lives, and society at large. For example, what does it actually mean to live in an "aging society"? That is, what does it mean to live in a "rectangularized," or even "top-heavy," population (due to low mortality and low fertility) and "feminized" population (due to the sex differential in longevity, in which women far outlive men)? How have these conditions altered the nature of experiences in the spheres of education, work, family, and leisure? For whom? How have social institutions in these spheres reacted to, or been shaped by, these changes?

New Possibilities for Work in the Last Third of Life

Several factors have also created the possibility that older adults may work, or need to work, throughout the last third of life: reduced morbidity (which makes the later years healthier ones), the lifting of the retirement cap in most occupations, new policies to accommodate workers with disabilities, the poor financial circumstances of many older adults, and concerns among the public and policy-makers about the viability of public pension systems (Burkhauser & Quinn, 1994; Kohli, 1994). In fact, many adults indicate that they hope to work beyond the typical retirement age, and many older adults who are already retired indicate that would like to be working and are capable of doing so (Christensen, 1990; McNaught, Barth, & Henderson, 1991; Quinn & Burkhauser, 1994). In addition, the possibility of work into later life may also make more flexible approaches to work earlier in the life course more attractive. This would seem especially attractive for adults at midlife, many of whom might like to return to school or retrain themselves, or need time to care for elderly parents.

New Routes to Retirement

At an organizational level, routes to retirement have also become more varied, as incentives are sometimes provided for early retirement due to disability, recession, or downsizing (Henretta, 1994; Kohli, 1994; O'Rand, 1996a). Periods of high unemployment may also create a demand for shorter workdays or workweeks in an effort to reduce overall unemployment. However, this does not reflect "flexibility" in the true sense of the word, but is instead "pseudo-flexibility" in that workers may be pressured to retire or reduce work hours before they wish (Rehn, 1990). These are only one set of factors that have been put forward to account for the fact that variability around the transition to retirement has increased. As O'Rand (1996a, pp. 194-195) notes, retirement is no longer "a narrowly demarcated and determinate sequence of events defined by straightforward exits from career jobs. We are identifying multiple pathways out of work that follow different schedules in later years. Employment in 'post-career' or bridge jobs, partial and intermittent work, under- and unemployment, and disability are among several alternative routes to retirement today that can be added to the traditional pension and health routes associated with recent cohorts of *men* in this economy" (emphasis added). Of course, it remains to be seen what the retirement experiences of more recent cohorts of *women* will be like in the future, as they have entered the labor market in unprecedented numbers and have had longer and more continuous work histories than their predecessors. The important point here is that increased variability around retirement may reflect, or even create, new possibilities for non-work activities during adulthood.

The Erosion of "Lifetime" Models of Work

Another important shift seems to be occurring in the organization of work itself. Age-based "lifetime" models of work are dissolving and are being replaced by "contingent" models of work (Henretta, 1994). In *lifetime* models of work, the employer and employee invest in a long-term partnership. In this scenario, the longer the amount of time the employee spends in the firm, the more the employee has gained important training, and the greater the individual's wages, job security, job mobility, and pension. Lifetime models contain a hierarchical sequence of positions, with a clear entry portal and a strong emphasis on promotion from within the organization.[29] As a result, these models are characterized by age- or tenure-based rewards and security. In addition, because much of an individual's training is firm-specific, the skills acquired may not be transferable to other organizations. This leaves little opportunity for work reduction or for temporary exits from work, and it reduces the incentive to receive training outside the firm, to shift to positions on other tracks within the same firm, or to completely change the direction of one's occupational career.

In contrast, *contingent* models of work are characterized by time-bound contracts with no promise of work beyond those parameters (Henretta, 1994). Among other things, the movement toward contingent models of work has been driven by technological change, foreign competition, concerns about the cost of labor, the decline of manufacturing, and the emergence of service-sector positions, which offer few benefits and low wages, and are generally not unionized.[30] The result is that employers keep fewer employees in their lifetime pools and more in their contingent

---

[29]These characteristics are typical of positions in the "internal labor market" (Doeringer & Piore, 1971) and of "primary jobs" in a "dual labor market" (Piore, 1971).

[30]Henretta (1994) notes that the purest form of the contingent model is the "day laborer" model, though contingent models need not be restricted to unskilled positions. In fact, many highly skilled positions are now filled in this way. Most part-time work does fit this model; part-time positions are also problematic in that these positions offer very limited, if any, health or pension benefits. So while part-time positions allow for flexibility, many adults, especially single parents or those in unmarried or alternative relationships, must work full-time in order to receive needed benefits.

THE STUDY OF LIVES / 57

pools. Relative to lifetime models, opportunities in contingent models are not tied as strongly to tenure (and therefore age), making recurrent education throughout adult life all the more important as a means for staying competitive in a rapidly changing market. In the end, contingent models of work may force more flexibility not only because individuals will move between many positions of uncertain duration throughout their work lives, but because limited health care and pension benefits may require them to work well into their later years.

Flextime Work Policies

In the late-1980s, political debates about rearranging (rather than reducing) work time surfaced in the United States. As part of these debates, flextime strategies were proposed and adopted by a select set of American work organizations and corporations.[31] Little is known about the availability of flextime policies and the proportion of workers who do or might take advantage of them. Perhaps *employees* are hesitant to take advantage of flextime policies if they fear that their employers or peers may view them as less committed to their jobs or to the organizations for which they work; or perhaps employees fear that they will subsequently lose important chances at promotion, or that they will be forced into lower level positions that are not as challenging or do not require full-time work commitments. Perhaps *employers* find flextime policies incompatible with their needs; employers need to know when their employees will be at work, and they need to minimize work disruption in order to meet deadlines. Nonetheless, flextime work policies do increase the potential for pursuits in other domains.

Growth in Adult Enrollment in Higher Education and in Educational Programs Aimed at Adults

The enrollment of adults, and of women in particular, has been an important force behind the exponential growth in higher education (Centre for Educational Research and Innovation, 1987; Davies, 1995). While educational attainment is generally regarded as the main vehicle for achieving occupational and social mobility, adults also cite other reasons for returning to school. In some cases, adults return to complete degrees previously abandoned, others wish to pursue advanced degrees in their current fields, and still others wish to train in completely new areas.

While adult-oriented and continuing education programs have become more prevalent in recent years and offer new possibilities for training, these programs also come with a set of concerns for both the student and the institution (student concerns were covered in the prior section on "Social Responses to the Adult Student"). Researchers have cautioned that in order for adult educational programs to be successful, educators must first identify and address the needs of different types of

---

[31] However, as few as 12 percent of American workers are on flexible schedules, though this proportion is expected to increase in years to come (Christopherson, 1991). For discussions of attempts at reforming working time in West Germany, France, the Netherlands, Belgium, the United States, and Japan, see Hinrichs, Roche, and Sirianni (1991).

adult students (Centre for Educational Research and Innovation, 1987; Davies, 1995; Schütze, 1987). Educational institutions have begun to recognize that adult students as a whole do not share a common set of needs and goals, and that they pose unique sets of concerns relative to those of traditional students (for a discussion of different types of adult students, and institutional responses to them, see Settersten & Lovegreen, 1998).

Individual Characteristics That Affect Life-Course Flexibility

In addition to the factors already discussed, several individual-level characteristics may promote or constrain life-course flexibility, depending on their direction. These factors are outlined in Table 3.[32] While these factors are classified as properties of individuals, this should not be taken to mean that they are congenital and permanent. Most of these factors interact with, are shaped by, and are even rooted in, meso- and macro-level social structures and processes, which themselves change over time.[33]

"Planful Competence"

Much of what Clausen (1991) calls "planful competence" is the ability to make informed, rational decisions and set realistic short- and long-term goals. Planful competence involves "knowing one's interests and developing them. It entails knowing about available options and thinking about how to maximize or expand those options, [and the] ability to make accurate assessments of the aims and actions of others in order to interact responsibly with them in the pursuit of one's objectives. Further, the person must have sufficient self-confidence to pursue his or her goal and desires" (p. 808). Clausen suggests that adolescents who possess planful competence fare much better over the life course than those who do not. Those with higher competence make more realistic and better choices in education, occupation, and marriage; these choices create more stable educational, work, and family lives in the long run, and they leave individuals feeling more satisfied with their lives.

What implications does planful competence have for the need for flexibility? As noted earlier, separate periods of education, work, and retirement now significantly structure the individual life course; more formal preparation is now needed to enter most occupations; and the structure of opportunities within occupations has changed dramatically. These factors make planful competence an increasingly

---

[32] Admittedly, this is not an exhaustive list of individual-level characteristics that may either promote or constrain life-course flexibility.

[33] Of course, social structures and processes also *generate* groups and individuals at risk, the events and conditions that are risky, and some of the coping, competence, and resilience that groups and individuals use to mediate risk (e.g., Link & Phelan, 1995; see also Chapter 5). Meso-level contexts and processes (e.g., in families, schools, peer groups, work organizations, communities and neighborhoods) seem particularly important in this regard; these settings often serve to connect micro and macro levels (Hagestad, 1990; see also Chapter 5).

Table 3. Individual Characteristics that Affect Life-Course Flexibility

- Planful Competence
- Motivation and Coping Skills
- Risk-Taking
- Time and Financial Resources
- Family Responsibilities and Support
- Employment Status and Occupational Position

valuable commodity.[34] Those who possess a high degree of planful competence likely reap the advantages, and *cumulative* advantages, of good decisions over their lives. For this reason, planful competence would seem a particularly good commodity to possess early in life. Because planfully competent individuals also seem to have more stable adult lives, they may therefore have little need for later flexibility in that they have chosen educational and occupational paths for which, and partners for whom, they are well-suited.[35]

Motivation and Coping Skills

Because of their more extensive life experiences, adult workers and students may be more inclined than their younger counterparts to adopt a proactive stance in gaining new experiences. For example, adult students seem to exhibit more rational and calculated decision-making tendencies, and greater drive and determination. Perhaps this is because adult students feel they must make up for lost time and realize they are faced with a more limited time horizon. Despite the obstacles they face, the prior life experiences of adults may provide them with a set of coping skills upon which to draw when faced with difficult situations. As a result, adults may be better able to handle the failures, disappointments, and pressures that accompany new pursuits.

"Risk-Taking"

One factor that creates resistance to flexibility is the common "aversion to risk-taking" (Rehn, 1977). Many adults may be content with familiar settings and the existing nature of their lives, and may neither desire nor seek change. This tendency may make new ventures, such as a return to school or a change of career, less likely.

---

[34] As Clausen (1991) notes, the "rational assessment of opportunities has to a large degree replaced tradition as the primary basis for choices to be made. Moreover, selection for professional or bureaucratic careers strongly favors those who show high potential and plan for the development of that potential early in their lives ... Higher education, and a reasonably clear idea of who and what one is and wants to be, now give not only a head start but an acceleration that makes it difficult for late bloomers without special talents to catch up" (pp. 806-807).

[35] At the same time, planful competence seems to come naturally with age, as "maturity tends to bring increasing skills in assessing what one must do to achieve success and smooth relationships with others" (Clausen, 1991, p. 809).

For example, adult students may fear that they are ill-equipped to return to school because they have long been absent from educational settings. They may be fearful of studying, writing papers, using computers, and competing with younger students. As a result, they may avoid educational experiences in adulthood, or they may choose less rigorous or less challenging educational experiences. These fears may be reinforced by the "frustrations and inappropriateness" of many admission policies and practices for adult students (Calloway & Jorgensen, 1994).[36] In addition, classes may be scheduled at times that conflict with family or work schedules; adult students may not feel supported by their younger peers, or by faculty or administrative personnel; and because adult students are generally on campus for limited periods of time, they may feel alienated from campus life.

Time and Financial Resources

Individuals often cannot reduce work time for other activities because they do not have the resources to make those activities possible, even if those activities would be most efficient or advantageous in the long-run (Rehn, 1977). For example, according to the Centre for Educational Research and Innovation (1987), older adults state that the lack of time and money are the two greatest barriers to obtaining education or retraining. (These factors have been discussed in previous sections.) An adult considering or making a return to school is faced with a complicated set of tradeoffs related to how educational experiences might be managed along with work and family priorities, particularly given limited time and financial resources to devote to these priorities.

Family Responsibilities and Support

Family responsibilities represent a considerable barrier for adults wanting to pursue educational, work, or leisure activities. For example, faced with competing demands, the adult student must simultaneously balance family, work, and educational responsibilities to the best of their abilities. Given these often conflicting responsibilities, it is not surprising that adult students demonstrate the highest attrition rate from college (Calloway & Jorgensen, 1994). Limited resources may be a particularly acute problem for single parents who generally possess fewer resources than their counterparts who are married or cohabiting. While family obligations may compete with the desire to pursue other activities, families may also be a source of tremendous support. For example, a supportive family environment may provide the necessary "infrastructure" to make a return to school possible and successful. Moreover, the presence of a working spouse or partner may provide financial backing for the pursuit of non-work activities. In addition, adults whose children are

---

[36]For example, older students may be required to take standardized college admissions examinations; those who write letters of recommendation may have little knowledge of the adult applicant's academic abilities; and requests are routinely made for information on the financial status and addresses of one's parents. While these practices are appropriate for students of traditional ages, they may be less appropriate for non-traditional students.

successfully launched may have additional time, energy, and financial resources to spend on other pursuits.

Employment Status and Occupational Position

The relationship between occupational position and the pursuit of other experiences in adult life is undoubtedly complicated. On the one hand, the level of complexity and stress associated with one's occupational position may seriously limit opportunities for other activities (Loessi-Miller, 1997). Workers faced with considerable job responsibilities may have neither the time nor the energy to devote to outside pursuits. On the other hand, individuals whose occupational positions are complex and challenging may be more resourceful, more competent at juggling multiple roles, and more likely to seek out and be successful at other kinds of activity.

Similarly, an individual's occupational position and the organization for which she or he works may also promote or hinder chances for retraining. On-the-job retraining programs are an important means for retooling adult workers. However, there is great selectivity in the kinds of workers who are chosen for training, and in the kinds of organizations that provide these opportunities (e.g., Brown, 1990; Knoke & Kalleberg, 1994). These types of experiences are likely to become increasingly important for organizations and workers, particularly in light of the many factors that make the pursuit of more formal educational experiences difficult during adult life.

The relationship between employment status and the pursuit of other experiences in adult life seems similarly complicated. Full-time work makes the pursuit of other activities, especially full-time schooling, difficult. However, cutting back to part-time work is not an option for many adults and their families. In addition, even if part-time work were a financial possibility, many could not afford the loss of benefits associated with this change of status. Therefore, while a shift to part-time status might offer the needed flexibility for adults to engage in other activities, it is not a viable option for many adults and their families.

Life-Course Flexibility and the Future

In the end, shall we take an optimistic view and emphasize new potentials for life-course flexibility? Or shall we take a pessimistic view and instead emphasize the many barriers that make the life course rigid? Future research must better explore how factors such as those discussed above might serve as opportunities or barriers to flexibility, and how any barriers might be overcome.

I would like to remain optimistic that concerns about flexible life scheduling will become increasingly important in policy debates, and that leaders worldwide will take seriously the challenge of developing policies and programs aimed at promoting flexibility. The absence of serious discussion of flexible life scheduling in American policy circles is both noteworthy and alarming. As Best (1990) notes, "beyond its apparent humanistic virtues, [policies aimed at building flexibility have] the potential to reduce a variety of social problems in the areas of education and training, family life, retirement, and unemployment" (p. 217).

Several factors ought to increase political discussion about flexibility (Best, 1990). First, the changing nature of work and education (e.g., technical and social change require retraining in the middle years; extended education in young adulthood may not be possible without intermittent periods of work; the emergence of "non-traditional" educational curricula and programs; fewer desirable occupational positions, especially in light of gains in educational attainment). Second, greater time pressures faced by families, especially dual-earner families (e.g., shifts in the need for both parents in intact families to be working, and in single parenting, create serious time pressures). Third, changes in unemployment (e.g., rises in unemployment may create the need to spread fewer jobs over a larger number of workers). Fourth, changes in retirement (e.g., public concerns about the viability and future of social security and pension systems; health and longevity trends make the extension of work into later life more possible and may promote more varied pathways to retirement).[37] Fifth, the prevailing values and political philosophy of the time (Best argues that in the 1960s and 1970s preferences emerged for "new balances" between work and non-work time and for improvements in the quality of working environments. What is the climate now?) And sixth, assumptions about cost effectiveness and the ability of work organizations to respond to hopes for flexibility (e.g., that proposals geared toward flexibility would "come at little or no cost" or might even be cost-effective; and that work organizations could easily "adapt their operations to allow for flexibility," p. 223). Whether proposals aimed at creating flexibility are supported will partially depend on these and other factors. The success of such proposals will first hinge on whether life-course *inflexibility* is perceived or defined as a political problem.

Several factors have also hindered major movement toward flexibility, particularly in the United States (Best, 1990). First, individuals' increasing concern over economic and employment security (e.g., while many people may be interested in sacrificing income for gains in free time, they may not be willing to gain free time at the cost of their long-term economic security, job security, or promotional chances). Second, individuals' growing concerns about savings and investment, and a resurgence of a strong "work ethic" that stresses the importance of work, not time away from it. Third, de-emphasis on issues related to social equity (e.g., concerns about the economy, and about financial and job security, have diffused concerns about other social problems). Fourth, limits of organizational adaptability. For example, organizations are generally preoccupied with concerns that they consider more important than restructuring work time. In addition, such concerns are even less

---

[37]Best (1990) argues that prior decades were characterized by growing resistance to early retirement. However, strong evidence contradicts this statement; there is a clear and marked historical trend toward earlier and earlier retirement in modern nations (e.g., Guillemard & Rein, 1993; Kohli, 1994), though there is some speculation that this trend may now have tapered off (e.g., Burkhauser & Quinn, 1994).

important to employers when there is a surplus of available labor. Many of these proposals also receive support from top-level administrators and managers, but not from the middle managers and supervisors who must actually deal with implementing such proposals in daily life, bear the burdens created by them, and be concerned about the unknown and negative impacts of these reforms. And fifth, diffusion of the issue, which may be brought about by several problems. These include the fact that it is difficult to agree on the need for, and feasibility of, flexibility; that there is no single program for achieving these aims; and that there is no clear consensus about who should bear the costs of these programs (workers, employers, the state), how the costs should be borne, and who should be responsible for implementing them.

There are several questions we might ask ourselves as we develop, implement, and evaluate programs and policies aimed at creating flexibility. For whom has the proposal been developed? What are the motivations behind it? How is flexibility to be achieved? What are important barriers to achieving flexibility? How will flexibility be used? What benefits will flexibility provide, and for whom? With what losses will flexibility come, and for whom? And who should bear the financial burden—the individuals and families that benefit from these policies and programs, all taxpayers, educational institutions, work organizations, the government?

Similarly, we might consider whether the proposal intends to increase a particular activity within a specific period of life or whether it instead intends to change the nature of life as a whole (see Habib & Nusberg, 1990). It is the latter type of proposal that is more comprehensive and adequately addresses the reorganization of education, work, and leisure over the life course. Yet few policies or programs are aimed at the entire life course and the ways in which the activities, opportunities, and constraints of one life period impact those in another period. Have various attempts at building flexibility actually broken up the rigid separation of training, work, and retirement? Or have they simply incorporated a few elements of flexibility?

Consider the question about the motivation for proposals aimed at reorganizing the life course. Different rationale and motivation may underlie various attempts at reorganization (Habib & Nusberg, 1990). One rationale, focused on the individual level, is that a better balance of education, work, and leisure at all phases would improve well-being, lessen burnout, and reduce technological obsolescence. Increases in longevity and the improved health of older people also strengthen this rationale. Another rationale, focused more on the level of society, is that extending worklife further into old age will reduce strain on the economy, and on public and private pension systems. (This rationale is also oriented toward a specific period of life rather than the life course as a whole.) Other rationale might exist on both the levels of the individual and the society.

We might also ask whether the approach simply creates a greater number of "standard" or state-sanctioned patterns for alternating between work, education, and leisure, or whether it genuinely attempts to maximize what Rehn (1977, p. 121) calls "the greatest possible freedom of individual choice" and what Sirianni (1991, p. 231) calls the "self-management of time." That is, whether it gives individuals more control over the allocation of personal time to various activities and leaves "wide margins" for "individual or group deviations."

We must thoroughly examine which elements of these proposals have already been implemented in other countries, and with what success; what individuals must trade off to achieve flexibility, and whether such tradeoffs are feasible given existing institutional constraints; the implications for overall economic productivity, or for productivity in specific sectors; and, finally, what existing experience and research can contribute to the evaluation of options, as well as what needs to be learned to make an informed evaluation of those options (Habib & Nusberg, 1990).

These are important questions around which developmental scientists, educators, and policy-makers must converge. Each of these groups must become more cognizant of the many factors that serve to promote or constrain lives, and of the multiple levels at which those factors operate and interact. These concerns are certain to become more important as time becomes a "contested terrain" (Sirianni, 1991) in international debates about the welfare of societies and of their citizens, and in debates about the nature and rhythm of the life course in modern societies.

CHAPTER
2

Challenges Posed by Age and Age Structuring

Age lies at the heart of most theory and research on human development, regardless of discipline. But because age is an integral dimension for the interdisciplinary study of human lives, and because of its simplicity, have we taken its importance for granted? Anthropologist Fry recently noted that even the most basic questions dealing with age have been given little attention because developmental scientists have rarely asked direct questions to members of any culture about how they think about, use, and experience age and the life course (Fry, 1994, 1996).

Nonetheless, age would seem important from the perspectives of both individuals and social structures, of self and society. For example, social psychologists and anthropologists have suggested that age functions as a convenient dimension with which to map social and cultural expectations about experiences and roles. Individuals use these age-linked "mental maps" to organize their own lives, the lives of others, and their general expectations about the life course (Elder, 1995; Fry, 1986; Hagestad, 1990; Hagestad & Neugarten, 1985; Hogan, 1985; Keith & Kertzer, 1984; Neugarten & Neugarten, 1986; Nydegger, 1986a; Riley, 1987). These maps, in turn, serve an important human need for order and predictability. Of course, lives as they are actually lived may sway from these cultural models of the life course (Rindfuss, Swicegood, & Rosenfeld, 1987). Nonetheless, individuals' perceptions of these models, and the degree to which age is embedded in them, may be powerful forces in determining how the life course is actively negotiated and experienced (Fry, 1996).

Similarly, age likely enters into and shapes everyday social interaction, affecting the expectations and evaluations of the individuals involved in those exchanges. However, little is known about the manner and degree to which it does so. Along these lines, age has been described as a "diffuse status characteristic," in that individuals may use cues about others' ages to make more general assumptions about their attributes and abilities (Boyd & Dowd, 1988). This practice would seem especially likely when little else is known about a person besides obvious "master status" and generally visible characteristics such as race, sex, and perhaps social class. As Boyd and Dowd (1988, p. 87) point out, the "diffusiveness" of these characteristics probably has its origin in their "portability" in that they always accompany the individual.

Personality psychologists have also debated about whether and how age is linked to personality attributes and behavioral dispositions (e.g., Block, 1993; Costa & McCrae, 1994), conceptions of the self (e.g., Markus & Herzog, 1991; Waterman & Archer, 1990), and processes of self-regulation (e.g., Brandstädter & Greve, 1994; Heckhausen & Schulz, 1995a). Additionally, sociologists, historians, and anthropologists have asked questions about the ways in which age functions in social structure: as a dimension organizing familial, educational, and occupational institutions, as well as the larger society (e.g., Buchmann, 1989; Chudacoff, 1989; Kohli, 1986a, 1986b; Riley & Riley, 1994; Sørensen, 1991).

As mentioned earlier, age structuring refers to the fact that every society has unique ways of thinking about, and organizing lives around, age. Age structuring may be *formal,* operating at the level of social structure and social institutions, or it may be *informal,* tapping the ways in which individuals and groups in a society divide the life course into meaningful segments, define the kinds of behavior considered appropriate for individuals of different ages, and designate the proper timing and sequencing of life experiences (Kertzer, 1989). The chapter opens with a discussion of the ways in which age and age structuring might differ by gender and along other social dimensions, across life spheres, and across cultures; and how these might be altered as a function of the dramatic change that has occurred in key demographic parameters in this century, especially longevity and mortality, fertility, and morbidity. Then, it addresses the measurement and uses of different types of age, including chronological, biological, psychological, and social age. These are followed by a discussion of subjective age identification; age norms and expectations; and developmental goal-setting. The measurement of age-related images and stereotypes, and of life phases, are also covered. The chapter closes with a brief discussion of the challenges of age and social policy, particularly whether we should advocate need-based rather than age-based approaches to social policies, and whether age-based policies bring the potential for age divisiveness in the population.

AGE STRUCTURING AND GENDER

Age usually operates interdependently with sex, and both age and sex are obviously universal categories (LaFontaine, 1978; Linton, 1942; Parsons, 1942). Most researchers have assumed that age structuring, whether formal or informal, may be quite different for men's and women's lives, with the strength of gender[1]

---

[1] Rossi (1986, p. 113) reminds us of the fundamental distinction between "sex" and "gender," with "sex" referring to the "reproductive and sexual characteristics that differentiate the female from the male, and with "gender" referring to "all social and psychological attributes linked to the social roles of men and women."

distinctions themselves conditioned by, and dependent on, age (Kertzer, 1989). In the words of Moen (1996, p. 177), "gender itself sets the context of lives," reflecting physiological, social, and historical conditions. Similarly, Hagestad (1991) has noted that anthropological research on transitions has suggested that men and women may attach different social meanings to age, and that men and women may use different guidelines to measure the progress of their lives.

Hernes (1987) even suggests that men and women may have different needs for predictability and order, and that they may experience different kinds of time.[2] Men's lives, Hernes says, are bound to linear time (and are therefore more bound to chronological age), while women's lives are instead more bound to cyclical (or at least non-linear) time (and are therefore less bound to chronological age). Cyclical time is time in which planning is limited, and is influenced more by "nature and deep cultural rhythms" (p. 106). Linear time, on the other hand, is man-made clock time, and runs independently of nature; it is future- and goal-oriented, easily-manipulated, rational time. Hernes' ideas mesh well with those of others who argue that the lives of women are more intimately tied to the lives of other people, and that women's lives are, therefore, less predictable and more discontinuous (e.g., Gilligan, 1982; Hagestad & Neugarten, 1985; Moen, 1996).

It is not surprising, then, that different social spheres have also been associated with different modes of time. The traditional lives of most men have been more strongly tied to the economic and political spheres; those spheres seem anchored in linear time; and the male life course may therefore be more constrained by age. In contrast, the traditional lives of women have been more strongly tied to the sphere of family; the temporal experience of the family sphere seems non-linear; and the female life course may therefore be less constrained by chronological age, with the exception of imposing biological clocks around reproduction. If we accept Hernes' argument, part of the "contradictions" of parenthood (Hays, 1996) that many working mothers, in particular, experience may result from the fact that men and women live on (or are oriented toward) different kinds of time, and that these temporal modes clash as individuals move between work and family spheres, which also operate on different kinds of time.

Much of what we know about the life course is focused on the "public" sphere, rather than the "private," and on male experiences in the labor market, in particular, at the neglect of women's experiences (Krüger, 1996, p. 143). This has resulted in significant "gender-blindness" in our research, and that it is important for us to "take a thousand steps . . . without the comfort of male shoes" to push our empirical and theoretical understanding of the life course. Life-course theory and research must become more sensitive to differences between men's and women's experiences.

---

[2] Hernes hints that these differences are natural to each sex, though this is likely a controversial stance. Others might suggest that these differences, if they exist, are instead socially constructed gender differences.

AGE STRUCTURING ALONG OTHER SOCIAL DIMENSIONS

Population-level behavioral patterns often show that the way the life course is actually experienced goes hand-in-hand with social location. The most common dimensions of social location examined in the literature include sex (as discussed above, with sex differences generally assumed to reflect gender differences), cohort, race (with racial differences generally assumed to reflect ethnic differences), and social class (education, occupation, income, or some combination thereof). While most scholars recognize that life-course patterns may differ along these social dimensions, little empirical research has examined this variability, particularly at the level of subjective experience (Fry, 1990a). As a result, developmental scientists must continue to describe and explain these multiple definitions and experiences, and our theory and research must allow for these complexities.

AGE STRUCTURING AND LIFE SPHERES

In most Western societies, many social institutions are formally organized by age, or at least to some degree. For example, primary and secondary educational institutions are heavily age-graded (Angus, Mirel, & Vinovskis, 1988), work institutions often structure prospects for promotion by age and seniority (Lashbrook, 1996; Lawrence, 1996a; Rosenbaum, 1984), and retirement policies and benefits are often structured around age (Henretta, 1994; Kohli, 1994).

The degree of both formal and informal age structuring may vary by life sphere. As discussed in Chapter 1, an emerging debate in the literature concerns the degree to which various life spheres (e.g., family, work, education) are more or less age-bound. For example, it has been argued that age is more salient in the economic and political spheres than it is in the family sphere. Within the economic sphere, age structuring has been linked to the emergence of the market. Within the political sphere, age structuring has been linked to the emergence of the nation-state, citizenship, and the welfare state. Clearly, chronological age is a convenient and practical administrative gauge. It is an easily-measured, objective, and universal attribute. Its use in these spheres may be linked to what sociologists, in the tradition of Max Weber (1904-5/1994), describe as the process of "rationalization": With the evolution of capitalism, human action became increasingly subject to measurement, calculation, and control, all with the hope of making society and its systems run most efficiently.

The family sphere, on the other hand, may not be structured by age to the same degree as the economic and political spheres. In fact, several scholars have suggested that family experiences are the most complex and diverse (Buchmann, 1989). An important exception here is that dramatic changes in mortality and morbidity have made patterns of illness and death among family members more predictable: At the turn of this century, most young people normally experienced the death of a parent or sibling; now, the experience of family-related deaths, whether of a parent, sibling, or spouse, is generally confined to the latter part of adult life (Hagestad,

1988; Uhlenberg, 1980). Age is not only strongly linked to mortality patterns, but also to morbidity patterns, and particularly to the emergence of chronic diseases and disability (Jette, 1996). However, social and demographic factors, especially sex and race, also affect these patterns significantly (George, 1996b; Markides & Black, 1996; Moen, 1996). These examples suggest that the degree of formal and informal age structuring may vary by life sphere. Because lives are lived out in multiple spheres, and because these spheres are often experienced in dramatically different ways, our theory and research must be sensitive to these differences.

AGE STRUCTURING ACROSS CULTURES

Most cultures and societies have their own frameworks for understanding age, age periods, and the life course as a whole, yet little is known about these frameworks. Cultural contexts structure and create variability in the ways in which lives are lived, represented, and assigned meanings. Indeed, much of human behavior would seem conditioned by the "time perspectives" of the individual and her or his culture (Frank, 1939). Project A.G.E. (Age, Generation, and Experience) is the only study of which I am aware of that has undertaken explicit cross-cultural comparisons of these frameworks across several continents. Project A.G.E. teaches us important lessons about the power of culture in shaping the life course. (In the field of child development, the monumental research of the Whiting's (1975) Six Culture Study is also noteworthy.)[3]

Lessons from Project A.G.E.

Project A.G.E. (a team of seven anthropologists) explored the meanings of age and aging in seven communities in four countries between 1982 and 1990 (Hong Kong, China; Swarthmore, Pennsylvania; Momence, Illinois; Blessington, Ireland; Clifden, Ireland; the pastoral Herero of Botswana, South Africa; and the !Kung Bushmen of Botswana, South Africa) (Keith, Fry, Glascock, Ikels, Dickerson-Putnam, Harpending, & Draper, 1994). These sites were chosen to maximize variability along several dimensions, including subsistence activities, resources, size

---

[3] In this study, the Whitings systematically explore how the cultural environments within which children are reared shape children's social behavior. I note it here for two reasons: first, because the initial impetus for their work was to understand the link between culture and the formation of the adult personality (and not to understand child development *per se*); and second, because their work, and that conducted by several generations of scholars whom they have trained, has critically shaped three decades of research in cross-cultural psychology, most of which has focused on child development. For a review of the cultural structuring of child development, see Super and Harkness (1997). In addition, Super and Harkness introduce three recent models developed in the field of child development that explicitly emphasize the role of larger cultural ecology: the "eco-cultural niche" model, the "developmental niche" model, and the "developmental micronichè" model. Life-course researchers might benefit from exploring the applicability of these models to periods other than childhood, and from taking seriously the challenge of building larger cultural ecology into theory and research. In fact, many of the issues discussed in this book have not been, but need to be, systematically compared within and between cultures (see also the section on comparisons in human development in Chapter 5).

and density of population, residential stability, and the complexity of roles in family and work.

Each investigator was fluent in the language of the community for which she or he was the primary investigator and lived in that community for at least a year, participating in activities and asking for detailed explanations about behavior. In each community, traditional field observations were gathered; interviews were conducted with between one to two hundred adults about work, family, community involvement, health perceptions, and attitudes about age; and detailed, verbatim life histories were conducted with at least twelve older people.

As noted above, the primary mission of Project A.G.E. was to map the meanings of age and aging in a variety of cultural contexts. In each site, investigators explored the *cognitive* meanings of age (e.g., What age categories do members of a culture perceive? How do they define, indicate, or signal these categories?), the *evaluative* meanings of age (e.g., What value is attached to different ages, age categories, or markers of age?), and age as a *criterion for social participation* (e.g., What informal and formal interactions are patterned by age? What are the norms for interaction between people of different ages? What are actual behaviors?)

One of the innovative strategies adopted by Project A.G.E. investigators is the "Age Game." In the Age Game, respondents are given a deck of cards that contain descriptions tailored to represent plausible *personae* for that site (e.g., "A male, high school graduate, single, is working, living with parents," "A female, working, married, two children both of whom have recently married," or "A male, widowed, retired, living with adult children"). Each respondent sorts the deck based on guesses about the ages of the people described on the cards (the decks for Blessington, Momence, Swarthmore, and Hong Kong had 24 female cards and 24 male cards, resulting in a total of 48 cards; the decks for Clifden, the Herero, and the !Kung had 15 female cards and 15 male cards, resulting in a total of 30 cards). Some characteristics on the cards were used in all sites (e.g., marital status, children's status, grandchildren's status, household composition, housing arrangements, work status), while other characteristics were site-specific (e.g., migration is a theme relevant to the life course in Ireland but not in any other site; great-grandchildren are not referenced in Botswana, nor was education beyond the primary grades, because these are rare).

The respondent first sorts the cards for her or his own sex, and then for the opposite sex. After respondents finish sorting the cards, they are asked: "What name would you give to the age-bracket or the age-group of the people you have placed in this pile? Are there any other words you might use to describe this general age group? Roughly, what is the age or range of ages in terms of years of the people described in this pile?" Using the respondent's own terms for these groups, the researchers explore differences between the age groups. They pay particular attention to the experiences that comprise each age period, those experiences that mark the transition from one period to the next, the best and worst things about each period, the core concerns of individuals in each period, and information about some of the actual people they know in these periods (Fry, 1994). For the American sites, the game was structured in a fashion similar to that of the parlor game "Twenty

Questions" in an attempt to guess the unknown person's age, though, as we will soon learn, this strategy did not work well elsewhere. (For an example of the Age Game and associated questions for one of the American sites, see the Appendix of Keith et al. [1994].) Across the sites, the number of divisions of the life course ranged from an average of zero to eleven divisions, with an overall average of about five divisions.

Where *cognitive* meanings of age are concerned, Project A.G.E. investigators generally found two kinds of results: either straightforward, affirmative responses to questions about age (indicating that age was a meaningful concept in that community), or clear indications that age was not at all a relevant dimension. Age was a meaningful concept in five of the seven sites (Hong Kong, both American sites, suburban Blessington, Herero of Botswana), though there was variation in the exact meanings of age, the number of life periods perceived, and the ages at which these life periods begin and end.

Age was largely irrelevant in two of the seven communities (!Kung and Clifden), particularly as indicated by their inability to play the age game. The investigators note that it is not that people in these communities completely lack a vocabulary to talk about age. It is simply that age has such "low salience as a marker of individual variability" in those communities (Keith, 1994, p. 204). For example, in response to questions about people of different ages, the !Kung say things such as "Oh, they have all kinds of names. There's John, Sue, Jane, George . . ." The !Kung actually define "*every* life transition" in terms of physical capability or functionality rather than chronological age (Keith, 1994, p. 206). (In fact, the !Kung do not use numbers, and questions about chronological age are meaningless. In addition, because the !Kung have no written language, the deck of cards designed for that site instead had icons. And while the Herero have a written language, the investigators discovered that many Herero were not very proficient and needed to have the cards read to them.) In rural Clifden, the other community in which age was largely irrelevant, only about half of the participants manage to "sort" the Age Game cards; those who do "sort" the cards actually arrange them in a single line until there is no room left on the table. They individualize each card and ask the investigator which members of the community the cards are meant to represent. Clifden respondents seem "uneasy with questions that presuppose age categories. For example, when the investigators asked questions about the difficulties that older people face in their community, Clifdenites tended to say things such as "Well, some do OK, and others don't. Which ones do you mean?" In contrast, chronological age had the strongest salience in communities that are part of modern, industrialized societies. These findings are in line with the "chronologization" and "institutionalization" theses introduced in Chapter 1.

An interesting methodological point noted by Project A.G.E. investigators is that as their project moved into Botswana and the two Irish sites (the two American sites and Hong Kong were begun first), the metaphor of the "Age Game" as a *game* may have been confusing, frustrating, and even alienating. In each community, the Age Game was revealing, but never an easy task; besides unexpected difficulties in its administration, it also brought unexpected difficulties in the interpretation of its results (Fry, 1994). Because age categorizations lie at the heart of the game, the game was particularly problematic in the two sites in which age categorizations were seldomly used: among the !Kung and those in rural Clifden. Even among the Herero, who promptly sorted the cards by sex and age, the results of the sorting process were difficult to interpret in that age categories are generally subsumed by kinship categories and are not categories in their own right. Data that result from the Age Game, even for those communities in which the Age Game worked reasonably well, present "great challenges to interpretation and parsimonious display of results because the units of analysis (the age groups or life periods) are specific to each participant" (Fry, 1994, p. 152). At the same time, one of the major methodological lessons of Project A.G.E. emphasizes the "importance of discovering the research questions that have significance for the people we study, rather than pressing them for answers to our own" (Keith, 1994, p. 205).

To analyze the Age Game, the investigators used techniques suited for data characterized by significant variability and based on individual judgments about similarity and dissimilarity: Multidimensional Scaling and Cluster Analysis (for Multidimensional Scaling, see Borg & Groenen, 1997; for Cluster Analysis, see Everitt, 1993; Romesburg, 1990). These techniques are also designed to display the structure of data geometrically.

In the end, Fry (1994) suggests that three factors seem to be important sources of variation where the *cognitive* meanings of age are concerned: (1) *characteristics of the social field,* especially the size of the field (where the social field is relatively small, there is no need to make assumptions about people based on age or any other characteristic because an individual knows, or knows about, most people in the community; as a result, individuals think in particularistic and not universalistic terms) and its permanence or stability (where there is little residential turnover, there is no need to rely on impersonal categories such as age; where turnover is high, such categorizations become useful and commonplace); (2) *education* (where they find that formal schooling "seems to facilitate the ability and/or willingness to make generalizations on the basis of scant data," and that less educated respondents are "more likely to use their own life experience as the basis for discussion of the life course in general—that is, they remain concrete rather than abstract in their approach to the questions" (pp. 191-192);[4] (3) the *predictability* of, and *variability* around, *life experiences* (in communities in which life experiences are more predictable and less variable, respondents are more willing to generalize about age and life periods); and (4) the *degree to which the life course is "waged"* (that is, organized

---

[4] This finding is surprising, given that one might also have predicted the opposite—that respondents with higher levels of formal education, higher incomes, or higher occupational statuses, might be *less* inclined to make simple generalizations based on age, and *more* inclined to think about the life course in more complicated ways. For example, we might have expected them to raise the problem of reference groups more often in response to generalized questions about age (that is, to say things like, "About whom, more specifically, are we talking?"). Given their greater resources, we might also have expected them to view a more flexible life course, one in which opportunities and experiences are not strongly related to age.

around work and the economy) and *"staged"* (through the state and its policies, many of which are age-based or relate to specific life periods).

Where *evaluative* meanings of age are concerned, all seven sites evaluated old age as the least desirable time in life. Surprisingly, the United States and Ireland held the least negative reactions to old age, especially from older people themselves. However, these responses were generally hedged by an important *if:* "If you have your health . . ."[5] The most negative reactions to old age were in the two African sites, presumably because life in those communities is significantly tied to health and vigor, and aging undoubtedly comes with some loss in physical capacity. Another interesting finding along these lines relates to dependence and independence in old age, concerns about which were often expressed in Hong Kong, the United States, and among the Herero. For Americans, being dependent on others, including children, was one of the worst potential things about old age. For the Chinese and Herero, on the other hand, dependence on others was one of the potentially good things about old age. And for the Herero, one of best things about being young is that it comes with the responsibility to care for elders.

Finally, where age as a *criterion for social participation* is concerned, significant variability in the "age borders" on interaction and behavior existed across the communities. The two American sites and the !Kung Bushmen were at two extremes. Among the !Kung, it was difficult to find any situation in which people of only one age category are present. Instead, "people of all ages worked, rested, played, and ate together—often touching and leaning on each other" (Keith, 1994, p. 210). On the other hand, in the United States, and especially in Swarthmore, Pennsylvania, age defined more and tighter social boundaries, with "fine age distinctions separating people" into age-graded social contexts.

In conceptualizing the types of constraints imposed by age, Project A.G.E. investigators make a useful distinction between physical and socio-cultural constraints. Physical constraints are generally imposed by biology, and were especially problematic in settings of smaller scale and lower technological development. In contrast, socio-cultural constraints are generally imposed by society (and can therefore presumably be changed), and were strongest in settings of greater scale and technological development. These investigators argue that we must be "vigilant to keep physical and cultural boundaries of age distinct," and be certain that socio-cultural age barriers do not prevent the full participation of anyone in a society (Keith, 1994, p. 216). Project A.G.E. stands as a strong testimonial for the power of cross-cultural differences and the need to be sensitive to these differences in our theory and research.

---

[5] It is also important to keep in mind that one of the two American sites, Swarthmore, Pennsylvania, is a relatively affluent suburb of Philadelphia, with 25 percent of its population over age sixty. Might their results have been different if they had studied other American cities, towns, or regions with different characteristics?

States and Their Policies

The state often relies on, and even creates, conceptions of the life course. Age rules and preferences are embedded within the laws, policies, and social institutions of the state (Cain, 1976; Eglit, 1985; Neugarten, 1982). These also create cross-national variability in the structure and experience of the life course. For example, in many countries rights and responsibilities are explicitly structured by chronological age. Examples of these rights and duties include age regulations around voting, driving, drinking, working (especially with regard to child labor), marrying, compulsory schooling, or seeking public offices. Eligibility for pensions, social services, or social insurance are also often dictated by age. Many of the discussions about legal age center around questions of how soon in life individuals should be granted the adult rights and obligations, or how late in life these rights and obligations should be maintained (Cain, 1976). General references to age-related categories without clearly-specified ages are also common in legislation (e.g., "minors," "the elderly") (Cain, 1976). As Mayer and Schöpflin (1989, p. 200) have noted, "age groups are a favorite way of dividing up social problems," and larger age groups are often targeted for service bracketing. A thorough examination of the state and its policies may provide further insights into the ways in which age and the life course are treated in a society (see also later sections in this chapter on "Social Policy and the Question of Age Versus Need" and "Social Policy and the Question of Age Divisiveness").

The Representation of Age and Aging in Cultural Materials

An additional strand of research explores images of age and aging as they are represented in cultural materials such as folktales and myths, customs and traditions, literature (novels, newspapers, magazines), photographs, greeting cards, music, television and movies, language and metaphors. For excellent examples, see recent volumes edited by Featherstone and Wernick (1995), Shenk and Achenbaum (1994), and Kenyon, Birren, and Schroots (1991), as well as Green's (1993) "discourse" analysis of gerontology and the construction of old age. The research in this tradition is tied more to the arts and humanities than to the behavioral sciences. As a result, most of these explorations are based on anecdotal data and are rarely comparative. However, these explorations provide important impressions of the meanings of age and aging in a culture. Images of aging, whether real or imagined, "shape as well as reflect reality," and the field of "gerontology is replete with images of which it is barely aware and has only begun to grasp the place of images in shaping the lived experience of aging" (Cole, 1995, p. S341). Cole argues that gerontology can be "greatly enriched by a deeper understanding of the omnipresence of [such] images" (pp. S342-343). Similar arguments can be made about the images of other periods of life and the scholarship on those periods.

The Cultural "Canalization" of Development

Apart from Project A.G.E., most research has focused on individual differences within a single culture. As a result, scientists have largely "bypassed the central question of how culture serves as an organizational framework for persons who 'belong to it'" (Valsiner & Lawrence, 1997, p. 80). To better address this question, developmental scientists might take an "individual-socio-ecological frame of reference" (Valsiner & Lawrence, 1997). This frame of reference provides "access to the systemic organization of culture (and of the person). It entails a direct empirical focus on the relationship between the person and the immediate life context, which is culturally regulated by internalized cultural meanings and social suggestions by 'social others'" (Valsiner & Lawrence, 1997, p. 80; see also Valsiner, 1989). Little is known about how culture leaves its imprint on the psychological functioning and social development of individuals. How do cultural phenomena guide and shape developmental processes? To get at this question, we must better study the transactions between individuals and their social worlds. However, our traditional methods limit our understanding of these transactions (see the discussion in Chapter 5 on bringing social contexts into our research). This requires us to better conceptualize and measure socio-cultural and individual transactions, and to better conceptualize and measure change in those transactions. It also involves taking account of the active roles of the person, specific social contexts, and culture (Valsiner & Lawrence, 1997).

To do so, we must better understand questions related to the "cultural canalization" of development (Valsiner, 1989, 1994; Valsiner & Lawrence, 1997). The metaphor of "canalization" is set within a "co-constructivist" framework, which emphasizes the joint and active roles that people and their contexts (including culture) play in shaping human development. Within this framework the person and the social world are conceptualized as "co-constructing agents" that set *mutual constraints* on each other. These constraints place limits on present and future possibilities for development. They are likely to be heterogeneous and operate on many levels; and they may constrain in synchronic ways (at a specific point in time) and diachronic ways (at a future point in time by pushing individuals forward in specific directions). The function of these constraints is "to reduce the unmanageable excesses of uncertainty" and specify possible developmental routes to be followed (Valsiner & Lawrence, 1997, p. 84). An actual course is then chosen from this set of possibilities. The canalization of development by social structures is not viewed as deterministic; while these forces do limit future activity, they are viewed as providing an acceptable arena within which the individual may develop and perform. The dialectic between social and personal constraints produces new syntheses in the development of both the person and the context.

An important aspect of culture relates to cultural *meanings,* which are "intricately interwoven with the constraining forces being exerted upon the person, and they too are remade through development" (Valsiner & Lawrence, 1997, p. 85). Individuals construct their own personal meanings for their life experiences, but they do this in conjunction with the meanings provided by social structures and other individuals. Members of a culture also share taken-for-granted meanings of objects, events, and relationships, and taken-for-granted norms, ideologies, and beliefs. As Valsiner and Lawrence (1997) point out, "each person's internal version of the social meaning attached to an experience can be said to constitute a 'personal culture,' and this personal sense of the life course agreed to a greater or lesser degree with a narrative form that fits the expectations circulating within social discourse" (p. 88). Individuals are also likely to rely on cultural "tools" for understanding and reorganizing the life course when they encounter periods of significant developmental change. This is in line with Turner's (1969) earlier anthropological writings on the dominance of cultural meanings and of social organization during periods of "liminality" or transition.

AGE STRUCTURING AND NEW TIME BUDGETS FOR THE LIFE COURSE

As discussed in Chapter 1, the demography of an aging society, particularly increases in longevity and decreases in fertility, may have changed the nature of family and social life (Gee, 1987; Hagestad, 1988; Riley, 1985; Uhlenberg, 1980; Watkins, Bongarts, & Menken, 1987). For example, roles may be prolonged, the sequencing of roles over lifetime may become more varied and complex, and family relationships may have become more active and intense (Riley, 1985). Changes in mortality and longevity, have created a shift from "life by chance" to a life of "new certainties" and securities (Imhof, 1986, p. 251). We can now count on a great deal of lifetime in front of us, making it possible to plan at both the individual and collective levels (Brose, 1989). However, we still have much to learn about the ways in which individual lives, family life, social institutions, and society at large have been transformed by new demographic parameters, and our theory and research must take these changes into account. The field of demography has a "mutual attraction" with life-course analysis, given that the life course "begins and ends with demographic events—birth and death" and is shaped by events such as migration, marriage, and childbearing (Uhlenberg & Miner, 1996, p. 226). In addition, as we try to understand demographic patterns, we must ask questions related to age, cohort, period, and social location, which are integral parts of the life-course framework (Uhlenberg & Miner, 1996).

In recent years, there has been a burgeoning interest in time use by individuals and households, particularly with respect to gender differences on time spent in paid work, child-rearing, and housework activities (for a review of data limitations and measurement issues in this area, see Avery, Bryant, Douthitt, & McCullough, 1996). Most countries now routinely collect data on time use, and these surveys offer exciting new possibilities to explore questions related to changing time budgets across and for the life course.

TYPES OF AGE AND TIME

Research on the life course hinges upon the effective measurement of age. As Bytheway (1991) notes, somewhere in the process of doing our research the questions "How old are you?" or "When where you born?" must be asked. The measurement of chronological age seems relatively straightforward, apart from error (e.g., difficulty remembering one's age or date of birth) or deception (e.g., intentionally misrepresenting one's age or birth date) on the part of a respondent. Chronological age can be measured in a number of ways, ranging in level of specificity (in days, months, or years). When the question is "How old are you?" the information gathered is normally expressed in "completed years." Of course, the same basic information is obtained with the question "What is the date of your birth?" However, Bytheway (1991) reminds us that this question is quite different from the question "How old are you?" First, date of birth is anchored in a past biographic event, while age is instead a current characteristic. Second, date of birth remains the same throughout life, while age is always changing. And third, *complete* birth date (in month-day-year) asks for more precise information. If only birth year is asked, the calculation of age involves some rounding error. (In some gerontological research, both the date of birth and age are often asked at separate points in the data-gathering process to check the consistency of the information provided.) Jolicoeur, Pontier, Pernen, and Sempé (1988) even make a distinction between *postnatal age,* measured from day of birth, and *total age,* measured from the day of conception (obtained by correcting postnatal age with average duration of pregnancy, 0.75 years). These examples serve as important reminders that we must ask ourselves *why* age is being measured and *how* it will be used; answers to these questions will dictate the best format for measuring age. Regardless of how it is operationalized, age is often the most powerful piece of information about an individual (Schroots & Birren, 1988).

At the same time, chronological age itself is an "empty" variable. We rarely assume that age *itself* causes a behavior; instead, it is whatever age presumably indexes that is important. In addition, most researchers do not use age as an index for a single underlying dimension or process, but for a host of dimensions and processes (Birren & Schroots, 1996). For example, age is often used as a predictor of an individual's physical and emotional maturity, readiness to assume certain responsibilities, or even of the probability of experiencing various medical or social problems (Chudacoff, 1989; Fry, 1986).

Tests of age differences are often tests of arbitrarily-defined age brackets, sometimes into very broad bands (e.g., 55 to 74, 85+), or into smaller five- or ten-year bands (see also the section on "Life Phases" later in this chapter for a discussion of the commonly used terms "young-old" and "old-old"). Ironically, all of the care taken to measure age accurately is lost when these brackets are constructed. Worse still, we habitually break down our data according to such brackets without compelling rationale. Why are a particular set of age brackets meaningful? And why should we expect to find important differences along these divisions? We must also begin to be more critical of the circumstances under which we "hold age constant" in our analyses and not routinely control for age without justification.

Rather than use successive finely-graded age bands, we might organize our data into age grades that are socially recognized in a society, if these are known. Here, we might rely on findings from studies such as Project A.G.E., discussed earlier, whose intention it is to uncover these age grades. However, as will be discussed below (see section on "Life Phases"), the ages used to define these segments likely vary within and between societies, and over time. Nonetheless, this approach requires the investigator to come up with a set of meaningful age groupings *a priori*, and then test them to see whether they reveal interesting effects in relation to data of interest. Another approach might be to array a select set of data for which we expect important age patterning (e.g., key characteristics or sets of items) and to search for demarcations in those data. The researcher might then use this information to make qualitative distinctions between age groups. Age bands of equal intervals may be required to meet the needs of some statistical tests or models, and a "bottom up" search for qualitative markers of age groups will not allow this. In addition, this method also requires dimensions to be chosen in non-arbitrary ways; a rationale must be provided (and ideally one based in theory) for why particular dimensions have been used.

As individuals grow older, and as variability among age peers may increase over the life course (Dannefer, 1987), chronological age may become less useful as an index. As a result, Birren and colleagues (Birren & Cunningham, 1985; Schroots & Birren, 1988) suggest that we develop alternative, and more specific, measures of age that are sensitive to individual differences. Birren and Cunningham (1985, p. 8), for example, discuss three distinct kinds of age: (1) *biological age,* which is defined by an individual's "present position with respect to his [or her] potential life span. Thus, an individual's biological age may be younger or older than his [or her] chronological age"; (2) *social age,* which is defined by an individual's "roles and habits with respect to other members of the society" of which the individual is part. This individual may be older or younger depending on the extent to which he shows the age-graded behavior expected of him by his [or her] particular society or culture"; and (3) *psychological age,* which is defined by the "behavioral capacities of individuals to adapt to changing demands."

Birren and his colleagues argue that while psychological age is tied to biological and social ages, psychological age is a larger concept. Birren suggests that these three types of age are highly independent from one another, except perhaps at their boundaries. While Birren's typology is helpful for explicating the concept(s) of age, he and his colleagues offer little specific advice on how these different types of age might best be measured.[6] (Some of what Birren describes as "social age" will be discussed below in the section on age norms and age expectations.) To my knowledge, most discussion about different types of age has been pitched at a

---

[6] Schroots and Birren (1990, p. 51) do suggest that the measurement of biological age would involve the "assessment of functional capacities of vial or life-limiting organ systems," while the measurement of social age would involve "such aspects as the individual's type of dress, language habits, and social deference to other persons in leadership positions" and the social institutions to which an individual belongs.

conceptual level, and no study has attempted to measure and empirically validate these types of age and their independence. Most research directed at developing more refined measures of age has been aimed solely at biological age, functional age, or both.[7] Even these attempts alone have generated significant controversy.

Functional age, at least as conceived in an earlier paper by Birren (1969), is defined in terms of an individual's ability to adapt to her or his environment. Most conceptions of functional age, however, are heavily tied to physical criteria. As a result, the line between functional and biological age seems thin. Yet functional age would seem perfectly legitimate as a fourth type of age in its own right, and an individual's capacity for functioning in daily life might be understood through biological, psychological, and social measures. Another conceptualization might be for functional age to exist as a subdimension of each of the three types of age, leading to specialized conceptions of biological, psychological, or social ages based on functional criteria.

In a review of the concept of functional age, Salthouse (1986) suggests that "function" and "functional" continue to be problematic concepts. Salthouse argues that functional age ought to be delineated into "occupational functional age" (linked to competency in an occupation), "biomedical functional age" (linked to the functioning of vital systems and organs), and "structural organization of human functioning" (linked to the interrelationships among multiple factors that impact the human organism). Any conception of functional age or functional capacity must be tied to a multitude of social, psychological, and biological factors.

Attempts to assign biological ages to individuals have also been controversial. Many of the problems noted in relation to measuring biological age also apply to the measurement of other types of age. When comparisons are made within a species, and especially within the human species, "the concept of different rates of biologic aging among individuals or among populations is less well-defined [than interspecies comparisons] and much more difficult to discern" (Ingram & Stoll, 1995, p. 707). These difficulties have led some researchers to consider any effort to measure biological age as futile. According to this view, individual aging is "too complex to be represented as a single index because different cell types, tissues, and organ systems age at different rates within individuals" (Ingram & Stoll, 1995, p. 707). These attempts typically assume that a "general aging factor" accounts for "all or most of the observable changes that occur with age" (a proposition against which empirical evidence is heavily weighted), but which is obviously not to say that

---

[7] Besides the review by Schroots and Birren (1988), readers interested in earlier work on *functional* age might consult Dirken & van Zonneveld (1969), Dirken (1972), Nuttall (1972), and especially Costa and McCrae's (1980, 1985) negative appraisals of attempts to measure functional or biological age and Dean and Morgan's (1988) defense of such attempts. Readers interested in *social* age might also consult an early paper by Rose (1972), and those interested in *biological* age might consult a pioneering paper by Benjamin (1947), a later monograph by Reff and Schneider (1982), special issues of *Experimental Aging Research* (Ludwig & Masoro, 1983) and *Experimental Gerontology* (Sprott & Baker, 1988), a collection of international clinical test batteries assembled by Dean (1988), and, most recently, a *Practical Handbook of Human Biologic Age Determination* edited by Balin (1994).

the cells, tissues, and systems of the body work independently of one another (Costa & McCrae, 1985, pp. 30-31).

Dean and Morgan (1988) counter Costa and McCrae's criticisms of this literature, arguing that (a) the development and use of biological age measures is not meant to replace chronological age, but to instead supplement it; (b) such measures need not be composite in form, but may be broken down for specific systems; (c) even though aging processes are independent, information on various organs or systems have significant predictive value; (d) only functions that are known to change with age should be used in such measures; and (e) researchers must be careful not to misinterpret measures of (absolute) biological age as measures of aging *rates*. Dean and Morgan also suggest that the reliability and validity of current test batteries be raised by improving techniques to measure biological age (rather than dismissing attempts to do so) and by replicating these measures in multiple studies and in longitudinal and cross-cultural frameworks.

There have been many attempts to build composite measures of an individual's "biological age" by measuring how an individual's appearance, and how her or his physiological, biochemical, and neuro-psychological conditions compare to the same-sex average for her or his chronological age (for a review, see Dean, 1994).[8] Another common approach to the measurement of biological age is that of "health risk appraisal": The leading causes of death at various ages are first determined, as are the risk factors associated with those causes; the risk factors are then measured, and an individual is assigned a "risk age" based on those data.[9]

We might also measure biological markers of aging without assembling them into a single index. There may even be good reasons to avoid the use of a composite index, particularly if one hopes to learn about specific aspects of physical aging. However, most discussions of biological age are aimed at how to summarize the multidimensional nature of physical aging in a single index. There is no consensus about the dimensions most important to measure, how to measure them, or how to combine them together. The conceptual and mathematical considerations of such measures are also underdeveloped. Indeed, as Ingram and Stoll (1995) suggest, the measurement of biological age requires "large samples and a multitude of tests" and is "useless without appropriate validation," with its ultimate validation being the "ability to predict the remaining lifespan of an individual or of a selected

---

[8] Dean (1994) reports that the first published empirical study along these lines was Murray (1951). Murray was apparently the first to use multiple regression techniques to derive a composite measure of biological age from a battery of tests to capture an individual's visual, auditory, blood pressure, and muscle force statuses. Benjamin's (1947) paper, published even earlier than Murray's, estimated biological age through a medical examination and a life history questionnaire. Benjamin began with the individual's chronological age and then added years to that age depending on hereditary and health risk conditions. As Uttley and Crawford (1994) note, these types of methods are subjective in that they hinge on the degree to which the clinician perceives them as serious. Regression approaches have been most common in the literature. Ironically, these approaches use chronological age as the dependent variable; yet it is chronological age that these researchers would ultimately like to replace.

[9] This approach apparently originated in the work of Robbins and Hall (1970), and has gained widespread acceptance. This approach has also been adopted by the Centers for Disease Control, and is even the basis for a professional society, The Society for Prospective Medicine (Dean, 1994).

population" (p. 708).[10] The concept of biological age has significant intuitive appeal. But to pose Ingram and Stoll's (1995) question: Are attempts to assess biological age worth the effort? Are our hopes to do so overly optimistic? Again, while I have highlighted some of the issues around the measurement of biological age, parallel issues might be raised for other types of ages as well. In fact, social and psychological ages may even pose greater problems in that they seem more difficult to conceptualize and measure.

Developmental research relies so heavily on chronological age as an index of biological, social, or psychological statuses, yet chronological age is often a poor indicator of these statuses (Neugarten & Hagestad, 1976). First, there are important individual differences in development. As a result, age is only a "rough indicator" of an individual's biological, social, or psychological development. Second, age is mostly "meaningful in relational terms, as in signifying that one is younger or older than someone else, closer or farther from birth or death, or in marking progress compared to other persons in one's reference group" (Neugarten & Hagestad, 1976, p. 36). Finally, chronological age is "meaningless unless there is knowledge of the particular culture and of the social meaning[s] attached to given chronological ages" (p. 36).

Given these problems, how might we move beyond the use of chronological age? We might begin by giving more thought to the dimensions and processes for which age serves as an index, and whether these might instead be measured more directly. This will require us to replace or supplement our use of chronological age as an independent (index) variable with "other independent variables that are sensitive to individual variation with age at biological, psychological, and social levels of the organism" (Birren & Schroots, 1996, p. 8; see also Birren & Fisher, 1992; Schroots, 1992). Such variables, Birren and Schroots (1996) suggest, will give us important clues about adult development. In addition, we should think more about the conditions under which age is a relevant dimension to begin with (Ward, 1984).

We must also be more cautious in the way we interpret the age differences unearthed in cross-sectional studies. While most developmental scientists are aware of the age-cohort-period problem, age *differences* nonetheless continue to be misinterpreted as age *changes* (see Chapter 3). We must work harder to specify the causes and consequences of age-related differences, and to identify the mechanisms through which age plays a role in producing these differences. In fact, developmental scientists have largely focused on producing static descriptions of differences and neglected explanatory processes of change (Dannefer & Perlmutter, 1990). While this strategy has resulted in a tremendous "catalogue" of age-related differences in behavior and factors that control behavior, it has provided little information about

---

[10] As Schroots and Birren (1993) point out, the two main strategies for validating measures of biological or functional age have been to relate them to two criteria: chronological age and length of life. Validation against chronological age is illogical (as explained in a prior footnote), and length of life is nearly impossible to measure at the individual level. The latter problem has resulted in researchers developing an alternative population-level variable, "probability of dying," which is "not a biological event but a statistical concept" (p. 27).

the processes responsible for observed differences. This neglect is likely driven by problems in conceptualizing and measuring the role of the environment in relation to individual development (and whether "the environment" can be dealt with scientifically in the first place), and the lack of an accepted "paradigm" relating person-environment processes (Dannefer & Perlmutter, 1990). (These issues will be covered in Chapter 5.) These problems are compounded by the fact that "unarticulated theoretical ideas" and "inconsistently defined terms" run rampant throughout the field (Dannefer & Perlmutter, 1990, p. 109).

Despite its problems, chronological age remains "an indispensable index" (Neugarten & Hagestad, 1976). It is especially convenient and practical as an administrative and normative gauge because it is easily measured, objective, and universal. As a result, it has become a prominent criterion for classifying and ordering society. Age remains "one of the most useful single items of information about an individual" (Birren, 1959, p.8), even though it is "diffusive" (Boyd & Dowd, 1988) and *in and of itself* contributes little to our understanding of human development. Yet because age is "such a powerful index, it will probably always be used to classify data while we are *en route* to explanations using variables other than the mere ages of individuals" (Birren & Cunningham, 1985, p. 12).

Conceptualizing Time

The meanings and uses of age draw attention to the fact that time can be conceptualized along different dimensions (Neugarten & Datan, 1973; see also Hareven, 1991; Kohli, 1986b; and Riegel, 1979). As an index of *life time,* age serves as a gauge for an individual's general position in the life course (e.g., infancy, childhood, adolescence, and early adulthood, midlife, old age), which we then take to be a proxy for biological, social, or psychological statuses. However, as discussed earlier, chronological age is at best only a rough indicator of an individual's position on biological, social, or psychological dimensions, and the use of age as a developmental index is host to an important set of conceptual and methodological problems.

Also as discussed earlier, chronological age takes on unique social meanings in a society; these meanings underlie *social time:* what age means for the social roles an individual holds, the events and transitions an individual experiences, or the behaviors that are expected of an individual. With what might be considered a subdimension of social time, scholars have used the term *family time* to designate the generation within which an individual is located in extended family structure. For example, in a four generation family, members of the eldest generation, G1, simultaneously hold roles as parent, grandparent, and great-grandparent; members of G2 as child, parent, and grandparent; members of G3 as grandchild, child, and parent; and members of G4 as great-grandchild, grandchild, and child. As generations "turn over" (that is, as older generations die and new ones are born), locations in family structure also change.

The term "family time" has also been used to denote shifts in parent-child relationships over time. For example, the nature of parent-child relationships changes as parents and children move from the earliest "Alpha" phase, in which parents are young and children are *little,* to the latest "Omega" phase, in which parents are elderly and "children" themselves are *middle-aged* or even *elderly* (Hagestad, 1982b, 1987). In both of these examples, an individual's changing place in family structure brings new identities, roles, and responsibilities. Family scholars have also used the term "family time" to refer to the interdependence of lives across family members, and the degree to which individual time meshes with family time (e.g., Hareven, 1991). Occurrences in the lives of one family member often have repercussions for other family members, and the scheduling of family events and transitions in one generation affects other generations. Many of these experiences are "counterpoint" transitions (Riley, Foner, & Waring, 1988), or experiences that are clearly outside of one's control (e.g., an individual becomes a grandparent when her or his children parent; an individual moves to the top level of family structure when the generation before her or him dies). Family or family-*like* relationships are the best examples of the powerful nature of "linked lives." These relationships carry the potential to be even more significant in the future because extensions in longevity have increased the period in which the lives of family members overlap.

Finally, as we think about *historical time,* we must consider its intersection with individual and family time. That is, we must consider how individual lives, and the collective lives of members in her or his family and cohort, are framed and uniquely shaped by historical time. Historical time is accompanied by both short- and long-term changes in economic, political, and social life, all of which may gradually or abruptly alter life circumstances. (The concept of cohort, which will be discussed in Chapter 3, attempts to link these levels of time.)

In addition to the types of time just described, we might also explore other types of time, such as biological or psychological time (at an individual level) or organizational time (at a meso-level). For example, serious illness prompts a loss in personal and social schedules, interrupts projects, and brings uncertainty about the future for oneself and others (Hagestad, 1996). As individuals and groups move through organizations, that movement is often rigidly calibrated by time: Educational programs require the completion of a specific number of credit hours; courses must be tackled at a specific pace and in a specific sequence; ultimate time limits are set for obtaining a degree. Work organizations operate on specific schedules and shifts; hours are clocked; production is timed; deadlines are set; sick, personal, and holiday time is monitored and negotiated; timetables are set for promotional tracks. The rhythm of experiences in medical institutions marches to the clock, as stays are time-bound, patients are scheduled, medicines are given, and rounds are made.

The many levels on which to conceptualize time call attention to the *dynamic* nature of human lives, as individuals and groups move through their lives, through the age strata of the population, through generations within their families, through social settings and institutions, and through the course of history; and as they take on the roles and behaviors that are expected of them across these points. Much remains to be learned about the many "times of our lives" (Hendricks & Peters, 1986)—the experiences, interaction, and synchronization of time at multiple levels.

84 / LIVES IN TIME AND PLACE

SUBJECTIVE AGE IDENTIFICATION

Research on subjective age identification examines how old a person feels, into which age group an individual categorizes her or himself, or how old one would like to be, regardless of actual age. This has been a lively tradition since the 1960s.[11] This body of research is important in that it generally does not anchor age in simple chronological terms, but instead in phenomenological, subjectively-experienced terms.

As Cutler's (1982) earlier review notes, subjective age is typically measured with a single item: "Do you feel that you are: young, middle-aged, old, or very old?" (e.g., Markides & Boldt, 1983). Across studies, there are slight variations in the item stem or the number and type of response categories. In many gerontological studies, subjective age identification is restricted to whether an individual defines her or himself as "old" or "very old." Often, this type of age is referred to as *identity age*.

Along these lines, Barak and Stern (1986) label as cognitive age the four separate aspects of identity age that comprise Kastenbaum, Derbin, Sabatini, and Arrt's (1972) "Ages of Me" instrument: *feel age* ("I feel as though I am in my . . ."), *look age* ("I look as though I am in my . . ."), *do age* "I do most things as though I were in my . . ."), and *interest age* ("My interests are mostly those of a person in his/her . . ."). Many of the items in the original "Ages of Me" instrument elicit specific ages. For Barak and Stern's items, the response categories are *decades* of life, starting with the 20s and ending with the 80s. Goldsmith and Heiens (1992) have recommended that the years from 0 to 10 and 90 to 100 might also be added if appropriate for the sample.

Heckhausen and Krüger (1993) also build on Kastenbaum's approach by asking about five separate aspects of subjective age identification: "the age I feel," "the age I look," "the age resembling my interests and activities," "the age other strangers would ascribe to me," and "the age my friends would ascribe to me." They use a 5-point response scale for these items, ranging from "much younger than my actual age" to "much older than my actual age." Other popular measurement strategies move away from identification with a larger age group, and instead ask for a specific age response. For example, another version of *feel age* is simply: "How old do you feel?" or "What age do you feel on the inside?" (Underhill & Cadwell, 1983; also see Cremin, 1992; Thompson, 1992). Similarly, *desired age* might be elicited through the question: "What age would you most like to be?"

In studies of *comparative* or *relative age identification*, respondents are normally asked whether they feel older, the same, or younger than most other people their chronological age (or even whether an individual feels a sense of solidarity

---

[11]For pioneering work from the 1960s, see Anderson (1967), Bell (1967), Bloom (1961), Guptill (1969), Jeffers, Eisdorfer, and Busse (1962), and Zola (1962). For the 1970s, see Ward (1977), Peters (1971), Kastenbaum, Derbin, Sabatini, and Arrt (1972), and Linn and Hunter (1979). For more recent studies, see Barak (1987), Barak and Gould (1985), Barak and Stern (1986), Baum and Boxley (1983), George, Mutran, and Pennybacker (1980), Goldsmith and Heiens (1992), Markides and Boldt (1983), Montepare (1991), Montepare and Lachman (1989), Thompson (1992), and Underhill and Cadwell (1983).

with her or his age peers; Sherman, 1994). Here, the comparison is generally between oneself and others of about the same age. However, a few investigators have examined a version of comparative age that has kept the comparison internal by asking whether an individual feels older, the same, or younger than her or his chronological age (e.g., Baum & Boxley, 1983).

In most studies, measures of subjective age are correlated with actual chronological age. In doing so, even more types of age may result (for examples, see Barak [1987], Barak & Gould [1985]). Besides chronological age, other commonly explored correlates of subjective age include physical and emotional health, sex, race, marital status, social participation, socioeconomic status, and retirement status (see reviews by Barak & Stern, 1986; Baum & Boxley, 1983; Montepare, 1991; Montepare & Lachman, 1989).

The measures described above are self-perceived ages: They ultimately reference the subjective ages of an individual him- or herself. One might also consider *other-perceived ages,* or the age status(es) of individuals as evaluated by others (e.g., Lawrence, 1974). For example, studies on subjective age identity among the elderly often find that older respondents will classify others of the same chronological age as old, but will use younger terms to describe themselves (Connidis, 1989). Younger adults tend to hold more negative views of aging than older adults, and many older adults who do view the aging process as negative do not apply this view to themselves. Generally, only those who are in poor health or isolated, or those who are very old, label themselves as old. This tendency may "lead to a focus on the denial of aging and the failure of older persons to accept reality," and may turn much-needed attention away from the negative sides of aging (Connidis, 1989, p. 8).

As a result, research has begun to examine the subjective *experiences* of aging. For example, to explore what an older person likes about being her or his current age, Connidis (1989) asks, "At each stage of life there are usually some things which people like about being the age they are. What do you like about being your age? By this I mean, the things you think are good about this stage of your life and the things you enjoy about being the age you are now." To explore what older people dislike about being old, Connidis asks, "Each stage of life has its troubles and problems. What things do you dislike about being your age? By this I mean the things you find difficult about this stage of your life, the problems you may have at the age you are now, and the ways other people treat you now that you don't like." And to explore any concerns about aging, Connidis asks, "When you look ahead are there any worries or concerns you have about growing older? (If "yes":) What are they?"

Similarly, Sherman (1994) has also explored *changes* in age identity, asking "Was there a particular time in your life when you started to feel older? What changes made you feel this way? Did any particular birthday have special significance to you? If so, which one and why?" After analyzing qualitative responses to these questions, Sherman finds four (overlapping) types of self that relate to age identity: the comparative self, the reflected self, the retrospective self, and the mature self. With the *comparative self,* individuals derive a sense of age identity by comparing themselves to age peers and family members. With the *reflected self,* age identity is shaped by the views that we believe others hold of us. With the *retrospective self,* individuals derive a sense of age identity by comparing their current selves to their former selves. Finally, the *mature self* relates to neither others nor to former (at least physical) selves but more to the "inside" and to an "inner maturity" and self-awareness (this "mature self" must be connected, then, to the "retrospective" self).

Most research on subjective age is based on adults at middle age and beyond. However, similar concepts might be explored for the periods that comprise the first half of life, and similar measures might developed for research on younger age groups.

AGE NORMS AND EXPECTATIONS

Elementary, ascriptive categories often conceal subtle, complicated processes and take on complex social meanings (e.g., influencing attitudes, behaviors, language).[12] Age is no exception, and one of the ways in which age exerts its influence is through age norms and expectations. Assumptions about the power of age norms and expectations underlie most theory and research on the life course. Sociologists, in particular, begin their work with the assumption that lives are socially structured, and that the most interesting aspects of age are the ways in which it becomes a social phenomenon. Life trajectories are conceptualized as being calibrated by a sequence of age-linked role transitions, times when social personae change, when new rights, duties and resources are encountered, and when identities are in flux (Hagestad & Settersten, 1994). As members of groups, we share notions about the "normal, expectable life," and we hold expectations about the timing and sequencing of life's changes. But of what are these expectations made?

Significant "conceptual ambiguity and theoretical uncertainty" surrounds the terms "age norm" and "age-normative" (Hagestad, 1990, p. 160; see also, Riley, 1985; Sherrod & Brim, 1986). At least three different meanings of age norms exist in the life-course literature, and the three are often blurred together. Most social-psychological research has used these terms in conjunction with investigations of the *optimal* ages ("best," "ideal," or "preferred" ages) at which to experience various life transitions (e.g., beginning with the classic study of Neugarten, Moore, & Lowe [1965] and extending to later studies by Plath & Ikeda [1975], Passuth & Maines [1981], Fallo-Mitchell & Ryff [1982], Zepelin, Sills, & Heath [1987], Gee [1990], and Peterson [1996] to name a few). The implicit assumption underlying most social-psychological theory and research in this area is that these optimal ages equip individuals with a "mental map" of the life course. This map lends individuals a sense of what lies ahead in their lives, and gives them a chance to prepare for those experiences. As such, it fulfills important human psychological needs for predictability and order (Hagestad & Neugarten, 1985; Neugarten & Hagestad, 1976).

---

[12] A longstanding distinction in the discipline of sociology is that between ascribed and achieved roles and statuses. *Ascribed* roles and statuses are those that are automatically assigned to an individual on the basis of characteristics that the individual cannot easily change, such as age, sex, or race. *Achieved* roles and statuses, in direct contrast, are acquired or developed on the basis of abilities and/or effort.

Within the field of psychology, "age norms" have not only designated frames of reference for orienting behavior, but also age evaluations and stereotypes (what individuals think about people of various ages; how they evaluate different life periods), age estimates (how individuals estimate the ages of other people based on physical and social cues), and age attributions (how individuals use age in explaining the behavior of others).

Demographers often use the terms "age norm" and "age-normative" to refer to *statistical regularity* in the actual timing of life transitions in the population at large or in subgroups of the population. However, when these transition patterns are observed, there are at least four possible explanations for these patterns: that they reflect universal patterns of development and aging that exist across societies; that they reflect structural conditions that create different opportunities and constraints for different age groups; that they reflect shared notions about the optimal timing of life experiences (as described above); or that they reflect actual social norms, whether formal (e.g., embedded in laws) or informal (described below) (Hagestad & Settersten, 1994).

This latter point captures the third use of the terms "age norm" and "age-normative": as age-linked *prescriptions and proscriptions* for when various life transitions ought, or ought not, occur. This use taps the essence of sociological theorizing about age norms. From this perspective, age norms lie at the heart of social organization and maintain social order. They are embedded in systems of social control, linked to the division of labor in society, and are a central means for the allocation of resources. For example, people of different "age strata" in the population structure are involved in different social roles and institutions; as individuals and birth cohorts grow up and older, they move through age-structured social roles and institutions (Riley, Foner, & Waring, 1988). Age is linked to role differentiation through the "3 P's": *prescription* (rules about when roles "ought" to be taken on), *proscription* (rules about when roles "ought not" be taken on), and *permission* (generally acceptable times to take them on) (Riley, Johnson, & Foner, 1972; Roth, 1963).

The first two P's, in particular, encompass what sociologists mean when they refer to age norms. Norms are defined by three components: (1) they are *prescriptions for,* or *proscriptions against,* engaging in certain behaviors and taking on certain roles; (2) there is *consensus* about these prescriptions and proscriptions; and (3) they are enforced through various mechanisms of *social control,* particularly positive social sanctions to keep people "on track," and negative social sanctions to bring "back into line" those individuals who stray from these tracks (Berger, 1963; Blake & Davis, 1964; Gibbs, 1965, 1981; Hawkes, 1975; Jackson, 1975; Morris, 1956; Reinharz, 1987; Strauss, 1959). If an age-normative system is operating, individuals within that system should be aware of the sanctions and consequences for violating norms, and be sensitive to social approval and disapproval (Neugarten & Datan, 1973). These sanctions may take several forms, ranging from the informal (interpersonal sanctions, in the form of persuasion, encouragement, reinforcement, ridicule, gossip, ostracism) to the formal (e.g., political, legal, or economic forms). For example, Krüger, Heckhausen, and Hundertmark (1995) suggest that when people depart from a norm, their behavior is not only evaluated negatively, but it is attributed to something negative about an individual's disposition. Similarly, Brandtstädter (1998), drawing on the research of one of his students (Kalicki, 1995), argues that deviations from a cultural script "arouse attention and a need for explanation and justification," and may, depending on the life experience at hand, be taken "as a sign of incompetence, irresponsibility, indifference, or carelessness" (p. 842).

While a handful of studies have intended to examine the presence of informal age "norms," their use and measurement of the concept "norm" has neglected its core prescriptive-proscriptive essence. Most investigators have used the term either in the statistical or optimal senses outlined above. Along these lines, Marini (1984) has criticized past research on age "norms," arguing that researchers have not actually measured social norms but instead have focused on the "ideal" and "preferred" domains. Researchers who have conducted their research at the optimal level have often assumed that notions about what is "best," "ideal," or "preferred" are synonymous with notions about what "should" or "ought to" be. Only a few recent studies have explored norms in the prescriptive-proscriptive sense (Settersten & Hagestad, 1996a, on family transitions; Settersten & Hagestad, 1996b, on work and educational transitions; Veevers, Gee, & Wister, 1996, on leaving home).

Interestingly, when demographers find regularity in life-course patterns at a population level, they often assume that the regularity reflects, and is driven by, cultural age prescriptions or proscriptions. For example, Hogan (1985, p. 70) argues that "in the United States, the appropriate ages for events are [not well-specified], but the statistical regularities in the timing of events are suggestive of underlying [informal] norms." Yet Marini (1984) rightly opposes such interpretations, noting that behavior that is statistically regular may not be socially "normative," just as behavior that is statistically irregular need not be socially non-normative.

Similarly, when *change* in transition patterns in the population is witnessed, we may be inclined to assume that these shifts are the result of significat *change* in social norms (and that increased variability in transition patterns, in particular, is the result of weakened age norms). However, social norms themselves may be reshaped as a result of new behavioral patterns. For example, with regard to marital timing, Modell (1980) has suggested that behavioral patterns first changed in response to economic conditions, which subsequently altered notions about the "best" time to marry. Both of these forces (new behavior may bring about new social norms, just as new social norms may bring about new behavior) are hopelessly entangled in an epistemological trap, and it is virtually impossible for scholars to adequately address the direction of the empirical link between them. Attitudes and behavior do not necessarily correspond, and the relation between the two is extraordinarily complex.

Part of the pioneering research conducted by Neugarten and her colleagues at the University of Chicago during the late 1950s and early 1960s explored age "norms" and age "constraints." Two of the instruments that were used in the landmark Kansas City Study of Adult Life[13] are most relevant here: "Timetables for Men and Women" and the "Age Norm Checklist." The eleven-item "Timetables for Men and Women" instrument asks respondents what they think the best age is for accomplishing a variety of transitions (e.g., "What do you think is the best age for a man to marry?" "What do you think is the best age for most people to leave home?"). For these items respondents give a specific age or age band. To measure consensus, they examined the proportion of individuals who cited an age (or ages) within a small band that "produced the most accurate reflection of the consensus that existed in the data." Depending on the breadth of responses given for any particular item, the age band used to calculate consensus ranged anywhere from two to fifteen years.

The forty-eight-item "Age Norm Checklist" asks whether respondents "approve of, feel favorable" or "disapprove of, feel unfavorable" about a variety of behaviors at different ages (e.g., "A woman who wears bikini on the beach—when she's 45; when she's 30; when she's 18" or "A man who buys himself a red sports car—when he's 60; when he's 45; when he's 25"). Responses are then scored to "reflect the degree of refinement with which the respondent makes age discriminations," with higher scores indicating greater age constraint.

One article in particular, Neugarten, Moore, and Lowe (1965), has become the single standard citation as the classic study of informal age norms. This research on which that article is based has been criticized for posing questions at the optimal level rather than the prescriptive level, and for not examining whether social sanctions or other consequences exist for violating these optimal-age timetables. However, they did examine whether respondents "approve" or "disapprove" of people of different ages engaged in a variety of more micro-level, lifestyle-related behaviors.

A later conference paper by Passuth and Maines (1981) essentially replicated Neugarten's approach, and is often cited as a follow-up study to Neugarten, Moore, and Lowe's (1965) landmark study. The research of Fallo-Mitchell and Ryff (1982), Gee (1990), Peterson (1996), Plath and Ikeda (1975), Settersten and Hagestad (1996a, 1996b), and Zepelin, Sills, and Heath (1987) has also used Neugarten's items in some capacity. However, these studies have (a) improved upon some of the original items (e.g., creating items about work for women that parallel previous items asked only about men; or splitting single items that asked about "people" into two separate items about men or women), (b) added new items (e.g., returning home) and eliminated others, (c) added follow-up questions, (d) altered scoring strategies, or (e) varied research and sampling designs.

Settersten and Hagestad (1996a, 1996b), for example, interviewed a random sample of 319 adults in the Chicago metropolitan area, and used a research design that addressed four different sets of perceptions: (1) men's perceptions of women's lives; (2) men's perceptions of men's lives; (3) women's perceptions of women's lives; and (4) women's perceptions of men's lives. The interviews explored

---

[13]The Kansas City Study had a profound impact not only on what was then a young field of gerontology, but its imprint remains evident in contemporary gerontological scholarship. For recent reflections on the legacy of the Kansas City Study, see a series of papers introduced by Hendricks (1994); and on the legacy of Neugarten, see an essay by Settersten (1997b).

individuals' thinking about age deadlines for a set of specific transitions. For example, six transitions related to the sphere of family (leaving home; [not] returning home;[14] marrying; entering parenthood; completing childbearing; and entering grandparenthood), and five transitions related to the sphere of education and work (exiting full-time schooling; entering full-time work; settling on a career/job area; reaching the peak of the work trajectory; and entering retirement). The structure of the interview schedule emerged directly out of the theoretical framework introduced earlier on the classical sociological question of norms. Respondents were first asked to identify the age deadline for each transition (e.g., "By what age should a man retire?"). Those respondents who mentioned a specific deadline were asked to discuss the reasons why a man or woman should meet the deadline (e.g., "Why should a man retire by that age?"), and the potential consequences for those who fail to meet the deadline (e.g., "Does anything happen to him if he doesn't retire by that age? Are there any consequences that come to mind?"). Interviewers used a series of open-ended probes to elaborate the discussion, and the respondent's core responses were noted verbatim and later coded into a set of categories that were developed both inductively and deductively. Many of the categories were based upon existing life-course concepts and principles, while other categories emerged out of the interviews. Categories included *interpersonal sanctions* (which tapped whether respondents perceived social pressure to adhere to a deadline and negative social sanctions for not doing so); *interdependence of lives* (which captured the notion that the timing of a transition can be affected by, or may have consequences for, the lives of others); *development* (where "psychological development" covered concerns about the development of the self and personality, and where "physical development" covered references to biological and health-related factors); *sequencing* (which linked the accomplishment of a single life transition to another transition or series of transitions); *synchrony* (which tapped the idea that an individual must keep pace with her or his age peers, or with some other important reference group, whose standards are used to anchor one's own progress); *opportunities and chances* (which captured concerns about staying "on-time" in order to ensure one's future opportunities); *economic considerations* (which related to concerns about pay, equity, financial stability, private pension arrangements, mortgage, or taxes); and *observed behavior* (which covered references to population means or modes for transitions).

Readers interested in additional information on research instruments related to age norms and expectations might also consult an earlier review by Hagestad (1982a). Hagestad's review covers other pioneering instruments, including Wood's (1972) "Age-Appropriate Behavior" and Bultena and Wood's "Normative Attitudes

---

[14]For returning home, respondents were asked to identify the age after which a man (or woman) should not be allowed to return to his (or her) parents' home. Unlike the other items, which ask about age *prescription*, this is an example of an age *proscription*. We were interested in asking our respondents about whether age limits should be placed on returning home because the demography (especially the prevalence and timing) of both leaving and returning home has changed dramatically in the past few decades. While leaving home remains a statistically normative event, a return home now also seems to be quite pervasive, occurring for roughly half of American young adults (White, 1994, p. 92).

Toward the Aged Role." Wood's (1972) "Age-Appropriate Behavior" instrument asks forty-one questions about the age at which a person is old enough to do various things (e.g., "At what age do you think a person is old enough to vote?," "After what age should someone no longer be required to attend school?"), or the age at which a person is too old to do other things (e.g., "After what age is a son too old to rely on his parents for some financial support?"). Bultena and Wood's (1969) "Normative Attitudes Toward the Aged Role" asks eight questions about whether it is proper for older men, women, or couples to engage in various activities (e.g., "Do you think a widower should remarry even if his children disapprove?").

Unresolved Issues and New Directions for Research on Age Norms

In explicating new directions for research on age norms, let me begin by building upon my recent work with Hagestad, described above (Settersten & Hagestad, 1996a, 1996b). First, that project focused most intensively on individuals' thinking about age when age deadlines were specifically mentioned. The interview schedule was structured so that our in-depth questions were focused on the transitions for which respondents thought age was an important dimension. Future research might begin to examine situations in which informal age deadlines are not perceived, and why age is not considered important in those situations.

The interviews in that project were also oriented around absolute upper age boundaries for accomplishing life-course transitions. An important direction for future research is to consider whether lower age boundaries on life transitions are also important: Are there age thresholds before which a transition should not occur? How old is old enough? Why?

In addition, our interviews focused on age deadlines for most men or women, most of the time. However, respondents periodically stipulated exceptions to these deadlines. Depending on an individual's circumstances, deadline extensions were occasionally granted. In a sense, these extensions gave certain individuals permission to be "late." Future research might begin to explore individuals' thinking about the circumstances under which, and why, such exceptions are made.

That project also focused on a specific set of sixteen life transitions and each transition was discussed separately during the course of the interview. However, respondents often clustered certain life transitions together in their minds, viewing them as interdependent (e.g., the timing of school completion may condition the timing of marriage which, may condition the timing of childbirth). Future research should not only consider other transitions, but it should also consider the intricate ways in which multiple transitions within and between life spheres are spun together. When we focus on separate experiences, we miss important questions about the density of, and distance between, multiple experiences, and the overlapping duration of these experiences. (The challenges of research on trajectories will be discussed in Chapter 4.)

That project was also a study of individual perceptions and social constructions. As the W. I. Thomas dictum reminds us, "If men define situations as real, they are real in their consequences." Whether individuals' thinking about age deadlines reflects reality, and whether these deadlines actually influence behavior remain important issues for future research. For example, sanctions and consequences may exist in reality but may not be part of an individual's construction of the situation. This may be because (a) the individual is genuinely unaware of these sanctions and consequences (e.g., sanctions and consequences may be hidden from the individual), or (b) sanctions or consequences for being off-time may be subtle or indirect, or they may be delayed until some later point in the life course. When we take a constructivist point of view, we must also pay more attention to the contexts in which social constructions take place, particularly with respect to meso-level contexts and processes (e.g., families, neighborhoods, work organizations).

Because scholars have called for research to explore variability in age norms, we decided to draw a random sample from a major, urban American city for that project. Nonetheless, our sample was limited in several ways. First, while the sample was random (e.g., random sample, random selection, random assignment), it was an American sample and, more specifically, a Midwestern and metropolitan sample. Second, the sample was fairly small and heterogeneous. Finally, because the study design was cross-sectional, potential age, period, and cohort confounds existed. Future research might focus on targeted subsamples of the population, subsamples for which variability along social dimensions is restricted. It might also examine thinking about informal age deadlines in other cultures and nations, particularly where both ideologies and institutional arrangements differ from those in the United States.

Perhaps the biggest problem we face is to clarify what exactly we mean by "age norms," explicate the levels at which we hope to study them (macro, meso, micro), and specify their form and content. For example, are age-related expectations really "norms" or simply "frames of reference" and "cognitive maps"? If the former, we must approach them as prescriptive and proscriptive phenomenon, demonstrate consensus, and find evidence of sanctions when individuals depart from them. This creates theoretical and empirical difficulties because norms and sanctions, in particular, cannot be separated: Identifying an age norm requires observing a sanction, so age norms cannot be studied independent of their enforcement mechanism (Lawrence, 1996b). Even if we generally accept the classical conception of norms, there will also be events and transitions to which this conception does not apply. For example, even though the death of a parent or the death of a spouse becomes more expectable in middle or later life, it would make little sense to think about these transitions in a prescriptive way (Hagestad, 1990).

In contrast, if we take norms to instead be "frames of reference" or "cognitive maps," they must be approached differently. In this conception, norms are not tied to societal requirements, but instead to individual needs for predictability and order. From this standpoint, we need not care whether they are truly "normative" (that is, complete with consensus and sanctions). We need only recognize that these frames of reference help guide and evaluate our behavior and that of others.

Either way, much remains to be learned about how "age expectations and timetables are constructed, transmitted, and learned" (Elder, 1998, p. 947). Little is known of the subjective experiences of age expectations and timetables, nor of how these take on important meanings for individuals. Both psychologists and sociologists alike assume that norms are "internalized," a process through which "meanings that are held out for the individual by social structures and social others are brought over into the individual's thinking . . . What originally [has] collective-cultural meaning . . . becomes intra-personal" (Valsiner & Lawrence, 1997, p. 95). However, the psychological and sociological viewpoints differ with respect to the role of external forces. Psychologist Heckhausen (1999) suggests that the "binding force" of age norms may come "precisely from the fact that they are not enforced by external institutional control but [are simply] internalized as frames of reference." In contrast, sociologist Kohli (1986a, p. 293) suggests that:

> By internalizing the requisite age norms, individuals are socialized to fit into the institutional life course program and bring [it] to life. It is indispensable that individuals play their part. There is of course the possibility that they do not—that they deviate. This is considered a failure of socialization, and there have to be sanctions as well as adequate repair mechanisms to deal with these unfortunate cases.

According to this view, norms therefore provide societies with a way of "constructing appropriate individuals," a goal that is viewed as particularly important in contemporary, individualistic societies (Meyer, 1986b). Similarly, sociologist Dannefer (1996) argues that the social structuring of age naturally becomes "mystified"; that is, societies make "conditions that are the result of *social organization or culture* appear to be part of nature" (p. 176, emphasis added).

Over time, the formal, external regulation of individuals by society created a set of rules that are now internalized and informally used by its members to govern their behavior (Elias, 1969), thereby reducing the need for society to formally regulate most of its members. As Heckhausen (1999) notes, these conventions may become so ingrained in people's thought that they become "institutionalized" in the mind, and seem, to individuals, to be part of nature itself. Age norms, as part of these conventions, may then have "committing power as internalized, naturalized, and thus unquestionable ways of thinking about human life."

For this reason, we often assume that norms are clear. However, in reality individuals often seem unaware of age expectations, either because the expectations are unclear or because they are simply part of the individual's taken-for-granted world, "so deeply held that they remain subconscious" (Lawrence, 1996b, p. 210). The question of whether and when age expectations are, or become, norms must be confronted. Not all age expectations need be normative, but all age norms by definition involve expectations. Normative or otherwise, age expectations are challenging to study in that it is difficult to get people to discuss the worlds they take for granted: When people are asked direct questions about the taken-for-granted, they may feel "ridicule, discomfort, embarrassment, or even hostility" (Lawrence, 1996b,

p. 210). The study of these phenomena therefore requires methods for making conscious information that is difficult to access.[15]

Another definitional problem relates to the fact that norms are necessarily group-level phenomena; they are collectively held. Yet whose norms are they? How clearly defined are the parameters of the group and what constitutes membership in it? In addition, because individuals are simultaneously members of multiple groups, how do they manage multiple norms? Individuals are embedded in larger social systems; some of those contexts may have similar norms, while others may not only be different, but conflictual (Lawrence, 1996a; Reinharz, 1987).

This also draws our attention to the question of how broadly or specifically norms operate, and whether they also operate at varying strengths for different types of experiences. For example, do "national" norms exist for "highly institutionalized" age-linked events such as entry into school or transition to retirement (Dannefer, 1996)? Do norms vary by occupation and organizational context (Lashbrook, 1996; Lawrence, 1996b)? Do norms for the transition to parenthood vary by family or across ethnic communities (Burton, 1996)? While meso-level contexts may have their own norms for moving individuals along predictable pathways, we probably cannot assume that these are developed solely from within; they are also likely shaped by larger, external expectations.

As noted earlier, researchers assume that there are important negative consequences for individuals who deviate from norms and that there are rewards and benefits for individuals who conform to norms. However, neither of these have been well explored. For example, falling "off-time" may have consequences for the lives of others around the individual, or for sequencing (where the larger life course may become "disorderly"), synchrony (where the individual may fall "out of synch" with her or his reference group), or the individual's opportunities and chances (e.g., in work, marriage, schooling). There may also be legal repercussions (particularly in instances where the state is directly involved in regulating life transitions and events), or consequences of an economic, physical, or psychological nature. Being "off-time" may make the experience of life transitions more stressful. Stresses

---

[15]Because age is so central to the experience of everyday life, and so common place, it may also produce indifference (Lawrence, 1996a). As Lawrence notes, "Everyone has one and everyone knows what it means to have one. Age changes but cannot be changed. It is there, a part of everyday life so entrenched in our awareness that it becomes invisible." Age is a taken-for-granted part of our worlds, at least in modern Western societies (Keith, Fry, Glascock, Ikels, Dickerson-Putnam, Harpending, & Draper, 1994). At the same time, several deeply held assumptions seem to exist about age, particularly in terms of how and under what conditions people use age to make distinctions between themselves and others (Lawrence, 1996a, pp. 16-18): first, that "age *makes me* similar to or different from other people" in certain ways, creating an age assessment in which we assume that age-similarity makes us similar as people and that age-difference makes us different as people; second, that "age *tells me* how I am similar to or different from other people," in which age serves as an index for a person's physical, psychological, or social development [as discussed earlier]; and third, that "age does not affect behavior," in which people may either not recognize or even deny the fact that age serves to pattern behavior in important ways. These three assumptions are, to a certain degree, inconsistent: "People recognize that they use age to differentiate themselves from others. Further, they recognize that they attach meaning to these differences. Yet, people simultaneously treat these differences and their meanings as irrelevant by believing that age does not influence behavior" (p. 18).

associated with new roles may be accentuated, socialization to new roles may be incomplete, or there may be negative reactions from peers or family.

We must also explore whether being off time may also have positive aspects. Lawrence (1996b), for example, notes that managers who are viewed by their superiors as being ahead of schedule are given higher performance evaluations; those who are behind schedule are penalized with lower evaluations. She also gives as examples a twelve-year-old who attends college and a twenty-two-year-old who receives an Academy Award nomination. In these cases, the individual receives high status because these accomplishments come early. (Lawrence also suggests that Americans may be particularly likely to reward individuals being ahead of schedule.) In some instances, individuals who might otherwise be dealing with multiple role transitions simultaneously may avoid that strain when one or more of these transitions are experienced off-time.

These examples illustrate the point that the violation of age norms may bring punishments, rewards, or both, and that much remains to be learned about the social and psychological repercussions of "untimely" behavior. The effects of timing probably depend on the degree to which it constrains or promotes later opportunities, whether it accelerates or delays experiences thereafter, or how well it fits within, or gives shape to, a trajectory or set of trajectories. Similar observations can be made about the effects of the sequencing, spacing, density and duration of experiences.

Finally, let me highlight Nydegger's (1986a) overlooked but useful distinction between "general timetables," "specialized timetables," and "personal timetables." I will also add a fourth type: "interdependent timetables." *General timetables* are widely-shared timetables for the major life transitions that most individuals experience. As I noted earlier, these timetables need not be "normative," nor must they be limited to age alone. For example, little is known about the normative sequencing of life-course experiences, which may be more important than norms related to age (Nydegger, 1986b).

In contrast, when age and sequencing patterns vary for some sub-population, timetables become *specialized*. The best examples of this are career schedules, which vary greatly between occupations. Specialized timetables are perhaps "most capable of fairly rapid change" because they must "respond most readily to situational and ideological pressures" (Nydegger, 1986a, p. 144). Along these lines, we might also consider *cohort-specific timetables* and their meanings, precursors, and consequences.

Finally, *personal timetables* are those that are "not shared and not normative" (p. 145). Little is known about personal timetables, the degree to which personal timetables do or do not mesh with specialized or generalized timetables, and their meanings, precursors, and consequences.

An additional type of timetable, and perhaps the most complicated form of all, is the *interdependent timetable*. The lives of individuals are intimately woven together, and little is known about how the timetables of intimates (whether general, specialized, or personal) do or do not mesh together, how they are negotiated, and at what consequences they come. Two forms of "interdependence" include the notions of "career contingencies" and "counter-transitions" (Hagestad & Neugarten, 1985).

"Career contingencies" are the expectations that an individual has for the ways in which the lives of significant others will unfold; these expectations shape they way in which that individual's own life is expected to unfold. "Counter-transitions" are experiences that an individual actually has as a result of changes in another person's life, regardless of whether those experiences are anticipated or unanticipated. A good example of either of these relates to entry into grandparenthood: The age at which one enters (or expects to enter) grandparenthood is a function of when any of one's own children become (or expect to become) parents for the first time.

Several recent papers reveal the importance of interdependent timetables. Hagestad's (1996) "personal ethnography" of illness examines how unexpected illness can create a struggle not to fall "out of time." Life-threatening illnesses create uncertainty in life; push people out of the predictable rhythms of social schedules; cause "ripple effects" throughout familial and social networks; and interrupt projects that are important for the maintenance of the self. Similarly, Cohler, Pickett, and Cook (1996) describe the ways in which schizophrenic adults and their families live "outside of time" as their lives are disrupted by episodes of hospitalization, discharge, and rehospitalization. Tobin (1996) also offers an interesting look at elderly parents with mentally retarded adult children. These "perpetual parents" experience time and aging differently than most parents: They must actively care for their retarded children all their lives, or at least until they can no longer maintain responsibility for care.

In closing, it is interesting to note that two of the major principles in developmental literature—one stressing the "normative," and one stressing "heterogeneity" (see Chapter 5)—are essentially oppositional. The emphasis of statistical norms and on consensual social norms "has had the effect of obscuring the realities of diversity and the need to study processes underlying diversity," while the importance of "taken-for-granted age norms . . . has also contributed to the neglect of diversity" (Dannefer, 1996, p. 176).

AGE AND DEVELOPMENTAL GOAL-SETTING

Normative or not, age-related expectations remain important factors in determining how people perceive themselves and evaluate others. They also play an important role in decision-making processes, particularly in shaping the kinds of goals people set and pursue at various points in life. Both of these are crucial areas for future research. These points are especially well reflected in the recent work of Jutta Heckhausen and her colleagues (e.g., Heckhausen, 1999; Heckhausen & Krüger, 1993)

Age norms may "strongly influence the choice of developmental goals, the investment of personal resources for realizing and elaborating chosen developmental tracks, as well as the process of adaptation after failing a goal" (Wrosch & Heckhausen, in press). Norms provide individuals with a general plan that guides the investment of resources. They give the individual information about the "opportunities and risks" associated with a developmental goal, push the individual to strive for those goals within a specific time frame, and prevent the individual from investing precious resources on developmental projects that are likely to fail or remain unfinished (which can be viewed as a highly adaptive function).

The basic proposition underlying Heckhausen's "theory" of developmental regulation is that "individuals profit from, and are challenged by, external constraints to their developmental potential that are provided by biological, socio-structural, and age-normative boundary conditions." *Biological* constraints include the impact of genes on developmental potential, and even the length of the human life span itself: As humans live longer lives, increased lifetime presumably brings more opportunities for development (though some might argue that the expansion of the life span has only created problems for societies and many individuals).

Socio-structural constraints relate to society and to social institutions. They may relate to lifetime (while lifetime has expanded, it imposes ultimate limits on developmental goals and life planning), chronological age (societies are age-stratified; they have age-based social clocks for life experiences which are partially created by, or reflected in, social institutions and organizations), and age-sequences (the possible range of sequence patterns is also limited, and certain sequence patterns may also be institutionalized in social structure).

Age-normative constraints relate to cultural conceptions about "typical" or "normal" development (though it would seem as if "age-normative" constraints are a subset of the socio-structural, since age expectations, normative or otherwise, are embedded in the socio-structural environment and become part of the developmental regulation process).[16]

Together, these three classes of constraints provide a "scaffold" for the individual, significantly reducing the range of potential options available and making an individual's life course more selective. These constraints lead to the "canalization" of the life course (see also the section earlier in this chapter on the "cultural canalization" of the life course). Processes related to the *socio-structural* "canalization" of the life course, in particular, allow for only a limited set of developmental pathways, and keep the individual focused on a specific track thereby maximizing potential gains along the way (e.g., to reap the accumulated rewards of one's skills and resources over time). These constraints create an age-graded framework in which individuals then seek to maximize developmental growth and minimize decline. Individuals strive to attain optimal levels of control over the environment, and over their developmental potential, throughout life. Because movement through life necessarily involves experiences of failure, Heckhausen and her colleagues are especially interested in "internally directed" strategies that individuals use to compensate for failure and remain motivated in the face of defeat; these compensatory strategies are also constrained by external factors that "help adjust frames of reference for self-evaluation."

---

[16] In her discussion of socio-structural constraints, Heckhausen includes references to what I earlier described as "informal" cultural age norms (Settersten & Hagestad, 1996a, 1996b). At the same time, Heckhausen describes "age-normative conceptions" as an entirely separate class of constraints. To keep things clearer in my brief explanation of each type of Heckhausen's "socio-structural constraints," I have restricted my examples to what might be described as "formal" cultural age norms.

It is interesting to note that in Heckhausen's framework external constraints or "socio-structural scaffolding" are nearly always conceptualized as positive factors precisely because they are limiting (that is, they relate to the "management of selectivity").[17] Many sociologists, on the other hand, consider the limiting function of the socio-structural world to be negative and, in many cases, oppressive. These constraints are especially problematic when individuals, and entire classes of individuals, are systematically denied certain options, or are forced onto negative pathways and given little or no opportunity to leave them. Nonetheless, Heckhausen's framework advances other important work on development-related action and goals (e.g., Brandtstädter, 1989; Cantor & Fleeson, 1991; Nurmi, 1992) because it explicitly takes structural constraints into account.

Where should our attention now be focused? We need to learn more about how processes related to the management of selectivity and the compensation of failure play themselves out temporally (within the context of the entire life course). We need to know more about the relationships between external and internal constraints, how these forces interact over time, and how individuals exert control over their development in the face of these constraints. We have much to learn about the ways in which individuals establish this control, whether through *primary* means, directed at changing the environment to better align it with the self, or through *secondary* means, directed at changing the self to better align it with the environment (Rothbaum, Weisz, & Snyder, 1982). More importantly, we need to know more about how these strategies, the balance between them, and the opportunities for different types of control, change over the course of an individual's life. And, ultimately we must learn about the ways in which all of these factors shape individuals' life decisions and goal-setting: how individuals set, regulate, and process short- and long-term developmental goals, the deadlines they set for them (a point after which attainment of the goal becomes very unlikely), and the positive and negative consequences they imagine for various experiences and pathways. A important task for future research is also to develop instruments that better capture the dynamic nature of developmental regulation, particularly via primary and secondary control strategies.

Future research on projected plans might also compare those plans with *actual* experiences later on. This is a fruitful area for understanding life-course dynamics: to understand how some people manage to "stay the course" and others not; to understand where, how, and why veering occurs, and whether it comes with any consequences; and to understand whether staying the course, comes with consequences (e.g., some may manage to adhere to the course at the expense of other opportunities). We might explore whether and why individuals with certain characteristics self-select themselves onto pathways that are realistic or unrealistic, and whether and why some individuals seem more disposed to plan than others. Research in this area might also distinguish between aspirations (projections related

---

[17]However, Heckhausen describes her stance on the nature of socio-structural constraints as "non-evaluative."

to what an individual *hopes* to see happen, and why) and expectations (projections related to what an individual *thinks* will happen, and why). In cases where one's aspirations and expectations do not match, important insights may be gained into the kinds of barriers individuals face (or think they face), be they psychological, social, economic, or of another nature, and how those barriers might be eliminated or overcome. In either case, a mismatch between projected plans and actual experiences, or between aspirations and expectations are important departures for understanding life-course dynamics.

I began this section with Heckhausen's work because her model is more comprehensive, its goals broader, and its time frame wider than important earlier work on "personal projects" (Little, 1983), "personal strivings" (Emmons, 1989), "personal life tasks" (Cantor & Fleeson, 1991), "personal goals" (Brunstein, 1993), "identity intentions" (Gollwitzer, 1986), and others. Little's (1983) method, in particular, set the stage for much of the work that followed, since it was later adopted, with slight variations, by many investigators.

Using both open-ended and standardized rating approaches, Little asked respondents to compile a detailed list of "personal projects," developmental in nature, and then evaluate each project along seventeen dimensions: *importance* ("how important each project is to you at the present time"), *enjoyment* ("how much you enjoy working on each project"), *difficulty* ("how difficult you find it to carry out each project"), *visibility* ("how visible each project is to the relevant people who are close to you"), *control* ("how much you feel you are in control of each project"), *initiation* ("how much you feel responsible for having initiated each project"), *stress* ("how stressful it is for you to carry out each project"), *time adequacy* ("how much you feel that the amount of time you spend working on each project is adequate"), *outcome* ("what you anticipate the outcome of each project to be"), *self-identity* ("how typical of you each project is"), *others' views* ("how important each project is seen to be by relevant people who are close to you"), *value congruency* ("to what extent is each project consistent with the values that guide your life"), *positive impact* ("how much you feel that each project helps others"), *negative impact* ("how much you feel that each project hinders other projects"), *progress* ("how successful you have been in a project so far"), *challenge* ("to what extent each project is demanding and challenging to you"), and *absorption* ("to what extent you become engrossed or deeply involved in a project.") Little gave respondents a matrix with rows in which to designate separate personal projects, and seventeen columns to place ratings (on a 10-point scale) for each of the dimensions just described. Little also included two additional columns, one of which asked the respondent to indicate the names of other people involved in the project, and one of which asked the respondent to indicate the setting in which the project would most likely be carried out.

The empirical research of Heckhausen and her colleagues is based upon the "Tenaciousness of Goal Pursuit" and "Flexibility of Goal Adjustment" scales developed by Brandtstädter and Renner (1990). In addition, she and her colleagues developed the Control Agency Means-Ends in Adulthood Questionnaire (Heckhausen, 1991; Heckhausen, Diewald, & Huinink, 1994) as well as an instrument aimed at tapping primary and secondary control processes in developmental regulation (Heckhausen & Schulz, 1995b). The empirical effectiveness of the latter instrument is currently being investigated (Heckhausen, 1999).

Examples of Brandtstädter and Renner's fifteen-item Tenaciousness Goal Pursuit scale include: "The harder a goal is to achieve, the more desirable it often appears to me," "I can be very obstinate in pursing my goals," "Even if everything seems hopeless, I still look for a way to master the situation," and "If I run into problems, I usually double my efforts." Examples of their fifteen-item Flexible Goal Adjustment scale include: "In general, I am not upset very long about an opportunity passed up," "I can adapt quite easily to changes in a situation," "After serious disappointment, I soon turn to new tasks," "I usually recognize quite easily my own limitations," and "Even if everything goes wrong, I can still find something positive about the situation." Psychometrically, these scales have been shown to be independent from each other and exhibit convergent and discriminant validity with several other well-established measures (see Brandtstädter & Renner, 1990).

As yet, there is inconclusive evidence about whether and how strategies of coping and control change with age. But in a series of cross-sectional comparisons, Brandtstädter and Renner (1990) provide some interesting evidence on the age patterns that emerge in the Flexible Goal Adjustment and Tenacious Goal Pursuit scales. These investigators show that flexibility scores generally increase with age, while tenaciousness scores generally decrease with age. An explanation for these patterns is that, with age, individuals are more often confronted with experiences that cannot be controlled and are related to irreversible losses (or are perceived as such)(see also Heckhausen & Baltes, 1991; Nurmi, Pulliainen, & Salmela-Aro, 1992). Along these lines, the research of Nurmi (Nurmi et al., 1992) shows that the goals and concerns cited by individuals reflect concerns related to themselves, their friends, and the "developmental tasks" of their ages.[18] Young adults are more likely to mention education- and family-related goals; middle-aged adults are more likely to mention goals related to their children's lives and property, and express concerns about their work lives; and elderly adults are more likely to mention their own health, retirement, leisure activities, and the world. In addition, the "temporal extension" of adults' goals related to education, family, and work declines across the age

---

[18]Nurmi administered a questionnaire to a sample of adults between the ages of nineteen and sixty-four. Nurmi first asked, "Would you please write down what kind of goals, hopes, plans, and dreams you have when you think about the future?" (followed by a space with 4 numbered lines), followed by, "Would you please write down what things you are afraid of or worried about?" (followed by a space with 3 numbered lines). Then, respondents were asked to designate the "temporal extension" of each goal or concern ("Could you please estimate how old you will be at the time [the specific goal or concern] will be realized?") Subjects were also asked about the degree to which each goal or concern is within the respondent's control ("Could you please indicate the extent to which you think you are able to influence the realization of the goal or concern you mentioned above?") using a response scale ranging from 1 ("totally due to factors other than me") to 4 ("totally due to me") (Nurmi et al., 1992). Each goal and concern was coded into one of fifteen content categories: profession/occupation, property, family/marriage, self, education, health, travel, children's lives, leisure activities, retirement, world, war, the health of others, friends, and other. These temporal extension scores were also aggregated across respondents (over the entire sample, and separately for five different age groups: 19-24, 25-34, 35-44, 45-54, 55-64) to create overall temporal extension scores, and across each of the fifteen categories noted above to create "domain-specific" extension scores.

groups (because most of the goals and concerns in these areas were closer to being realized), and beliefs about the controllability of events become more external across the age groups.

Brandtstädter argues that these empirical patterns suggest a shift from assimilative to accommodative coping strategies with age. With *assimilative* strategies, discrepancies between the actual and desired course of development can be reduced by actively adjusting developmental and life circumstances to personal preferences. With *accommodative* strategies, these discrepancies are handled by adjusting personal preferences to situational forces and constraints. This shift helps "optimize the balance of gains and losses in development" by improving or maintaining the aging individual's sense of well-being and satisfaction (Brandtstädter & Renner, 1990, p. 58). If we accept Brandtstädter's (1998) proposition that the resources available for actively creating development tend to decline in later life, then the personal goals and identity projects in which one invests must not only be more restricted, but, as such, these goals and projects may take on even greater significance.

For further discussion of measurement strategies related to developmental goals, see Heckhausen (1999). In addition to the work discussed here, Heckhausen covers Dittmann-Kohli's (1991) research on younger and older adults' hopes for their personal futures, Nurmi's (1991, 1992) work on the orientations of adolescents toward their futures and on the life goals of adults, Rapkin and Fischer's (1992) approach to developing goal profiles among older adults, and Markus' concept of "possible selves" (e.g., Cross & Markus, 1991).

AGE-RELATED IMAGES AND STEREOTYPES

Another body of research has examined the images associated with people of different ages, especially their personality traits and characteristics. The most prominent of these instruments were included in Hagestad's (1982a) earlier review, including Hickey and Kalish's (1968), Neugarten and Peterson's (1957) "Age Association Items," and Cameron's (1972, 1976) "Comparisons of Age Groups." Hickey and Kalish's (1968) "Perceptions of Adults" prompts young respondents to give the ages that they associate with people who are "mean or unkind," "lonely," or "busy"; people who "like children and young people," or people they "like to help." Neugarten & Peterson's (1957) "Age Association Items" is a thirty-four-item instrument that asks for the age that respondents associate with a variety of feelings or behaviors, such as "a man who gets the most pleasure from his children," "when a woman gets most pleasure from sex," or "the prime of life for a man." Cameron's (1972, 1976) "Comparison of Age Groups" asks respondents to compare young, middle-aged, and old adults on dimensions of masculinity and femininity, and on dimensions of fun and happiness.

Along these lines, the recent work of Heckhausen and her colleagues (Heckhausen, Dixon, & Baltes, 1989, Heckhausen & Baltes, 1991) is also noteworthy. With the goal of examining perceptions of developmental gains and losses throughout adulthood, Heckhausen begins with a checklist of 385 "psychological" adjectives covering various personality (e.g., "impulsive"), social (e.g., "friendly"), and cognitive (e.g., "ready-witted") characteristics. Respondents rate the extent to which the characteristic is perceived to increase across adult life ranging from "not at all" to "very much." Increases in positive characteristics are viewed as developmental gains, and increases in negative characteristics are viewed as losses. In a second session, respondents rate a reduced set of items (those found to be sensitive to change in the first round), this time in terms of the desirability of the developmental change ranging from "very undesirable" to "very desirable." Finally, respondents rate the degree to which they think the psychological change is controllable, "Do you think that one can facilitate or hinder the increase of [the attribute], or do you think that one does not have any influence on the increase of [an attribute]?," with a response scale ranging from "not at all" to "very much."

In Heckhausen's later work, of which I will now give an example, both increases and decreases are more explicitly examined. For example, Heckhausen and Krüger (1993) use a list of 100 adjectives of psychological attributes, and ask respondents to rate each attribute on six dimensions: (1) *desirability* ("How desirable is the attribute? ranging from 'very undesirable' to 'very desirable' "); (2) *expected change in adulthood* ("Does the attribute increase 'a little,' 'medium,' or 'very much'; decrease 'a little,' 'medium,' or 'very much'; or remain stable during seven decades of adulthood (i.e., the 20s, 30s, 40s, 50s, 60s, 70s, and 80s)?"); (3) *perceived controllability* ("How much can one control the modification of the attribute? ranging from 'not at all' to 'very much' "); (4) *self-description* ("How characteristic is the attribute for you? ranging from 'not at all' to 'very much' "). In addition, Heckhausen and Krüger use this list of attributes to ask respondents about their (5) *developmental goals* ("Mark up to 10 attributes for which you intend a change," using a plus symbol to indicate an intended increase of the attribute and a minus symbol to indicate an intended decrease in the attribute); and (6) sense of the *"normative"* age of their developmental goals ("Give for each of your 10 selected developmental goals the age at which people typically would hold this developmental goal").

Some of the research mentioned above might fall under the category of *age stereotypes*, since it draws on common images of, or perceptions about, what people of different groups are like (e.g., physically, psychologically, socially) and what it means to be of a particular age. However, most research on age stereotypes deals with stereotypes of aging and older people, regardless of whether older people themselves or those of younger age groups are asked to make the evaluation (for a compilation and review of instruments used between 1953 and 1977 that measure perceptions of old people, see McTavish, 1982). Three instruments are very popular but widely criticized. These include two early instruments, one by Tuckman and Lorge (1953) on attitudes toward old people, and the other by Rosencranz and McNevin (1969) titled the Aging Semantic Differential (ASD). The other popular instruments are Palmore's two Facts on Aging (FAQ) quizzes (for the 25 item FAQ1, see Palmore, 1977; for the 25 item FAQ2, see Palmore, 1981). Palmore's two quizzes have also been converted from true-false to multiple-choice format, which resulted in stronger instruments (for the conversion of the first quiz, see Harris &

Changas, 1994; for the conversion of the second, see Harris, Changas, & Palmore, 1996).

Scales used in the recent empirical research of Braithwaite (e.g., Braithwaite, Lynd-Stevenson, & Pigram, 1993) show great promise for overcoming the limitations of prior instruments. These self-administered scales measure attitudes toward the elderly (8 items, e.g., "I really enjoy talking to older people"), attitudes toward the aging process (16 items, e.g., "In my old age I will be as enthusiastic about life as I am now"), stereotypes of sociability-antisociability (10 items, e.g., "Elderly people are as capable as ever of concentrating on any given task"), stereotypes of capability-incapability (8 items, e.g., "Older people are the most friendly toward strangers"), and awareness of ageism (10 items, e.g., "This a youth-oriented society").

Another new instrument is the Age Group Evaluation and Description (AGED) Inventory developed by Knox, Gekoski, and Kelly (1995), which was designed to overcome the limitations of the ASD. The AGED Inventory allows for a self-administered assessment of both age stereotypes and of attitudes toward age-specified targets. A confirmatory factor analysis produced two seven-item "evaluative" factors, one on "Goodness" (e.g., positive adjectives: generous, sensitive, considerate, patient, honest, wise, sincere) and the other on "Positiveness" (e.g., positive adjectives: productive, optimistic, flexible, hopeful, involved, sociable, imaginative). It also produced two seven-item "descriptive" factors, one on "Vitality" (e.g., positive adjectives: independent, busy, active, expectant, assertive, adventurous, sexy), and the other on "Maturity" (e.g., positive adjectives: satisfied, trustful, other-oriented, accepting, dignified, modest, even-tempered). The investigators argue that four factors replicate across young ("mid-twenties"), middle-aged ("mid-forties"), and old ("early seventies") targets, but that the factors are strongest when male and female targets are combined. Knox and colleagues suggest that if one is interested in the respondent's evaluative attitudes, the Goodness and Positiveness dimensions may be used as a reliable proxy. If one is interested in the degree to which age stereotypes are endorsed, the investigator might use only Vitality and Maturity (which are relatively independent of attitudes toward the target), all four dimensions (but with caution, since they are not orthogonal factors), or combine Vitality and Positiveness (which are orthogonal and together seem to assess "Youthfulness") and combine Maturity and Goodness (which are also orthogonal and together seem to assess "Agedness").

While many stereotypes of aging seem negative, they need not be so. Positive stereotypes also exist, such as stereotypes that older people are wise, dignified, friendly, patient, calm, and nurturing; these positive stereotypes are important counterparts to the negative stereotypes that many gerontologists deem as "ageist" (for a review, see Heckhausen & Lang, 1996). Heckhausen and Lang's (1996) review also suggests that when respondents are asked to make evaluations of older people in general, their responses are largely negative. However, when respondents are instead asked to ground their evaluation by keeping in mind a specific older person (or people) they know, or when older respondents use themselves as an anchor, responses are much less negative, and even positive. In addition, in some cases, such as the characteristics noted above as positive stereotypes, older people are even regarded more favorably than young people.

LIFE PERIODS

Theorists and researchers have relied on stages or phases as a favorite way of conceptualizing human lives from birth to death (e.g., Eisenstadt, 1956; Erikson, 1980). The differentiation of life phases has been viewed as an historically emergent property of modern societies, beginning with "childhood," "adulthood," and "old age" (Ariès, 1962; Borscheid, 1992; Ehmer, 1990). Childhood was eventually differentiated into "early childhood," "youth and adolescence," and "post-adolescence." Adulthood was also segmented into "early adulthood," "midlife," and "old age." Old age was further split into the "third and fourth ages" (Laslett, 1991), or the "young-old" and the "old-old" (Neugarten, 1974a/1996) and, more recently, the "oldest-old" (e.g., Suzman, Willis, & Manton, 1992).

Neugarten brought us these latter terms in a 1974 essay on "Age Groups in American Society and the Rise of the Young-Old," and in a 1979 essay on "The Young-Old and the Age-Irrelevant Society" (Neugarten, 1974a/1996, 1979/1996). Since then, gerontological researchers have routinely used these terms and have defined them in purely chronological ways with the young-old defined as those between sixty-five and seventy-four, or between sixty-five and eighty-four; and with the old-old defined as either those aged seventy-five or older, or aged eighty-five or older. However, Neugarten's original formulation of "young-old" and "old-old" was not exclusively bound to age. Neugarten does say that "at the risk of oversimplification, the young-old come from the group composed of those who are approximately 55 to 75, as distinguished from the old-old, who are 75 and over" (Neugarten, 1974a/1996, p. 37). But, her intention was to separate elders who are relatively healthy, affluent, and active from those who are not, regardless of their ages. Indeed, "the terms young-old and old-old were originally suggested as a gross way of acknowledging some of the enormous diversity among older persons" (Neugarten, 1979/1996, p. 48).

How do individuals in a society divide the span of time from birth to death into distinct categories and what age boundaries and markers do they use to define these categories and designate movement from one phase to another? An earlier review by Hagestad (1982a) outlined a number of measurement strategies which, with slight modifications, remain the most dominant approaches to measuring life phases. However, there has been little research on this topic since the mid-1970s (apart from Project A.G.E., which was discussed earlier in this chapter).

Research in this area began with Neugarten and Peterson's (1957) "Phases of Adulthood" instrument, which is representative of these measures. It asks, "What would you call the periods of life, the age periods most people go through? At what age does each begin, for most people? What are the important changes from one period to the next, for most people?" For strategies of this sort, respondents must provide their own divisions and labels.

Another common strategy is to provide respondents with predetermined labels and ask them to generate the age parameters they associate with those labels.

Cameron's (1969) "Age Parameters" questions ask for the ages at which "young adult," "middle-aged," "old," and "aged" begin. Similarly, Drevenstedt's (1976) "Onset of Adult Phases" questions ask for age parameters, but also make distinctions between men's and women's lives. It asks for the ages at which a man becomes a "young man," a "middle-aged man," and an "old man," and the ages at which a woman becomes a "middle-aged woman" and an "old woman." Some of Neugarten and Peterson's (1957) "Age Association Items" are in this format as well.

The simplest strategy has been to provide respondents with the label for the life phase *and* a number of preset response categories. The National Council on Aging's (1975) "Onset of Old Age" adopts this approach, asking "At what age do you think the average man becomes "old"? "Under 40 years, 40 to 44 years, 45 to 49 years, (et cetera in 4-year brackets), 90 years or older." Respondents were also given the options of "Never," "It Depends," "When he stops working," "When his health fails," "Other," or "Unsure." A follow-up question asks respondents to give their reasons for choosing a particular age band. In addition, a similar series of questions were asked about women. Of course, the primary drawback of this strategy is that it imposes both categories and labels on respondents. In contrast, the innovative "Age Game" developed by Project A.G.E. investigators (Keith et al., 1994; discussed earlier in this chapter) allows respondents to generate categories and labels in subjective, phenomenological ways.

Another approach is to divide the life course into a series of positions vis-à-vis the welfare state: As non-recipients and non-contributors (e.g., children, housewives), contributors (e.g., the economically active), and recipients (e.g., elderly, unemployed, disabled, maternity leave) (Mayer & Schöpflin, 1989). For example, "old age" is often defined by eligibility rules for the receipt of pensions or Social Security benefits, or by the legal or actual retirement ages. However, as a measure of "old age," age at retirement entails a number of obvious problems. First, many older people remain employed in some capacity after retirement, while others do not have gainful work from which to retire. Second, the receipt of pension payments and Social Security benefits may not coincide with age at retirement. Third, age at retirement tells us little about an individual's level of physical and mental functioning, degree of autonomy or dependency, or level of social participation, which may also be used to define life stages. Where this last point is concerned, there are now several good examples of strategies for measuring the multidimensional process of aging using interview or survey methods (see Berkman, Seeman, Albert, Blazer, & Kahn, et al., 1993, from the MacArthur Foundation Research Network on Successful Aging; and Baltes, Mayer, Helmchen, & Steinhagen-Thiessen, 1993, from the Berlin Aging Study). Nonetheless, well-developed indicators for measuring transitions to dependency in old age are not available. While measures related to Activities of Daily Living (ADL, IADL) capture declining abilities for self-care (Fillenbaum, 1995), these measures do not take support structures and social settings into account. In this area, measurement strategies might be improved by adopting the logic of life-course analysis (see Chapter 4). For example, one might conceptualize the transition to dependency as a series of different states (e.g., first being unable to work, followed by the receipt of informal help, the receipt of formal help, and institutionalization). The duration of time spent in these various states could then be used to better understand the course of this process.

AGE AND SOCIAL POLICY

Social Policy and the Question of Age versus Need

The state plays a significant role in structuring the life course, and its policies often use age or life stage as a basis for providing opportunities and allocating resources in the spheres of education, work, family, or health care. Yet with *Age or Need? Public Policies for Older People* (1982), Neugarten first began to advocate a need-based rather than age-based approach to social policies, even for those policies originally conceived as old age policies. Neugarten questions whether social policies and the needs of the aged will be "congruent" in the future, particularly if we continue to grant government assistance on the basis of age without acknowledging the possibility that age may become increasingly irrelevant in Western societies. The aged are a heterogeneous group on biological, psychological, social, and economic indicators alike (the "Mathew effect," to be discussed in Chapters 3 and 5, emphasizes the cumulative nature of advantage and disadvantage over the life course and is offered as an explanation for heterogeneity among the aged).

As a result, it would seem unreasonable to use age alone to determine eligibility for benefits and entitlements. While age-based policies may elevate the status of an age group as a whole, they overlook differences across subpopulations within the group, some of whom may be in much greater need than others and remain at a relative disadvantage even after receipt of age-based benefits and entitlements. An age-based approach to social policies may also have the unintended consequences of labeling specific age groups as problematic, institutionalizing new forms of ageism, and creating age divisiveness. At the same time, several characteristics of chronological age make it perfect for use in social policies: It is convenient, easily measured, practical, objective and universal. Pitfalls may also occur if we instead adopt need-based approaches without clearly defining what is meant by "need," and without considering whether our means for demonstrating need will demean or stigmatize the very people we are trying to help.

More recently, Binstock (1996) has hinted that purely age-based policies may be eroding. These are mainly instances of age being *combined* with economic status to determine benefit levels (e.g., the Social Security Reform Act of 1983, the Tax Reform Act of 1986, the Medicare Catastrophic Coverage Act of 1988, and the Omnibus Budget Reconciliation Act of 1993). In addition, several long-term care proposals have been introduced since the late 1980s (e.g., the Long-Term Care Act of 1989; a long-term program proposed by Clinton in 1993), and each of these initiatives has *eliminated* age as a criterion for coverage.

We have much to learn, particularly through cross-national comparisons, about the ways in which states and their policies structure the life course. As we explore this link, we might ask the following questions: How exactly does a program or policy improve people's lives or life chances? What dimensions does it address (e.g., physical, psychological, social, economic)? How exactly does the improvement come about? Is the improvement temporary or permanent? What is supposed to happen in the short-term and the long-term? How can we evaluate whether the policy or program succeeds or fails? Does it relate to a certain segment of life or to the life course as a whole? Is its vision of the life course rigid (i.e., with certain kinds of work, family, and leisure experiences confined to specific segments) or flexible (promoting meaningful opportunities in work, education, family, and leisure across the entire life course)? Who is targeted, who is excluded, and why? Are there assumptions about who should be helped (or who is worthy of help)? What are the assumptions about who is "at risk," and why? Even among those "at risk," are some at greater risk than others? Who foots the financial costs? Are there other kinds of costs? And are there costs associated with *not* developing these policies and programs? To effectively answer questions such as these, we must better combine basic research on human development with applied research on intervention design, delivery, and evaluation (Lerner, 1995, p. 32).

Social Policy and the Question of Age Divisiveness

As noted above, an issue related to age-based social policies concerns the potential that these policies carry for age divisiveness. Early on, Neugarten (1974a/1996) warned us of the possibility that politics based on age-divisiveness may be exacerbated in an aging society as younger groups lash out against the unprecedented numbers of older people. As for whether anything came of Neugarten's early warnings, we need only remind ourselves of the controversial intergenerational equity debate that surfaced in the 1980s (for reviews, see Cook, Marshall, Marshall, & Kaufman, 1994; Marshall, Cook, & Marshall, 1993).

Intergenerational equity refers to the idea that different generations should receive similar treatment and have similar access to societal goods and services. This debate was spurred by demographer Samuel Preston's presidential address to members of the Population Association of America, in which he argued that elderly people receive more than their fair share of the federal budget, particularly in light of their economic status, and that they ultimately receive these benefits at the expense of groups that are more needy and deserving, especially children (Preston, 1984). Preston's thesis is linked to the fact that the elderly, as a group, have experienced increases in their economic well-being over the last several decades, while younger age groups, and especially young children, have experienced declines. This has fostered the perception that the elderly are "greedy geezers" who are self-absorbed and only concerned about meeting and satisfying their own needs. Proponents of this thesis have also argued that the elderly have coupled their gains in economic power with gains in political power, granting them the ability to secure a greater share of public services for themselves.

On the other side of the debate stand those who believe that this logic is predicated on nothing but false assumptions. These include the assumptions that (a) older people, by virtue of the fact that they are old, have the same needs and share the same interests as a group; (b) older people are self-interested; (c) older people represent a tremendous economic burden; and (d) given the chance, both the public and legislators would happily decrease or even eliminate old age benefits and entitlements.

Where the first assumption is concerned, research has consistently shown that older people are not only very heterogeneous as a group on biological, psychological, social, and economic indicators; they are also more heterogeneous than any other age group (Dannefer, 1987). Where the second assumption is concerned, the elderly do vote at a high rate, but their voting choices are "rarely, if ever, based on age-group interests" and do not dominate the political arena (Binstock & Day, 1996, p. 368). Where the third assumption is concerned, most evidence (and anxiety about the economic burden of older people) is linked to the fact that there are increasing numbers of retirees relative to the working population. However, policy experts have stressed that this will *not* ultimately lead to the collapse of entitlement programs that are dependent upon employee-employer contributions. In addition, dependency ratios often do not include children and unemployed adults, which seriously misrepresents burden caused by elders (Binstock, 1996). Where the fourth assumption is concerned, Cook (1996) has charted support for programs for older Americans throughout the 1980s and into the 1990s, and shows that while views in the *media* and among *policy elites* were often negative, *public* support for entitlement programs that target older people has remained strong.

Questions related to the development of age- versus need-based social policies, and to their possibilities for age divisiveness, are complicated and have no clear solutions. These challenges pose important, and even serious, costs and benefits. Our research must fully explore their impact on individuals, families, age and other groups, social institutions, and society at large.

CHAPTER
3

Challenges Posed by Generation and Cohort

This chapter addresses the challenges posed by the concepts of generation and cohort. After a brief discussion of the common uses of the concept of "generation," this chapter turns to several landmark essays that remain critical for contemporary thought on cohort. It then examines issues related to measuring and analyzing cohort, including challenges associated with demonstrating cohort effects, handling the age-period-cohort problem, linking lives and history, examining cohort trajectories, and understanding the societal significance of cohort. As the chapter nears its end, it entertains a few metaphors of cohort aging that exist in popular culture and social science theory. It closes with a discussion of the problem of "historical specificity." That is, because most developmental research is cross-sectional, and because even the most long-standing of longitudinal studies are typically composed of members of a single birth cohort, little is known about the extent to which developmental knowledge is historically specific. Yet our theory and data are discussed as if they are valid across historical periods. The problem of historical specificity has been largely disregarded, but is serious and runs throughout developmental research. It is a problem to which we must now respond.

COMMON USES OF THE CONCEPT OF "GENERATION"

The concept of generation is used by social scientists in multiple and inconsistent ways (Kertzer, 1983). First, the term generation is often used to designate levels in extended kinship structure, and several scholars have suggested that the term "generation" be reserved strictly for that use (e.g., O'Rand & Krecker, 1990; Riley, Johnson, & Foner, 1972; Ryder, 1965). Second, it is used to designate the general "stage" or segment in the life course that a group occupies (e.g., the current "generation of old people," the "college generation"). Third, it is used to refer to a large group of people alive in the same historical period (e.g., those born before the war versus those born after the war). Fourth, it is used to refer to a special age group in history, or to a "political" generation, which becomes aware of its uniqueness and joins together to work for social or political change (e.g., generations that begin with capital letters, such as the "Beat Generation" or the "Hippie Generation" [Braungart & Braungart, 1986]). Each generation may have its own *Zeitgeist*, reflected in its ideas, values, emotions, and behaviors. Of course, because multiple generations exist at once, multiple *Zeitgeist* exist simultaneously and are, to some degree, interdependent. Each generation defines itself in relation to, and often sets itself against, other generations.

Finally, the term generation is often used to denote circumscribed, age-based strata in the population. This use of generation, when combined with pieces of the second and third uses, comes closest to what developmental scientists consider *cohort*. While birth and death dates mark an individual's historical presence, the concept of cohort is reserved for an *aggregate* of individuals, generally defined on the basis of birth year, whose lives move together through historical time. As they do, they occupy a unique place in the life course, and in historical time, relative to older and younger groups. Given the multiple meanings of generation and cohort abound in the literature, the uses and measurement of these concepts must be clarified.

LANDMARKS FOR CONTEMPORARY THOUGHT ON COHORT: A DISCUSSION

The nineteenth-century writings of Comte, Cournot, Dilthey, Ferrari, Lorenz, Mill, and von Ranke all contain important theoretical observations on the nature of social and political "generations," as do the early- to mid-twentieth-century contributions of Eisenstadt, Ortega y Gasset, Halbwachs, Mannheim, Marías, and Pinder. Of these, Mannheim provided the foundation for most contemporary thought on cohort.

The Problem of Generations

Mannheim (1928/1952) was concerned with the "problem of generations": how generations, whose emergence and ultimate disappearance are based in the *biological* rhythms of birth and death, become meaningful in *social* and *cultural* ways. Mannheim distinguished between three different concepts of generation. The first, and simplest, concept denotes a set of people who share a location in the "social and historical process," such as a "class" of people on the basis of their birth year (*Generationslagerung*). A "tendency inherent" in this *common locational status* create in them the *potential* for "definite modes of behavior, feeling, and thought" (p. 291). This concept of generation comes closest to the way in which the concept of cohort is most often used in developmental science.

Mannheim's second concept of generation (*Generationenzusammenhang*) moves a step beyond the simple co-presence of individuals with a shared locational status. Here, individuals are subjectively aware of their membership in a particular generation, and they are united as an *actual generation* in that they at least passively experience the social and intellectual currents of this group.

Mannheim's third concept of generation (*Generationseinheit*) moves beyond that of an actual generation still further. Here, subgroups of individuals within the actual generation "work up the material of their common experiences in different specific ways" and become separate *generational units* (p. 304). Generational units are able to organize and act in a concerted fashion. At their nucleus, generational units are *concrete groups* composed of "naturally developed and consciously willed ties" (p. 289). In addition, the separate generational units that form within an actual generation may even be oppositional. This serves as a reminder that experiences and meanings within a generation need not be uniform and may actually be diverse.

In the case of both actual generations and generational units, some degree of consciousness emerges among members; this consciousness is important because it has socializing effects. Both of these concepts are substantively meaningful and carry strong assumptions. In contrast, the use of cohort in contemporary research comes closest to Mannheim's first concept of generation: It is purely categorical and carries few assumptions.

In considering the fundamental principles of generations as *social* phenomena, Mannheim asks us to imagine how human social life would feel if one generation lived on forever and was never succeeded by another. We must compare this to the dynamic processes operating in real societies, in which new cohorts are continuously born and others continuously die.[1] As a result, "members of any one generation can participate only in a temporally limited section of the historical process" (p. 292). This creates the need for a continuous process of generational transmission, in which one generation passes on "accumulated cultural heritage" to the next. Each generation that emerges not only makes "fresh contact" with that heritage (it meets that material in new ways), but because members of a generation are similarly located in historical time, they are "in a position to experience the same events and data, etc., and especially that these experiences impinge on a similarly stratified consciousness" (p. 297).

For Mannheim, this stratified consciousness is the result of *dialectically articulated experiences,* in which early experiences are crystallized into a world-view, and later experiences are then understood in light of earlier ones. At times, later experiences confirm earlier experiences; at other times, they negate them. As a result, a generation's early experiences—in childhood, adolescence, and early adulthood— are viewed as being particularly important in shaping its world-view. For Mannheim, like other theorists of social and political generations, young adulthood is a particularly important period. As new cohorts come of age and come into fresh contact with traditional ideas, they often provide a "market for radical ideas and a source of followers, and they are more likely than their elders to criticize the existing order" (Ryder, 1965, p. 850).

---

[1] These dynamic processes have been referred to as "demographic metabolism" (Ryder, 1965), "cohort replenishment" (Waring, 1975), and "cohort succession" (Riley, 1973).

Finally, the *pace of social change* is probably the most important element in Mannheim's framework. Not every generation forms its own style or "entelechy" (p. 309). When an entelechy does occur, it is likely linked to the pace of social change. When the pace of social change is rapid, traditional modes of experience, thought, and expression may no longer be possible. Under these circumstances, each generation, and especially younger generations, may produce new modes of experience, thought, and expression. When the pace of change is slow, the evolution of a new generational style, even if it may be emerging, is not visibly different from its predecessor because these changes are so gradual. Whether and when the tendencies inherent in a generation are therefore realized "depends entirely on the trigger action of the social and cultural process . . . The biological fact of the existence of generations merely provides the *possibility* that generation entelechies may emerge at all" (pp. 310-311).

Cohort as a Concept in the Study of Social Change

Later in this century, a second landmark occurred in the evolution of contemporary thought on cohort: demographer Norman Ryder's (1965) essay on the "Cohort as a Concept in the Study of Social Change." Ryder stresses the importance of understanding the significance of cohort at *multiple levels of analysis* (e.g., for individuals, families, and society). Ryder links the concept of cohort to the *aggregate processes* of life and death in society: to the "massive process of personnel replacement" (or "demographic metabolism"), in which new materials are put into the social system (via fertility processes) and in which old materials are discharged (via mortality processes). These processes are a central force behind social change, though changes in an individual over the course of his or her life are nonetheless "distinguishable from changes in the population of which he [or she] is a component" (p. 843).

Like Mannheim, Ryder emphasizes the fact that each new cohort makes fresh contact with "contemporary social heritage and carries the impress of the encounter through life . . . [But because] it embodies a temporally specific version of the heritage, each cohort is differentiated from all others . . . [and] each fresh cohort is a possible intermediary in the transformation process, a vehicle for introducing new postures" (p. 844). However, for Ryder, as for Mannheim, new cohorts only create the *possibility* that social change will occur; they do not automatically *cause* it. When social change does occur, it creates differentiation between cohorts, and the effects of social change can then be examined by comparing the life experiences and trajectories of different cohorts.

Ryder conceptualizes cohort more broadly than birth year, defining cohorts as an "aggregate of individuals (within some definite population) who experience the same event within the same time interval" (p. 845). However, Ryder indicates that nearly all research up to that point (1965) limited its definition of cohort to birth year. The same observation can safely be made today, over three decades later.

Ryder points to cohort *size and composition* as especially important factors in determining its implications for society and its institutions, and for the opportunities and constraints that members of a cohort face in life. Abrupt changes in cohort size result from significant shifts in fertility, migration, or mortality. As an example of the strain that large cohort size may have on the social system, consider the "baby boom" cohort. As this group has grown up and older, it has strained educational institutions and job and housing markets. Similarly, there is great concern among both the public and policy-makers about the effects that the baby boom cohort will have on the health care system and Social Security program when it reaches old age. Another good example of the importance of cohort size is Easterlin's (1987, 1996) "birth and fortune" hypothesis, which emphasizes the link between cohort size and the economic fate of its members.

Just as the size of this cohort impinges on the social institutions that must assimilate it, its size may also have implications for the experiences and opportunities of its members as they move through social institutions. They may find themselves in overcrowded schools, and they may face many more competitors in a restricted job and housing market. These factors, in turn, may also shape other life decisions, such as whether and when to marry, whether and when to have children, or how many children to have. These experiences may also have cumulative effects over time, shaping the social, family, and economic circumstances under which individuals find themselves in later life. Issues such as these are underexplored in contemporary scholarship on the life course.

The issue of *relative* cohort size is also a reminder that cohorts do not stand in isolation from one another. In addition to examining the ways in which the characteristics of a cohort set parameters on the lives of its *own* members, we must also examine their implications for adjacent and distal cohorts. The lives of members of multiple cohorts are inextricably linked within the social settings of daily life, such as schools, work places, social groups and organizations, and communities.

It is important to remember that just as cohorts change in size and composition, so, too, does society and its organization. As each new cohort encounters social institutions, its experiences are likely different from those of previous cohorts because the social institutions are themselves different. For example, changes in the indexing of Social Security may have an inequitable impact on the financial benefits paid to members of different cohorts (see Schultz [1995] for a discussion of the so-called "notch" problem). Similarly, changes in the organization of state-supported medical programs such as Medicare and Medicaid likely create different health care experiences and options for members of different cohorts.

As noted earlier, the *tempo* or *pace* of change is an important factor in many theories of social change. How might this be linked to the salience of generational distinctions? On the one hand, when the pace of social change in a society is rapid, life experiences within and between cohorts may become more variable. This may be partially due to the fact that the "diverse institutional structures in which life takes place, and the normative patterns of interpreting an acceptable normal biography, [may] change much faster than otherwise" (Weymann, 1996b, p. 46). (However, as noted in Chapter 1, social change may also create "structural lag" as social structures fail to keep pace with rapidly changing ideas and behaviors [Riley,

Kahn, & Foner, 1994].) In this case, differences between generations may be reduced or even eliminated.

On the other hand, rapid social change may, as Mannheim suggested, serve to crystallize (or create solidarity within) a cohort, and it may also carry the potential to create or strengthen chasms between cohorts. For Ryder, social change emerges in the city and through the process of urbanization; and it is ultimately driven by *technological development*. Dramatic technological change has an age-differentiated impact on the population, serving to distance cohorts from one another by making the past irrelevant. For example, rather than retrain older workers to keep their skills up-to-date with new technology, companies may more easily (and more efficiently) recruit workers from younger cohorts who already hold these skills.

However, a recent television commercial illustrates the fact that technological change may also *foster* ties between cohorts. In the commercial, a kindergarten girl sits with her mother in front of their home computer. The mother is at the keyboard, and the little girl calls out an internet address for her mother to enter. The mother is confused by the terminology the girl uses: "http:," "double slash," "tildé," "dot." As the girl explains the syntax to her mother, she looks up and says, "Mom, what *did* they teach you in kindergarten?!"

Along these lines, I am also reminded of a recent visit to the Rock and Roll Hall of Fame, which is for some a multi-media wonder, and for others a high-tech nightmare. Hundreds of monitors fill the walls and project video clips and short films; sounds and lights bombard visitors from every direction; displays are often interactive, as people choose the music they would like to hear or the entertainers about whom they would like to learn. In the middle of this environment stand two elderly women—clear outliers in this 40s-and-under, and largely 20s, crowd. While this technology is foreign to them, they seem actively interested in it: They bravely approach displays, ask younger people for help in operating them, and giggle their way through the museum. In both of these examples, technological change does not distance cohorts from each other but instead provides an opportunity for them to, quite literally, join hands.

The pace of social change has also been linked to how often new generations emerge. For example, increases in longevity may slow the rate of social change, given that the dominance of a generation is extended; if the conservatism of a cohort also increases as it grows older, the ability of the younger "rising" generation to create social change is also likely weakened (e.g., Comte, 1839). On the other hand, increases in longevity may not only extend the period of youth, but also intensify the resentment of younger generations toward older generations, and intensify the impulse of the younger generation to force change. As a result, the time that elapses between generations may actually shorten with increases in longevity and during periods of rapid social change (e.g., Berger, 1960). When the pace of social change is rapid, generations defined in large time segments (such as 15 or 30 years, which were suggested by Comte [1839], Dilthey [1875], Ferrari [1874], Mannheim [1928/1952], and Ortega y Gasset [1933]) are less meaningful. Under such conditions, it may be more appropriate to define generations in shorter spans of time.

While the historical circumstances associated with the period of young adulthood may be especially important in shaping individuals' world-views or in bringing about generational *mentalités,* one might also hypothesize that periods of social change, especially periods of extreme social change, may take their largest toll on *older* adults. In the case of older adults, extreme social change may seriously shatter lifelong assumptions, beliefs, and values on which identities have long been based.

On the other hand, one might argue that social change has its weakest effects on older people. In fact, Ryder (1965, p. 858) argues that:

> Social change ordinarily touches older persons less closely. They lead a more restricted social life, they read less, they attend fewer movies, and their friends, books, and movies are more carefully chosen to conform to their biases. Their residences and friendships become more stable. The longer a person persists in an established mode of conduct, the less likely its comprehensive redefinition.

At the heart of Ryder's statement is the view that aging is accompanied by inevitable disengagement, withdrawal, and rigidity. Of course, Ryder's essay was written over three decades ago, a time at which most theories of aging posited movement in these directions. Propositions along these lines have long since been abandoned in favor of propositions that emphasize activity, integration, and other potentials associated with aging (see Lynott & Lynott, 1996; Schroots, 1996). Nonetheless, Ryder speculates about social change, the groups most likely to spark it, and its differential effects on various cohorts in the population. What might we propose now? Contemporary research must address these important questions.

What is a Cohort and Why?

Finally, Rosow's (1978) essay "What is a Cohort and Why?" stands as a third landmark for contemporary thought on cohort. While Rosow's essay has not received the attention it deserves, the issues raised therein remain among the most challenging questions with which we must wrestle today. Little has changed in the two decades of theory and research since Rosow's critique, or since Schaie's (1984) proclamation that "the time has come to remedy the lack of substantive attention given to the specific meaning[s] of historical time and cohort" (p. 2). As a result, developmental scientists must attend to both the conceptual and empirical problems associated with cohort.

What exactly is a cohort, and why? And how exactly should cohort be measured and its effects analyzed? Rosow raises three problems associated with these questions. First, consider the problem of *cohort boundaries.* When we refer to a cohort, who exactly do we mean? The crux of this problem comes down to how to construct a "series of discrete cohorts from a continuous flow of people" emerging in time (p. 68).[2] In the process of defining a cohort, where do we draw the line between the

---

[2] Fortes (1984) makes a similar point, arguing that when we analyze cohorts, we are inherently faced with a tension between continuity and discontinuity as we search for "ostensible discontinuities between successive generations in a framework of overall continuity" (p. 109).

end of one cohort and the beginning of another? How do we decide who is in a cohort and who is not? How can these successive groups be meaningfully distinguished from one another? Because cohorts often do not "naturally announce themselves" with "loud and clear" differences in social behavior, researchers must ultimately set somewhat arbitrary upper and lower limits in defining the group of people to be designated as a cohort (Knoke, 1984, p. 192).

Second, cohorts are supposed to be defined on the basis of their unique historical experiences. This brings the problem of *distinctive experience:* What are these unique experiences, and how can they be demonstrated? Third, the experiences of a cohort are supposed to be markedly different from those of other cohorts. This brings the problem of *differential effects:* We must show that each cohort, relative to those adjacent to it, responds in its own way to a phenomenon of interest. It is this unique response that constitutes a "cohort effect." For example, the impact of an historical event or period of change[3] should generally depend on the age at which it is experienced by an individual or cohort. This is what Elder (1995) has described as the "life-stage principle." As a *specific* birth cohort grows up and older, its members encounter an historical event or period of social change at roughly the same point in their lives; and as *successive* birth cohorts encounter those same events or changes, they experience them at different points in life. As a result, the impact of a specific historical event or change is likely contingent on the position of a cohort when the event or change occurs. This is an example of *inter-cohort differentiation,* which emphasizes variability *between* cohorts in "size, composition, patterns of aging, characteristics of its members, or experiences associated with the differing historical eras spanning their respective lives" (Uhlenberg & Riley, 1996, p. 299).[4]

With respect to the problem of distinctive experience, can we, or should we, ever assume that members of a cohort have uniform experiences? While the same historical event or change may impinge on members of a cohort, the nature of individual experiences with it, and the meanings that result, may vary significantly as a function of their personal characteristics and resources. This is an example of *intra-cohort differentiation,* which emphasizes variability *within* a cohort and denotes subcohorts with shared life-course patterns and experiences. Subcohorts may be defined by characteristics such as "gender, race, or class, or by exposure to particular historical trends or events" (Uhlenberg & Riley, 1996, p. 299).

These three problems—of cohort boundaries, distinctive experiences, and differential effects—bring important challenges for developmental scientists. How might history be taken into account in the study of lives? How might we build history into our research designs and analyses? How might we better unearth important inter- and intra-cohort variability, its sources, and its consequences?

---

[3] Following Schuman and Scott (1989), I use the term "historical event" to designate discrete events that are of relatively short duration and easy to mark in time, such as a war or economic crisis. I use the terms "historical change" or "periods of change" to designate larger changes for which precise years are more difficult to determine, such as the civil rights or women's movements.

[4] The essence of inter-cohort differentiation is well-captured in the Arab proverb, "Men resemble their times more than they do their fathers."

MEASURING AND ANALYZING COHORT

The definition of cohorts according to birth year is simultaneously the most common and problematic use of cohort. If we choose to define cohorts this way, what is our rationale for why a particular span of years is important? Similarly, a common analytic strategy is to subdivide a cohort into finer birth year-brackets or according to social location variables such as sex, race, income, educational attainment, or occupational status. If we subdivide a cohort in these ways, what is our rationale for choosing a particular set of dimensions? Most importantly, how might any differences that result be explained?

We should also keep our core variables of interest in mind as we consider possible cohort comparisons. Are these variables for which we expect to observe great or little differentiation between or within cohorts at a particular point in time? Are these variables that are likely to be susceptible to historical forces? (For example, some types of variables, such as attitudes, values, or beliefs, may be more susceptible to historical forces than other types, such as cognitive development [Caspi, 1998]). How might this differentiation (or lack thereof) change over time? (These questions call attention to the issues of both stability and change, which will be discussed in Chapter 4.)

First and foremost, the concept of cohort should be tied to the fact that the individuals in it share an experience. Cohorts need not be defined in terms of birth year; other definitions are often more useful. For example, we might define as a cohort a group of students entering a doctoral program in the same autumn term; a group of managers who begin their training within an organization at the same time; a group of women who give birth to their first child in the same year; or a group of men called upon for military service during World War II. In each of these cases, the age distribution within the cohort may be highly variable. For example, it is common for incoming doctoral students to differ in age by ten, fifteen, or twenty or more years; or for a group of first-time mothers to vary in age to the same degree.

There are several recent examples of interesting attempts to construct more meaningful cohort groups in empirical ways, even with cross-sectional data. For example, following the framework offered by Elder and Caspi (1990), Settersten and Hagestad (1996a, 1996b) constructed a variable to capture meaningful cohort groups based upon the year in which the respondent came of age (turned 18): 1920-1934; 1935-1945; 1946-1959; 1960-1973; and after 1973. This approach links the period of young adulthood with the historical conditions associated with those years, an intersection which, at least in terms of theory, is believed to be particularly influential in shaping the world-views of a cohort and its members.

Settersten and Hagestad develop their demarcations along the following lines: Those entering adulthood between *1920-1934* came of age during a time of both changing sexual mores and swings in economic stability (a general economic boom from 1923-1929, the onset of the Great Depression during 1929 and 1930, and the depth of the Great Depression during 1932-1933). Those entering adulthood between *1935-1945* came of age during partial recovery from the depression, an economic slump, the incipient stage of wartime mobilization, and World War II; men who returned home after the war had new opportunities (particularly educational) provided by the GI bill. Those entering adulthood between *1946-1959* came of age during post-war economic growth, the Korean war, the McCarthy Era, the onset of the civil rights movement, and new family patterns of the 1950s. Those entering adulthood between *1960-1973* came of age during the mobilization of civil rights, civil strife, the Vietnam War, changing patterns of labor force participation for women. Those entering adulthood *after 1974* came of age during a time of growing disillusionment about the role that government could play in instituting social change (e.g., what some policy analysts have described as the failures of the Great Society), disillusionment about faith and trust in the government (e.g., Watergate, questions about the role of the United States in the Vietnam War), growing problems in the economy (e.g., restricted employment opportunities, the oil embargo of 1974, the stock market crash of 1987, the expansion of the service economy, and America's standing in the global economy), and heightened consumerism and materialism of the mid-1980s. Of course, more or different boundaries might be drawn depending on the age distribution of the sample, its size, the research questions, or other factors. This approach, however, nonetheless involves constructing more meaningful cohort groupings *a priori,* and then tests them to see whether they reveal interesting effects in relation to data of interest (outcome variables).

Another strategy is to overlay birth year or age atop historical dimensions such as political administrations or regimes, military ventures, or swings in economic prosperity and decline. For example, a common strategy for American political researchers is to construct cohorts of four-year or eight-year bands to "reflect the span of presidential administrations, starting at the age of enfranchisement" (age 18) (Knoke, 1984, p. 192).

Another interesting idea is to group cohorts on the basis of their exposure to, and use of, different technologies. For example, Weymann (1994) examines the "diffusion" of technological innovation in everyday life, especially with respect to "household technologies" (e.g., computers, microwaves, VCRs, video cameras, CD players, televisions, telephones, dish washers, refrigerators, freezers). Drawing on data from East and West Germany, he compares East-West respondents, men and women, and, especially relevant to the discussion here, cohort differences in technological diffusion. More importantly, Weymann examines how respondents classify themselves as members of technology "generations," especially based on the technological changes that occurred during their formative years. Weymann finds that "certain technologies are crucial symbols of generational identity, depending on cohort membership"—for instance, the "computer generation," and the "car and dishwasher generation" (p. 32). Other research by Weymann with Sackmann (Sackmann & Weymann, 1989) shows that West Germans are able to comfortably classify themselves and other people into one of four "generations": The "generation of the Third Reich/war," the "post-war generation," the "post-1968 generation" (as the starting point of the "cultural revolution"), and the "generation of labor market- and environmental-crisis." Once classified into these groups, respondents can also be clearly distinguished on items related to life style, educational values, and knowledge of social science.[5] This strategy draws attention to a factor which, from a theoretical standpoint, is viewed as a driving force behind the formation of generations or cohorts: technological change. Surely, both the degree and type of technological change must affect cohorts differently. For example, developments in the fields of medicine and public health may differentially change the survival patterns and functional health of cohorts. Similarly, developments in communication may differentially change the degree to which, and the manner in which, cohorts have contact with others or access to information (Uhlenberg & Miner, 1996). This strategy also offers an alternative method for identifying generations or cohorts: It allows respondents to define, or classify themselves into, generation or cohort categories.

Finally, a strategy discussed earlier with respect to the analysis of age differences might also be extended to the analysis of cohort differences: One might begin with members of adjacent single-year birth cohorts and then, moving outward, search for ways in which they differ qualitatively from others on a set of variables. In this way, the researcher arrays information by birth cohort, looking for important patterning in data that might then be used to define the cohorts. Again, a limitation of this approach is that it is purely an empirically-based strategy. In addition, such a strategy would require us to reverse our approach to analyzing generations and cohorts: Rather than examine attitudes and behaviors as *outcomes* of generation or cohort, generations or cohorts would instead be *defined* on the basis of attitudes and behaviors. However, because the very definition of a generation or cohort would then be intimately tied to both the particular characteristics of a sample and content of its data, these definitions would vary dramatically across studies, thereby making the synthesis of findings across studies a difficult task.

While definitions of cohort based on substantive criteria (such as their distinct historical experiences) are attractive in theory, the groupings that result may often not meet the assumptions of statistical tests. As Knoke (1984) wryly notes, "empirical researchers usually designate all birth cohorts in a population as having equal widths, but conceptually such straight-jacketing is not warranted, since the formative historical events that mold each generation do not erupt with monotonous regularity" (p. 192). The popular practice of using five- or ten-year bands may be more a function of "our use of the decimal system" rather than any "meaningful dimension," psychological, social, or otherwise (Schaie, 1984, p. 4). In addition, researchers often even convert arbitrary age bands into corresponding birth-year cohort categories for purposes of the convenience of computation. In such cases, the resulting cohort categories are even less credible. Nonetheless, cohorts of variable width may create serious methodological problems for quantitative analytic strategies.

Many of the problems associated with measuring and analyzing cohort ring similar to the criticisms raised in Chapter 2 around the use of age as an "empty" or

---

[5] Sackmann and Weymann (1989) suggest that younger generations have been more exposed to the social sciences, and that social science ideas play an important role in shaping world-views.

amorphous variable. Cohort, like age, sex, social class, and other "social location" variables, has explanatory power because it serves as a "surrogate" index for the common ideas, values, emotions, or behaviors of many people (Ryder, 1965). However, we must move away from defining cohorts in arbitrary ways and instead find ways to make cohort more meaningful in our research. What exactly does cohort serve to index, and why? Might the factors for which we use cohort as an index be measured more directly?

While the typical measurement of cohort (in terms of an arbitrarily defined span of birth years) may be practical, it is atheoretical and of little value when used in this way. In these cases, cohort is "not a theoretical concept but a methodological one. *It is a way to organize data*" (Marshall, 1984, p. 208).[6] (Marshall actually argues that cohort is an atheoretical concept and should only be used as a methodological concept. His conceptualization of cohort is therefore very different from what I, following Rosow, am suggesting cohort ought to be about.) As such, cohorts, like age groups, are generally used as statistical categories and not as substantively meaningful groups.[7]

This has led some to suggest that cohorts are nothing but "statistical artifacts," and that only generations are sociological realities. (However, as noted earlier, cohorts certainly do take on sociological realities, as their characteristics alone have important consequences for individual lives and for society at large. Later in this chapter, the importance of understanding the societal significance of cohort will be further explored.) For example, Braungart and Braungart (1986) argue that while a cohort is a group of people who share a common birth year, a generation (1) not only shares cohort membership, but also (2) develops an "age-group consciousness," (3) is characterized by distinct attitudes and behaviors, which are also counter to those of other "age groups" in society, and (4) is actively involved in bringing about social change. Thus, Braungart and Braungart argue that "a cohort represents a category 'in itself,' while a generation acts as a social group 'for itself' " (p. 213). If distinctions such as these are accepted, they carry important consequences for our research, and particularly for our operational definitions of generation and cohort. Must each of these components be in place to constitute a "generation"? To what degree? How can these components be measured adequately? At what point does a cohort (or some subgroup therein) become a generation, and vice versa? These distinctions are also at odds with the earlier point that cohorts need *not* be defined in terms of birth year (and may, in fact, be highly age-variable), even though they are normally defined this way in empirical research.

---

[6] However, Marshall argues that when birth cohorts are shown to be qualitatively different on social variables they are instead "generations." As such, Marshall's conceptualization of generation, then, comes closer to my conceptualization of cohort. It is also noteworthy that Marshall's definition of generation is data-driven and does not presuppose any degree of consciousness or interaction.

[7] The term "age cohort" is commonly used in the literature but is not particularly useful (even though at any given point in time, a birth cohort does occupy an age category in the population). When individuals from different age categories in cross-sectional data are being compared, it would be more accurate to label these categories as "age groups" or "age strata" (Uhlenberg & Miner, 1996).

However, even Marshall (1984), who views cohorts as nothing more than statistical artifacts, also takes the optimistic stance that "even though age is fully determined by birth cohort, and vice versa, when one speaks of cohort, one is led to think in terms of the historical period of birth and the historical circumstances experienced by the cohort" (p. 208). However, a quick glance through volumes of scholarly journals will undoubtedly render Marshall's stance questionable: Researchers seldom demonstrate, or even discuss, how a cohort's unique place in historical time is (or might be) important or through what processes or mechanisms detected "cohort effects" are (or might be) brought about. Instead, the typical approach to analyzing cohort differences is identical to that for analyzing age differences: Simple, arbitrary five- or ten-year brackets are developed and tested without much thought to why a particular set of brackets are used, what exactly those brackets are believed to reference, and how any differences might be explained. This is why Rosow's critique is so important: It encourages us to be more mindful of what we mean by cohort, how we measure it (and whether the dimensions cohort serves to index might instead be measured more directly), and how we use cohort in our analyses. Similarly, Marshall's commentary is important in that it encourages us to look more closely at how, to use Mills' (1959) phrase, the "intersection of biography and history" produces empirical clusters of behavior and attitudes. Those clusters, as Berger (1984, p. 220) points out, *suggest* the "probability of real interaction, and that probable interaction suggests the sources of a common culture." These clusters are also made more complicated, and are likely weakened, once they are overlain with variables such as race or sex, or indicators of social class (educational attainment, occupational status, income). Even when it can be shown that by virtue of a common birth date that a cohort has been subjected to "common formative influences from the massive social facts of a given era" (Berger, 1984, p. 220), we ought not assume that all its members were equally exposed to those influences, that those influences were experienced in similar ways or held similar meanings, or that they came with similar consequences. Much remains to be learned about the degree to which members of a cohort interact with a common set of influences in *dissimilar* ways, and how much dissimilarity is permissible before they no longer constitute a cohort.

Whether the historical location of cohorts *in and of itself* induces important and significant empirical clusters of behaviors and attitudes remains an empirical question. As noted earlier, little research has used empirical clusters of behaviors and attitudes as a means for defining cohorts. Instead, investigators first define cohorts and then search for empirical clusters of behaviors and attitudes; beyond this, few actually attempt to explicate what exactly it is about historical location that produces (or fails to produce) empirical clusters.

In the end, shall we restrict our use of the term "generation" to indicate lineal position in the family, as some have suggested, and refer to those positions as "familial generations"? Generational boundaries are clearest where familial generations are concerned. At the same time, the generational position of an individual in extended kinship structure (such as "grandparent," "parent," or "grandchild") provides only a crude sense of an individual's life stage, and says nothing certain about age and even less about cohort membership. Generations within families are not always neatly organized by cohort (Hagestad, 1981). In fact, in modern families generational position begins to crumble as a potential proxy for age or cohort. For example, high divorce rates lead to large numbers of second and third marriages, often giving parents (especially fathers) several "generations" of children, often dramatically varied in age, some of whom may even be older than their new stepmothers or step-fathers.[8]

Or shall we reserve the term "social generations" for subgroups of a birth cohort that are conscious of themselves as a group, exhibit a collective *mentalité*, and are united together for the purposes of social change (that is, what Mannheim called "generational units" and what Braungart and Braungart call "political generations")? If so, how do we measure and operationalize concepts such as "collective consciousness" or "collective *mentalité* "? In addition, how do these come about, and with what consequences do they come?

Shall we instead use the term "cohort" only for birth year groups that lack consciousness as a group and are not active in creating social change? Shall we also use the term cohort for arbitrary birth year groups, which is most often done? Or shall we attempt to make cohort substantively meaningful, and force ourselves to illustrate their distinctive experiences and differential effects? (And if we use these effects to *define* cohorts, what, then, will we use as outcomes?)

Answers to these questions carry significant implications for both theory and research, and developmental science will benefit from greater sensitivity to cohort. Greater sensitivity to cohort may also be particularly helpful in explaining results that run counter to our expectations or conflict in the research literature (Uhlenberg & Miner, 1996). However, greater sensitivity to cohort also restricts our ability to generalize results; it will force us to temper our desire to generalize what we learn about specific cohorts to other cohorts. When we generalize our findings in this way, we commit sins of "cohort-centrism" (Riley, 1987) or "tempero-centrism" (Nydegger, 1986a).

Cohort Effects and the Age-Period-Cohort Problem

Ideally, the concept of birth cohort does more than simply mark the historical location of a group of individuals. It is used as a basis for searching for collective properties—cohort effects—brought about by the fact that certain historical events and conditions impinge upon a group of individuals anchored at the same point in the life course. For some developmental scientists, especially sociologists, cohort effects are of central interest and even the primary phenomena for which they search. These scientists are interested in examining the ways in which history marks the trajectories of cohorts in unique ways. For others, especially life-span psychologists and those searching for universal laws of human development and aging, cohort is instead the very thing they seek to control. From the standpoint of these scientists,

---

[8] In fact, the English language does not even contain words to describe new and complicated forms of family relationships brought about by multiple divorces and remarriages within and across family generations (Riley & Riley, 1994).

cohort is a nuisance; it is something that confounds the pure age changes they hope to uncover.

These confounds are especially problematic for investigators with cross-sectional data. With cross-sectional data, one can never be certain whether the age differences they find are the result of genuine age change (due to maturation) or whether those differences are instead the result of either cohort or period effects.[9] In cross-sectional data, age, period, and cohort effects are hopelessly entangled. Ultimately, the problem of disentangling age, cohort, and period comes down to the fact that each one is a function of the other two (see Schaie, 1965; Baltes, 1968).[10] As a result, attempts to control any one variable, whether through *a priori* research design controls or *post hoc* statistical controls, leaves the other two inseparable and confounded.[11] We are simply examining the time span in two different ways. As Nydegger (1981) puts it, these measures have:

> the same starting point (the year of birth of respondents) and the same terminus (time of measurement). Time of measurement may be any point along this single age/cohort time span. There is only one span of time involved, no matter how we measure it. It is as if we used a triangular ruler, each side in a different metric: the faces show different intervals but, since the length is the same, the correlation between the faces is perfect. Any two sides yield the third (p. 7).

Yet even longitudinal data, especially cohort-specific longitudinal data, are problematic in that age change (maturation) is confounded with historical (secular) trends (Schaie, 1992). (The challenges associated with gathering and analyzing longitudinal data will be discussed in Chapter 4.) Besides cross-sectional and longitudinal strategies, a third developmental model is the "time-lag" model (Palmore, 1978), in which two different samples are compared when respondents were of equivalent age, but in which the calendar year (time of measurement) is different (Schaie, 1992). In this model, cohort differences are confounded with historical trends.

Analytically, developmental scientists typically approach cohort and its effects in one of three ways (Baltes, Cornelius, & Nesselroade, 1979). First, cohort variability may be treated as "*error*" or transitory "*disturbance*," and viewed as "irrelevant" to the phenomenon or theory of interest. Second, cohort may be treated as a

---

[9] *Age effects* are changes due purely to maturation and should therefore exist across all cohorts. *Period effects* are a function of time of measurement and presumably affect all cohorts uniformly.

[10] However, cohort is a "higher-order concept" than age because it attempts to capture person-environment interaction. As a result, it is both more interesting and more complicated than age as an explanatory factor in research (Maddox & Campbell, 1985). Like cohort, period-related forces are also anchored outside of the individual, making them more difficult to study.

[11] It is important to note that this type of confound is not restricted to developmental research, nor is it restricted to the age-period-cohort problem. It emerges whenever multiple time-related measures are used in a single analysis. Good examples of this confounding with other types of variables include the following triads: age, timing of parenthood, and age of the first born child; age, timing of marriage, and duration of marriage; or age, timing of a job promotion, and years in rank (Nydegger, 1986a).

"dimension of generalization." From this standpoint, cohort variability is important to consider if we hope to generalize a behavioral principle or theory, though this approach does not treat cohort as a "full-fledged" theoretical variable. Only the third treatment does so. It explicitly takes cohort to be a "theoretical" and "process" variable, which it is meant to be. However, investigators seldom use cohort in this way, and it is from this standpoint that my earlier critique of the use of cohort in developmental science stems.

Baltes and his colleagues have wavered on the degree to which developmental scientists need to understand and explain cohort differences (though they consistently hint that sociologists are overly concerned about cohort). At times, Baltes and his colleagues seem to downplay issues related to cohort, suggesting that it is often legitimate to simply interpret cohort differences as "error" or "historical disturbance." At other times, they claim such interpretations as unacceptable. The prior approach avoids "the kind of fundamental issues that must be addressed for the 'constructive dialogue between sociologists and psychologists' to move toward any kind of real synthesis" (Dannefer, 1984, p. 849). These differences remain an important barrier to the advancement of developmental science.

Nonetheless, recent methodological developments have provided a means for better dealing with the age-period-cohort problem. Some of these developments attempt to disentangle age, period, and cohort effects *a priori* through research designs. In particular, the cross-sequential research design, which combines aspects of both cross-sectional and longitudinal designs, has been heralded as the ideal design for disentangling these effects (e.g., Schaie & Baltes, 1975).[12] However, these designs are often neither practical nor feasible for many reasons (e.g., time, money, other resources). Surprisingly, Schaie (1992) himself, one of the pioneers of the cross-sequential design, argues that "it is always prudent to commence with an age-comparative cross-sectional design. However, in those instances where such a design cannot answer the question of interest, additional data must then be collected across time," within a cross-sequential framework. At the same time, it is clear that cross-sectional designs simply *cannot* answer most developmental questions. As Ryder (1965) noted decades ago, cross-sectional designs and analyses imply that "the past is irrelevant," prevent "dynamic inquiry," and foster "the illusion of immutable structure" (p. 859).

Other developments attempt to disentangle age, period, and cohort effects *post hoc* through statistical procedures. These statistical advances, especially within the context of sequential data matrices, allow us to estimate age, period, and cohort effects through ANOVA and regression models, under the assumption that their effects are additive and not interactive (Schaie, 1992). However, in many cases, statistical strategies that rely on additive assumptions are also problematic,

---

[12] Of course, our designs must be related to our theoretical propositions; they must allow us to analyze both the hows and whys of age-related developmental changes (Brandtstädter, 1993). While cohort-sequential strategies are heralded as the best strategy for disentangling age, period, and cohort effects, they do not themselves identify the processes and mechanisms that bring about these effects.

given that aging, cohort, and period effects may be *interactive*. The problem of identification can be handled if the researcher is able to assume one of the parameters is not operating. However, in most cases such an assumption is likely unrealistic or unwarranted. Even where this assumption is realistic or warranted, small amounts of measurement error, or error in specifying constraints for any of the three parameters, can result in inaccurate estimates (Rodgers, 1982).

Purely statistical attempts to disentangle age, cohort, and period effects are futile in that solutions to the age-period-cohort problem depend "at least as much on theories of aging and of recent history as on technical [statistical] expertise" (Glenn, Mason, Mason, Winsborough, Knoke, & Hout, 1976, p. 900; see also Campbell & Alwin, 1996). In addition, statistical solutions to the age-period-cohort problem are themselves problematic in that they simply treat period and cohort as residual control variables, and give them little substantive meaning, treatment, and interpretation (Mayer and Huinink, 1990). Elder (1998) makes a similar point, noting that "even when history is substantively important, it may be operationalized as a period or cohort effect that provides no clues as to the precise nature of the process" through which it becomes important (p. 963). These are central challenges for future research.

For both classic and recent discussions of the age-period-cohort problem and its possible solutions, see Donaldson and Horn (1992), George, Siegler, and Okun (1981), Labouvie and Nesselroade (1985), Mason, Mason, Winsborough, and Poole (1973), Mayer and Huinink (1990), Rodgers (1982), and Schaie (1986). These challenges serve as a powerful reminder that time creates its share of "developmental middles" (Donaldson & Horn, 1992) for those interested in the study of lives and that developmental scientists get "caught up in time willy nilly" (Nydegger, 1981, p. 3).

Rather than invest more effort in finding statistical and design solutions to these problems, we might take a more "radical" approach and:

> abandon the computer, sit down in an armchair, and examine our thinking about time and question our premises. Just what is the *meaning* of time in our various studies? . . . From a strictly logical point of view, [many of our models] are tautologies. But are the meanings tautological? Are they truly confounded? Or do we confound ourselves by indexing so many different referents by a single measure? Is time really the index of choice, or merely convenience? . . . Perhaps it is time to stop inferring psychological and social phenomena from the calendar. Instead, why not specify just what it is that we are trying to capture when we use time measures? Once identified, we can measure these phenomena more directly. In the process, some of our confounds should unlock . . . It will not be easy, but the alternative is to remain calendar-bound in our riddle-models—literally caught up in time" (Nydegger, 1981, pp. 10-11).

Where the meaning of time in developmental science is concerned, no other single strategy will serve us better today, nearly twenty years after Nydegger's recommendation.

Linking Lives and History

Research has often focused on the more *general* impact of historical events on human lives, including the civil rights movement (e.g., McAdam, 1988), political activism on college campuses and the counter-cultural movement of the late 1960s (e.g., Flacks, 1988; Whalen & Flacks, 1989), the Vietnam War (e.g., Kulka, Schlenger, Fairbank, Hough, & Jordan, et al., 1990), the women's movement (e.g., Carden, 1978), and the rural farm crisis of the 1980s (e.g., Conger & Elder, 1994). However, as discussed earlier, underlying the concept of cohort is the expectation that members of a cohort are supposed to have had shared historical experiences; their experiences are also supposed to be unique relative to the experiences of other cohorts. Where the *differential experiences of cohorts* are concerned, we know most about two large-scale historical events: the Great Depression (e.g., Elder, 1974) and World War II (e.g., Clipp & Elder, 1995; Elder, 1986, 1987; Elder & Bailey, 1988; Elder & Meguro, 1987; Elder, Shanahan, & Clipp, 1994; Maas & Settersten, 1999; Mayer, 1988).

Much remains to be learned about precisely how, and through what mechanisms, historical events, large or small, play themselves out in proximal and distal ways in the lives of individuals; their differential effects both within and between cohorts; and how their effects are moderated by personal and familial characteristics, circumstances, and resources. It is one thing to acknowledge that cohort and cohort differences are critical for understanding the life course. It is another thing to demonstrate their effects, and to know how, why, and for whom they come about. In addition, we might classify historical events and changes according to their characteristics and effects. For example, we might consider the pace at which they occur, the levels of their effects (e.g., population, individual); domains or types of impact; directions of impact; the temporal range of various effects (e.g., proximal or distal); desirability; prevalence; duration; or whether and how cohorts are affected similarly or differently (e.g., Reese & McCluskey, 1984; Schaie, 1984). In this way, historical events might be approached in ways similar to "critical" or "stressful" life events, though that body of literature is faced with significant challenges (see Chapter 4).

When we consider the historical events and changes that have occurred since the turn of the century, it would seem as if the lives of members of all cohorts in modern societies have been, and continue to be, conditioned by many of these events and changes. Yet not all cohorts have experienced the same events or changes, nor experienced them to the same degree. It is important that developmental scientists take seriously the challenge of exploring how historical events and changes take on personal meanings or leave their imprint on individual and aggregate lives, especially from a subjective, phenomenological standpoint. Little attention has been paid to the "phenomenal" aspects of experiencing social generations (Nydegger, 1986a; Nydegger, Mitteness, & O'Neil, 1983): What is the meaning of a cohort experience to its members? What is shared? Who shares it? Which cohorts perceive themselves as such?

The research of Schuman and Scott (1989) begins to explore questions such as these. Schuman and Scott interviewed a randomly drawn national sample of 1410

Americans, eighteen years or older, to examine perceptions of important historical events and changes (for a replication in Britain, see Scott & Zac, 1993). Respondents were asked the following question: "There have been a lot of national and world events and changes over the past 50 years—say, from about 1930 right up until today. Would you mention one or two such events or changes that seem to you to have been especially important [to our nation]?" Up to three historical events or changes were then noted. For each event or change mentioned, respondents were asked "What was it about [that event or change] that makes it seem especially important to you?" Up to three reasons per event were then noted. If any personal effects were mentioned as part of an individual's response to the question just described, those reasons were noted as such. If no clear personal effects emerged in response to that question, respondents were asked, "Would you say that [this event or change] had any important effect on your own life or that of your family—I mean on how you have lived or how you have looked at things?"

While Schuman and Scott's study offers an important first look at the link between lives and history, their approach provides only a limited understanding of these connections. In a recent pilot project, I therefore built on Schuman and Scott's instrument in an effort to get older adults, in particular, to discuss how their own lives, and the lives of their contemporaries, have been shaped by the historical time in which they have lived. The interviews were focused on whether, which, and how historical events and changes hold important personal meanings and have affected them in important ways. In addition, I explored the subjective sides of cohort and cohort membership. I chose to study contemporary cohorts of older adults because they have witnessed both rapid and dramatic social change, and have long histories behind them as they look back on their lives. At the same time, I could not assume that the individuals in this group of older adults had uniform experiences. In fact, one of my intentions was to explore how experiences differed across members of this group. Recent gerontological research, in particular, has emphasized the need to better explicate the variability that exists among older adults, which is assumed to be greater than that for younger age groups. (This will be discussed briefly later in this chapter and at length in Chapter 5.)

In this project, I, along with two of my doctoral students, conducted in-person semi-structured interviews with a sample of 100 Cleveland elders (age 69 to 94) drawn from a GAO-funded longitudinal study that was begun in the 1960s. Our interviews averaged seventy-five minutes and were tape-recorded and transcribed. We opened our interviews by stating, "You were born in [birth year], which means that you were 'coming of age' between [see grid], if we use the ages of 18 to 20 as a benchmark. Would you tell me a little about what was going on in your life at that time?" We probed by asking questions such as "What were you doing?," "What was happening in the world around you?," "What were you thinking and feeling?," and "What were your hopes and dreams for your life?" These questions got respondents thinking about their personal pasts, national and world history, and the intersection between the two.

To explore subjective aspects of cohort and cohort membership, we began by asking the question, "We often use the term 'generation' to refer to a group of people born at about the same point in history. We tend to think about people from the same 'generation' as being very similar—as having similar attitudes; similar opportunities and chances in life; and similar experiences as they grow older. Think for a moment about your 'generation'—people born around the year [birth year]. What would you say characterizes people from your generation? (Are there attitudes and experiences you share? Are there ways in which you are all pretty similar?)"

We then turned to a series of questions meant to tap the ways in which the experiences of the respondent's cohort were similar to, or different from, adjacent ones: "How were the circumstances that people your age were facing at that time different from those who came before you? [Interviewer: Explore expectations and opportunities related to family life, work life, education, and optimism about the future. If necessary, you may use the same-sex parent of the interviewee as an anchor for this discussion]." We also asked, "Compared to when you were a young adult, how is life *more difficult* for young adults today? [Interviewer: Probe similar expectations and opportunities. As a frame of reference for this discussion, you may use a same-sex young adult whom the interviewee knows, if necessary]," and "Compared to when you were a young adult, how is life *easier* for young adults today? [Interviewer: Probe similar expectations and opportunities. As a frame of reference for this discussion, you may use a same-sex young adult whom the interviewee knows, if necessary]."

Finally, to probe the link between their own biographies and history, we began with a question similar to the core question used by Schuman and Scott, already noted. But for each historical event or period of social change mentioned, we asked in-depth questions about how the event or change shaped the respondent's life or took on personal meanings, including:

- Did it have an impact on how you have lived or how you have looked at things?
- Why was that event especially important to you or your family?
- How exactly did it change your life? For example:
  Did it change you in psychological or emotional ways? How?
  Did it change your physical health? How?
  Did it change your opportunities (work, education, marriage, parenting)? How?
  Did it change the way you thought about life and the world around you? How?
  Were there negative effects? Were there positive effects? What were they?
  Were there short-term effects? Were there long-ranging effects?
- Were others affected?
- How old were you/they when the event or change happened? Do you think your age was important in shaping your experience?
- Do you think most people your age had similar experiences and feelings?
- Can you imagine how your life would have gone if this event or change had not occurred?

These questions bring us closer to more fully exploring history, biography, and the relationship between the two. In fact, George (1995) notes that references to "rapid rates of social change characteristic of modern societies are common in aging research. Rarely, however, do [gerontologists] attempt to empirically link changes in social structure with changes in aging or in the older population. More effort should be devoted to . . . observing [the] differential effects of [social change] on both subgroups of the older population and the aging process itself" (p. S2).

Much of what we know about generational or cohort identity is based upon historical literary texts or colorful personalities (taken to be the voices of and for their "generations") or survey research (in which behavioral or attitudinal data on many people of different cohorts are compared) (Newman, 1996). These approaches have left important gaps in our understanding: Little is known about "broad, deep mental structures" that are thought to lie at the heart of generations or cohorts— "world-views," basic values, mind sets, and characteristic ways of thinking (Esler, 1984, p. 106). We cannot assume that the lives and ideas of public intellectuals, especially writers, adequately represent the lives and ideas of an entire group of ordinary people; and survey research data, while more representative than that of "iconic" authors and intellectuals, lacks the "interpretation and meaning, cultural elaboration and historical experience [that] cannot be answered to anyone's satisfaction using fixed choice surveys" (Newman, 1996, p. 372). As a result, we must, as suggested above, couple these methods with life-history and ethnographic methods to better illustrate the link between historical experience, generational or cohort identity, and personal identity. In addition, we might turn to forms of verbal evidence, probing "usages, idioms, and slang" for their "deeper connotations or associated meanings," and forms of nonverbal evidence, probing fads, fashions, rituals, gestures, and modes of interaction (Esler, 1984, p. 107).We might also select the subjects of developmental studies with the exploration of generational cohort differences in mind.

Some scholars have advocated for research that focuses on the ways in which these generational or cohort differences cause "disjunctures" in modern societies: The ways in which the "values, expectations, beliefs, and socially constructed meanings" diverge across these groups (Newman, 1996, pp. 373-374). However, I would also argue that it is equally as necessary to explore solidarity between generations or cohorts, and the ways in which the values, expectations, beliefs, and socially constructed meanings *converge* across these groups. The assumption that generations or cohorts differ along these dimensions and that these differences bring tensions in their path has long existed in this literature. Significantly less explored are the ways in which these groups are similar along these dimensions, bringing intergenerational cooperation and solidarity with them. Perhaps the potential for solidarity across these groups is also tied to whether social settings are age-homogeneous or age-heterogeneous. Age-homogeneous settings may create generational differences by concentrating similarly-aged people together and encouraging them to interact and communicate. At the same time, it seems plausible to argue the reverse: In age-homogeneous settings, there is no variability in age and therefore no other group *against* which to mark one's own position. As a result, there may be little awareness of generational or cohort distinctions. In contrast, in age-heterogeneous settings, individuals of similar ages may be keenly aware of how they differ from those of older and younger generations or cohorts.

We also need to know about the meaning of generational or cohort identity and experiences, how these meanings vary or are cross-cut by characteristics of the individual (and what may be "competing," and even conflictual, forms of solidarity and identity, including race, sex, social class, or other dimensions), and how these meanings are reflected in behavior. In addition, we need to understand the dynamic nature of these identities, and their associated meanings and experiences, exploring the ways in which they are reformulated or reconstructed over time.

Cohorts and Trajectories of Heterogeneity

As noted in Chapter 1, developmental scientists emphasize the importance of studying any segment of life within the context of the entire life course. Nowhere is this orientation more important than in gerontological research and practice. Individuals arrive at old age with many decades of life behind them, and individual differences observed in later life are critically linked to times past—times, for example, when individuals were launching or developing their educational, occupational, marital, or parenting trajectories. In the discipline of sociology, the life-course framework partly has its roots in status attainment models (e.g., Blau & Duncan, 1967), which emphasize the cumulative effects of processes of social allocation over lifetime. As members of a cohort grow older, their trajectories likely become more different. This process has come to be known as the "Matthew effect" in the sociological literature on the life course (Dannefer, 1987; Dannefer & Sell, 1988).

Drawing on a passage from the Gospel of Matthew ("for unto every one that hath shall be given and he shall have abundance, but from him that hath not, shall be taken away even that which he hath"), sociologist Merton (1968) first described the "Matthew effect" as a more general principle of social life: Advantage breeds further advantage, and disadvantage breeds further disadvantage. Dannefer (1987) uses the principle of the Matthew effect to explain why variability among older people is often greater than variability within any other age group (a phenomenon that Dannefer labels "aged heterogeneity"). As advantages and disadvantages cumulate over the life course, members of a cohort become increasingly different from each other as they grow older.

In the aged heterogeneity scenario, these social processes may continue to generate increasing inequality through advanced old age, creating a *divergent* trajectory. However, trajectory variance might take other forms as a cohort moves through life (Dannefer & Sell, 1988; O'Rand, 1996a). Consider Figure 1. Depending on the characteristics or processes under study, we might also consider trajectories of other forms. For example, we might consider trajectories for which the level of heterogeneity remains *constant* for a cohort over time; a trajectory of constant heterogeneity would be likely for characteristics that are largely fixed (genetically) at birth and are not associated with mortality (this latter point is especially important in that characteristics associated with mortality are likely to create declines in heterogeneity over time, especially in the latter third of life).

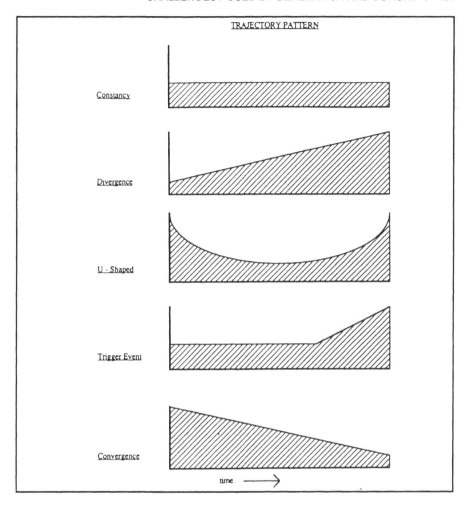

Figure 1. Alternative trajectories of diversity over the life course.
Source: Dannefer, D., & Sell, R. (1988). Age structure, the life course, and "aged heterogeneity": Prospects for research and theory. *Comprehensive Gerontology, 2.* p. 3.

We might also consider trajectories of heterogeneity that are *U-shaped,* in which a cohort exhibits high variability on a characteristic both early and late in life, but low variability in the middle of life; in this case, members of a cohort become more "homogenized" during their middle years. Similarly, we might consider trajectories that take the shape of an *inverted-U,* in which a cohort exhibits low variability on a characteristic early and late in life, but high variability in the middle of life; in this case, members of a cohort are relatively homogenized during their early years, drift apart, and become homogenized again during their late years. Empirically, these patterns may also result when subgroups of the population, each characterized by different trajectories, are aggregated together (Dannefer & Sell, 1988).

Trajectories characterized by a *trigger effect* might also be considered. In the case of a trigger effect, the level of heterogeneity remains constant up to a specific point, but then suddenly rises or falls at a critical juncture. Here, for example, we might consider the roles that age-related life events and transitions potentially play in increasing or decreasing the degree of heterogeneity within a cohort.

Finally, we might consider the opposite of the divergent trajectory: a *convergent* trajectory, in which the amount of heterogeneity declines over time, exhibiting great variance during the early years and dropping continuously as the cohort ages. Decreasing heterogeneity might result from natural processes, such as age-related physical changes or characteristics related to morbidity or mortality; it may result from exposure to specific social settings that discourage or even reduce the salience of individual differences, such as nursing homes or medical institutions; or it may result from specific social policies or programs that at least partially reduce the degree of inequality between individuals at different points in the life course, such as TANF (Temporary Assistance for Needy Families, which replaced AFDC) or the Head Start program for children, or Social Security and Medicare for older people. Given the multi-dimensional nature of human lives, a cohort will be characterized by multiple forms of variance trajectories, thereby creating significant challenges for the study of cohorts as the move through time. (Other challenges associated with studying heterogeneity will be discussed in Chapter 5.)

The Societal Significance of Cohort

We might also better explore the *societal* significance of cohort. Uhlenberg (1988) asks us to conduct an experiment in our minds: "Suppose," he says, "that all members of a five-year birth cohort were removed suddenly and permanently from the population. In what ways would the lives of those remaining in the population be altered? Or, alternatively, how much reorganization would occur in the lives of the survivors?" (p. 405). Of course, our responses depend on a few other pieces of information, such as the general life stage at which the disappearing cohort is positioned, its characteristics, the society in which it is embedded, and the historical time in which it disappears. But this question is intriguing. For example, what if that cohort is aged forty-five to forty-nine? Major reorganization would be required in all spheres of life. In families, children and adolescents will have lost parents. Work organizations, the media, and the government will have lost employees, many of whom may be in important positions. Now, what if that disappearing cohort is between seventy-five and seventy-nine? In contrast to the previous scenario, this loss would require significantly less structural reorganization, though the loss would most certainly be felt emotionally by kin and friends. Some caregiving support would be lost, as older adults provide important care to their family members (especially to their spouses and, increasingly, to their grandchildren). The status of, and enrollment in, hospital and nursing home settings would certainly change.

Governmental resources would also change, given the array of welfare state programs and policies for older people.

These examples suggest that the societal significance of a cohort changes as it grows older, that its significance declines over time, and that it is close to zero when it has only a few remaining members in its very latest stages. Part of this decline is the result of biological changes, and part of this decline is the result of social factors (e.g., age stratification of social institutions; the ways in which cohort characteristics change over time).

Uhlenberg's use of the term "significance" does not refer to the "moral value" of a cohort. Instead, it refers to the "level of productive contributions that are valued in the contemporary society. As such, the term 'societal significance' could be replaced by 'societal importance' or 'societal contribution' " (p. 423). Nonetheless, there is a danger in such an argument, much like the danger inherent in arguments about intergenerational equity, that as a cohort ages it becomes less useful and, worse still, a social and economic liability. These arguments overlook the important ways in which older adults make important contributions to their families and friends, their communities, and society at large. Nonetheless, because the old are not economically self-sufficient as a group, they are vulnerable. Only a cohort that is completely self-sufficient in late life can "afford to become societally insignificant without running any major risks" (p. 422).

Uhlenberg suggests that the societal significance of a cohort be measured not "by aggregating the feelings of significance held by its members, nor . . . by aggregating the frequency with which others identify members of a cohort as significant others. Rather, the societal significance of a cohort refers to the degree of control that members of the cohort exert over the lives and behavior of others in the population" (p. 406). This control is revealed through how much structural reorganization would be required if the cohort mysteriously disappeared, as demonstrated in the examples above. While this may be an interesting conceptual exercise, how might empirical indicators of a cohort's "depth of control" over other cohorts be developed? (While Uhlenberg focuses on the ways in which one cohort exerts control over another cohort, he notes that we should not overlook the ways in which members of a cohort exert control over members of their own cohort.) In our search for indicators, Uhlenberg suggests that we explore any mechanisms that bring people together in dependent or interdependent relationships, and look to activities that involve direct or indirect interaction with others in several different domains (families, work organizations, the polity, the media, voluntary organizations, and friendships).

In addition, the characteristics of a cohort, especially relative to those of other cohorts, are also likely to play a role in its significance. These characteristics include its size, level of physical and mental vigor, and level of wealth and "useful knowledge." Cohort size and its levels of physical and mental vigor decrease throughout life (though the link between social participation and physical and mental vigor is surely complicated). Level of wealth and useful knowledge, at least among healthy individuals, may increase throughout life. (Yet if we know that physical and mental vigor are generally decreasing, we might also expect wealth and useful knowledge to decrease?) While Uhlenberg posits that societal significance of a cohort declines over time, current and future cohorts of older people bring the potential, at least relative to cohorts past, to make greater contributions in later life, given both their increased size and (presumably) vigor. Uhlenberg offers little in terms of possible empirical indicators of significance within these domains (whether separately or in combination), nor of the thresholds that distinguish societal significance from insignificance. However, his provocative framework provides an exciting avenue for advancing theory and research on cohort.

METAPHORS OF COHORT AGING

Cohort is a collective phenomenon, and, as already discussed, is important in at least three ways: as an *index of social change* (as the lives of these aggregates of individuals are marked by a set of historical events and changes), as a *reference group* (as the cohort forms its own norms against which individuals judge the progress of their own lives), and as an *interactive system of age-peer relationships* (Dannefer, 1991). Drawing on the metaphor of a race (or variants thereof), Dannefer (1991) explores conceptions of collective (cohort) aging in both popular culture and in social science theory. Where *popular culture* is concerned, several interesting examples relate to the notion that life is a race, and that members of a cohort, as they move together in time, compete against one another (e.g., "the race is to the swift," "fast track," "the rat race," "survival of the fittest," "it's a dog-eat-dog world," "every man for himself").

In terms of *social science theory,* three concepts are most important: "convoy," "contest," and "tournament." The idea of a "convoy," particularly salient in the gerontological literature, is that individuals move through life with a social network, or group of intimate others, at their sides. The concept of a convoy is different from a race in that these relationships are viewed as supportive, not competitive, and are actually meant to buffer individuals from negative experiences. The concept of a convoy is also different from traditional ways of conceptualizing cohort in that a convoy need not be composed of similarly-aged peers and may actually be composed of people of varied ages (especially parents, children, and other family members).

In contrast, the terms "contest" and "tournament," dominant in the literature on the sociology of work, education, and social mobility, emphasize the potential for conflict or competitiveness among members of a cohort. For example, opportunities and chances may be structured as a function of competitions, some of which are open to everyone, and others of which are closed to certain types of individuals; early "losses" or "wins" may close off or open up future opportunities; or individuals may be tracked in schools and work organizations (some tracks may be explicitly acknowledged, while others may remain hidden).

THE PROBLEM OF HISTORICAL SPECIFICITY

A limitation of much developmental research is its "historical specificity" (Caspi, 1998). That is, because most developmental research is cross-sectional, and because even the most long-standing of longitudinal studies are typically composed of members of a single birth cohort, little is known about the extent to which developmental knowledge is historically specific. However, our theory and data are discussed as if they are valid across historical periods. The problem of historical specificity has been largely disregarded, but is serious and runs throughout developmental research. It is a problem to which we must now respond.

Thus far, responses to this problem have taken three forms: metatheoretical, methodological, and social-historical (Caspi, 1998). At a *metatheoretical* level, the problem of historical specificity is dismissed by taking the view that *all* social-scientific theory and data are obviously "historically conditioned and socially constructed." After all, if the severity of this problem were to be acknowledged, it would threaten our scientific quest to predict, explain, model, and even search for laws related to individual and social behavior. At a *methodological* level, the response has been to find ways to deal with age, cohort, and period confounds through design or statistical controls (as described elsewhere in this chapter). A *social-historical* response has been promoted by a select group of life-course sociologists who have attempted to take history more seriously and better trace the ways in which macro-level historical events and changes play themselves out in human lives, as described earlier.

CHAPTER
4

Challenges to Understanding Lives the Long Way

This chapter begins by introducing central concepts and parameters for describing and analyzing the life course. It then turns to a discussion of the many conceptual and methodological challenges associated with understanding lives the "long way" (Block, 1993), including the use of life-history calendars and matrices, retrospective and prospective strategies, and secondary and archival data; handling trajectories; characterizing continuity and discontinuity, and measuring change.

CENTRAL CONCEPTS AND PARAMETERS IN THE STUDY OF THE LIFE COURSE

Life Events, Transitions, and Trajectories

Life events, transitions, and trajectories are central concepts in the study of the life course (Elder, 1998). The distinction between life events and transitions was discussed in Chapter 1. The concept of a life *trajectory,* or *pathway,* is similar to that of a career. A trajectory is long in scope, charting the course of an individual's experiences in specific life *domains* (or *spheres*) over time.[1] The individual life course is composed of multiple, interdependent trajectories (for example, work, family, and educational trajectories).

Given their more gradual nature, transitions may involve a series of "mini-transitions or choice points," with different factors influencing each of the phases that comprise the larger process (Elder, 1998). As an example of mini-transitions or choice points, Elder (1998) cites the transition from marriage to divorce, noting that this is a gradual process that "begins with disenchantment and extends across divorce threats, [through] periods of separation, and [to] the filing of divorce papers"

---

[1] However, Pearlin and Skaff (1996) warn us that while the metaphor of the life course as a trajectory is useful, it should not be taken too literally: "A trajectory, like a ballistic missile, is propelled by some explosive force that sends it on its way in some straight or arching track. By contrast, the life course most typically approximates a pattern of forward movements, pauses, loops, and shifts in directions" (p. 244).

(p. 958). Transitions and events are always embedded within a larger trajectory, and the trajectory gives them "distinctive form and meaning" (Elder, 1985, p. 31).

Key Parameters for Describing and Analyzing Lives

The parameters of *timing, sequencing, spacing, density,* and *duration* are often used to describe a set of experiences that comprise a larger trajectory. As such, the researcher must first identify the *life domains* and *state spaces* to be measured. *Timing,* the most frequently explored of these concepts, refers to the age at which experiences occur. *Sequencing* refers to the order in which experiences occur, *spacing* to the amount of time between two or more ordered experiences, and *density* to the compression of transitions within a bounded period of time. *Duration* refers to the length of time spent in any particular role or "state." The timing, sequencing, spacing, density, and duration of earlier transitions may have important "domino" effects that shape the nature of later transitions.

As Nydegger (1986a) has also noted, most research along these lines does not focus on how these parameters play themselves out in individual lives, but instead describes one of these parameters in aggregated, and even simulated, cohort data. In addition, most research has focused on a handful of discrete, major, and statistically-normative experiences (e.g., marriage, fatherhood) rather than on transitions of lesser magnitude, more gradual changes, or experiences not as widely shared. Part of the problem of studying these latter types of experiences relates to the fact that they are often difficult to define or describe. For example, the "norm" may be hard to determine, and therefore those "off norm" equally hard to designate; beginning or end points may not be easily marked in time; experiences may be so gradual as to be unnoticeable or indescribable; or, because these experiences are not widely shared, they may not only be difficult to sample, but their precursors and consequences may be difficult to trace over time. Nonetheless, research must be designed and conducted to help us better understand these experiences. An examination of "modal" or "typical" experiences is insufficient for understanding the complex patterning of the life course within and across cultures.

The age patterning of life experiences has long been of particular interest to developmental scientists. In their "purest" form, *age transitions* are "changes in social status due solely to the attainment of particular chronological ages" (Nydegger, 1986a, p. 132). Good examples of such transitions are the onset of puberty[2] or the ages at which individuals are legally deemed "adult" and must assume the rights and responsibilities associated with adult status. In reality, there are few transitions in which a change in social status is based on age alone. Most age-related transitions are also *role* transitions. As a result, when we explore the age patterning of experiences, we must consider whether "(1) we are dealing with *age qua age;* (2) the change is primarily a *role transition* and age is simply a concomitant

---

[2] However, in complex modern societies, the onset of puberty does not bring the clear change in social status that it did in many simple or primitive societies, in which puberty marked an important rite of passage (see the classic anthropological work of van Gennup, 1908/1960).

due to customary role sequencing; or (3) age, though not primary, exerts an independent influence to *modify* the role transition in some significant way" (Nydegger, 1986a, p. 132). We should first approach these experiences by taking *as an empirical question* their degree of age-regularity (or, its flip side, age-variability) rather than assume their age-relatedness *a priori*, and then consider *why, for whom, and at what benefits or costs* age-regularity (or age-variability) exists. We should also clarify what we mean by "role" and "transition." Both of these concepts are important, but our use of them is generally imprecise. For example, at what level is a role important (e.g., macro, meso, micro), and why? What are its properties? How is the role experienced, by whom is it experienced, and with what benefits and costs are roles acquired or relinquished?

Turning Points

In addition to events and transitions, researchers have raised the concept of a *turning point*, about which there is little agreement. Intuitively, turning points would seem to be points at which a trajectory shifts significantly in direction or is "discontinuous" in form, whether "objectively" defined as such by an investigator who has examined its shape, or "subjectively" defined as such by the person who has experienced it. Where subjective perceptions of discontinuity are concerned, there has been discussion as to whether an individual's life need have entailed an *actual* change in direction to have the *feeling* that life has new meaning(s). As a result, one conception of a turning point is that it need only involve the *perception* of "new possibilities for self-realization" or mark the place at which a "new sense of identity" begins to take shape (Clausen, 1993, p. 17). As turning points are subjectively experienced, they are also often tied to context and depend on whether contexts are chosen or assigned, whether contexts provide opportunities for the development of the self and that of others, and whether contexts serve to protect individuals from other negative settings and relationships (Clausen, 1995). (The challenges of context will be discussed later in this chapter.)

To make these points, Clausen draws on an initial set of questions related to turning points that he and his colleagues developed for the Berkeley Growth Study and Berkeley Guidance Study, and which were asked of participants when they were in their mid-50s to early-60s. These interviews broadly covered circumstances and experiences in middle adulthood. As part of these interviews, subjects were given a life chart and asked to plot their "basic life satisfaction" from early childhood through the present. The interviewer then asked, "As you look it over, can you pick out any point or points along your life course that you would call 'turning points'— where your life *really* took a *different* direction?" Starting with the most important turning point, subjects then talked about each turning point and what they thought had caused it. At the conclusion of this discussion, subjects were asked to again review their entire lives and quickly choose the turning point they felt to be most important.

Reflecting on his experiences in posing these early questions to respondents, Clausen (1995) notes that "it quickly became apparent that we could say very little about the relative importance of turning points from the *order* in which they were reported" (p. 370, emphasis added). In one of the interview excerpts, the subject struggles with the term "turning point," and the interviewer explains that the intent of the question is to get at the "*unexpected* changes in direction rather than [those] which were part of the plan" (emphasis added). In response to the question, however, the subject actually reports several different kinds of experiences. In one instance, she acquires a new sense of who she is; in other instances, she sets new goals for herself, becomes involved in new activities and makes new discoveries, or feels a new sense of fulfillment. In each case, the subject also reports turning points that were *self-initiated* (and therefore *expected*) and *positive* (that is, they led to an increase in life satisfaction). While these investigators intended to get at unexpected changes, the formulation of their question (". . . where your life *really* took a *different* direction") also solicited responses in the directions just noted and might have prompted negative turning points as well. In retrospect, Clausen notes that interviewers needed more time to adequately review the stated turning points and probe why and how these turning points were so important. In addition, experiences that the *interviewer* might have classified as turning points during the course of the interview were often not mentioned by the *subject* when the question about turning points was asked.

In later research, Clausen and his associates again used the life chart to get at turning points, but instead allowed more time for more complete questioning around each one. Clausen suggests that the *number* of turning points can generally be increased the more the interviewer probes the twists and turns in the life chart. The more individuals review their life histories, on their own or via interview occasions, the more they may see changes in their lives and identities. Extensive probing is therefore required to collect sufficient information on turning points. In addition, the development of coding categories to capture the resulting information is a daunting task. Their most elementary coding schema, which they found wholly inadequate, was to classify turning points in terms of the *major role affected* (e.g., educational, occupational, marital, or parental), the *type of event that caused the turning point* (e.g., illness, death of a family member, geographical move, or a religious conversion), and the *nature and extent of change* (e.g., expected versus unexpected experiences, with subcategories for changes in self-concept, life satisfaction, interests and goals).

In contrast, Pickles and Rutter (1989) provide a very different conceptualization of turning points. They suggest that turning points are instead "everyday events or happenings that bring about a potential for *long-term psychological change*" (p. 133, emphasis added). Pickles and Rutter distinguish between two types of turning points: (1) those resulting from "an opening up or closing down of opportunities," or (2) those resulting in "radical lasting change in life circumstances" (p. 133). Yet they *eliminate* from their discussion "rare dramatic 'internal' psychological experiences" (such as religious conversions), "rare dramatic 'external' experiences" (such as earthquakes or being taken hostage), and "universal age-defined transitions" (for which they give the example of a midlife crisis, the existence of which, as an aside, is highly debated; in addition, the category "universal age-defined transitions" presumably includes most of the major life experiences that have been examined in the literature, such as those that comprise the transition to adulthood).

There are several problems with this definition, which also differs dramatically from that of Clausen and his colleagues. These problems raise important questions for future research in this area. First, how significant must an experience be to be classified as a "turning point"? Are they "everyday events or happenings," as Pickles and Rutter suggest, or something greater? Second, need turning points only create psychological change, as Pickles and Rutter argue, or might they also create other types of change for the individual—social, economic, familial, or otherwise? Third, need turning points merely create the potential for change in these directions, as Pickles and Rutter suggest, or should they actually entail change? And should this be judged from a "subjective" or "objective" standpoint? Fourth, need turning points only create long-term effects, as Pickles and Rutter argue, or are short-term effects just as relevant, even in the absence of long-term effects? Fifth, are the two classes of turning points that Pickles and Rutter specify—those that relate to a change in an individual's opportunities *or* to a change in life circumstances—mutually exclusive? (It would seem not.) More importantly, might turning points also stem from purely internal sources? (It would seem so.) Finally, if both dramatic "non-normative" experiences (whether external or internal) *and* more typical "age-normative" experiences are eliminated as turning points, what else remains?

These problems aside, it is also important that we begin to conceptualize turning points as part of a longer temporal process, with "chain effects" leading up to and occurring after the turning point. As Pickles and Rutter note, "it would be misleading to conceptualize what happens as a once-and-for-all change that stems from some event that arises out of the blue" (p. 134). It is also important to recognize that part of this process also involves some degree of decision-making. We must better study the critical junctures "at which alternatives present themselves. At each point, some individuals choose one way; others choose another, and it is necessary to examine both the consequences of their choices and the mechanisms resulting in one choice rather than the other" (Pickles & Rutter, 1989, p. 134). Similarly, researchers must also ask about the consequences that turning points hold for later development. When turning points are conceptualized in this way, they must be analyzed within larger trajectories which, as will be described later, brings an important set of challenges.

Turning points may also be more likely to occur at certain points in the life course than at others. For example, the transition to adulthood may be a time when turning points are especially likely to emerge, given that many important and interdependent decisions and experiences occur at that time. We also cannot assume that content and meanings of a "transition" are similar for those who experience it (Pickles & Rutter, 1989). (The use of the word "transition" here also raises an important conceptual and empirical question: When exactly does a transition become a turning point?) In addition, the fact that transitions are experienced in personal ways need not draw our attention away from the fact that some part of that experience may nonetheless be shared. The timing of a transition may also be important in raising its potential as a turning point. (See also the discussion of "critical" or "stressful" life events later in this chapter.)

It is important to recognize the fact that we must generally rely on a person's *own story* to understand how turning points are defined, how they came about, and what consequences they entailed. And, as Clausen (1995) reminds us, "people cannot always tell us what beliefs and experiences led to seeing one kind of change as a turning point . . . Asking a person about pathways taken and the course of particular roles is a necessary condition for understanding how that person makes sense of his or her life, but it may not permit us to assess the full meaning or consequences of turning points or the contextual influences involved" (pp. 386-387).

Much remains to be learned about the precursors, consequences, and meanings of turning points, and about variability therein. These examples illustrate our need to continue wrestling with the concept of a turning point. While this concept seems straightforward at first glance, it becomes quickly complicated as we attempt to explicate and measure its components.

"Critical" or "Stressful" Life Events

Within the larger field of research on life events and transitions, a body of work focuses on "critical" or "stressful" events (Cohen, 1988; Inglehart, 1991). This tradition begins most notably with Holmes and Rahe (1967) and their Social Readjustment Rating Scale (also referred to as the Schedule of Recent Events). Holmes and Rahe ask respondents to indicate whether they experienced any number of forty-three different events during the past twelve months, ranging from events as major as "death of a spouse" or "jail term," to events as minor as a "vacation" or "minor violations of the law."

Many later inventories essentially seek to improve upon Holmes and Rahe's earlier measure, by expanding the scope of items, rewording existing items that are ambiguous, or altering scaling procedures. These include the Life Events Inventory (Cochrane & Robertson, 1973), the PERI Life Events Scale (Dohrenwend, Krasnoff, Askenasy, & Dohrenwend, 1978), the Paykel Scale (Paykel, Prusoff, & Uhlenhuth, 1971), the Life Experiences Survey (Sarason, Johnson, & Siegel, 1978), and the Life Events Questionnaire (Chiriboga, 1984; Chiriboga & Dean, 1978). Other measures move away from major life events, and instead focus on everyday hassles (e.g., "concerns about owing money," "home maintenance") and uplifts (e.g., "daydreaming," "feeling healthy," "laughing") (Holahan, Holahan, & Belk, 1984; Kanner, Coyne, Schaefer, & Lazarus, 1981; Lewinsohn, Mermelstein, Alexander, & MacPhillamy, 1985; Wagner, Compas, & Howell, 1988). Most of these inventories have been used primarily with adult (but non-aged), and often clinical, populations.

To remedy the age-bias of these inventories, several investigators have incorporated items that are more appropriate for elderly populations (e.g., "age discrimination," "trouble with Social Security"). These inventories include the Elders Life Stress Inventory (Aldwin, 1992), the Geriatric Scale of Recent Life Events (Kahana, Fairchild, & Kahana, 1982), the Geriatric Social Readjustment Rating Scale (Amster & Krauss, 1974), the Louisville Older Persons Event Scale (Murrell

& Norris, 1984), the Small Life Events Scale (Zautra, Guarnaccia, Dohrenwend, 1986), modified versions of the Schedule of Recent Events (Mensh, 1983; Wilson, 1985) and the Pleasant and Unpleasant Events Schedules (Teri & Lewinsohn, 1982). However, many of the items in inventories for elderly populations weigh heavily toward declining physical and mental health (e.g., "loss of hearing or vision," "difficulty walking," "painful arthritis," "move to home for the aged"), though the onset of illness and/or physical impairment is one of two kinds of stressful events that become more common with advancing age (Pearlin & Skaff, 1996). The other kind is the death of loved ones, and especially the death of parents, older siblings, spouse(s), and similarly-aged peers. Some measures also include events that happen to other people to whom one's life is intimately bound, especially children or grandchildren (e.g., "child married," "death of a grandchild"). It has been hypothesized that such events, described as "nonegocentric" (Aldwin, 1992), may be more likely or particularly difficult for older adults (Pearlin & Skaff, 1996).

At the other end of the life course, several investigators have discussed difficulties in either studying stressful life events or in creating inventories appropriate for children and adolescents (e.g., Compas, Davis, Forsythe, & Wagner, 1987; Johnson & McCutcheon, 1980; Newcomb, Huba, & Bentler, 1986; Sweeting & West, 1994; for a review of these inventories, see Compas [1987] and Williams and Uchiyama [1989]). Special items included in inventories on childhood or adolescence cover successes and failures in school (e.g., "poor school report," "praised for good work"), successes and failures in sports and extracurricular activities (e.g., "failed to get into sports team," "joined a new club"), and relationships with teachers, parents (e.g., "serious row with parents"), siblings (e.g., "got a new sibling," "sibling left home"), girlfriend or boyfriend (e.g., "new girl/boyfriend," "broke up with girl/boyfriend"), friends (e.g., "close friend moved far away," "close friend seriously ill or injured"). Other occurrences in child or adolescent life are covered in these inventories (e.g., "passed driving test," "taken to court," "attacked or injured"), as are occurrences in the lives of others to whom the child or adolescent is tied (e.g., "parents decided to separate," "parent lost job," "serious illness in family member"). Older children who work part-time may also be asked about an additional set of items related to their employment experiences (e.g., "promoted," "trouble with boss/supervisor," "changed job"). Of course, researchers are confronted with additional ethical concerns in gathering data on minors, especially data on negative life experiences.

Several problems are often associated with research based on these inventories. First, a very select set of the larger universe of possible events is sampled (as one would expect), but events that are more common for young adults, men, whites, and the middle class are over-represented. In addition, negative and undesirable events are over-represented, and "non-events" (events that are expected to happen, but never occur) are omitted. Some people are also never "at risk" to experience certain events (e.g., an individual cannot experience the death of a child if the individual has not parented). In addition, the items in many such inventories have been criticized for being too vague or for allowing too much room for subjectivity in their interpretation.

Second, not all events are equally important, and the procedures used for weighting events vary dramatically between studies. Some investigators develop weights using independent raters, while others ask respondents themselves to weight their own events; here, response scales of differing types have also been used (e.g., dichotomous measures, Likert scales of varying points, bipolar scales with neutral points). Others derive weights empirically, using group mean ratings or regression techniques. Still other (and perhaps most) investigators altogether abandon the complexities associated with weighting, and opt not to use weights (especially for those populations for which extreme life events have a low rate of occurrence).

Third, there are problems associated with the reliability of recall, especially over long periods of time. However, most of the measures intend to tap events that have occurred within a limited span of time, usually occurring within the prior year. Recall bias seems most problematic for events more than one year in the past, and the amount of bias generally seems to increase in step with the period of time being recalled. For those interested in the life course, the issue of recall is therefore problematic, since the unit of time becomes an individual's *lifetime*. The problem of recall is a more general problem that wreaks havoc for developmental scientists (this problem will be discussed later in this chapter). Besides problems related to recall, there are general concerns about the reliability and validity of these instruments: Evidence on the psychometric properties of these scales is seldom presented, as is evidence related to various types of validity.

Fourth, a number of problematic assumptions run through this literature. Four of these assumptions are especially noteworthy. One is that life events cause psychosocial disturbance, rather than vice versa (for example, that those with higher levels of psychosocial disturbance are more likely to experience stressful events). Instead, we must better explore whether psychosocial states instead predispose individuals to experience a certain set of events. The emphasis on psychosocial disturbance as an outcome is likely exacerbated by the fact that some of the items in these inventories are similar to items included in common outcome measures of physical or emotional distress (that is, they are symptoms or consequences of illness rather than precursors), thus confounding the predictor and outcome variables. In addition, when some sort of later pathology is the outcome of interest, dating the onset of illness is very difficult, and the nature of the illness itself may exacerbate problems with recall, particularly when its nature is mental.

A second problematic assumption is that the direction of change is almost always negative. In part, this emphasis is a function of the fact that most inventories focus on negative rather than positive events. Instead, following the time-honored adage that "good things can come out of hard times," we must better explore any positive change that may result from negative experiences (what Aldwin [1994] calls "transformational coping"). Similarly, we must also better explore any negative change that results from positive experiences. A good example of positive outcomes resulting from life crises is reflected in Lieberman's (1996) research on widowhood. While the loss of a partner may create a state of crisis and cause grieving, it may also create new potential for growth as these women revise their self-concepts, take on new interests, develop new relationships, and become more self-sufficient. Another good example comes from Elder's research on military service for men (Elder & Pavalko, 1993; Elder, Shanahan, & Clipp, 1994). For some men, military service during wartime may promote social independence, offer an acceptable time-out from age-graded careers, provide new skills and training, and broaden life experiences. Similarly, Lieblich (1989) suggests that positive personality development may take place as a result of military service, including the acquisition of active coping strategies and the expansion of personal boundaries through encounters with death, people, and values.

A third problematic assumption is that effects are primarily additive in nature—that is, that the greater the number of events experienced, the greater the impact on the individual. Instead, we must better explore whether relationships of other nonlinear (and especially curvilinear) forms might also be appropriate. For example, "eventless lives" may be just as problematic as those filled with many changes (Theorell, 1992).

A fourth problematic assumption is that the impact of life events is usually direct and short-term. Instead, we must better explore whether and how their effects may be delayed, dissipate, or grow over time. However, delayed or "sleeper" effects, in which there is a substantial lag between a cause and an effect, and in which a clear mechanism links the two, are difficult to handle theoretically and methodologically.

In addition, when the effects of transitions are studied, we must consider how much of what we find is the result of self-selection (that is, due to the characteristics of the people who experience certain transitions), and how much is the effect of the transition itself (independent of selection effects).

Fifth, researchers might better classify events or cluster items along multiple dimensions, including major versus minor; anticipated versus unanticipated; controllable versus uncontrollable; typical versus atypical; desirable versus undesirable; and acute versus chronic. For example, Sweeting and West (1994) attempted to classify events based on their desirability (desirable, ambiguous, or undesirable), degree of control (whether the event might have been associated with the respondent's own behavior in any way, or whether it seemed likely to be independent of the respondent's behavior), and the "likelihood of occurrence" (which they define empirically in terms of whether the event is reported by 10 percent or fewer or by more than 10 percent of the respondents in their sample).[3] Another possibility might be to classify events not in terms of their properties *per se,* but in terms of the types

---

[3] It is unclear why these investigators chose 10 percent as a threshold for "likelihood of occurrence." This approach seems dangerous in that it is completely driven by sample characteristics, and most research in this area has been conducted on nonrepresentative, and often clinical, samples. In addition, for many of the items in their inventory, whether an item is deemed "common" or "rare" would seem dependent on the respondent's age. For example, the likelihood of an affirmative response to "started college/university," "left home," "got engaged," or "got married" presumably increases with each year through adolescence and early adulthood. An interesting approach to studying rare life-course events, or even those events that are relatively common but rare in single studies (e.g., serious illness, widowhood), is to form "synthetic" cohorts by pooling observations from panel studies (see Campbell & Hudson, 1985). This strategy results in a multi-wave data set that is focused on the event of interest and contains fixed data both before and after the event (though the timing of the event of interest itself is obviously variable).

of effects they have on individuals. This approach addresses one of the criticisms running through this literature: that the same event may be experienced in dramatically different ways depending on the person's characteristics, circumstances, and resources. However, a constant problem in this literature is how to define life events (or stressful situations) in ways that are independent of outcomes for the individual. As Dodge (1993, p. 285) points out, it is "tautological to identify events as being stressors by their outcomes in individual adjustment." What, then, turns a circumstance into something stressful or problematic?

Whatever the strategy, the task of classifying events in multiple ways is difficult to handle empirically, regardless of whether the researcher or the respondent makes these judgements. This is especially true when the investigator hopes to build a composite index of an individual's exposure to many different types of events. Besides gathering data to help facilitate the classification of experiences along multiple dimensions, researchers must gather information about the resources to which people have (or had) access as a means for coping with difficult experiences.

At a conceptual level, Brim and Ryff (1980) provide an eight-cell classification of life events, with one dimension being those events experienced by many versus those experienced by few. These two dimensions are subdivided into those events that have a high probability of occurrence versus a low probability of occurrence, which are, in turn, further divided into those experiences that show strong correlation with age and those that show weak correlation with age. Brim and Ryff also call our attention to the importance of discovering "hidden" events (those that occur in an individual's life but are left "unrecognized" or "unnamed," whether by the individual, by the culture of which the individual is part, or by larger humanity). This search should reinforce the importance of conducting cross-cultural research and studying subcultures within single, heterogeneous societies.

Brim and Ryff (1980) also urge us to be cautious of common fallacies in making causal attributions about life events. We should not assume that the most "attention-grabbing vivid event" matters most in causing personal change. We should also not assume that more recent events are most influential, nor that a single "big" event is more important than the cumulation of more minor ones. In addition, we should not simply consider classes of life events singly, but instead search for interaction effects among them. As discussed earlier, we must also pay greater attention to larger trajectories in an effect to examine the configuration of the timing, sequencing, spacing, density, and duration of multiple events, multiple risk and protective factors, and ultimately their combined and interactive impact on outcomes of interest.

Finally, following Elder's "life course principle" and the principle of the "interdependence of lives," we must better examine the degree to which the impact of life events varies as a function of the life stage of the individual and as a function of experiences in the lives of others to whom the individual is tied. As Brooks-Gunn, Phelps, and Elder (1991, p. 901) ask, "Do environmental events occurring at one life phase have more of an effect on individuals or families than similar events occurring at another life phase? Do prior events have persistent effects in subsequent life phases, and under what conditions and in what life phases do such effects persist?"

These questions must be explored more thoroughly, and some of the secondary longitudinal data sets now available or in progress will allow this. These data sets may also afford us an important opportunity to study the *precursors* of especially negative or relatively uncommon events (whether positive or negative), or of larger pathways that seem especially negative. Similarly, they may allow us to better study the precursors of pathways that seem particularly positive. (New opportunities for conducting life-course research with secondary and archival data sets will be discussed later in this chapter.)

In the literature on "critical" or "stressful" life events, two measurement instruments stand out as exemplars: The Standardized Life Events and Difficulties Interview (SL), developed by Kessler and Wethington (1992) at the University of Michigan in the United States; and its predecessor, the Life Events and Difficulties Schedule (LEDS), developed by Brown and colleagues (Brown & Harris, 1978) at Bedford College in England. The LEDS has been used in England, Europe, Canada, and Africa. Both schedules provide a comprehensive understanding of severe life events, ongoing stresses and difficulties, and life turning points. The SL is a more structured version of the open-ended, semi-structured LEDS, and is more in line with conventional survey techniques. Both schedules, however, are very long and require the extensive training of interviewers. Unlike many of the investigators cited earlier, neither Kessler and Wethington nor Brown and his associate seek to develop composite measures of events based on their inventories.

Researchers in the "critical" or "stressful" life events tradition must pay greater attention to the issue of *temporality*. Because social stress can be viewed as a temporal process, researchers will greatly benefit by framing stress and stressful life events within a life-course perspective (Elder, George, & Shanahan, 1996; Kahana & Kahana, 1999; Pearlin & Skaff, 1996). For example, the general models developed by Pearlin and colleagues emphasize three conceptual components of the stress process: (1) stressors, (2) moderating resources, and (3) outcomes (Pearlin, Lieberman, Menaghan, & Mullan, 1981; Pearlin & Skaff, 1995, 1996). In their framework, stressors may be "eventful" or "chronic." Eventful stress is strain caused by life events, which may decrease in prevalence at midlife and beyond. Chronic stress may be one of three types: (1) "ambient" strain, which comes out of interaction between the person and her or his immediate environment; (2) "role" strain, which relates to "institutional roles," which include the family and interpersonal relationships; and (3) "quotidian" strain, which arises out of the circumstances of everyday life (what were earlier described above as "daily hassles"). Aneshensel (1992) also makes a distinction between "systemic" and "random" strain, and links systemic strain to an individual's social location.

In Pearlin and colleagues' framework, *moderating* resources typically include "coping" (which they describe as the selective use of adaptive skills and the management of meaning in difficult situations), "social support" (the social relationships from which people draw support), and "mastery" (which they define as a global sense of control, which regulates the impact of stressors). Finally, stressors and moderating resources are considered in relation to an outcome, the "final major component of the stress process" (Pearlin & Skaff, 1996, p. 244). Several recent applications of their model relate to caregiving for close relatives with Alzheimer's disease or for AIDS patients, which may be of interest to many readers (e.g., Pearlin, Aneshensel, Mullan, & Whitlatch, 1996; Pearlin, Mullan, Aneshensel, Wardlaw, & Harrington, 1994; Pearlin, Mullan, Semple, & Skaff, 1990).

To extend research on stress and coping to a life-course framework, these models must become more temporal, which they have rarely been. The kinds of stressors, resources, and outcomes to be considered will vary as a function of life period. Stressors, resources, and outcomes must be measured continuously as the individual grows older, and their many connections must be charted over time. The classification of variables as stressors, moderators, or outcomes is also more difficult when the model becomes temporal. In a dynamic model, not only are these variables changing in quantity and quality, but what is classified as a stressor, resource, or outcome at an earlier point in time may be classified as something different at a later point.

In these models, characteristics of social context are also generally thought to moderate (and also mediate) the link between stress and various outcomes. The characteristics of "context" most often examined include socioeconomic status, social integration, the composition of an individual's social network, degree and types of support provided by that network, and social-psychological resources (e.g., self-esteem, locus of control). Several of these are characteristics of individuals, not contexts. In addition, we must move our attention beyond the structural aspects of social context and toward a more complete examination of the *processes* through which contexts moderate or mediate the impact of stress. Advances in statistical procedures, namely multi-level and event-history analyses, hold great promise for stress research, the first for modeling the effects of individual and contextual factors on outcomes, and the second for better exploring the timing, sequencing, spacing, density, and duration of various events and their relationships to outcomes of interest. Social contexts also differentially *expose* individuals to stress and create differential *reactions* or *vulnerability* to stress. And while stress itself has long been conceptualized as a process, we have only recently begun to study it as such, in part because we have only begun to examine these issues using longitudinal data (Elder, George, & Shanahan, 1996).

To close this section, let me describe an interesting life-event strategy for examining *societal* well-being. Using individual data from the 1991 General Social Survey conducted by the National Opinion Research Center (NORC) of the University of Chicago, Smith (1992) examined the incidence of sixty-six negative life events or problems experienced by individuals during the prior year, as well as the severity of those events. The events or problems tapped the domains of health, work, finances, material hardships, family and personal life, law and crime, housing, and "other." The severity of each event or problem was measured using both "categorical" and "magnitude" techniques. The categorical technique asked individuals to rate the "seriousness" of each problem on a 100-point scale, with 0 designating the "very least serious" and 100 the "very most serious." The magnitude technique asked individuals to rate, choosing any number to their liking, the seriousness of each problem relative to an anchor ("being fired or permanently laid off," which was assigned a value of 200). Smith then multiplied the incidence by seriousness scores to get an individual-level measure of the "amount of troubles" experienced by each person. Trouble scores were calculated for each life event, each larger life domain, and overall. Smith then examined the "societal associates of troubles," exploring the degree to which these problems are concentrated across a variety of social groups (e.g., sex, age, race, income, education, occupation, marital status, communities, regions). As a result, Smith offers, through this extension of the life events approach, an interesting way to study societal well-being and the (uneven) distribution of problems across social groups.

GATHERING, ORGANIZING, AND ANALYZING LIFE-COURSE DATA[4]

Standardized, quantitative life histories from large samples have been collected since the late 1960s (Balan, Browning, Jelin, & Litzler, 1969; Blum, Karweit, & Sørensen, 1969; Rogoff-Ramsoy, 1973). But it was not until a decade later (and thereafter) that adequate methods for data organization, retrieval, and analysis finally became available (e.g., Allison, 1984; Blossfeld, Hamerle, & Mayer, 1989; Courgeau & Lelievre, 1992; Flinn & Heckman, 1982; Griffin, 1993; Mayer & Tuma, 1990; Petersen, 1995; Singer & Willett, 1991; Yamaguchi, 1991).

Regardless of whether the experiences being analyzed come from prospective or retrospective projects, they must be dated to be used optimally with multivariate methods and adequately placed within a life-course framework. It is always best to gather as precise a date as possible so that experiences can be clearly arrayed over time. For some experiences, it may be possible for the respondent to provide a complete date (month-day-year); for other experiences, the respondent may only be able to provide a less precise date (month-year; or year). In addition, many experiences are not discrete, but instead extend over a period of time. In these cases, the investigator should gather information on the beginning and end points of the experience, to the extent that this is possible. The important point here is that the investigator must do everything possible to ensure that the timing, sequencing, spacing, density, and duration of experiences can later be arrayed completely and accurately. This is especially important if the investigator plans to use techniques such as survival analysis, event-history analysis, or structural equation modeling.

The recent sociology of the life course has almost made it its mission to show that lives are differentiated, event-related, and episodic, and must be analyzed in a step-by-step piecemeal fashion. In practice, the study of the life course has, by and large, been a study of transitions in the first third of life, particularly those that mark movement into adulthood (e.g., Buchmann, 1989; Hogan, 1981; Kerckhoff, 1990; Modell, 1989; Wadsworth, 1991). One good reason for this is that, indeed, the period of early adulthood is filled with a large share of events and transitions, not only those

---

[4] An early version of part of the framework outlined here was developed in Settersten and Mayer (1997).

that are highly institutionalized (e.g., around educational and occupational training, entry into work organizations, and job shifts), but also those related to family formation (e.g., finding partners or spouses, having children), migration and residential change.

Descriptive techniques for survival data and stochastic models for discrete events in continuous time (known as hazard rate or event-history models) have been shown to be especially useful in analyzing life history data. A major charge of critics has been that these methods atomize lives into unrelated transitions and episodes. In contrast, these critics have called for a methodology to better represent total trajectories with typologies (Abbott, 1983; Abbott & Forrest, 1986; Abbott & Hrycak, 1990; Chan, 1995), which is one of the most important challenges currently facing developmental scientists. The technical problems associated with shifting the focus of our analyses from one or two transitions to entire trajectories are daunting. These challenges will be discussed later.

Life-History Calendars and Matrices

Life histories provide the basic data needed for research on the life course. Life-history matrices plot life domains, and specific experiences within them, over time (Balan, Browning, Jelin, & Litzler, 1969; Caspi, Moffitt, Thornton, Freedman, Amell, Harrington, Smeijers, & Silva, 1996; Frank & van der Burgh, 1986; Freedman, Thornton, Camburn, Alwin, & Young-DeMarco, 1988). A natural and convenient way to do this is to structure data collection on activities in the domains of *family* (e.g., parents, siblings, spouses or partners, children), *education and training* (e.g., schools, training places, credentials), *employment* (e.g., employment contracts, occupational activities, firm membership, sector location), and *residence and household* (e.g., places of residence, household composition). (Other domains might also be considered.) While researchers seem drawn to primary activities in these domains, a more complete picture of the life course must also include *marginal* periods and events, such as brief periods of training, second or part-time jobs, periods of unemployment or sickness.

In most life-history matrices, the first column calibrates time (the unit of measurement, whether in days, months, or years, depends on the purposes of the project), and the remaining columns specify domains and experiences of interest. The date an event began is indicated in the appropriate row, and its duration is then charted vertically. This procedure produces the essential information needed to examine the timing, sequencing, spacing, density, and duration of experiences along a trajectory or set of trajectories.

The advantage of this type of instrument is that activities in multiple life domains are simultaneously mapped onto one frame, and the relationships between them are easily seen. Rather than view experiences in isolation, this strategy places experiences within larger "streams" of events, to use Caspi et al.'s (1996) term. Most of the time, the interviewer and the respondent construct and view the calendar together during the interview. Because of its visual nature, inconsistencies are easily detected and can be double-checked immediately. The calendar may also assist the interviewer in further probing specific experiences and the connections between experiences. As respondents anchor their discussion in these experiences, they may also recall other less easily-remembered experiences from the same time period. It is also important to note that many of these instruments can be self- administered and have excellent potential in applied or clinical settings as assessment tools or therapeutic aids (see Caspi et al., 1996).

The biggest disadvantage of these approaches is that little information can be noted directly in matrix cells (e.g., it is difficult to note detailed information about occupational titles or duties). However, more elaborate matrices can be developed and used in conjunction with interview schedules designed to gather extensive data on the experiences noted therein. This strategy is exemplified by the Life History Questionnaire applied in six surveys of the German Life History Study (Mayer & Brückner, 1989), which built upon the landmark Norwegian Life History Study (Rogoff-Ramsoy, 1973). In the German Life History Study, the goal was not only to extract monthly data on an individual's "states" in several life domains, but also to obtain a wide variety of contextual information on each state. For these purposes, complete event histories (from birth to the present) were collected in each life domain, beginning with the residential history. In the case of residential history, for example, data were gathered on every residential location, including the month and year that mark the beginning and end points, the size and type of residence, geographic location, and the composition of household. The residential history was taken first, since it provided a good anchor for the recollection of information on other domains. In a similar format, general schooling, occupational training, primary employment, secondary employment, and military service trajectories were charted and reviewed for any unaccounted periods. As one can see, the main content of these surveys becomes the life course itself; it results in rich and accurate time-continuous data (for theories, rationale, and applications, see Blossfeld, Hamerle, & Mayer, 1989; Mayer & Tuma, 1990).

In the German Life History Study, this technique was applied in both personal and computer-assisted telephone interviews with people between the ages of 29 and 103 (Brückner, 1994). Of course, there are high costs associated with interviewing time (in most cases, between 1.5 and 3 hours), the editing process (including return calls to respondents to clarify inconsistencies), and the training of interviewers and editing staff. When respondents agreed, their personal and telephone interviews were also audio-taped; those recordings were used successfully during the process of editing data. Abbreviated versions of these instruments are possible when either the number of life domains or the range of contextual variables is restricted.

Retrospective Versus Prospective Strategies

Data collection in most retrospective studies is cross-sectional in character: A sample is interviewed only once, and respondents are asked retrospective questions related to most, if not all, of her or his life. At least in principle, the information that results approaches that obtained in a long-ranging longitudinal study. One-time retrospective studies offer an excellent alternative to prospective longitudinal designs, especially for those interested in the entire life course, given that the gathering of life-history data requires respondents to reflect on, and offer a detailed account of, the past. And because respondents are interviewed only once, an investigator does not face an ongoing struggle with attrition. It is also possible to use this strategy with larger, and multi-cohort, samples, if desired.

This approach, like any, comes with its own set of concerns. The most common problem associated with retrospective data relates to the accuracy and precision of recall (Dex, 1991). Recall error may result from forgetting (this leads the investigator to be unaware of important precursors or outcomes), reversals (in which the order of reported experiences is accidentally reversed; this leads the investigator to misspecify cause and effect), or invention (in which the respondent reports experiences that did not happen or exaggerates their seriousness) (Robins, 1988). In addition, there seem to be two other systematic biases related to recall, namely, the tendency to look back on the past more positively than it was experienced and the tendency to build more continuity between the past and the present in an effort to create more orderly and self-preserving life stories. As a result, what people say about the past and what actually happened may be two different things (Caspi, 1998; Henry, Moffitt, Caspi, Langley, & Silva, 1994).

The reliability of recall may also depend on whether the types of data being gathered deal with experiences that are readily available in the respondent's memory, or whether they instead deal with information that must be "rehearsed" if it is to be remembered with accuracy. Some difficult-to-retrieve information (e.g., precise dates that mark important experiences or periods) may be aided by the use of formal documents or with the help of significant others who may be able to confirm or disconfirm that information. The reliability of data resulting from retrospective questioning may also vary by age group, with data gathered from children and adolescents and from the very old being most fallible; it may also vary by the life period being recalled, with data gathered on childhood and adolescence being more fallible than data gathered on other periods (Brewin, Andrews, & Gotlib, 1993; Henry et al., 1994). Data gathered on subjective psychological states and family processes may also be more fallible than data obtained in response to straightforward questions about the course of an individual's educational, occupational, residential, marital or fertility histories (Henry et al., 1994).

When retrospective data are cross-checked against data from archival sources (e.g., registry, school, or firm records) some degree of inconsistency is likely to emerge. This incongruence is often taken as evidence that retrospective data cannot be completely trusted, even though archival data may be equally, or even more, fallible. While the biases associated with recall data may result in inaccurate or misleading findings, extreme concerns about the unreliability of retrospective data seem "exaggerated" (Brewin, Andrews, & Gotlib, 1993). Once common sources of error are known, these errors can be taken into account as research instruments are being designed; this results in a substantial reduction of measurement error (Brewin, Andrews, & Gotlib, 1993; Brückner, 1990). In addition, *structured* life-history instruments gather complete histories in a systematic fashion, embedding experiences in both diachronic and synchronic life contexts; this also alleviates many of the potential sources of recall error. Other strategies for reducing error are to gather data from other sources to corroborate retrospective self-report data (e.g., draw on family members and significant others, formal documents), make questioning more specific, and increase sensory and contextual detail, including recognition cues.

It is important to remember that criticisms about the fallibility of retrospective data apply to any type of biographical data, including most of the "background" questions that are routinely asked of respondents. As data are gathered on lives, we must rely on "the person's own report of his or her life: his or her perceptions of the influences on it as these have been experienced" (Clausen, 1995, p. 367).[5] For this reason, even longitudinal designs are not exempt from problems associated with retrospective measurement: Information is usually gathered on the period of time before the survey began and, at any particular wave, researchers are often interested in gathering data not only on the present, but on the period of time that has elapsed since the last measurement point. Otherwise, prospective longitudinal studies run the danger of providing only "sequential snapshots" of lives with "gaps in the record of events" rather than continuous information (Caspi et al., 1996, p. 102; Featherman, 1980, p. 158). Relative to single-occasion retrospective designs, however, the potential problems related to recall error are significantly reduced in prospective designs, given that the interval of time being recalled is not only much shorter, but is generally closer to the present.

The major disadvantage of longitudinal frameworks is, of course, that many years must pass before a sufficient span of the life course can be described. This may be particularly problematic if a mission of a project is to identify individuals with specific behavioral patterns or with various types of disorders. It may take many years before the patterns or disorders surface, and one must also begin with a very large initial sample to compensate for this problem, and for attrition, if one is to have a sufficiently large sample of "positive" cases to later study. Beyond this, a sufficient range of information must be collected routinely along the way so that the researcher can eventually look back on earlier assessments to examine when, why, how, and for whom these patterns or disorders develop (Robins, 1988). What is more, many of the

---

[5] The narrative approach to studying lives has rapidly grown in the past decade, and across the human sciences (for a review, see Mishler, 1995). This approach examines people's stories of their lives, and these accounts become text to be analyzed. Yet, as we tell our life stories to ourselves and others, we are likely to tell stories that are more coherent than they were actually experienced. While we do not necessarily create fiction, we search for, and even impose, continuity amidst discontinuity. Is this a by-product of what we take to be the art of good story-telling? (That is, that every story must be structured around themes, told chronologically, and coherent to listeners?) Or is this a by-product of the fact that as we grow older, we need to look back on our lives and integrate our pasts in orderly ways to achieve a sense of unity and purpose? Similarly, as discussed in Chapter 2, cultural scripts for the normal, expectable life meet human needs for predictability. These scripts give us a sense of what lies ahead and, as such, take a *prospective* view of the life course. Yet do these scripts also play a role in shaping retrospective views? For example, Hagestad (1990, p. 155) wonders whether these scripts are not as important in creating "accounts of lives that have [already] run their course, because such stories are built on the understanding that experience brings." To illustrate this question, she quotes the Danish philosopher Kierkegaard, who observed that "life can only be understood backwards. In the meantime, it has to be lived forwards."

"negative" cases at any point in time may eventually turn positive; this makes the continuous study of the negative cases crucial, and it renders our understanding tentative—at least until certain periods of risk, if known or applicable, have passed so that we may be fairly confident that most of the negative cases are, in fact, true negatives. Long-term risk-oriented studies are also unlikely to involve the study of multiple cohorts, given that the study would then have to cover the youngest cohort's movement through all risk periods as well. This also raises the question of generalizability, though this problem is not restricted to risk-oriented longitudinal studies, but is a concern for any single-cohort prospective study.

Finally, because longitudinal designs necessitate many decades of study, they are very expensive. As the duration of a study expands, the interval between its follow-up waves is likely to make it increasingly difficult to (a) take a complete inventory and assess all partially relevant factors in the intervening period, (b) connect together relevant factors at multiple points in time, and (c) specify the mechanisms through which these factors are associated. Nonetheless, longitudinal research is essential for understanding not only *proximal* processes and outcomes, but especially those that are *long-ranging*. Research on the life course must better explore how an individual's present has been shaped by the past, and how an individual's anticipated future is shaped by both the past and the present, especially from a subjective standpoint. For longitudinal studies to be effective, they must not only cover many important developmental periods and functions, but observations must be made continuously during these periods and on these functions so that important changes are not missed (Magnusson, 1985).

Longitudinal studies can be classified into three basic categories: real-time, microgenetic, and simulation studies (Kruse, Lindenberger, & Baltes, 1993). *Real-time* longitudinal studies may be of the single-cohort "classical" type, or they may involve multiple cohorts (e.g., full-blown cohort-sequential strategies). We routinely hear the claim that longitudinal analyses allow us to make causal inferences. However, while some cohort-related designs allow us to describe maturation effects (age change), they may nonetheless render causal inferences difficult in that the researcher has no control over antecedent conditions. (At the same time, relative to cross-sectional studies, longitudinal analyses certainly do permit us to make causal inferences with greater certainty.) As a result, real-time longitudinal methods should ideally be coupled with methods that allow the researcher to more adequately control antecedent conditions (Kruse et al., 1993).

In particular, we might combine real-time strategies with either microgenetic intervention or developmental simulation strategies. *Microgenetic intervention* approaches generally involve (a) the observation of individuals through a period of change (this period is relatively short compared to most longitudinal studies); (b) a high density of observations relative to the rate of change within that period; and (c) intensive gathering of data at each observational point, particularly aimed at making inferences about the processes that bring about the change (Siegler & Crowley, 1991; see also Kuhn, 1995). While this type of strategy is very costly in terms of time, effort, and money, it allows finer-grained understanding of short-term change functions (qualitative or quantitative), which may also help illuminate medium- or longer-ranging functions.

Developmental simulation approaches attempt to create experimental conditions that mirror the age-related change trends observed in real-time longitudinal studies; this is done with the hope of better explaining and understanding age-related changes (Kruse et al., 1993, p. 155). These simulations are guided by theory, and involve at least five steps: (1) to identify and define the age-related change function to be explained; (2) to formulate hypotheses about the variables that might produce this function; (3) to manipulate the relevant variables experimentally; (4) to test the set of data (which involves comparing simulated data against the target); and (5) to examine external validity and search for alternative causal mechanisms.

The *combination* of real-time longitudinal studies with either microgenetic intervention or developmental simulation strategies is ideal, but seldom possible. As noted above, real-time longitudinal studies pose tremendous costs themselves, let alone in combination with other approaches. In addition, some developmental processes may not be easily studied via microgenetic or simulation approaches, whether because they cannot be time-compressed or simulated. Nonetheless, the combination of a variety of methods is necessary if we are to achieve a complete understanding of the nature of human development, and the great nexus of factors and mechanisms that comprise it. We must therefore seize all opportunities to combine "longitudinal observations with experimental process research, biographical analyses, case studies, simulation techniques, and other strategies of investigation that may help to illuminate the dynamics of development over the life span" (Brandtstädter, 1993, p. 212).

Of course, the demands of longitudinal research bring challenges related to selection and attrition. These challenges pose serious problems for students of aging, in particular. Those who survive into later life, and especially advanced old age, are a select group, and the very things that create attrition in longitudinal studies with older people (e.g., physical or mental illnesses or incapacities; death; migration) are often related to the very topics in which gerontologists are interested. In addition, declines in physical or mental functioning also create serious problems with measurement error and response bias. Important strides have been made with respect to our ability to deal with some of these problems (Campbell & Alwin, 1996). For example, these include advances in imputing missing data,[6] in modeling the sources of error with structural equation approaches, in design strategies that involve the use of proxies, and in methods for improving data collection and quality. However, it is important to remember that "these methods are no panacea; we will find that the theoretical demands they place on the research are at least as difficult as the

---

[6] In longitudinal research, missing data may exist for several reasons (Campbell & Alwin, 1996). Respondents initially selected for a study (a) may not participate, whether they refuse or cannot be located (*non-response*); (b) may have been part of the study in an earlier wave, but in a later wave refuse, are incapacitated or dead, or cannot be located (*loss to follow-up*); or (c) may not have responded to all items, whether by choice, accident, or because of time constraints (*item non-response*). Recent developments in techniques for imputation relate to this last type of missing data (see especially Little and Rubin, 1987).

technical demands," which are already astounding (Campbell & Alwin, 1996, p. 35). Problems of selection and attrition have important implications for generalizability of findings (for an overview, see Nesselroade, 1988). In aging research in particular, problems of selective survival and selective sampling plague the representativeness of both cross-sectional and longitudinal research samples (Kruse et al., 1993).

Sampling in longitudinal studies, like that in cross-sectional studies, is often problematic because non-random samples are drawn due to practical considerations. At the same time, there are also problems associated with using standard, experimental designs to study "multi-determined, dynamic phenomena of social development" (Cairns, Costello, & Elder, 1996, p. 231). This may be especially true of designs that use random assignment because, in real life, not only are developmental phenomena not random, but developmental risks are not normally distributed. Nonetheless, longitudinal studies of any type pose a special problem in that they require intensive and expensive data collection, which often eliminates the possibility of a large sample. Those who conduct longitudinal researcher must worry about the matter of attrition, particularly if the study is a long-ranging one, thereby shrinking (often characteristically) the size of an already small sample. This may render the generalizability and interpretability of findings based on a small, non-random sample not only problematic from the start, but increasingly problematic with the passage of time. Some scholars have suggested that the attitude toward sampling in developmental research is too lax and sampling problems must be taken more seriously (e.g., Bergman, 1993). The lack of attention to sampling may be exacerbated by our emphasis on modeling, especially structural equation modeling. "Modellers" tend to defend themselves against this charge, claiming that a "model is assumed to hold for everyone and hence is tested also for non-random samples" (Bergman, 1993, p. 223). This position is dangerous because the assumption on which it is based seems unreasonable in most circumstances.

Time constraints make the collection of *long*-ranging longitudinal data (as opposed to a few measurement points in the short-term) difficult for individual researchers in other ways. Investigators must have long-term commitment to the project; the skills and staff to plan, implement, monitor, and administer the project; and the great cooperation of many people, including staff, universities, funding agencies, and the subjects themselves. These interests require the duration of a research project to continue well beyond the career spans (and often the desired commitments) of individual researchers, who are confronted with the "real-life demands of academe and their own aging," to use Brooks-Gunn, Phelps, and Elder's (1991, p. 900) phrase. The structure of science does not reward long-ranging longitudinal research: Longitudinal research demands great patience and effort, and the complicated nature of longitudinal questions makes quick-and-dirty answers either impossible, uncertain, or slow in coming; in addition, the "risk of failure [is] often high . . . an error in a longitudinal project may result in wasted years of work, and in errors that are often irreparable" (Magnusson, 1993, p. 19). The career stage of an investigator may also be at odds with the costs of a longitudinal project especially for junior scholars faced with heavy tenure demands and "hard and fast" evidence of productivity (Block, 1993).

More importantly, these strategies demand continuous, long-term funding commitment from federal agencies and private foundations, which is particularly difficult in times, like the present, of serious retrenchment. This makes many scientists reluctant to pursue longitudinal research projects, even when the nature of the questions they pose requires such a design. In addition, in some countries legal concerns have surfaced around the collection, storage, and retrieval of data on the same individuals over long periods of time; these concerns have created obstacles for the conduct of effective longitudinal research (Magnusson, 1993).

As a result of these many barriers, research on human lives seldom covers long periods of time. The bulk of primary "longitudinal" research tends to be composed of only two data points with a short interval between them. Even "longitudinal" analyses based on large-scale, multiple-wave, secondary data sets have been based on "*at most* two waves of the data, or have used the longitudinal aspects of the surveys to construct independent variables that take time, transitions, sequences, and so on into account to *predict outcomes at some fixed point*" (Campbell, Mutran, & Parker, 1991, p. 480; emphasis added). As Rogosa (1988, p. 171) suggests, the biggest *myth* with respect to longitudinal research is that two observations constitute a longitudinal study and are adequate for studying change. "Two waves of data," he says, "are better than one, but maybe not much better . . . Longitudinal designs with only two observations may address some research questions marginally well— but many others rather poorly." While two observations allow an estimation of change, they tell us little, if anything, about an individual's growth curve, and the amount of change estimated is often misleading (see also Rogosa, Brandt, & Zimowski, 1982; Rogosa & Willett, 1985).

Yet as we shall later see, the analysis of two time points itself is significantly more complicated than it seems at first sight, and the analysis of more than two time points even more so. However, our methods for dealing with longitudinal data, and even three or more time points, have improved significantly in the past decade (Campbell & Alwin, 1996; Campbell, Mutran, & Parker, 1991), which makes the deficit of longitudinal analyses all the more bothersome. Opportunities to study lives "the long way" (Block, 1993) are also beginning to improve as we take seriously the need to invest in the gathering of longitudinal data (Campbell & Alwin, 1996), and as we recognize that the most pressing and intriguing questions about human development require "a corpus of data that traces the lives of individuals over [many] decades of childhood, adolescence, and adulthood" (Tomlinson-Keasey, 1993, p. 65).

Several longstanding longitudinal projects now span a significant number of years. But because the life-course framework was not well developed when many of these studies were designed and conducted, they did not gather extensive information on life experiences, preparation for them, and adaptation to them. These studies are also largely focused on cohorts of people born before 1930 and who are now in later phases of adult life. We must have reservations about the degree to which we can generalize what we have learned about the life course from these subjects to current cohorts of young people whose adult lives will span the next century. As a result, new longitudinal projects are needed that cover earlier phases of the life course, beginning with those who are now young. As Thomae (1993) reminds us, "man does not live within an abstract life space which is as identical as Skinner boxes are for many generations of rats. He grows up under specific cultural and historical conditions which may change considerably during his lifetime. We should contribute to the design of our grandchildren's lives in old age by starting to gather the basic knowledge for this with new longitudinal studies" (p. xiii).

In addition, one of the most important contributions of recent research on the life course is that it has raised our awareness of the importance of historical forces in shaping human lives. However, this recognition has not significantly altered the kinds of data that have been gathered, or are scheduled to be gathered, in longitudinal studies. This point has also been made by Elder, Pavalko, and Clipp (1993), who note that cohort studies are not generally driven by concerns about the influence of historical forces on lives. Instead, these studies are driven by a desire to test assumptions about developmental invariance; that is, they are designed to assess the degree to which developmental patterns can be generalized (see Chapter 1).

For those interested in embarking on a longitudinal study of development, Block (1993) offers a set of recommendations. Where does most contemporary longitudinal research stand with respect to these recommendations? A longitudinal study should:

(1) "Be an intentional rather than accidental study, not a study begun for other reasons and only subsequently (and belatedly) declared to be a longitudinal study" (p. 16). This goes against the ways in which many longitudinal studies come into being, in that they are often simple extensions of existing cross-sectional samples.

(2) "Make public and communicable just what was done during the course of the study, how observations were made, how categories or numbers were generated, and how conclusions and interpretations were formulated" (p. 17) These are lacking in many scholarly publications that report results based on longitudinal projects or archival data sets (given that investigators who do not expect to later make their data available to others often do not document these issues thoroughly). This requires extensive journaling of both major and minor decisions made along the way, a task which is often considered a "distraction" or is difficult to coordinate in larger project groups (most of us who have worked in such groups will quickly attest to the fact that some participants take the task of documentation more seriously than others).

(3) "Be sufficiently extended in time so that developmental processes, continuities, and changes can be discerned" (p. 17). As noted earlier, most "longitudinal" studies are focused on the *short term* (generally two measurement occasions with a short interval between them) rather than the long term, and on *outcomes* rather than processes.

(4) "Involve a sample of reasonable initial and continuing size" (given problems related to the attrition of subjects) and be "of reasonable relevance" in composition (p. 18). Block argues that researchers who hope to pursue the "close and continued study of development" simply cannot aspire to study a random or representative sample of subjects ("representative of what, pray tell?") but should at least avoid "unusual, severely disproportionate subject selection." In contrast, manuscript and proposal reviewers often express grave concerns about (and often

even seem obsessed with) the effects of sample attrition and selectivity on the integrity and generalizability of longitudinal data. While these are legitimate concerns, have they been taken too far?

(5) "Have a conceptual or theoretically integrating rubric directing its doings and progression rather than be blandly or blindly eclectic" (p. 18). This, too, goes against what often occurs as multidisciplinary longitudinal studies are planned and executed. Rather than pay attention to research questions and analyses that are genuinely *inter*disciplinary in nature, investigators from a variety of disciplines each negotiate for a core set of their own variables to be represented in the research instrument. This is especially true of projects that are eventually meant to serve as secondary data sets in the public domain.

(6) "Be broad and deep," and include inquiry aimed at unearthing developmental processes and mechanisms (p. 19). In the face of limited resources, this is a serious challenge: It is difficult for any single study, longitudinal or otherwise, to be both broad and deep, and to do both well.

(7) "Be methodologically competent," which is not the same as "knowing statistics" (p. 19). Unfortunately, many researchers equate the two, creating serious barriers to advancing scholarship on human development. (This problem will be discussed later in this chapter, as well as Chapter 6.)

(8) "Be innovative" (p. 20). In Block's view, many longitudinal studies have been conducted in "plodding, unthinking ways." We often focus on variables that are easy to measure; we often rely on a bank of measures that are ready-to-use without giving much thought to the concepts and issues to be studied; and, worse still, we repeatedly administer measures simply because they were administered in the past, giving little thought to how useful those measures have been or whether they remain appropriate as respondents age or as new historical circumstances emerge. (Issues related to the reliability and validity of measures of change will be raised later in this chapter.)

(9) "Be able to sustain the quality of the enterprise over the long period of time required" (p. 21). An "endemic disease" of longitudinal studies is that they generally reach a point after which they "begin to falter, lose their vitality, and perhaps even their *raison d'être*" due to staff demoralization, "busy-ness without purpose," personnel replacements, loss of funds or institutional support, or the long delay in payoff.

While these recommendations set high (and, some might argue, unachievable) standards, they are nonetheless important to consider in designing longitudinal studies, particularly in light of the fact that longitudinal research to date has seldom occurred in these ways. While longitudinal methods have long been recognized as essential for the study of lives, they have been criticized as being "relatively sprawling, untidy, costly, difficult to integrate both with respect to data processing problems and conceptual matters, and sometimes excessively prolonged" (Block, 1993, p. 36). While these criticisms may be more or less true, Block argues that the longitudinal approach is, in the long run, "more science-effective, more cost-effective, and more time-effective" than conducting many "small, compartmentalized, incomplete, and hit-and-run" studies on "conveniently and quickly accessible" phenomena, which characterizes most contemporary developmental research (p. 36).

Longitudinal Strategies and Our Understanding of Trajectories

To understand trajectories, especially those related to developmental "risk," longitudinal research strategies are particularly advantageous (Rutter, 1988). (The challenges associated with defining and measuring risk-related factors and processes will be discussed in Chapter 5.) First, longitudinal strategies reduce bias because they record events and their expressions as they actually occur (or at least relatively close to their occurrence), depending on the precision with which those events and expressions are measured in time.

Second, longitudinal strategies offer opportunities to study prospectively those individuals whom, at an earlier point, are disadvantaged in some way but manage to avoid negative outcomes despite their risk(s). Longitudinal strategies turn our attention to the processes that buffer or protect individuals against negative outcomes as they actually occur. (This approach stands in direct contrast to strategies that begin by identifying subjects who already exhibit negative outcomes and then, through retrospective questioning, attempt to construct a causal chain of earlier conditions that might have brought about the negative outcome.) This point draws attention to the issue of reference points, and to "follow-up" versus "follow-back" strategies for analyzing prospective longitudinal data (Caspi, 1998; Rutter & Garmezy, 1983). (These are similar to what Reese and McCluskey [1984, pp. 31-32] label "anterograde" versus "retrograde" methods.) In the *follow-back* strategy, the investigator begins with those subjects who have a specific outcome by some point, and then traces their pathways back in time in an effort to search for common origins or earlier characteristics that predict the later outcome. In the *follow-up* strategy, the investigator instead begins with those who share common origins or early characteristics and traces their pathways forward in time to later outcomes. These two strategies provide different types of important information, some of which may not converge. In fact, causal chains that develop from "looking forwards often differ markedly from those looking backwards" (Rutter, 1988, p. 3). However, those interested in understanding and predicting developmental risk generally find data from follow-up strategies more interpretable than that which results from follow-back designs. At the same time, because follow-up strategies begin with *common* origins and early experiences, they often overlook the fact that common outcomes can be brought about by *diverse* origins and experiences.

Third, a longitudinal approach allows us to better plot the multitude of outcomes that may result from a specific risk factor or set of risk factors. If we search only for the risk factors associated with a single outcome, there is a "danger of assuming that the risk is specific for that outcome when in fact the risks may apply to a much broader range of sequelae" (Rutter, 1988, p. 4). Similarly, longitudinal strategies allow us to better plot the multitude of processes and pathways through which the risk factor may bring about an outcome or set of outcomes. As such, they provide the possibility of exploring feedback mechanisms, circular processes, chain effects, and "delayed" or "sleeper" effects over the short or long term, though our methods for analyzing these remain limited. In addition, processes and effects of these types also pose an important challenge to our theories, which seldom propose or account for them.

Fourth, longitudinal approaches allow us to examine the *persistence* of specific effects of sequelae over time, as we explore the complex causal connections between them and as we attempt to delineate the mechanisms involved in the persistence or non-persistence of these effects. Yet in order to be useful, explicit theory and associated hypotheses must govern the connections drawn between an earlier set of variables and their later outcomes. While this seems obvious, it is an important point to make, particularly in relation to developmental risk. As Rutter (1988) notes, "most research on developmental risk focuses on risk indicators which have, at best, an ambiguous relationship with a set of risk mechanisms, if any mechanisms are stated at all" (p. 12). Despite some of its weaknesses, structural equation modeling is advantageous in this way because it forces the researcher to think about underlying constructs, and to explicate in advance the connections between variables. However, these approaches do not provide a "cure-all" where the causal mechanisms are concerned, given that including risk *indicators* in our models, which is most often done, is something very different from understanding risk *processes*, about which little is known.

Fifth, as we follow at-risk individuals over time, we are likely to find that individuals develop negative outcomes or disorders at different points. This will allow us to subdivide subjects according to the *timing* (age) of onset, and to study how its precursors and consequences vary with timing. This approach need not be restricted to understanding risk; it may be applied to gain an understanding of the precursors or consequences of any life event or transition.

Sixth, longitudinal strategies allow us to examine changes over time within individuals (intra-individual change) as well as differences between individuals and groups (inter-individual differences in intra-individual change). Causal models that result from analyses that focus on inter-individual differences need not be synonymous with those that result from analyses that focus on intra-individual change. In fact, in some situations, the two approaches may lead to opposite conclusions, even when based on the same set of data. Of course, the strategies associated with these two types of analyses also address different causal questions. (Issues related to measuring and analyzing change will be addressed later in this chapter.)

Regardless of our approach, we must be cautious of "third variable effects" as causal chains are created and analyzed (Rutter, 1988). That is, as we link one variable to another, we must increase our certainty that the link between the two is a genuine causal effect and not the result of another variable associated with both the prior factor and the later outcome. As with cross-sectional data, investigators will want to partial out or control for the confounding effects of third variables. At least with longitudinal data, the temporal relationships between the variables is clearer (though the investigator must nonetheless select which variables to include from different wares of data, which is often based on assumptions about the temporal order of variables). Investigators also likely have the chance to examine change over time in both the outcome variable and the confounding variables. At the same time, it is seldom possible to include, and measure well, all confounding variables. In addition, confounding variables may be differently distributed between comparison groups, which may lead to inadequate statistical adjustment for those variables.

Seventh, statements about cause and effect inherently involve time. An examination of change requires a time axis and at least two points of data along that axis. Most importantly, it requires the specification of the *temporal order* (the cause must precede the effect), the *temporal interval* (the interval necessary for the cause to bring about the effect), and the *temporal form* (or shape) of the causal effect (Blossfeld & Rohwer, 1997). Unfortunately, only very rarely are the latter two issues addressed in our theory or research, and it is here that significant advances are also needed. The cause and effect may be immediate (or be characterized by *apparent simultaneity*, particularly when the observation intervals are crude, as is the case in social science research), or there may be a delay or lag between cause and effect (though most social science theory cannot sufficiently specify or explain lagged effects) (Blossfeld & Rohwer, 1997).

For example, as illustrated in Figure 1, we might consider effects that are immediate but remain constant thereafter (panel 1); those that are lagged in time but remain constant thereafter (panel 2); those that are immediate but continuously increase (panel 3); those that are immediate, rise shortly, decline, and eventually disappear (panel 4); or those that are immediate but oscillating (panel 5) (Blossfeld & Rohwer, 1997). Other forms might also be considered, though again, most social science theory is inadequate to specify these shapes *a priori* or explain them *post hoc*.

Finally, as we attempt to advance our understanding of trajectories, it would also seem just as important to examine what does *not* replicate across studies as it does to examine what *does* replicate. Similarly, we should search for and highlight the *provocative,* and not simply (or necessarily) the confirmatory (Krüger, 1998). Indeed, non-confirmatory findings are often most provocative.

Life Review

The continuity of subjective identity, and of personality characteristics and behavioral dispositions, provides a sense of integrity in life. While individuals may engage in reminiscence and life review activities throughout the life course, these activities seem especially salient during middle and old age, functioning to bridge earlier and later segments of life (Erikson, 1980; Levinson, 1986; Neugarten, 1968b; Staudinger, 1989).[7] In addition to their research value, reminiscence and life review techniques are also popular therapeutic tools (e.g., Butler & Lewis, 1982; Coleman,

---

[7] Staudinger (1989) notes that while the terms "life review" and "reminiscence" are often used synonymously, they should be recognized as distinct. Reminiscence is the simple recalling of life events, something that can be "triggered quite unwillingly by the reminiscer"; life review, on the other hand, involves the interpretation and evaluation of those events and often requires more "active engagement of the person who is reviewing his or her life" (p. 71). Butler (1963, p. 67) also reminds us that life review "is not synonymous with, but includes, reminiscence."

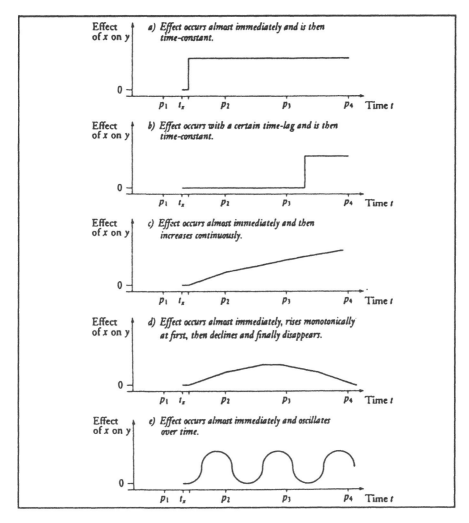

Figure 1. Different temporal shapes of how a change in a variable x, occurring at point in time t$_x$, effects a change in a variable y.
Source: Blossfeld, H.-P., & Rohwer, G. (1997). Causal inference, time, and observation plans in the social sciences. *Quality and Quantity, 31*. p. 368.

1986; deVries, Birren, & Deutchman, 1990; Haight, 1991). Life review and reminiscence activities may help individuals achieve a sense of self-worth, coherence, and reconciliation with the past; maintain perceptions of competence and continuity; and pass on cultural heritage and personal legacy (Wong & Watt, 1991).

The most common approaches to life review and reminiscence involve unstructured or semi-structured interviews. Interviews are usually conducted with individuals, but family and group sessions may also be conducted (e.g., Birren & Deutchman, 1991; Botella & Guillem, 1993; deVries et al., 1990). Examples of central questions include "What do you see as important or significant in your life?" (Lewis, 1971), "What family members have had a major impact in shaping your life? Why?" (deVries et al., 1990), "Describe three memories that you've been thinking about lately" (David, 1990), "What were the most important events? What were the most difficult decisions?" (Tismer, 1971), "Tell me something of your past that is most important to you—that is something that has had the most influence on your life" (Wong & Watt, 1991). Others have had revealing discussions around cherished objects (e.g., photographs, jewelry, books, paintings) (Sherman, 1991).

In addition to examining the *content* of reminiscence, investigators have also asked about the *frequency* and *affective quality* of reminiscence activity. For these purposes, Havighurst and Glasser's (1972) questions are commonly used: "Looking back over the last several weeks, would you say you have done a great deal, some, or very little reminiscing?" and "Would you most often characterize your reminiscence activities as most pleasant, pleasant, or unpleasant?"

Another interesting approach to life review is to ask a series of questions about life *revision;* that is, to ask respondents to identify what they would do differently if they had their lives to live over again. For example, DeGenova (1992) created a life revision index based on thirty-five questions with the stem "If you had your life to live over again, how much time would you spend . . ." and with the response categories "much more, more, same, less, much less." The items in DeGenova's index cover seven different life domains: family (e.g., "developing close relations with your children"), work (e.g., "worrying about your job"), friendships (e.g., "keeping up with good friends"), health (e.g., "taking good physical care of your body"), education (e.g., "pursuing your education"), leisure (e.g., "traveling"), and religion (e.g., "developing your spirituality"). Additional depth could be gained through a series of follow-up questions on what exactly respondents would do differently, and why they would allot their time in new ways.

A related approach is to ask subjects to graph a specific aspect of their lives over time (e.g., work histories, life satisfaction). For example, Runyan (1980) and several earlier studies (e.g., Clausen, 1972; Pressey & Kuhlen, 1957) gave respondents a graph with ages five through forty calibrated on the horizontal axis, and personal morale (spanning from 0 or "rock bottom," to 9 or "absolute tops") on the vertical axis. Respondents were asked to draw a curve indicating their degree of happiness over those years, and were then asked to discuss the reasons for their ratings. Similarly, others have administered blank-grid life graphs with only five-year age demarcations (from 0 through 80) on the horizontal axis, and have asked subjects the following question: "Can you visualize how your life could be put into a graph? That is, ups and downs, level periods, rises and declines, etc. Assuming that you live until at least 80 years of age, how do you think that a graph of your life will look?" (e.g., Back & Averett, 1985; Back & Bourque, 1970; Bourque & Back, 1977). However, this question is vague, and we might find the resulting data easier to understand if we were to ask the respondent to generate separate graphs for specific dimensions (e.g., physical health, psychological well-being, social activity). In addition, depending on the age of the subject and the age-span of the graph, some subjects will respond in terms of how they think their lives will unfold (prospectively), how their lives actually did unfold (retrospectively), or both. While these graphs may be used with any age group, this method may be especially useful in research with middle-aged and aged respondents, particularly to help structure life review discussions or to gather life histories. Questions can be asked about the overall contour of the graph; the notable movements along it (e.g., swings up, swings down, plateaus) and its sources; and the nature, precursors, and consequences of various turning points. This strategy may also help respondents recall additional experiences and the larger contexts within which specific experiences took place. Life graphs can also be evaluated along the dimensions just noted, but it is difficult to analyze the graphs themselves in systematic ways, partially because their patterns often seem idiosyncratic. Readers interested in other applications of reminiscence and life review methods might consult two recent edited volumes by Haight and Webster (1995) and Hendricks (1995).

Prospective Life-Course Questions and Future Time Perspectives

In contrast to the widespread use of retrospective questions among gerontologists in particular, investigators interested in childhood, adolescence, and early adulthood have begun to ask *prospective* questions of respondents in an effort to understand the life course as it is projected. For instance, there is now a tradition of such questions among sociologists of education who are interested in examining educational and occupational *aspirations* (how far an individual would like to go in school, or what kinds of jobs she or he would like to hold), *expectations* (how far an individual thinks she or he will actually go), the *match* (or *mis*match) between aspirations and expectations, and, ultimately, their connection to actual later attainment.

Let me provide examples from a few recent studies that have employed prospective questions about specific life experiences or about the life course more generally. In the Monitoring the Future study (Bachman, Johnston, & O'Malley, 1994; Johnston, O'Malley, Bachman, & Schulenberg, 1993), seventeen consecutive nationally representative samples of high schools seniors (spanning 1976 through 1992) were asked about their attitudes toward family and work. A few of these questions tap future expectations around marriage and childbearing. For example, respondents were asked about their desires for the timing of marriage (e.g., "If it were up to you, what would be the ideal time for you to get married?" ranging from "within the next year or so" to "over five years from now"). Questions such as these could be revised to ask about age, and to elicit specific ages so that continuous rather than categorical variables result. In addition, it might be interesting to ask young adults why they hold these timing desires and whether they expect their lives to match these desires. These investigators also asked about the desired number of children ("If you could have exactly the number of children you want, how many would you choose to have?" ranging from "none" to "six or more"). As with the question on marriage, it would have been interesting to follow this question with other questions about the desired timing and spacing of childbirth.

Similarly, in the 1980 Senior Cohort base year of the High School and Beyond study, high school seniors were asked "At what age do you expect to . . . Get married? Have your first child? Start your first regular (not summer) job? Live in your own home or apartment? Finish your full-time education?" Response categories included "Don't expect to do this," "Have already done this," "Under 18," a category for each age from eighteen through twenty-nine, and "30 or more." This survey also asked "How many children altogether to you eventually expect to have?" with response categories ranging from "None" to "Four or more." Like the questions from the Monitoring the Future study, it would have been informative to follow these questions with probes about why high school seniors hold these expectations, whether they think their lives will mirror them, what barriers might prevent these experiences from occurring, or whether an inability to meet these expectations will come with anticipated costs or benefits.

Several other good examples of questions about the future come from the Middle School Family Survey Study conducted by Eccles (1993). As part of a set of comprehensive interviews, with questionnaires administered to early adolescents and their families, Eccles asks early adolescents to project their futures, including whether they worry that they "will be discriminated against at work when you grow up because of your race," or "because of your sex"; what the chances are that they will experience a series of twenty events (e.g., "have a nice group of friends when you are in high school," "enter the military," "find a stable and well-paying job when you become an adult"), many of which are largely negative (e.g., "become pregnant or get someone else pregnant before you finish high school," "get involved in drugs," "be sexually assaulted or raped," "have limited opportunities due to the economy"). For most items, Eccles uses 5-point Likert scales from "very low" to "very high," with an additional column to indicate whether the event "already happened." Again, it would have been interesting to follow up middle school students' responses to these questions with other questions aimed at understanding when, why, and with what consequences they think these will come.

Eccles also includes an interesting series of generally open-ended questions about the type of person the pre-adolescent would and would not like to become in the future. For example, Eccles asks the following: "Many people know what they would like to be in the future. They have a picture in their minds of a person they would like to be. Please tell me *four* things about the kind of person *you most hope* to be when you are in high school." A similar question is asked about the "*four* things *you do not want to be true of you* when you are in high school." These are followed by questions about the person they "hope to be when you are grown up," the "kind of job you would most like to have when you are grown up," the likelihood that "you will have this kind of job," the "kind of job you think you will really have," the kinds of things that "will keep you from getting the job you want" (including questions about race and sex discrimination), and an interesting question that asks the child to "describe what you think a typical weekday will be like" as a grown-up, specifying "what things you think you will usually be doing from the time you get up until the time you go to bed."

Another area of research explores "future time perspectives" and is worthy of significantly more attention. An individual's sense of the future likely relates to her or his current developmental state and future developmental chances, to her or his well-being, and to the well-being of the society to which she or he belongs. Research along these lines will become increasingly important as recent cohorts of young people now face futures that are dramatically different from those of cohorts past, particularly in terms of economic and occupational opportunities.

Along these lines, Bouffard and Bastin (1996) explore age differences in the extension and content of future goals and hopes. To collect data on the personal goals of their respondents, they use twenty-three sentence beginnings from the Motivational Induction Method (Nuttin & Lens, 1985), such as "I hope . . . ," "I wish . . . ," and "I would like to . . ." Respondents may express any type of aspiration that comes to mind. In analyzing the temporal extension of the aspirations cited, these investigators use three categories: *short-term future* (those that may be achieved before the end of the year), *long-term future* (those that are in the distant future and extend as far as the remainder of the individual's life), and *open present* (more general aspirations, such as "to be happy" or "peace in the world," that cannot be placed into a specific time period). They also create an *extension index* to tap the ratio of the number of short-term future goals to long-term future goals. In analyzing goal content, they classify aspirations into ten "motivational" categories. These relate to the *self* (general self, personality traits, self-preservation, health preservation, autonomy), *self-development* (or self-actualization), *activity* (general "useful," professional, or academic activities), *contact with others* (general, intimate, or altruistic contact), *contact from others* (to receive affection, support, consideration), *wishes for others, exploration* (gain knowledge, life experience), *possession* (acquire money, comfort, material things), *leisure* (recreation, vacation, sports), and *transcendental* (religious aspirations, hopes for a good death).

Similarly, Staats, Romine, Atha, and Isham (1994) also explore "future time perspectives," but instead measure these perspectives in terms of expected psychological affect and anticipated happiness (the Expected Balance Scale, or EBS) and hope for specific positive outcomes or circumstances (the Hope Index). The EBS, which is a descendent of Bradburn's Affect Balance Scale, is an 18-point scale with nine positive (optimistic) and nine negative (pessimistic) items such as "Will you be annoyed with someone?" or "Will you feel that things are going your way?" For these scales, they explore the following time frames: "in the next few weeks," "in the next year," "in the next 5 years," and "in the future." The items in the sixteen-item Hope Index, used here on college-age adults, were developed by asking young adults and their parents to list things for which they hoped. Eight items tap hopes for the self (e.g., "to do well in school or job"), and eight items tap hopes for others or for larger world circumstances (e.g., "other people to be helpful"). Respondents pass through these items (on a 5-point scale) twice, the first time evaluating how much they wish for the outcome, and the second time evaluating how much they expect it to occur.

Taking a more qualitative approach, Greene and Wheatley (1992) analyze the "future narratives" of young adults. Using a task called the Density of Future Events, they ask respondents to spontaneously discuss their futures and the events they think might occur, allowing them to alter, delete, or reorganize events as they choose. In the process, the interviewer asks the respondent to identify the age at which the event will most likely occur. The narratives are analyzed in terms of *density* (absolute number of events described), *spontaneous extension* (the oldest age provided for the events described), *constrained extension* (the median age), and *content* (especially with respect to four "superordinate" event categories of achievement, relationship, experiential, and existential events).

This strategy is similar to O'Rand and Ellis' (1974) early measure of the "Social Time Perspective" (STP), which built on even earlier measures developed by Wallace (1956), Kastenbaum (1961), Lessing (1968), and others. O'Rand and Ellis' STP instrument asks respondents to report seven things that they think will happen sometime in the future (including things they are "looking forward to" or would "not like to see happen"). These investigators then probe to determine when the respondent expects the event to happen, and whether the event will likely be pleasant or unpleasant. O'Rand and Ellis analyze the time perspective in terms of "extensity" (how distal the latest episode is) and "sequence" (the degree to which the order of reported future events reflects the "normative life-cycle model," a comparison which indexes the respondent's "ability to order his future systematically") (p. 56). However, these investigators note that other dimensions might also be analyzed, including "clarity, coherence, directionality, duration, and reality-irreality" (p. 56).

Research on the life course will significantly benefit from projects designed to assess the visions that children, adolescents, and adults hold of their futures: the hopes and fears they have for their own lives, the opportunities and barriers they perceive and how barriers might be overcome, and the ways in which they see their lives as being similar to or different from past cohorts or generations in their families; and their hopes and fears related to the nature of human life more generally. Cross-national research along these lines would also be particularly insightful, given the dramatic social change that has occurred in recent decades, and its presumed variable effects on individuals within and between nations.

Analyzing Secondary and Archival Data

There are two basic considerations when deciding whether an existing (secondary) data set is appropriate for a set of developmental questions (Brooks-Gunn, Phelps, & Elder, 1991). First, one should consider the length of time, if any, over which an individual or family has been followed. In research on children and adolescents, longitudinal research typically examines repeated measures in a specific life phase or captures movement between two phases, and involves a few waves (often only two) separated by short time intervals. In research on adult life, the time frame studied is often much wider, but each wave is typically separated by a longer interval of time in part because of the *assumption* that changes during adulthood are not as rapid as those during childhood and adolescence. Regardless of whether the researcher assumes that change during adulthood is minimal or great, important action will be missed when the time interval between waves is large.

Second, one must consider whether the data set was gathered to examine specific research questions and hypotheses or whether it was gathered for more general purposes. If data were originally gathered with specific research questions and hypotheses in mind, they may not be well-suited for other applications, particularly if the measures are limited. In contrast, several longitudinal studies have been planned and implemented for the benefit of the social science community as a whole. The content of these studies is often intentionally broad and multidisciplinary. This allows developmental scientists exciting opportunities to conduct interdisciplinary research and to examine relationships between a wide range of variables. At the same time, because large scale secondary data sets are now collected for general purposes, many measures may not be of sufficient depth to entertain certain research questions or hypotheses. When we use secondary data sets, we are restricted by their content and design, and this may seriously restrict our inferential scope.

The analysis of existing data sets may provide opportunities to extend our research questions to other types of samples. It may also provide opportunities to examine the strengths and weaknesses of questions asked in previous research, and to explore hypotheses before new data are collected (James & Paul, 1993). The analysis of secondary data is also an attractive option in times of limited funding. Secondary data can be analyzed at relatively low financial cost, and this may encourage investigators to better tap existing resources before they collect new data. This factor is likely an important force behind the recent explosion of interest in secondary data analysis in the social sciences, and in the resources that have been channeled toward archiving collections and making them widely available to the scientific community.

Despite their attractiveness, secondary data sets come with a set of costs and limitations (Brooks-Gunn, Phelps, & Elder, 1991; McCall & Appelbaum, 1991). Users must critically asses the reliability, validity, completeness, and portability of data, as well as the appropriateness of the research design (David, 1991). For example, can results published by the initial investigator be reproduced? Are the design and execution of data collection clear? Can logical inconsistencies be detected and clarified? Can responses and response values be unambiguously interpreted? Can the data set be moved to a local computer environment with ease?

Contrary to expectations, the use of secondary data sets normally requires substantial investments of time up front to prepare it for use and to understand its contents, which are not always well documented. In addition, secondary data sets are generally *not* readily suited for the particular needs of an investigator. They must be approached in imaginative ways and "radically restructured" (James & Paul, 1993) or "recast" (Elder, Pavalko, & Clipp, 1993) in order to shed light on new questions. In the process, the investigator should expect to spend a significant amount of time seeking information on the many fine-grained decisions that were made by the original investigator during the process of collecting and coding data. These decisions have an important impact on the subsequent recoding of data, their reliability, their use in analyses, and their interpretation and ultimate meaning. The investigator must also invest time in understanding the nature and consequences of missing data. Some secondary data sets come with missing data already imputed in some fashion, whether through simple mean substitution, LaGrangian linear interpolation-extrapolation, multiple imputation, or more advanced methods for estimating missing data (see Little & Rubin, 1987). Related to missing data is the problem of attrition, which is an important concern for secondary data sets that are longitudinal in nature. These time investments are even greater in the case of secondary data sets that are longitudinal, not only because of problems related to attrition, but because each wave often varies in content (e.g., different questions may be asked, or questions may be asked differently) and because data must be extracted and carefully matched across waves.

Secondary data sets pose several additional challenges. The researcher must consider the methodological challenges posed by the time and manner in which data were collected. For example, data gathered many decades ago are often regarded as "simplistic, unsystematic, and parametrically questionable" (Tomlinson-Keasey, 1993, p. 76). And because data were gathered before the research questions were posed, the researcher must take extra caution not to capitalize on chance (this can be facilitated by specifying a set of hypotheses and an analytic plan *before* examining data).

Several ethical issues also emerge when data are made available to others, including concerns about informed consent (and possible breaches therein), confidentiality and anonymity, and to whom access should be granted. These concerns may be even more problematic when the set of data being shared is sensitive in nature (Boruch, Reiss, Garner, Larntz, & Freels, 1991). (These concerns are discussed further in the next section.) For a review of issues involved in conducting secondary analyses, see McCall and Applebaum (1991), and in working with archival data, see Elder, Pavalko, and Clipp (1993) and Hill (1993).

There are several valuable guides to widely available secondary data sets and archives. The "Guide to Resources and Services" issued by the Inter-university Consortium for Political and Social Research (ICPSR) at the University of Michigan contains basic information on hundreds of secondary cross-sectional and longitudinal data sets that are housed there and available to ICPSR members (most research universities subscribe to ICSPR). The ICPSR data sets span a wide variety of general topics of interest to researchers interested in the life course, including data on educational, economic, health care, political and social behavior. Each entry in the Guide, which is updated every few years, contains a paragraph summary of the data set, its universe, its sampling, the extent of its collection, and its format and structure. Each year the ICPSR also publishes a similar resource book on "Data Collections" from the National Archive of Computerized Data on Aging (NACDA). The NACDA archive, which is also housed at the University of Michigan, is sponsored by the National Institute on Aging and includes data on the social, economic, psychological, and physical characteristics and needs of older adults.

Another important archive about which readers should be aware is the repository at the Henry A. Murray Research Center of Radcliffe College. The "Guide to the Data Resources of the Henry A. Murray Research Center" and "Index to the Guide" include information on hundreds of data sets in that archive. Several members of the Murray Center research team also compiled a more general inventory of longitudinal data in the social sciences (Young, Savola, & Phelps, 1991), which updated two earlier volumes published by the Social Science Research Council (Migdal, Abeles, & Sherrod, 1981; Verdonik & Sherrod, 1984). Each entry includes information on the primary investigators, substantive topics covered, characteristics of the original sample, attrition, constructs measured and instruments used, representative references of published research based on those data, and current status of the study (e.g., whether further waves are planned, whether data are in machine-readable format and available for secondary analyses).

Data Sharing

The sharing of data within the larger scientific community would seemingly encourage more explicit comparisons across studies with similar types of data, across disciplinary boundaries, and across cultures and nations. In addition, the widespread sharing of data may result in original findings being refuted or refined (Colby & Phelps, 1990), which is good for scientific progress. Several technological changes have also increased our ability to share data and reduced the costs of doing so, including advances in computer storage, memory, networks, retrieval programs, and statistical packages.

While shifts toward open scientific communication and data sharing have occurred in recent years, these have long been "ideals" and not "norms" of science as it has actually been practiced (Sieber, 1991a, p. 4). Scholars may be hesitant to distribute their data too widely, whether out of fear of criticism or that their findings will be refuted, or because they feel they need not "give away" their hard work to others who will profit from it with little effort (Sieber, 1991b). Investigators may also resent attempts to regulate what they and others do with their data, particularly when they must spend time and money preparing, documenting, and distributing their data for use by others (David, 1991; Tomlinson-Keasey, 1993).

At the same time, there now seems to be ethical consensus that scientists ought to make their data available to peers for scrutiny, especially when findings are controversial (Sieber, 1991a). In addition, the sharing of data has been mandated by the federal government and strongly advocated by major scientific foundations (e.g., National Science Foundation, National Academy of Sciences; see Sieber, 1991a; White, 1991). These mandates and statements suggest that scientific research, especially *funded* research, may be regulated by new rules in the future (Sieber, 1991a). Several questions highlight the need to establish norms and ethical standards with which to guide the sharing of data (see Sieber, 1991b; Weil & Hollander, 1991). Should scientific institutions and gatekeepers (e.g., funders, journals, professional associations) reward investigators for preparing and sharing data files? If so, how? Who should pay the costs associated with documenting and duplicating data files? Who "owns" the set of data? Who should have access to them? Should funded data be controlled by the investigator, the institution, or the funder? For what purposes should the use of secondary data be approved? How should we deal with the matter of informed consent, especially when data were not originally intended to be shared? How might confidentiality be breached in the process of sharing data? Do secondary users have obligations to their donors? At what point must data be released? In large-scale collaborative efforts, who controls the set of data and is ultimately responsible and accountable for it?

Analyzing Trajectories

Developmental scientists are (or ought to be) especially interested in understanding lives over time, and the antecedents and consequences of various experiences. We must therefore generate theories and use methods that allow a more complete examination of long-ranging trajectories. This involves examining the critical "bifurcation" points at which trajectories branch out and lead, through specific sequences of events, to various outcomes, whether "old" or "novel" (Valsiner, 1989).[8] The concept of a trajectory has a long tradition in the sociology of work and occupational careers, as individuals move through sequences of (often hierarchical) positions over time, as movement through these positions determines later opportunities for advancement, and as the structure of these pathways varies across organizations and occupations (e.g., Kaufman & Spilerman, 1982; Kerckhoff, 1993; Rosenbaum, 1984, 1987; Spenner, Otto, & Call, 1982; Spilerman, 1977).[9] Similarly, sociologists of education have a longstanding interest in high school tracking, as an individual's social status and personal characteristics play a role in determining the track onto which she or he is placed, and as track placement determines later educational and occupational chances (e.g., Jencks, Bartlett, Corcoran, Crouse, Eaglesfield, et al., 1979; Jencks, Smith, Acland, Bane, Cohen, et al., 1972; Rosenbaum, 1976).

To advance our ability to handle entire trajectories, methods that generate and describe whole trajectories must first be developed; these methods must simultaneously incorporate data on timing, sequencing, spacing, density, and duration. Then, we are faced with the formidable challenge of how to analyze trajectories: to connect multiple experiences along a given trajectory, and multiple trajectories within individuals; and to aggregate and compare trajectories across individuals. For example, how do we handle problems posed by the fact that lives, and trajectories within lives, differ in length?

As the span of time to be analyzed increases, the number of experiences to be handled, the possible connections between them, and the mechanisms that link them together, become infinitely complicated, particularly as we attempt to approximate the span of an entire life. This also makes it difficult to describe "typical" courses (which, as we will see below, may not be our best strategy in any case). The number of possibly relevant variables to be considered, and the ways in which they may be plotted over time, are virtually endless. For example, we must select *a priori* from that list of enormous possibilities those variables that we deem to be most important.

---

[8] Valsiner (1989) discusses bifurcation points as points of "irreversible choice," though they need not be conceptualized as irreversible nor as a matter of choice.

[9] However, the concept of the work "career," and related theory and research, has been based largely on the experiences of men, not women (Moen, 1996).

As Nydegger humorously notes, this amounts to the same problem faced by a child in a candy store: "limited means confronting unlimited choice. The result is often the same: paralysis of decision, finally resolved by a wild grab for the nearest, or the prettiest, candies" (1986a, p. 137).

This process is also made difficult because there is little temporal life-course theory to guide the selection process. Significant theoretical advances, whether through the development of new theories or through the revision and extension of existing ones, are necessary for us to answer the following questions: *which* is the most critical set of variables, *when* is each variable from that set most important (given that the same variable may be available at different time points), *how* might those variables then be arrayed in some sequence of relationships over time, and *what mechanisms* drive these relationships? In addition, we must consider the ways in which our variables might be multiply confounded not only at a single point in time, but especially across multiple points in time. In the absence of temporal theory, these linkages become major "leaps of faith," especially when the time interval between them is dramatic and when very distal experiences are included. Yet these leaps of faith are often made in the analysis and interpretation of longitudinal data (see also Cairns, Costello, & Elder, 1996). Future theoretical advances can only be made to the extent that measures and observations over time can be meaningfully connected (Brandtstädter, 1993).

Not only has much research on the life course been *atemporal*, but even those variables that have been examined at two or more points in time have not been critically evaluated in temporal terms: Does the validity and reliability of a construct and its measures change as individuals grow older? Do they change across different historical periods? Should we expect this? How might these changes affect our measurement and interpretation of these constructs?

As noted in Chapter 2, we know little about how age expectations and timetables are subjectively experienced, and how these take on important meanings for individuals. We must begin to examine how these factors impact the dynamic process of "selving," as experiences are continuously organized, interpreted, integrated into the self; and how these factors impact, or are conditioned by, larger "selfways"—culturally constructed patterns of "thinking, feeling, wanting, and doing" (Markus, Mullally, & Kitayama, 1997, p. 16; see also Gubrium, Holstein, & Buckholdt, 1994; Kling, Ryff, & Essex, 1997; Whitbourne, 1996). These issues are raised again because they must also be extended to our analyses of long-ranging trajectories: How are pathways through the spheres of family, work, education, health, and the like, subjectively experienced? That is, what does particular constellation of experiences along a pathway—their timing, sequencing, spacing, density, and duration – feel like from the standpoint of the person who experiences it? More importantly, how does the nature of a trajectory, as a larger entity, take on meaning above and beyond the meanings associated with the specific experiences that comprise it? Finally, how is the interaction of trajectories (for example, between family and work) subjectively experienced and assigned meaning?

As noted above, most research on trajectories relates to experiences that comprise the passage to adulthood, given the compression of many events and transitions within that relatively brief period. However, research on childhood has begun to explore achievement trajectores through the elementary and middle schools years (e.g., Alexander, Entwistle, & Dauber, 1994), and research on aging has begun to explore trajectories related to retirement (e.g., Elder & Pavalko, 1993; Henretta, O'Rand, & Chan, 1993; Mutchler, Burr, Pienta, & Massagli, 1997), health status and disability (e.g., Clipp, Pavalko, & Elder, 1992), and caregiving (e.g., Aneshensel, Pearlin, Mullan, Zarit, & Whitlatch, 1995).

For example, Elder, Pavalko, and Clipp (1993; Clipp, Pavalko, & Elder, 1992) offer five models for classifying about physical and emotional health trajectories over four-and-a-half decades for men in the Terman Longitudinal Study (starting in 1945, when the men were in the 30s, and continuing in 1950, 1955, 1960, 1972, 1977, 1982, and 1986). Drawing on all information pertaining to physical or emotional health, Elder and his colleagues first develop physical and emotional health measures (5-point Likert scales) for each survey year and for the periods between survey points. They then separately classify each subject's data on physical and emotional health into one of several different typologies (see Figure 2). The first trajectory is of *constant good health,* in which an individual's level of health remains consistently "good" or "excellent" at each survey point and between them. In direct contrast, is a trajectory of *constant poor health,* in which an individual's level of health remains consistently "fair" or "poor" at each survey point and between them. A third trajectory is of *decline and recovery,* in which an individual experiences a marked decline (one or more "fair" or "poor" ratings) after having a period of good health, then recovers and restores the prior level of functioning. A fourth trajectory marks *linear decline,* in which an individual begins in good health, but falls either markedly or subtly (the codes for each survey point, and for the intervals between those points, decrease over time). Their final trajectory is of *decline at end of life,* in which an individual has good health throughout most of life but declines, whether dramatically or incrementally, in old age, and from which the individual never recovers (by 1986, or ending with death if it occurred before 1986). For emotional health, they also offer a sixth typology, *mild emotional,* depicted as a wavering line, in which the subject describes her- or himself as having some sort of mild emotional trouble that is a continual source of distress, but for which the subject shows no evidence of having ever sought treatment.

Good examples of recent exploratory research on trajectories associated with work and retirement can be found in Elder and Pavalko (1993) and Mutchler, Burr, Pienta, and Massagli (1997). Again, using life-history data on two cohorts of men in the Stanford-Terman study (those born before 1910 and those born after 1910), Elder and Pavalko (1993) analyze patterns of work (and work exit) in later life. Building on follow-ups from 1960, 1972, 1977, 1982, and 1986, they assemble employment data at each of these points to plot men's work trajectories. They classify these trajectories into five possible patterns: *gradual,* in which work time is gradually reduced at least once without a complete exit, or in which two or more reductions are followed by a complete exit; *one-step* (abrupt), in which full-time employment is followed by a clear and permanent exit out of the labor force; *sporadic,* in which employment is reduced to 50 percent time or less at some point but then increased at

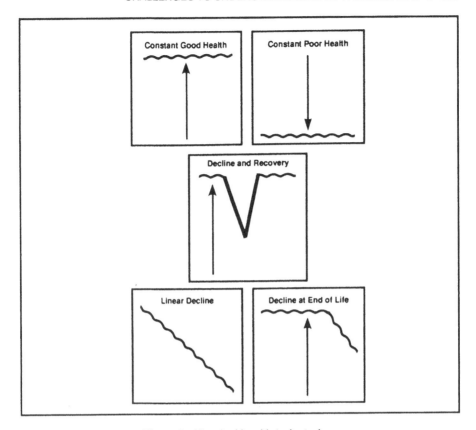

Figure 2. Physical health trajectories.
Source: Elder, G. H., Jr., Pavalko, E., & Clipp, E. (1993). *Working with archival data.* Newbury Park, CA: Sage Publications. p. 34.

a later point, or in which men completely exit and then re-enter; and *not reduced,* in which no or little reduction in work effort takes place.

Similarly, Mutchler, Burr, Pienta, and Massagli (1997) draw on retrospective work-history data from the 1984 Survey of Income and Program Participation (SIPP) to examine twenty-eight-month pathways of labor force activity (8 observations, with each separated by 4 months) for men aged fifty-five to seventy-four. They explore the extent to which men's work patterns are non-transitional, for which there are two patterns, continuous work and continuous non-work (across all data points), and the degree to which men's exit patterns are transitional, for which there are also two patterns, crisp exit (a clear transition from continuous work to continuous non-work) and blurred exit (alternating between periods of work, unemployment, non-work).

Regardless of whether the forms of a trajectory are specified *a priori* or *post hoc,* and regardless of whether they are an heuristic device or something to actually be analyzed, these examples point to the need to characterize both the level and slope of a variable, and changes in level and slope, over time.

The Complexities of Sequencing

To highlight some of the other technical challenges of analyzing trajectories, let me turn to a brief discussion of the complexities caused by sequencing alone. One recent technique for examining whether common sequence patterns exist in data—"optimal matching"—has been proposed, but it remains to be seen whether it holds its promise in the social sciences (in addition to the research of Abbott, Chan, and others noted above, see Kruskal, 1983; Mishler, 1996). Sequence comparisons, which are widely used in the natural sciences, examine sequence structure on a case-by-case basis and then seek to unravel larger patterns by measuring "sequence resemblance" across cases. The most common means of comparing two sequences (that is, a *source* and *target* sequence) are to examine the *substitution* or *replacement* of one element in the sequence for another, the *insertion*, *deletion*, or *"indel"* (both insertion and deletion) of elements into and from the sequence, the *compression* of two or more elements into one element, the *expansion* of one element into two or more elements, and the *transposition* or "swap" of two adjacent elements in the sequence (see Kruskal, 1983).

Three primary modes for analyzing and presenting these differences—at least those based in more elementary substitutions, deletions, and insertions—are the "optimum" modes of tracing, alignment (or matching), and listing. Optimum modes are contrasted with "distance" modes which, as the name suggests, are aimed at calculating the *distance* between sequences; that is, the smallest number of substitutions or indels to change one sequence into another (see Kruskal, 1983). Procedures for calculating distance are particularly useful in that they produce "a set of intermediate 'interval-level' measures of resemblance between sequences,' which may then serve as inputs to clustering or multidimensional scaling analyses to determine typical sequence patterns" (Mishler, 1996, p. 81).

Many of these procedures can be applied to either continuous or discrete variables; they can be used on large numbers of cases (but require complex programming and computations); and, most importantly, they not only retain the individual as the unit of analysis, but begin to represent long-ranging trajectories.

To illustrate the complexities of sequencing, let me draw three examples, beginning with Hogan (1980), and then turning to Rindfuss, Swicegood, and Rosenfeld (1987) and Ravanera, Rajulton, and Burch (1994). Hogan's (1980) research on the transition to adulthood as a "career contingency" analyzes 1973 data from the Occupational Changes in a Generation II survey. Using responses from 18,370 ever-married white men between the ages of twenty and sixty-five that year, Hogan examines variability in the sequencing of only three events during the transition to adulthood—finishing education, starting work, and marrying—and the effects of these early sequencing patterns on later occupational status and earnings returns to educational investments. Hogan is especially interested in comparing the patterns of men with "normative" or "orderly" trajectories to those with "non-normative" or "disorderly" trajectories. *Normative sequencing* is defined as finishing education, then taking a first career job, and then marrying (fully 11,288 men held this pattern). *Intermediate non-normative* sequencing is defined as a single inversion in this sequence—taking a job before finishing school, or marrying before finishing school or taking a job (3,379 men held this pattern). *Extreme non-normative* sequencing is defined as two inversions in the sequence—marrying before finishing school (3,703 men held this pattern). Hogan finds no difference in the occupational attainments of men in these groups, but men who experience a disorderly pattern do experience lower earnings returns to their educational investments and deficits in the total earnings. The "normative" sequencing of the transition to adulthood, whether in terms of actual behavioral patterns or in terms of prescriptions, seems much less clear today. Recent cohorts of young adults face a different set of educational and occupational needs, experiences, and circumstances than cohorts past. How quickly complex sequencing patterns would become if we were to analyze them for contemporary cohorts of young men and, especially, women; and if we were to also build other events into the profile (e.g., first birth).

A more complicated attempt at analyzing sequence patterns in the transition to adulthood is provided by Rindfuss, Swicegood, and Rosenfeld (1987). Using data from the NLS High School Class of 1972, these investigators analyzed the major role activity for each of eight years following high school graduation. Simply coding each of the eight years into one of five statuses (work, education, homemaker, military, other), they examined the degree to which sequence patterns were "consistent" with a "normative" pattern of *non-family* transitions in early adulthood.[10] If each event has an equal probability of occurring in each of the eight years, there are 5^8, or 390,625 possible sequences! Rindfuss, Swicegood, and Rosenfeld found that it took fully 1,100 sequence patterns to capture the experiences of 6,700 young men, and fully 1,800 sequence patterns to capture the experiences of 7,000 young women. On average, they found about six men in each of the male sequences, four women in each of the female sequences, and many sequences with only one or two individuals in them.

---

[10] The sequences of non-family transitions that they define as "apparently consistent" with the "normative" model are: "(1) Worked the entire eight years; (2) In school the entire eight years; (3) School followed by work. Treating time in the military as a form of work adds: (4) In the military the entire eight years; (5) School followed by military; and (6) School followed by military followed by work. Because taking time out from school to 'fulfil one's military duty' is considered conventional in some contexts, we include as well: (7) Military followed by school; and (8) Military followed by school followed by work." Adding in homemaker as a status (which one might also consider a form of work) adds five more "consistent" possibilities: "(9) Homemaker the eight years; (10) School followed by homemaker; (11) School followed by military followed by homemaker; (12) School followed by work, followed by homemaker; and (13) Work followed by homemaker." An additional possibility exists—school followed by military followed by work followed by homemaker—though there was no one in this category. For a description of "inconsistent" sequences, see Rindfuss, Swicegood, and Rosenfeld (1987, p. 789).

These authors note that the "normative" model of the transition to adulthood in the literature is "leaving school, entering the labor force full-time, getting married, and then having a first child. It is almost as if parent and student were mutually exclusive roles. The problem with this past strategy for sequencing is that individuals can simultaneously hold both family and non-family roles" (p. 786). While individuals hold roles in both spheres at once, these investigators argue that to combine family and non-family roles in their analyses would create "theoretical confusion," they chose to first restrict their analyses to non-family roles. They also argue that each sphere has its own expected sequencing (e.g., marriage comes before parenthood; completion of schooling before entering full-time work).

It is important to emphasize that these complexities exist even *after* the investigators made several decisions in an effort to simplify their approach. They examined only *non-family* roles; they considered only *five* possible roles, and coded only *one* role per year; and they covered only an *eight-year* period. Imagine how much more complex these patterns would become if we were to account for (a) a greater number of work and educational statuses, and statuses in other spheres (e.g., family, community); (b) the fact that individuals hold more than one role, even in a single sphere, simultaneously; and (c) a longer span of time, or other life periods.

In addition, definitions of "orderly" versus "disorderly," or of "consistent" versus "inconsistent," must be defined relative to an overall standard. Yet can we assume that such a standard is clear, or that it even exists? Are there instead different standards for men and women, for different social classes, race or ethnic groups, age or cohort groups, or specific combinations of these? If so, whose standards should be used (or imposed)? We must also more fully explore how disorder comes about, whether it comes with any short- or long-term consequences, what kinds of consequences it entails, and for whom disorder and its consequences come in modern societies. Besides observing disorder and its effects from an "objective" standpoint, we must also more fully explore the subjective sides of disorder: Do individuals actively choose to live "disorderly" lives, or does it simply happen? Do individuals deemed to have experienced transitions in a disorderly way think (or realize) that they have done so? If so, what are their stories about how disorder came about, and what consequences it entailed? Do these perceptions vary by social location? Along these lines, Rindfuss and his colleagues (1987) end with a plea to better understand "the nature and importance of sequencing in the life course [by] analyzing what the roles themselves mean and how they are causally linked" (p. 799). A decade has passed since their landmark paper, and we know little else about these important matters.

A third example of a project in which the investigators wrestle with the complexities of sequencing is that of Ravanera, Rajulton, and Burch (1994). Using life history data gathered as part of the 1990 Canadian General Social Survey, these investigators examine the sequencing of ten different family-related events and transitions for six cohorts of Canadian men and women (1910-20; 1921-30; 1931-40; 1941-50; 1951-60; 1961-70). The events and transitions they analyze are (1) leaving the parental home, (2) first-cohabitation or common-law union, (3) first marriage, (4) first separation and/or divorce, (5) death of spouse, (6) second marriage, (7) birth of first child, (8) birth of last child, (9) home-leaving of first child, and (10) home-leaving of last child. What might be perceived as a "typical" of "classic" family, is to move from launching (leaving the parental home) to family formation (first marriage) to family extension (first birth) and completed extension (last birth) to family contraction (home-leaving of first child) to completed contraction (empty nest; home-leaving of last child). These investigators examine patterns for those men and women for whom a maximum of six of these transitions have occurred (higher-order sequences occur mostly in relation to changes in marital status). Of the three eldest cohorts, and for both men's and women's lives, they find that only between one-fourth to one-third experience what is considered the "typical" or "classic" sequence. In addition, the patterns of the latter three cohorts, and again for both men and women alike, show even greater diversity. As a result, the assumption on the part of the family scholars that a "typical" sequence of family-related transitions exists in contemporary societies seems questionable. This research, like the two prior examples, suggests that future work should seek to better understand the nature of diverse sequences and the factors that influence the sequential structure of life-course experiences. As noted earlier, this also requires us to improve our techniques for handling trajectory data.

Continuity and Discontinuity

Neugarten (1969) opens her classic paper on "Continuities and Discontinuities of Psychological Issues in Adult Life" by noting that she is "more impressed by the discontinuities than by the continuities of psychological issues into adult life"; we cannot understand adulthood simply by "projecting forward the issues that are salient in childhood" (p. 88). Neugarten begs us to consider the many *new* psychological issues that emerge during adulthood, particularly in middle and old age. Among other things, Neugarten notes the "changing time perspective," as individuals begin to think about their lives in terms of time-left-to-live rather than time-since-birth; the "personalization of death," as women rehearse for widowhood and men rehearse for illness;" and a gender-related crossover in personality, with traits more often considered "feminine" emerging for (or being reclaimed by) men at midlife, and with traits more often considered "masculine" emerging for (or being reclaimed by) women at midlife.[11] In this and other work, Neugarten has also pushed us to consider the unique changes that accompany midlife—changes in family, work, body, mind, and personality.

The theme of continuity and discontinuity throughout adult life is one of the great themes of developmental scholarship. However, seldom are explicit theoretical or empirical models for understanding continuity and discontinuity offered in the literature. In fact, Chiriboga (1996, p. 174) notes that developmental scientists "have long decried the lack of theoretical guidelines for investigating continuity and change over time," and can offer only Gergen's (1977) three underlying models of adult development as a way to frame these questions. These are the developmental stability model, the orderly change model, and the random change model.

---

[11]On the latter age- and gender-related personality changes: The first project Neugarten conducted along these lines was done with Gutmann as part of the Kansas City Studies of Adult Life (1958/1996). An elaboration of that thesis, and the replication of those findings, would become Gutmann's life work (see Gutmann, 1997). After all, the personality shifts observed in the cross-sectional Kansas City data, if they were to be claimed as a universal developmental process, would not only need to be paralleled in diverse settings the world over, but they would need to be anchored in longitudinal data. Over the course of his career, Gutmann expanded his work by pursuing the Navajo (of the southwestern United States), Druze (of Galilean Israel and the Golan Heights), and Mayan peoples (of Mexico, including both the Lowland and Highland Maya). Gutmann links this personality shift to the "universal requirements of human parenthood," with men and women expressing "conventional" characteristics during early and peak parenting years, and releasing these conventions thereafter.

Gergen (1977) begins by arguing that four criteria should be used to evaluate "theories" of human development. First, we must consider the degree to which a theory provides a comprehensive understanding of human development. A good theory should give a "broadly inclusive description of a developmental sequence" and an "efficient rational or explanation for those sequences within the description" (pp. 136-137). Second, we must consider the degree to which a theory can aid in the process of prediction. Most social science theorizing is "emergently" predictive: It should be a "reasonable forecaster" of future events under the assumption that current conditions remain stable; if those conditions change, the theory must be revised to accommodate the new conditions. Third, we must consider the "prescriptive valuation" of a theory; that is, we must assess not only how well a theory describes and explains phenomena, but also the position it implicitly advocates. Finally, we must consider the theory's place in the scientific enterprise, and especially the degree to which it is consistent with traditional conceptions of science.

With these four dimensions in mind, Gergen evaluates the three models noted above. For a classic introduction to models and theories of human development, see Reese and Overton (1970).[12] First, Gergen considers the *stability template*, which emphasizes the stability of "behavioral patterns" (and presumably traits, attitudes, and the like) over time. In the stability framework, "whatever exists tends to endure" (p. 141). Second, Gergen considers the template of *ordered change*, which emphasized change over time, but change that is patterned, orderly, forward-moving, and essentially invariant across time and place. Finally, Gergen considers the *aleatory change* template, which takes the view that there is little about development that is "preprogrammed."[13] That is, "we enter the world with a biological system that establishes the *limits or range* of our activities, but *not* the precise character of the activities themselves" (p. 148, emphasis added). To this point, we might also add the fact that we enter the world, and live out our lives, within a *social* system that does

---

[12]Reese and Overton's review highlights the tensions between (a) *organismic* models, which tend to emphasize the holistic nature of the human organism, changes intrinsic to and guided by the organism, and movement through a universal sequence of stages toward some ultimate end state, (b) *mechanistic* models, which tend to emphasize specific aspects of development, changes driven by factors external to the individual, and the "openness" of the organism to develop at any age, and (c) models of *contextualism*, which have since been promoted more fully in the developmental literature. Contextual models, which were introduced in Chapter 1 and will be discussed further in Chapter 5, emphasize the "reciprocal and bi-directional relations between organisms and contexts, and the balances between processes of constancy and change across life, [and] tend to state the multiplicity of causes and their probabilistic variations with age or time" (Featherman & Lerner, 1985, p. 661). The latter two frameworks, and especially models of contextualism, take a view of development that is "probabilistic" in nature. For example, they posit capacity for developmental change throughout life as a "potential that may be achieved in whole or in part at any one historical moment by the species or at any one time in a cohort's or individual's life history . . . [T]o what extent, how, and when that potential is realized depends on historical and situational circumstances over time" (Featherman & Lerner, 1985, p. 661).

[13]Similarly, Alwin (1995) suggests that it is helpful to distinguish between aleatoric and persistence views of development over time. *Aleatoric* views posit a high degree of plasticity and adaptability throughout life, which is characterized by constant changes and challenges. *Persistence* views, on the other hand, normally take the human organism to be flexible and susceptible to influence early in life (through early adulthood), but increasingly rigid and stable thereafter. The persistent view is similar to what was described in Chapter 1 as the traditional conception of development.

this as well. In addition, some *dis*advantages, regardless of their type, may also be transcended. This makes the course of development contingent on many factors in both the individual and the environment, and, as a result, highly variable. After all, change in the individual may be driven by change in the environment (Clausen, 1993). (This issue will be discussed at length in the next chapter.) For example, the socio-cultural transformations that come with historical change expose individuals of different ages to new norms, opportunities, and constraints. As individuals move through life, they take on new roles, responsibilities, and relationships; and they encounter, and adapt to, stressful or traumatic circumstances. Of course, the ways in which these changes affect individuals will depend on the personal and social characteristics and resources individuals bring to those situations.

Twenty years ago, Gergen argued that the aleatory template was significantly less developed than the stability or ordered change templates. Twenty years later, most contemporary developmental research now seems to advocate a position in line with the aleatory template, though much more in principle than in practice. Because human lives are considered neither stable nor orderly, nor valid beyond specific groups of people in specific environments in specific periods of historical time, theory in line with aleatory template also becomes significantly more difficult, if not impossible, to develop. Similarly, because individuals and the worlds in which they live are ever-changing, our empirical work becomes increasingly difficult, and the task of prediction becomes nearly impossible. As developmental science becomes increasingly aleatoric, is it destined to become a science of simple description? Will our research do little else but contribute to the historical record?

Empirical evidence on continuity and discontinuity generally centers around consistencies or changes on dimensions of interest within an individual or between groups of individuals (Hinde, 1988). This may involve the emergence of a qualitatively different pattern, a marked change in rate, a notable change in the magnitude of correlations between different dimensions of concern, or a change in the rank ordering of individuals.

There are several problems with evidence of these types (Hinde, 1988). One problem relates to the fact that these types of evidence are distinct from each other. Any continuity or discontinuity observed with one approach may not necessarily be found with another approach. Second, evidence based on correlations or on the rank ordering of evidence is tainted by ceiling and floor effects and by individual differences. A third and related problem is that when group data are used, any discontinuity (or continuity) observed may be driven by a select set of individuals and may mask potential continuity (or discontinuity) for subgroups. Fourth, there are problems related to the effects of the environment in bringing about continuity or discontinuity. That is, as we study development, we must consider the interdependent and simultaneous changes in both the individual *and* her or his environments; this is especially problematic when our evidence is based on group-level data. Finally, there may be problems related to the use of higher-order measures (e.g., composite measures based on several lower-order variables may mask differences in the directions of those variables), the nature of variables (e.g., an individual's status on a particular measure at different ages may reflect completely different factors and processes), "coherence" (e.g., the same developmental "propensity" may manifest itself differently at different ages), and linking earlier and later experiences (e.g., early and later experiences may be related through complicated, subtle, and indirect pathways). Despite these many problems, once continuities or discontinuities have been identified we can begin to understand the mechanisms (physiological, psychological, social, or otherwise) that drive them, and, most importantly, their short- and long-term effects.

Caspi (1998) explores several different types of continuity: differential, absolute, structural, and ipsative. These are examples of "homotypic" continuity, which deals with the continuity of behaviors or phenotypic attributes over time.[14] The most common definition of continuity, indexed by a correlation coefficient, is *differential continuity*. Differential continuity refers to the "consistency of individual differences within a sample of individuals over time, to the retention of an individual's relative placement in a group" (p. 345). This type of continuity generally tends to increase with age (at least with respect to many personality variables), and to decrease as the time interval between observations increases. Because differential continuity is usually indexed through a correlation coefficient, it is especially sensitive to, and will depend on, the sources and amount of variability in the sample and measures.

Absolute continuity refers to the "constancy in the quantity or amount of an attribute over time. Conceptually, it connotes the continuity of an attribute within a single individual, but it is typically assessed empirically by examining group means" (p. 346). Most of this research is atheoretical and focused on age-related mean-level changes. While a sample of individuals may preserve their rank over time (differential continuity), they may nonetheless shift in mean levels (absolute continuity).

Structural continuity refers to the "persistence of correlational patterns among a set of variables across time. Typically, such continuity is assessed by examining the similarity of covariation patterns among item and factor relations across repeated measurements" (p. 348). (This technical work is best accomplished through structural equation modeling.) Structural changes, therefore, may indicate that a transformation has occurred.

Regardless of the fact that differential, absolute, and structural continuity are meant to address the *individual* level, they are generally analyzed using procedures that characterize a *sample* of individuals. In contrast, *ipsative continuity* refers explicitly to continuity at the individual level, must be analyzed at that level, and is dependent on having an identical measure available at multiple points in time (though, as discussed later, the reliability and validity of many measures may nonetheless be questionable at multiple points, especially over long periods of time).

---

[14]Phenotypic attributes are observable and result from interactions between the genotype (the genetic constitution of the organism) and the environment. Caspi (1998) also discusses a fifth, and more complicated, type of continuity: *coherence,* which refers to the "continuity of an inferred genotypic attribute presumed to underlie diverse phenotypic behaviors" evidenced over time (pp. 349-350). A claim of coherence "requires a theory that specified the basis on which the diverse phenotypic behaviors can be said to cohere" (p. 364).

Just as the concept "continuity" is ambiguous and has many meanings and measurements, so too is the concept "change." In fact, some of the evidence on continuity, especially that which examines correlations, can also be taken as evidence on change. At some point, the line between continuity and change becomes both fine and subjective. As Caspi (1998) asks in his discussion of personality, "Do correlations of .5 over a 10-year period highlight connectedness in development, or do they underscore the malleability of personality? Do seemingly inconsistent behaviors reflect personality transformations or the changing but lawful expressions of personality dispositions?" (pp. 361-362). These questions draw attention to the tricky business of conceptualizing, measuring, and assessing continuity or change.

At least three different conceptions of "change" can be found in the literature: as measurement error; as the absence of continuity (versus change as systematic); and as a turning point (Caspi, 1998). When we analyze change, we make the assumption that the amount of measurement error is relatively small, that the measures are sensitive enough to capture change, and that any change observed reflects true change. These are questionable assumptions. Better methods for handling measurement error must be developed, though several techniques are available for continuous variables via structural equation modeling (e.g., Bollen, 1989). In longitudinal analyses, simple corrections for measurement unreliability may not be sufficient, particularly where unreliability may vary as subjects age and with the length of the study. There is also the additional problem, discussed elsewhere in this chapter, of developing identical if not parallel measures of the same construct as subjects move through different life periods. This is a challenging task not only for the period spanning childhood through the early adult years, but also for the many decades that comprise adult life. It also renders the measurement of continuity or change all the more problematic, in that even measures of the same construct may vary depending on the age of the subject, thereby creating uncertainty about the comparability of measures and measurement error at different points in time.

In addition, need our conception of change require it to be *systematic?* Or need it only involve the absence of continuity? A claim that change is the absence of continuity is far easier to make and illustrate than a claim meant to demonstrate and explain systematic change.

Finally, change can be conceptualized as a "turning point," as discussed earlier, in which life trajectories are altered or redirected in significant ways. Caspi (1998) states that "real people show real change over time, and the trajectories of real lives can be altered both by chance events and by planned interventions. However, these real changes are more likely to be discovered and explained *after* researchers account for error-caused changes and for changes that are little more than the absence of continuity" (p. 366, emphasis added). We might therefore ask ourselves several questions about change: Does the observed change result from chance? Is the change itself systematic? Is it systematically linked to individual or structural characteristics, or to interactions between them? Are there predictable individual differences in who responds, and how they respond, to events that have the potential to create change or become turning points? (Sampson & Laub, 1993).

Questions about the relative importance of continuity *versus* discontinuity or of stability *versus* change in human development seem silly and even dangerous when they are framed as if a choice must be made between one *or* the other. It is clear that "individuals are neither infinitely malleable, hostages of whatever winds of fortune they encounter, nor are they rigidly consistent, maintaining an identical psychological [or social, or biological] structure" as they move through life (Hinde, 1988, p. 367). Because our conception of the developing person is multi-dimensional, that conception must include the possibility of both continuity and stability on the one hand, and of discontinuity and change on the other. Little is also known about whether the processes and conditions that foster continuity or stability are merely the opposite of those that foster discontinuity or change (Caspi, 1998).

The term "continuity" is often used synonymously with "stability," just as the term "discontinuity" is often used synonymously with "change." (This is evidenced even in my discussion thus far.) Yet are these the same? Some scholars have suggested that they are different concepts and should not be used interchangeably. For example, Shanan (1991) argues that "stability" is often used in one of two ways, both of which "fit easily into the realm of traditional psychometrics" (p. P309). First, the term stability is used to indicate the absence of change in population averages over time; and second, it is used to indicate similarity in the position of an individual or group of individuals on a specific variable as indexed by $t_1(-):t_2$ correlation coefficients. Whereas stability implies the virtual absence of change, the term "continuity" allows some amount of change: It is typically "defined mathematically as change by infinitesimal increments (i.e., by steps so small as to be separately unnoticeable)" (p. P310). (However, aspects of development that are "recognizably similar" at two or more points in time may be a "far cry" from being "identical" at two or more points in time [Light, Grigsby, & Bligh, 1996, p. 168].) With respect to "continuity," Shanan suggests that we should not only concern ourselves with "identifying discrete bits of behavior" in this more narrow use of the term, but especially the "behavior recognized by others and interpreted by them as so similar to a previously perceived act, that intuitively the observer is compelled to view both acts as identical, . . . [therefore] representing a lawfulness different from that of stability . . . [in that it focuses on] continuous quality or meaning of any aspect of personality functioning or development" (p. P310). Shanan therefore seems to be arguing that concepts of stability and change are linked to "objective," quantitative, empirically-driven measures and definitions, whereas continuity and discontinuity are linked to "subjective," qualitative evaluations and definitions. Regardless of whether we agree with Shanan's distinctions, the meanings and uses of these concepts must nonetheless be clarified. Are continuity and stability, and discontinuity and change the same? How do we know these phenomena when we see them? How might they be defined, measured, and validated? Along these lines, there is an emerging literature on how more sophisticated, and more meaningful, measures of change might be developed in longitudinal research (e.g., see Collins, 1996; Collins & Horn, 1991; Engel & Reinecke, 1996; Gottman, 1995; Willett, 1989). These issues will be discussed next.

The Measurement of Change

Many critical questions about the measurement of change remain unanswered (or are at least not handled well in developmental research), and must be overcome for developmental science to advance. How shall change be conceptualized? What is it that changes? How much change occurs, and in what forms? Why does it occur? How shall change be represented, measured, analyzed, and interpreted? How much change is *meaningful* change? How much is "true" change, and how much is measurement error, random, or idiosyncratic? How much change is needed for "development" to occur? From what influences does development arise and where does development lead? Why do some individuals develop in certain ways and others not? Why do individuals change in different directions, and still others not at all? Why do individuals develop at difference paces? What specific conditions facilitate or prohibit these pathways? Is development a property of individuals, collectives, or both? Three recent volumes have begun to tackle some of these challenges and present recent advances and applications (Collins & Horn, 1991; Gottman, 1995; Engel & Reinecke, 1996; see also Willett, 1989). Many of these challenges are decades old, as evident in the early volumes by Harris (1963) and Bloom (1964) and in other classic papers (e.g., Bohrnstedt, 1969; Cronbach and Furby, 1970; Lord, 1956, 1958; McNemar, 1958).

Given that definitions of development, change, and the link between them are blurry at a conceptual level, it is easy to understand why they are difficult to handle at a practical level. Researchers differ substantially in the degree to which they emphasize the direction, rate and/or level of change; and the degree to which they emphasize qualitative and/or quantitative shifts. Developmental scientists are generally concerned with one of four different types of change: individual change, universal change, aggregate change, or differential change (von Eye, Kreppner, & Wessels, 1992).[15] As noted earlier, any discussion of change must have an anchor: It must be relative to something. Questions about *individual change* are focused on the way an individual changes in relation to a specific variable or set of variables. (As a subset of this category, we might also consider "directed change." Directed change is active change, directed at a specific set of goals, that the individual strives to achieve.) Questions about *universal change* relate to whether most or all individuals change in the same way. *Aggregate change* is average change for members of a population (and averages are, of course, swayed by the variance of a distribution, and especially by outliers in a distribution). Questions about *differential change* are aimed at whether smaller subgroups of a population exhibit different patterns of change.

Developmental scientists are (or ought to be) especially interested in studying *dynamic* latent variables rather than static ones. However, the procedures traditionally used to study differences in development between individuals (interindividual differences) are not appropriate for studying change within the individual

---

[15]These types of change are not mutually exclusive.

(intra-individual change). The study of intra-individual change requires its own set of methods that allow us to trace and model individual trajectories of growth, which are explicitly temporal. (The term "growth" in growth curve models is not used to indicate positive change. It is used to simply indicate the study of a larger trajectory, the curve of which may be characterized by periods of increase, decrease, and stability.) Several recent advances have been made along these lines, especially through latent growth modeling and hierarchical linear modeling. Intra-individual analyses of growth might then be more appropriately used to guide inter-individual analyses. In fact, Collins (1996, p. 38) argues that the "precise and valid measurement of intra-individual change" should be a "prerequisite to assessing inter-individual differences" in development. If new procedures are to fulfill their potential, the precision and validity of measurement must be improved (Collins, 1996). Of course, the entire study of quantitative change is dependent on the assumptions that dimensions of development can be easily quantified, that that quantity is part of a larger continuum, that that continuum does not change across age or over time, and that our measures are sensitive enough to accurately place individuals, and detect change, along that continuum. In many circumstances, these assumptions are unrealistic and unwarranted.

The most basic approach to measuring individual change between two time points is to calculate the *simple difference* or raw "gain" score, in which one observation is subtracted from another. The difference is then retained and analyzed as a dependent variable. Cronbach and Furby's (1970) influential article sparked decades of debate about the reliability of simple difference scores, and established widespread belief that these scores are unreliable. Collins (1996) and many others have since argued that "assuming there are no ceiling or floor effects, there is nothing inherently unsound about difference scores" (p. 39). Paradoxically, unreliability in difference scores need not imply that differences scores are imprecise measures of intra-individual change; difference scores can be both reliable and valid (see expositions by Collins, 1996; Willett, 1989).[16] Nonetheless, there are also means available for adjusting difference scores for measurement unreliability, normally at Time 1 only.

While simple difference scores can be very informative, researchers must also confront the problem that individuals have different starting points. We lose sight of this when we use simple difference scores. A strategy for dealing with this problem is to calculate a *residualized* gain score, in which the later score is regressed on the earlier score, therefore allowing the researcher to control for initial status. The residual is then saved and used as the dependent variable. However, relative to simple difference scores, residualized gain scores are very difficult to interpret because they essentially assign all individuals a common initial status (and this may be especially problematic from a theoretical or substantive standpoint). As with

---

[16]The fundamental problem of reliability relates more to the analysis of, and its dependence on, inter-individual differences. This makes it a "misleading criterion for evaluating the measurement qualities of an instrument, as it *confounds* the unrelated influences of group heterogeneity in growth-rate and measurement precision" (Willett, 1989, p. 595).

difference scores, there are also means available for adjusting residualized gain scores for measurement unreliability, and, again, normally at Time 1 only. For a comparison of the advantages and disadvantages of simple and residualized gain scores, and the circumstances under which one may be more appropriate than the other, see Allison (1990).

Both simple difference scores and residualized gain scores are based on only two time points. The task of understanding change becomes far more complicated when we wish to analyze change over three or more occasions (and move toward the description and modeling of longer-ranging growth trajectories), and when the functional form of these changes is neither clearly upward, clearly downward, nor constant. This is likely why most researchers choose to analyze change between two time points, or between various permutations of two time points, even when more than two data occasions are available.

To examine change in continuous variables over three or more data occasions, latent growth models are appropriate. Latent growth models can be analyzed with software packages that permit either covariance structure modeling or hierarchical linear modeling (e.g., Bryk & Raudenbush, 1987; Rogosa, Brandt, & Zimowski, 1982; Rogosa & Willett, 1985; Willett & Sayer, 1994; for a general overview, see Collins, 1996). As Collins (1996) notes, these models are conducted in two steps, with the first step analyzing the individual growth "curve" or trajectory in light of the functional form of a pre-specified model, and the second step using individually-fitted growth parameters as dependent variables. These procedures handle multiple assessments and non-linear growth functions, and allow us to estimate the correlation between the intercept and the slope and predict the intercept with other variables. This helps us deal with the problem of initial status, and permits us to model the relationship between change and initial status (and the reliability of these parameters). A common and problematic practice in the developmental literature is to "represent" group-level growth by charting group averages over time. Methods for analyzing individual-level growth trajectories consistently show that this practice produces a very misleading representation of the "overall tendency" in those trajectories.

I have thus far focused on quantitative change. Most conceptions of change view it in purely quantitative ways. Relative to ordinal, interval, or ratio-scale variables, much less is known about how to conceptualize and measure change with nominal-level data (though scholars have begun to explore strategies to do so using Configural Frequency Analysis, latent class or variable analysis, and log-linear modeling) (e.g., von Eye, Kreppner, & Wessels, 1992). Change may also be qualitative, in which an individual's "state" becomes distinctively different in structure or function. For example, these new forms may be driven by a process of accumulation or agglomeration of skills or capabilities, upon which the new structure or function may emerge; new structures or functions may also modify or transform themselves in non-cumulative ways (that is, without being dependent on cumulative processes) (Widaman, 1991). We must turn our theoretical and empirical attention to the possibilities of qualitative change, and critically examine what distinguishes quantitative from qualitative change (Widaman, 1991).

Three limited empirical procedures are most common for analyzing qualitative change in development (Schroeder, 1992). One approach is to simply examine the averages or frequencies of a developmental variable (or set of variables) between individuals in different age groups or to examine differences in the same group of individuals at different measurement points. When differences are discovered, they are assumed to indicate qualitatively different types of development. (Of course, when individuals in different age groups are compared at a single point in time, age and cohort differences cannot be disentangled; that is, age differences should not be misinterpreted as age changes.) In addition, when the averages of the same group of people at multiple points in time are found to differ, we cannot assume that the overall trends in change for the group also hold for each individual in the sample. A second approach to analyzing qualitative change in development is to use correlations, which can be misleading if they are used to justify "order-theoretical" relationships (that is, relationships that are composed of, or dependent upon, the sequencing of qualitatively different developmental states over time).[17] A third approach is to Guttman-scaling procedures, which do take "individual patterns into account, but cannot model within-person changes over time" (Schroeder, 1992, p. 4). But when we expect change over time to be quantitative *and* form of a series of sequential categorical stages (or to have some qualitative aspects), a fourth alternative is likely most appropriate and desirable: latent transition analysis. This method extends latent class analysis to longitudinal frameworks (e.g., Collins, 1996; Collins & Wugalter, 1992).

The tension between *statistical* significance and *substantive* significance deserves greater attention. Change that is statistically significant may not be substantively significant, just as change that is statistically insignificant may not be substantively significant. The over-reliance on testing for statistical significance is not a very useful "decision rule" for determining meaningful significance. As Alsaker (1992) also notes, the emphasis on statistical significance is flawed in two important ways. First, "null" results may be interesting and important from a developmental standpoint, but they are seldom reported in the literature (largely because of publishing norms). Null results may also lead to very fruitful hypotheses. As a result, we must better examine and explain the *absence* of change, especially when change might have been expected. More extensive probing of these situations may be as important as the study of change itself. Second, given the emphasis on large sample sizes (also because of publishing norms), even minor changes may reach statistical significance and result in "partly unfounded interpretations and expectations" (Alsaker, 1992, p. 92).

In one of the most important papers of the last decade, Rogosa (1988; updated in 1995) challenges many classic assumptions about longitudinal research and the analysis of change. Rogosa (1995, p. 6) effectively argues that the following nine points are *myths* about longitudinal research and the analysis of change:

---

[17]If we take an "order-theoretical approach" to qualitative shifts in development, two kinds of sequences become apparent: prerequisite and precursor sequences. *Prerequisite sequences* require that one developmental state be in place before a subsequent state can occur, while *precursor sequences* "merely represent the empirical order" in which states are, or are likely to be, experienced (Schroeder, 1992, p. 3).

1. Two observations a longitudinal study make.
2. The difference score is intrinsically unreliable and unfair.
3. You can determine from the correlation matrix for longitudinal data whether or not you are measuring the same thing over time.
4. The correlation between change and initial status is (a) negative, (b) zero, (c) positive, (d) all of the above.
5. You can't avoid regression toward the mean.
6. Residual change cures what ails the difference score.
7. Analyses of covariance matrices inform about change.
8. Stability coefficients estimate (a) the consistency over time of an individual, (b) the consistency over time of an average individual, (c) the consistency over time of individual differences, (d) none of the above, (e) some of the above.
9. Causal analyses support causal inferences about reciprocal effects.

Rogosa also effectively argues that, despite its popularity, structural equation modeling should generally be avoided in the analysis of longitudinal data and change, and that other analytic approaches are more useful. In addition, Rogosa provides advice on how "meager" two-point data might be analyzed (this is in line with his earlier motto, "Two waves are better than one, but not much"), and argues that problems associated with regression toward the mean should not serve as an impediment to assessing change.

Most thought on the challenges posed by change relates to change in *dependent* variables. There has been little discussion of change in relation to *independent* variables, and of conducting analyses in which change in independent variables is used to model change in dependent variables (change-on-change analyses). Cohen (1991) raises a problem related to this issue: the problem of the "premature covariate." In longitudinal investigations, we are often concerned with studying the effects of (a usually temporally prior) X on (a temporally latter) Y, and even with reciprocal mechanisms in which Y, in turn, produces effects on X; we may also be concerned with studying the effects of *changes* in X on *changes* in Y. In these circumstances, we would ideally like to match the interval of our design to the effect period; that is, we would like to match the design interval to the point at which X exerts its influence on Y, or to the "amount of time required for a change in X to produce a change in Y" (p. 19). In practice, however, these "effect periods" or "equilibrium periods" will rarely match the longitudinal interval, even when theory can help us specify these periods in advance. The problem of the premature covariate is created by the fact that the covariate itself is changing over time, and if it is not measured at the time at which its causal influence is exerted, it will not be as effective in partialling out its effects on the dependent variable. This makes our ideal design one with many repeated observations with short intervals between each observation. Yet as discussed earlier, this strategy is generally not possible in practice. Even if it were possible, we would likely be faced with high attrition and the problems it brings, and with assessments that may be "too reactive and often lead to a deterioration of the quality of responses, or even a psychological restructuring of the phenomena under investigation" (Cohen, 1991, p. 20). In addition, when the interval between observations is too short, we may capture only trivial intervening events and trivial change in our variables with which to estimate effects.

While traditional procedures for assessing the validity of measures are appropriate for *static* latent variables, these procedures may be inappropriate for *dynamic* latent variables (Collins, 1991, 1996), which are (or should be) of primary concern to developmental scientists. In addition, one cannot be certain that instruments sensitive to inter-individual variability will be sensitive to intra-individual variability, both of which are also (or should also be) of central importance to developmental scientists. With dynamic variables, our questions about validity must be revised to somehow incorporate change and assess the individual level. For example, consider *criterion validity*, in which a measure is considered valid if it correlates significantly with those criteria (a set of variables) it should logically correlate. In the case of *concurrent criterion validity*, in which the criteria are collected at the same time as the measure being validated, we must not only examine whether the variables correlate at their initial point, as we would normally do, but we must also examine whether the variables "track together" across multiple time points. In the case of *predictive criterion validity*, our measure at an earlier point in time must predict well the criteria at a subsequent time point; we are interested in the temporal lag between our measure and the criteria. As we move toward studying lives over sufficiently long periods of time, and as the time between our measurement points lengthens, predictive criterion validity will be more difficult to establish.

Similarly, with *construct validity*, we are interested in whether our measure of a larger theoretical construct can be used to predict a theory-based relationship to another construct. In the case of dynamic variables, our theory must make a change-over-time prediction, and our measure should be able to demonstrate or reflect this change. In addition, the multi-trait multi-method matrix, which is also often used to assess construct validity with static variables, will not only be difficult to assemble for multiple waves, but it may be wholly inappropriate for variables that are dynamic.

With *content validity*, we are especially interested in the degree to which the items in a measure tap the entire domain of interest. With dynamic variables, as with static variables, we are concerned about the range of items being measured. However, in the case of dynamic variables, we must concern ourselves with the questions of whether the items, and the range of items, adequately tap the domain of interest, tap them in the same way, or hold the same meanings over time (and whether we should even expect any of these to occur).

Where these questions are concerned, it would help to develop two exploratory procedures for use with longitudinal data and dynamic variables (Collins, 1991, 1996). One procedure, analogous to factor analysis, must help us identify and test the properties of higher-order dynamic constructs. The other procedure, analogous to cluster analysis, must help us identify groups of individuals with similar growth curves or stage sequences. At present, there are few strategies for analyzing multi-wave longitudinal data and dynamic variables in these ways.

In addition to the challenges that dynamic variables bring for validity, the very concept of "reliability" of measurement, and the standards we use to gauge it, may also be inappropriate for dynamic variables. If we expect people to change significantly on a dimension (or set of dimensions), we should not expect a measure used at one point to be reliable at another point, especially if the measure is used over a long period of time. The same operationalized measure may tap different constructs at different ages; in addition, the same construct may require different operationalized measures at different ages. For example, what seems a reliable and valid measure for children will not likely be a good measure for teens or adults; and even measures developed for adults may not be reliable over many decades of adult life. The same operationalized measure, and the items that comprise it, may also tap different constructs and hold different meanings at different points in historical time. These issues create serious difficulty for the estimation of the reliability of a variable or larger construct, which is necessary to demonstrate before examining change (otherwise, change observed may simply be measurement error). Herein lies the paradox: It is necessary to establish reliability before we examine change; yet change in the dimension of interest—the very thing we want to study—may render our measures unreliable. In addition, the interpretation of change scores is affected by whether (a) the same quality is, in fact, measured at both time points (if not, the meaning of the change score is questionable), and (b) the correlation between the same variable is high across time points (Bergman, 1993). If the same quality is, in fact, measured at both time points, one should expect the correlation between them to be very high; yet a high correlation will make the reliability of the change score psychometrically unreliable. This creates another paradox for the researcher.

CHAPTER
5

Challenges Posed by Place and Other Issues

This chapter begins by turning our attention to the challenges associated with understanding lives in place—that is, to questions of how social contexts affect human lives, and how we might better bring them into our research. The chapter then explores other strategies for analyzing lives, including variable- versus person-oriented approaches; general versus differential approaches; outcome- versus process-oriented approaches; approaches that emphasize the person, the environment or the link between them; formal versus naturalistic approaches; and comparative approaches. The final section comments on several other important issues that are emerging in the developmental literature—questions about the relative roles of social structure and human agency in shaping lives; the documentation and explanation of heterogeneity; and what constitutes "successful" development.

BRINGING CONTEXT IN: THEORETICAL AND METHODOLOGICAL ISSUES

Human lives must be understood in light of the many social spaces and interrelated systems in which they unfold—what Bronfenbrenner (1979) called the "ecology of human development." Yet despite the basic premise of "contextualized development," most theory and research does not specify well how social contexts shape individual development (see also Valsiner & Lawrence, 1997). Greater attention must be paid to the structural properties of those settings and the processes occurring within them (Levy, 1991). While developmental scientists have, in the past few decades, paid greater attention to social contexts, this attention has largely been focused on the development of children and adolescents (Lerner, 1995). Much of this attention has also focused on the relations between children and their parents, and on the bi-directional relations between the family and other social settings within which children and parents function (e.g., work, day care, educational, recreational settings in neighborhoods) (for examples, see Kreppner & Lerner, 1989).

In fact, one of Dannefer's (1984) criticisms of research in developmental psychology can be applied to most developmental research: "To state that the environment is important, to mention it often, and to include in it definitional statements does not together mean that research will be designed, nor findings interpreted, in a way that apprehends social structure as a constitutive force in development, and that views the social environment as more than a setting that facilitates maturational unfolding" (p. 847). At the same time, it is difficult to both conceptualize and measure social environments, not only in terms of their structural characteristics, but especially in terms of the processes occurring within them. In the end, these difficulties prevent us from understanding how and why variations in social environments are differentially linked to developmental outcomes. The lack of attention to these issues is also a result of the fact that we have neither a comprehensive system of concepts nor a "scientific language" for dealing with the environment (Magnusson, 1985).

The meanings of context and their relation to human development must therefore be clarified. Four separate and generally unrecognized approaches to context exist in developmental science (Dannefer, 1992). The first approach is to consider context *functionally unimportant* or *analytically trivial* in bringing about developmental outcomes. This view is taken, for example, by organismic theorists who posit a universal and fixed sequence of age-bound stages of human development that transcend both time and place. This view is also taken by many developmental psychologists who emphasize the shared, predictable "ontogenetic" or "age-graded" changes experienced by the human organism.

The second approach is that context is *powerful but unorganized*. That is, context may be important, but its effects are random and unpredictable. Because contextual forces cannot be organized or ordered, they are viewed as being impossible to study scientifically. This view of context is prevalent among developmental psychologists and biologists, both groups of which are naturally more focused on the developmental processes occurring *within* the organism than those occurring outside of it. While these scholars may nod to the fact that interactions between the individual and the environment may be important for development, the assumption is made that environmental forces, in all their complexity, boldly resist theory and research. The "non-normative" influences in Baltes' framework are in line with this view, in that they have a significant impact on individual development but are also considered random and unpredictable.

The third approach is to consider context *organized but passive*, constituting a *congeneries* (or "pile") of influences that can be identified but are exogenous and static. These "ordering principles" are presumably captured by many of the independent and control variables with which developmentalists routinely analyze their data (e.g., "social location" variables). Another good example of this approach is the "master contextual variable" in much work on the life course: cohort. In Baltes' framework, cohort is the only "contextual" variable that is assumed to have an organized, orderly, independent effect on development.

The fourth and final approach is to consider context as a set of *dynamically* or *systematically organized* processes that have significant effects on developmental outcomes. This perspective is the "standard view of context from a sociological perspective, but one that has received only limited attention in relation to aging and human development" (Dannefer, 1992, p. 91). While there have been important attempts to bring context into developmental research in a more systematic way, these attempts typically do not identify social dynamics beyond what can be reduced to individual-level phenomena. These views use context as a descriptive typology rather than treat it as an active system. Because the "dynamic aspects of the environment remain unrecognized and unacknowledged," context remains a *congeneries* (as in the third view of context). These advances have pushed us to consider the link between ecology and the person, but they have not provided a "framework for understanding interaction as a systematic *process* in which human action and integration are integrally embedded" (Dannefer, 1992, p. 90; emphasis added). As discussed earlier, several ecological frameworks do emphasize, at least *heuristically,* the dynamic and bi-directional nature of relationships between people and their environments, and that environments exist at different levels that are not only *interrelated* but themselves *interact* and *change* over time. At the same time, too strong an emphasis on contextual influences or on variability poses a serious threat to classic views of development, which posit the universal movement of individuals through a fixed, irreversible, linear sequence of qualitatively different stages toward some ultimate end state. Some critics even suggest that too great an emphasis on context or variability comes with the potential to render *any* concept of development useless, even though most "theories of development do believe that context, or some locus of influence rather obviously related to 'context' (e.g., environment or experience), is related intimately to development" (Lerner 1985, pp. 157-158). This point serves as an important reminder that we often leave implicit (perhaps because we are unclear about) our definition of "development," the shapes and forms it takes, and the processes through which it occurs.[1]

According to the fourth view, then, context is an explicitly structured and interactive set of relationships and processes that significantly shape development. Social systems must, by definition, be characterized by a relatively stable set of dynamics that become institutionalized and therefore endure over time (Dannefer, 1992). This assumption is problematic in that many, if not most, aspects of social contexts likely change. And it is change that provides the most interesting nexus for studying human development, and particularly for studying the adaptability and plasticity of the human organism. Is the notion of a relatively stable set of dynamics therefore incompatible with the notion that the environment is ever-changing? The assumption that these dynamics become "institutionalized" also creates the impression that they become formal and explicit, yet they need not be: Some dynamics may be unintended, unrecognized, and implicit. These dynamics are not well-captured by

---

[1] Our approaches to the concept of "development" must become more explicit. We might even move beyond the restrictive definitions of individual scholars and create a standard definition for developmental science at large. At the very least, this will require us to set minimum criteria for defining "development" (and other common concepts) within and across disciplines (Alsaker, 1992; see also Bronfenbrenner, 1988).

general context variables, such as their structural characteristics, which are most easily measured. In addition, any conception of the environment as a social system must also capture the ways in which its subsystems interact. This means that we must not study single social contexts as isolated entities, as we generally do, but that we must study multiple contexts, and study them as interdependent and interactive entities.

The most intriguing part of this fourth view of context is that it forces us to consider the ways in which the environment is not only systematically organized, but also operates on its own accord through social processes that are "largely independent of human volition" (Dannefer & Perlmutter, 1990, p. 120). As such, this view requires us to move well beyond simple (and prevalent) views of the environment as "amorphous and unclearly differentiated." It also emphasizes the need to understand the ways in which differential developmental patterns are produced by environmental processes.

The first three views of context, abound in the literature, neither raise nor facilitate important questions about the linkages between contexts and development (though each increasingly acknowledges the importance of this linkage); only the last view adequately does so. And while the fourth view of context may often be advocated, particularly among sociologists, seldom does our theory or research offer an explicit formulation of the important structural characteristics of contexts and the processes operating within them, and the mechanisms through which these characteristics and processes actually shape individual development.

However, as noted elsewhere in this chapter, research on adolescent development has explored person-context linkages more than research on any other period of life. Here, discussions of "successful" development have been tied to discussions about what constitutes "good" (or "bad") school, family, neighborhood, and peer group contexts (Cook, Degirmencloglu, Phillips, Settersten, & Shagle, forthcoming; Crockett & Crouter, 1995; Furstenberg, Eccles, Elder, Cook, & Sameroff, 1999; Jackson & Rodriguez-Tomé, 1994; Jessor, 1993; Silbereisen & Todt, 1993; Winegar & Valsiner, 1992). While these discussions are based on the questionable assumptions that "good" contexts can be explicated and measured, and that these contexts are uniformly good for all adolescents, they have nonetheless pushed scholars to consider the aspects of context that foster development.[2]

For example, a good *school* environment might be characterized by an academic environment that promotes learning through better curricula, homework, and professional development; school climates that are characterized by adults who care about children, children who respect each other, and curriculum materials that value different types of achievement and different social groups; decentralized and cooperative governance structures; and high parent involvement in schools. A good *family* environment might be characterized by parenting styles that emphasize

---

[2] The task of explicating and measuring the multidimensional nature of context, and of determining what constitutes a "good" environment, is accompanied by a set of conceptual and analytic challenges identical to those for "successful" development (outlined elsewhere in this chapter).

warmth, parental control, and the promotion of autonomy. Also relevant might be the ways in which a family supports the school and various cultural activities, the degree to which a child relies on family members for social support, and the kinds of financial and other stresses the family is or is not under. A good *neighborhood* environment might be characterized by social cohesion, social control, value consistency, few problems around drugs and crime, high levels of organizational resources, high levels of civic participation, high stability of residents, and high satisfaction with the neighborhood in general. A good *peer group* environment, at least from the standpoint of most parents and of public policy, might be characterized by friends who are involved in more wholesome activities, envision conventional futures for themselves, avoid negative activities (e.g., crime, sex, drugs), are mutually supportive, and are stable in composition (including some who are deemed as "close" friends and not many who are older). The emerging portrait of a good peer group seems less well-articulated than that emerging for schools, neighborhood, and even families.

Contexts, like individuals, are changing, multidimensional, interactive, and interdependent. They must be studied as such. In addition, if the proposition of reciprocity is taken seriously, then changes in context may bring about changes in the individual, just as changes in the individual may bring about changes in the context (a few hypotheses related to the former proposition will be explored shortly). Therefore, the very problems encountered in studying individual lives within a temporal framework can be extended to the environments in which lives are lived. As we attempt to map changing individual lives onto a changing context, or, still harder, *multiple* contexts, and try to examine interactions across these levels, our theoretical and analytic work becomes immensely complicated.[3] These are the most significant problems in advancing the fourth view of contexts. However, our ability to analyze contexts has improved in recent years, particularly through advances in multi-level modeling and social network analysis.

It is also important to note that while people may be systematically sorted into, or excluded from, specific contexts (through processes of social allocation), they may also *self-select* themselves into specific contexts. George (1996a, p. 252) argues that one aspect of this self-selection is that people choose contexts that are "compatible with their subjective perceptions and desires—and, by doing so, are happier and healthier than they would be otherwise" (p. 252). George's view, which heavily emphasizes the role of individual choice in determining the environments in which they find themselves, suggests that "in the absence of rare and highly powerful external forces," people experience the kind of lives they desire, which also means that lives are bound to be very heterogeneous (p. 252). As a result, the important issue, for George, is whether the environments people choose allow them to "implement their behavioral choices." This view, however, de-emphasizes the facts that

---

[3] Very little theory or empirical research has addressed the link between changing environments *and* changing individuals. In fact, I am aware of only one other paper that explores some of the analytic challenges posed by this link (Kindermann & Skinner, 1992).

(a) many people often cannot select environments well or, still worse, cannot control these environmental assignments; (b) many people do not have a full range of options open to them; (c) early life experiences (whether by choice or otherwise) may severely restrict later options; and (d) what happens to an individual is often not the result of one's own doing, but is instead the result of something that happens in the lives of significant others. George's argument is interesting because it suggests that when people have experiences that they choose, they are also likely to experience positive subjective well-being. Yet this overlooks the fact that a person may not be happy, or at least not equally happy, with all of their choices. In addition, it overlooks the fact that individuals may be happy with their choices but nonetheless have low subjective well-being for other reasons, including factors over which they have had no control. It is also true that individuals are encouraged or discouraged along certain pathways, or into or out of certain social contexts, via socialization processes. This seems especially true during childhood, as parents, relatives, teachers, peer groups, neighborhoods, and society send messages to children about what they should be working on, and working toward, in their lives. Along these lines, little is known about the conditions under which adult socialization experiences may override the effects of childhood socialization (George, 1996a).

In what directions might research on social contexts move to advance developmental science? We must better conceptualize the multi-dimensional and interactive nature of contexts and their influences on individuals. We must move toward more explanatory models of context, and toward the processes that occur within contexts (rather than descriptive models and models of "passive exposure" [Wohlwill, 1983], which focus more on whether individuals have been exposed to certain features of the environment). We must pay more attention to the issue of human agency within contexts (rather than conceptualizing environments deterministic all-powerful social forces that impose on lives, what Wohlwill [1983] calls "monolithic entities"). Along these lines, we must also learn about individuals' perceptions of their environments, and how these perceptions shape their actions, reactions, and interactions in their environments. This draws attention to the possibility of comparing the environment as it actually is with the environment "as it is perceived, constructed, or represented" in the minds of individuals. (Of course, one might raise the question of whether an "objective" reality can ever really exist, at least apart from a perceived one. Yet sociological research on educational institutions and work organizations, for example, is replete with examples of how certain aspects of these environments are often kept "hidden" from many of the individuals in those settings, and how environments are constructed and manipulated to foster or maintain images that run counter to the reality that exists below the surface.)[4] We might also explore the characteristics and processes needed to create "optimal" environments, given that environments serve as both a source of information and stimulation; they not only shape individuals but are actively and purposefully created *by* individuals (Magnusson &

---

[4] This also brings to mind Goffman's (1959) "dramaturgical" ideas about "front-stage" and "back-stage" behavior.

Stattin, 1998). Each of these points to the need to better examine the *unique, reciprocal,* and *dynamic* nature of relationships between individuals and their environments over time (see also Kindermann & Skinner, 1992).

In addition, the ways in which contexts are conceptualized and believed to have an effect on development will hinge on the aspects of development being examined. As Kindermann and Skinner (1992) point out, "the dimensions, components, and levels of the environment that are of interest will vary depending on the target phenomenon" under study (p. 160). Yet it is not enough to explicate relevant aspects of context. It is important to specify how and why these aspects of context have a significant connection to the phenomenon under study. This is true not only of *spatially* proximal environments, and of *temporally* proximal influences, but especially of environments and influences that are more *distal* in space and time. We should also not assume that distal environments and processes are less significant than proximal ones (though distal environments and processes do pose bigger theoretical and analytic challenges).

It is also important to consider whether the "target phenomenon" of interest is especially open to the influence of the environment at particular points in time, whether (and how) certain contexts are particularly influential at different points in life, and whether (and how) the strength of their effects on target phenomena change for individuals over time. If possible, we should therefore try to identify a "developmental frame" within which environmental factors, and particular types of environmental factors, play a clear role in shaping development (Kindermann & Skinner, 1992, p. 160). Once identified, the points of measurement in a study should be timed appropriately to best capture those influences. However, for many phenomena these windows may not be known or clear, or they may vary across individuals.

Kindermann and Skinner (1992) point out that the concept of a "developmental frame" for studying person-environment linkages is, at first glance, similar to the idea of a "critical" period. The concept of a critical period captures the idea that there are important junctures at which person-environment interactions are particularly powerful (e.g., if the individual is at an age deemed to be sensitive, she or he may be especially susceptible to environmental stimulation or deprivation, which in turn may leave a lasting impact on the individual if either occurs). A "critical period" implies that the "window" for studying certain aspects of development is open only for a certain amount of time and then closes permanently. The consequences of the critical period are assumed to change the individual in significant, permanent, and unchangeable ways. In contrast, a "developmental frame" for studying person-environment linkages can reoccur, and its effects may be even minor, temporary, and modifiable. It would also seem important to not only consider *when* and *how* critical periods or developmental frames are important, but also *for whom* they are important and how they may differ between individuals and groups.

In terms of life periods, most research on the effects of social context has focused on development during childhood and adolescence. Relatively little work has systematically explored the effects of social contexts, past or present, on development during periods of *adult life* (beyond general experiences related to work and family, which is different than examining the effects of specific configurations of context and the processes occurring within them). Interestingly, Clausen (1995) suggests that the number and diversity of settings in which adults can participate, without damaging their major responsibilities, is limited. And while a variety of roles in adulthood may be enriching (as it is in childhood), too diverse a variety of roles may lead to "the attenuation of one's sense of identity" (p. 369). This suggests that the number and diversity of social contexts in which individuals exist *changes* as individuals move through life, and that contexts have different effects on individuals depending on the individual's age or life period. In addition, the likelihood of experiencing disparity between contexts would also seem to change as individuals move through life. For example, upwardly mobile adults from working class or poor families experience a chasm, or even a clash, between the social worlds in which they live and those from whence they came. To move forward, they may distance themselves from, and even hide, their origins. Similarly, many individuals, especially women, experience significant tensions as they move between, and attempt to meet often contradictory role expectations in, work and family settings. Issues such as these are underexplored in scholarship on the life course.

As I noted earlier, very little theory or research has addressed the link between changing environments *and* changing individuals. The standard, and most prevalent, model for incorporating context is what Kindermann and Skinner call the *launch model*. This model completely ignores contextual change. Instead, it incorporates the distribution of a context variable (or set of variables) at an earlier point in time (T1), and uses the context variable as a predictor of a later developmental outcome (T2). If the dimensions of context are, in fact, changing, these changes are assumed to be irrelevant to the outcome of concern (which may not be a warranted assumption). The term "launch" is used to describe this model because the temporally prior contextual variable is viewed as "catapulting" into motion a set of forces that determine the later outcome.

Another model, the *developmental transition model,* views individuals as experiencing "systematic changes in environments, but not because environments themselves are changing, but because people are moving across age-graded contexts" (p. 169). As individuals move through life, they move through a sequence of (often) age-graded settings. For example, as children grow older, they move in and out of classrooms and schools; young adults transition from school settings into the workplace, leave home and start their own families; older adults transition out of the workplace and into retirement, or out of their homes and into other residential institutional settings. Again, the key point here is that while *individuals* move between different contexts as they move through life, the *contexts themselves* are not necessarily viewed as changing. As noted, some contexts are "culturally designed" or age-graded social institutions, while other contexts are self-selected.

As alternatives to the launch and developmental transition models, in which changes in context are absent, three models are proposed for relating changes in context to changes in individuals. The weather model of co-development, the developmental co-adaptation model, and the developmental attunement model. The *weather model of co-development* (see Figure 1) considers change in the environment that is not initiated by the individual but that has an important effect on changes in her or

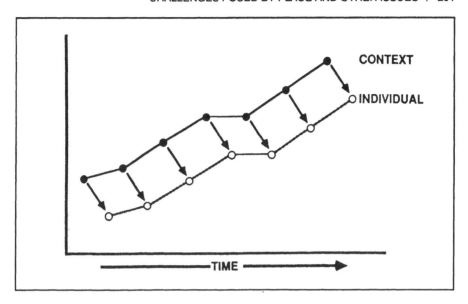

Figure 1. The study of individual-context co-development with the "weather model": Individual development influenced by contextual change.
Source: Kindermann, T. A., & Skinner, E. A. (1992). Modeling environmental development: Individual and contextual trajectories. In J. B. Asendorpf & J. Valsiner (Eds.), *Stability and change in development: A study of methodological reasoning*. Newbury Park, CA: Sage Publications. p. 173.

his developmental pathway. As a result, the figure implies a *lagged effect* between environmental change and individual change, with environmental change being temporally prior. The effect also seems focused on the relationship between the level of the contextual dimension(s) and the subsequent level of the developmental dimension(s) rather than the rates of change.

The *developmental co-adaptation model* (see Figure 2) focuses on the ways in which change in the environment and change in the person shape each other (there is reciprocal interaction between them). However, the model actually seems to emphasize the *contemporaneous* levels of the dimension(s) of context and the dimension(s) of individual development, rather than either the level or rate changes between the prior and current points (in either the environment or the individual) or the interaction of level or rate changes between the environment and the person.

Finally, the *developmental attunement* model (see Figure 3) also focuses on the reciprocal interaction between change at both levels, but "changes in the environment are calibrated to the development of the individual" (p. 172). Kindermann and Skinner describe attunement models as models in which "the development of the individual is an agenda item for the context" (p. 178). That is, environmental changes are instrumental in that they are designed around an individual's level of development. Relative to the prior figure (Figure 2), Figure 3 does, in fact, illustrate

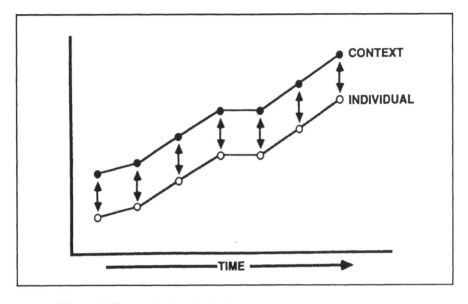

Figure 2. The study of individual-context co-development within the "developmental co-adaptational model": Reciprocal relations between developing persons and changing environments.
Source: Kindermann, T. A., & Skinner, E. A. (1992). Modeling environmental development: Individual and contextual trajectories. In J. B. Asendorpf & J. Valsiner (Eds.), *Stability and change in development: A study of methodological reasoning.* Newbury Park, CA: Sage Publications. p. 173.

reciprocal interactions between the environment and the person, and a clear, alternating pattern between the level of individual development shaping the level of context, which in turn shapes the next point of individual development. These effects are again portrayed as lagged, and are focused more on changes in level rather than on the changes in rate.

While the models that Kindermann and Skinner propose are neither free of problems nor entirely clear (for other commentaries, see van Aken, 1992; Rossetti-Ferreira & de Oliveira, 1992), developmental scientists must turn their attention to the dynamic nature of social contexts; this is an important area in which theoretical and empirical advances are desperately needed. As Kindermann and Skinner point out, to assume that contexts do not change is just as dangerous as assuming that individuals do not change. By ignoring the dynamic nature of contexts, we (a) lose sight of the ways in which individuals develop in the process of adapting to the changing demands of the social contexts around; (b) downplay the ways in which individuals themselves actively shape and initiate change in these contexts; and (c) underestimate the degree to which contexts themselves respond to the developmental levels and pace of the individuals in those contexts.

So while it is clear that an appreciation of context is crucial for understanding human development, few scholars have managed to conceptualize or measure

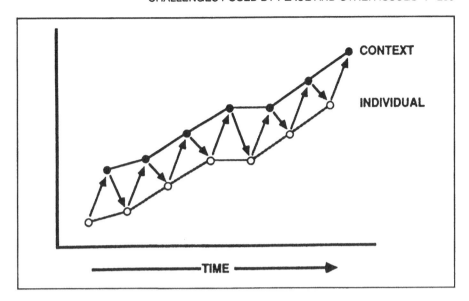

Figure 3. The study of individual-context co-development within the "attunement model": Reciprocal exchanges between developing persons and changing environments within a developmental agenda.
Source: Kindermann, T. A., & Skinner, E. A. (1992). Modeling environmental development: Individual and contextual trajectories. In J. B. Asendorpf & J. Valsiner (Eds.), *Stability and change in development: A study of methodological reasoning.* Newbury Park, CA: Sage Publications. p. 173.

context, even in static ways, adequately in their theories or applications. As a result, context-related questions have remained at the periphery of developmental research. This is a serious problem in that *we take the "life" out of the "life course" when we neglect or control context* (this latter criticism applies to many of the variables for which we routinely control, not only those related to context). How can we better attend to, rather than do away with, social context?

To a large extent, this is dependent on overcoming the methodological barriers associated with studying person-environmental relations. More appropriate methods must be devised for examining these relations by either (a) extending or generalizing the traditional methods used to study non-interactive phenomena, or (b) creating new methods based on alternative epistemological and methodological assumptions (Thorngate, 1995). The first solution is inadequate because the kind of data required of traditional methods (e.g., counts or measures of variables) and the kinds of techniques used to analyze them (e.g., aggregation across people or environments) are inappropriate for *interactive* phenomena or are misleading summaries of the nature of, and changes in, *reciprocal* influences.

To develop alternative methods for studying person-environment relations, some of our epistemological and methodological assumptions must change (Thorngate, 1995). First, we must seek good accounts of *specific* relations between people and their environments. We should do this *not* with our immediate sights set on generalization, but with genuine interest in learning about these specific relations in and of themselves. To do so, we must reduce our concerns (perhaps obsessions) about random sampling, the manipulation of variables, and statistical significance, and instead move more slowly toward generalization.

Second, we must let go of the common belief that a single and best account exists for the phenomena that interest us, and of the desire to eliminate all but a single account. It is "certainly desirable to devise methods for separating the good accounts from the bad ones, and for combining those that say the same thing. At the same time, there is no reason to believe that all the good accounts will be related, and that they will eventually fit together to show us the Big Picture" (Thorngate, 1995, p. 42).

Third, we must change the way we think about the nature and amount of data, letting go of the idea that our work will be more scientifically valid and important if we use bigger samples and make it as quantitative as possible. In stressing quantity over quality we have committed an error of "misplaced precision." That is,

> [A] bad idea cannot be improved through complex measurement models or statistical manipulation. In addition, most ideas can be tested without resorting to fancy empirical or statistical procedures . . . In our rush to SPSS we usually overlook the power of *careful observation, compulsive description,* and *skeptical thinking*. These are three good habits, and we would benefit from acquiring them, especially if we choose to explain phenomena as resistant to numerical summary as person-environment interactions (Thorngate, 1995, p. 42, emphasis added).

Finally, we must realize that "descriptions and explanations are not only ends of science; they are also means of communication" (Thorngate, 1995, p. 42). Both description and explanation can take a wide range of forms. At the very least, we must be more considerate of our audiences. For whom, and for what purposes, do we conduct our research? We should find clearer, simpler, and more interesting ways to communicate than those means that our disciplines, and the scientific enterprise at large, now advocate. We might all heed this advice, regardless of discipline, method, or area of inquiry. Developmental science, and the behavioral and social sciences more generally, will benefit tremendously from movement in these directions, particularly if that movement advances our knowledge about, and methods for studying, person-environment relations.

In the end, one thing is certain: We cannot simply deal with context by simply dismissing it as "error variance" or "background noise," nor can we simply "control" for it with distal "background variables." We fail to take context seriously if it affects neither the framing of our questions nor the expectations or interpretation of our findings (Modell, 1996).

Does Environmental Change Create Individual Change? Competing Hypotheses

Recent work by Caspi and Moffitt (1993) offers a challenge to the traditional hypothesis that periods of change in the social environment are likely to bring about, or bring the potential for, change in the individual. Instead, they suggest that *"characterological continuity* is most likely to emerge during periods of *social discontinuity"* (p. 247). Their perspective is paradoxical because most behavioral and personality theory assumes the opposite: It assumes that individuals may be inclined to develop *novel* behavioral responses to the environment when faced with unfamiliar circumstances. Certain circumstances may, in fact, make novel responses more likely, especially where previous responses are actively discouraged or where there is clear information about how to behave adaptively. These circumstances, however, seem few and far between. Instead, individuals may be more often confronted with new situations in which a response is demanded but where there is no information about how to behave adaptively. These conditions favor continuity over change in that individuals may simply attempt to assimilate the new conditions into already-existing cognitive and action frameworks rather than revise or completely reconstruct these frameworks. Caspi and Moffitt argue that when individuals experience significant disruptions in their "total life space," individual differences are magnified. Like Elder and Caspi's (1990) accentuation principle, Caspi and Moffitt's hypothesis is that periods of social disturbance may increase interindividual variability *not* because it causes differential change in individuals, but because it accentuates already-existing and stable personality characteristics. In an effort to transform their experiences in uncertain environments into "familiar, clear, and expectable encounters," individuals search for and choose responses that "work, . . . work quickly, and . . . require little energy" (pp. 249-250).

The basic methodological implication of Caspi and Moffitt's thesis is that individual differences should be assessed during times of transition because they pose novel, ambiguous, and unpredictable situations to which individuals must respond. This implication parallels a problem that plagues longitudinal research: the problem of the appropriate intervals at which to make observations (the spacing of measurement points, as described earlier). This problem is also exacerbated by the fact that the behavioral manifestation(s) of a personality trait or disposition probably change over time but may nonetheless be *consistent* with earlier ones. In addition, the "continuities of personality are [often] expressed not through the constancy of behavior across time and circumstance but through the ways persons characteristically modify their changing contexts as a function of their behavior" (Caspi & Moffitt, 1993, p. 258). Therefore, if what is most important is the consistency with which individuals confront new situations, we should target our assessments in that direction (that is, to examine the ways in which individuals respond to changing situations). These approaches require us to search for characterological and behavioral continuity amidst a background of environmental or social change. Approaches in line with this thesis probably do not need to be as concerned with the time interval between observations as with the degree of similarity between "environmental demands" at different measurement occasions. It is this similarity that will largely determine the magnitude of the stability coefficient.

In addition, this thesis is in line with another observation in the literature: that traits better predict behavior "in situations in which the individual's *maximal* performance is assessed than in situations in which the individual's *typical* performance is assessed" (Caspi & Moffitt, 1993, p. 259; emphasis added). That is, we should set out to examine what individuals are capable of doing in response to a new challenge rather than focus on what they generally do. (This is also in line with Baltes' "testing-the-limits" strategy for tapping an individual's developmental capacity.)

It is also clear that not all life transitions are created equally: Some pose more turbulence than others. Transitions that are "highly ritualized" and accompanied by "rites of passage" are not as likely to accentuate individual differences, given that such transitions, by definition, are not only expected but are accompanied by social rituals that make them less stressful and demanding. Methodologically, this also creates problems in that the very transitions that are easiest to capture and study, especially with any prevalence in a sample, are those transitions that are "normal and expectable," to use Neugarten's (1969) phrase.

As a result, Caspi and Moffitt argue that three crucial aspects of situations facilitate the observation of characterological continuity: ambiguity, uncertainty, and, especially, novelty. Yet as Dodge (1993) points out, too strong an emphasis on the novelty of a situation implies that personality differences vanish upon repeated assessments in a particular context, which need not be true. Surely, a situation can be problematic without being novel. The line between ambiguous and uncertain also seems hard to draw. In addition to these aspects, Caspi and Moffitt also refer to "threatening," "arousing," "stressful," "negative," and "complex," situations, as well as those that are "filled with information overload," "strong situations," and "discontinuous with previous experience" (Dodge, 1993). What, then, are the most important characteristics of contexts that reveal individual differences? In addition to this question and the question of *"when* individual differences matter," we must also turn our attention to questions of *how* and *why*. Where the latter two questions are concerned, we might begin by better exploring how and why individual differences interact with different environmental contexts to produce different outcomes (Dodge, 1993). Despite these limitations, Caspi and Moffitt's thesis turns our attention to the importance of context, especially changing and unstable contexts, in an effort to discern aspects of the stable or "true" self. In addition, this thesis turns our attention to the study of life-course transitions as an important window for examining personality.

Like Caspi and Moffit, Dannefer (1993) also challenges conventional wisdom that the effects of the environment on the development of individual differences are most relevant during periods of social change. But Dannefer argues the inverse of Caspi and Moffit's proposition, suggesting that the influence of the environment is best viewed *not* during periods of social change, but instead during periods of *environmental stability*.

Taken together, these two stimulating propositions offer exciting avenues for future theory and research. As Dannefer (1993) points out, these propositions force us to realize that "an adequate account of increasing inter-individual differences . . . will require consideration of *socially* generated differentiation that occurs during periods of environmental stability, as well as *individually* generated accentuation permitted by social discontinuity" (p. 282, emphasis added). These propositions therefore require us to more systematically attend to "(a) social-structural sources of individual differentiation that are part of the individual's immediate context and (b) the powerful role of early experience (as distinct from genetic predispositions) in shaping stabile individual characteristics" (p. 282).

Individuals, Contexts, and "Risk"

Implicit in many "social address," "personal attribute," or "social niche" models of human development (which will be discussed at greater length later in this chapter) is the notion that certain individual and contextual statuses, especially certain *combinations* of individual and contextual statuses, come with different types and degrees of developmental "risk." This makes some locations more or less favorable than others (e.g., a child in a family with two or more children that is headed by a single mother with low income or little education; a young adult Black male in an impoverished neighborhood).

Some have viewed the "at-risk" label as a "wolf in sheep's clothing" to use Tyack's (1989) phrase. These authors charge the "at-risk" label as being "implicitly racist, classist, sexist, and ableist, a 1990s version of the cultural deficit model which locates problems or 'pathologies' in individuals, families, and communities rather than in institutional structures that create and maintain inequality" (Swadener & Lubeck, 1995, p. 3) (for a discussion aimed at deconstructing the "at-risk" label, see Swadener, 1995). Instead, these critics suggest that we adopt an alternative label— "at promise"—to acknowledge the fact that all individuals face significant challenges in their lives, many of which may be overcome. This seems an inadequate solution to the problem, and may even worsen it. While the "at-risk" label may be damning, the "at promise" label may be overly idealistic. And its idealism may have a damaging unintended effect: With its emphasis on possibilities and promises, this label may place even greater blame on individuals who do not, or cannot, overcome difficult circumstances, and whose chances might have been furthered by policies and programs designed to assist them. The developmental opportunities of individuals are, *in reality,* limited by social processes that create and maintain inequalities. Herein lies the paradox: To define groups of people as "at-risk" can be damaging in the ways noted above; yet it is clear that policies and programs must, for practical reasons, be targeted toward clearly defined groups of people. To change the label from "at risk" to "at promise" serves only to change the wolf's clothing rather than expose him. The *real* challenge lies in eliminating the social processes that create and maintain inequalities. Until then, we are confronted with the problem of finding sophisticated but convenient ways of targeting groups of people in need of assistance without basing those groups on superficial, ascriptive characteristics. This discussion also serves as a reminder that interventions aimed at improving human development and welfare can have both intended *and* unintended consequences (Lerner, 1985). For an overview of issues related to intervention in human development, see Rothman and Thomas (1994), and for an overview of issues related to the evaluation of such interventions, see Chelimsky and Shadish (1997).

Significant attention has been devoted to identifying the factors that place individuals "at-risk" for a variety of negative developmental experiences or "disordered behaviors" (especially during childhood and adolescence). To do this, we must first have a solid conception of what constitutes "normative" development as a benchmark against which to measure deviations (Garmenzy, 1993a). Apart from the fact that "normative" can be conceptualized in several different ways (see Chapter 2), any trend toward the individualization of life patterns (see Chapter 1) makes the definition of "normative" increasingly difficult. This also makes clear definitions of "successful" or "optimal" development more difficult, given that these definitions might also serve as standards against which to measure "risk."

As we search for factors that distinguish those who have negative developmental outcomes from those who do not, it is often *not* that their prior experiences, or risk factors themselves, differ greatly, but that the ways in which individuals respond to stressors differ (Garmenzy, 1993a). Adaptable responses may temper would-be risk factors. This has led to the concept of "resilience" or "stress-resistance," in which functional behavior is either maintained or soon recovered in the face of major stressors and adversity. It is not that resilient individuals are invulnerable to stressors. Instead, it is that certain processes (internal, external, or both) allow the individual to maintain or restore a prior level of functioning during or after a taxing period.[5] Similarly, Rutter (1993) suggests that the very factors that influence "normal" development may also influence "abnormal" development; for example, abnormal developmental processes may simply be distortions or exaggerations of normal developmental processes. This is a good example of how the *maintenance* of a level of functioning, particularly during a period of turbulence, might also be considered "development" (though most conceptions of development would not include this). In this case, an individual does not exhibit positive change along a pathway, but positive developmental processes nonetheless allow the person to hold steady rather than fall.

The field of epidemiology has greatly increased our inventory of risk factors, though this has not necessarily improved our understanding of the processes and mechanisms through which risk factors bring about negative outcomes. The catalog of risk factors examined in the literature is diverse and includes variables related to genetic, biological, psychological, social, and economic realms. However, the risk factors most often examined are those variables we often consider "background" or "demographic" characteristics (especially race, sex, age, socioeconomic status, or some combination thereof). As a result, most risk factors are anchored purely in individual characteristics (and often ascriptive characteristics), and they seldom tap aspects of the environment that may also serve to place individuals at risk. In practice, because risk-related research is generally aimed at populations, it assumes that individuals who possess a risk factor (or set of factors) are at equal risk.

---

[5] How are vulnerability and resilience related? Is one a "protective" factor and the other a "risk" factor? Are they opposite sides of the same coin? One perspective, offered by Garmenzy (1993b), is that *vulnerability* "represents a heightened probability for maldevelopment ostensibly because of the presence of a single or of multiple risk factors" (p. 379). While vulnerability often "provides a singular emphasis on risk elements, *resilience* is defined by the "presence of any or many of these self-same risk factors, but the accompanying adaptive outcomes are now presumed to be a function of evident, or unidentified, positive elements within the individual and external environments that serve a protective function" (p. 379).

Again, this neglects not only the individuals larger constellation of personal characteristics, but also those characteristics related to the social settings in which an individual exists. These settings themselves may place individuals at risk or buffer them from it. In fact, rather than a personal characteristic uniformly becoming a risk (or a buffer), it would seem that these characteristics become risks (or buffers) largely *in conjunction with* a set of social contexts. Individual risks grow out of these environments and out of the transactions between individuals and their environments.

As noted above, risk-related research also often assumes that all risks are created equally and are interchangeable. That is, it often assumes that the *number* of risks to which an individual is exposed matters significantly more than the *type* of risks or the *degree* of exposure; and it often assumes that the functional relationship between risk factors and outcomes is linear (the greater the number of risks, the worse the outcomes). Both of these assumptions are clearly questionable.

Risk-related research also often focuses on the link between a single risk factor and a single outcome. Yet a single risk factor may predispose an individual to multiple negative outcomes, just as a single negative outcome may be linked to multiple risk factors. This makes longitudinal research essential. We must explore the full set of outcomes that may be associated with a specific risk factor over time, some of which may result not because it raises the risk of any specific outcome or set of outcomes *per se,* but because it may instead disturb psychological functioning, which may, in turn, bring about a separate set of outcomes (Rutter, 1993). (This also raises our awareness of the importance of studying the interrelated, or nested, nature of negative outcomes over time.) We must also explore the ways in which a single risk factor might manifest itself differently in different age periods. In addition, while single factors may be powerful in producing an outcome or set of outcomes, we have underexplored whether particular *constellations* of factors, in combination, are instead most powerful. This is in line with Magnusson and colleagues' "person-centered" approach to studying development, to be discussed later, and with approaches to studying co-morbidity (the search for associations between two presumably different disorders).

Longitudinal research also allows us to (a) examine "escape" from risk (in that some individuals exposed to a risk or set of risks manage to move through life without serious problems, presumably buffered in whole or in part by a set of "protective" factors);[6] (b) direct and indirect chains of effects (as noted above); and (c) important junctures at which individuals change direction along a developmental

---

[6] In reviewing the literature related to children's adaptability, Garmenzy (1993a, 1993b) identifies four classes of "protective" factors that promote resilience in children: (1) *temperamental attributes* such as a child's level of activity, reflectiveness, responsivity to others, sociability, communication, internal locus of control; (2) *intelligence* and the good use of one's cognitive skills; (3) the nature of *family and affectional* ties, especially the level of cohesion, warmth, and concern in the family; and (4) sources of *external support* (e.g., in schools, neighborhoods, social agencies, churches). Similar factors have also been emphasized in Werner and Smith's (1992) landmark research on resilience among at-risk children of Kauai, Hawaii, a project which now spans over thirty years. How might these classes of protective factors change as individuals move through life?

trajectory (whether onto, or off of, an adaptive or maladaptive path). Along these lines, extremely "high risk" situations may offer a particularly important lens through which to study developmental processes (Rutter, 1993).

The nature or extent of risk may also be contingent upon the age at which the risks impinge on individuals, just as certain kinds of risks may be age-related. While contemporary developmentalists now largely reject the idea that there are fixed "critical" periods of development, there may nonetheless be "sensitive" periods or "developmental frames" during which individuals may be particularly susceptible to positive or negative influence, bringing out either marked developmental gains or losses. However, if these critical periods are not "fixed," but are instead highly variable or individualized, how might they be identified and their influences tracked? Despite Baltes' (1987, p. 613) proposition that "no one age period holds supremacy in regulating the nature of development," might sensitive periods or developmental frames nonetheless be more likely during the period spanning childhood and adolescence rather than in adult life? An important challenge for the future is to "design research that can test such hypotheses and delineate the circumstances and limits of their operation" (Rutter, 1993, p. 142). We must work harder to "disaggregate" age effects: to specify age-related vulnerabilities (whether biological, social, or psychological in nature), to show how they come about, and to show how they play themselves out over time.

We must also learn more about the origins of psychosocial risk factors and their distribution in the population, neither of which are likely random. For example, certain types of individuals may be sorted or self-select themselves into multiple contexts that are all of poor quality, and whose presumably negative effects may cumulate across contexts and over time. Similarly, certain types of individuals may be sorted or self-select themselves into multiple good contexts, and these presumably positive effects may also cumulate across contexts and overgwime. Still others may develop in contexts of discrepant quality, some of which may be negative and place the individual at some developmental "risk," and others of which may be more positive and "buffer" or "protect" the individuals from these potentially damaging factors. Much of the relevant research along these lines emphasizes the role that genetic factors (G) play in determining individuals' behaviors, particularly those behaviors that shape and select their environments (E) (e.g., Scarr, 1993). Yet inquiry into the origin of risk-related life experiences must be much broader than $G \rightarrow E$ conceptualizations.

Research on risk is likely to increase as we further explore the possible factors that protect individuals, or propel them forward on positive developmental paths, despite the fact that they may be disadvantaged or at-risk in important ways, and as we extend these concepts and questions to the study of *adult* life. However, to move forward, it is important that we better clarify the conceptual and empirical boundaries between (a) "risk factors" and "protective factors," (b) between "vulnerability," "resilience," and "adaptability," and (c) between the former and the latter. Better knowledge of risk, its mechanisms, and its consequences, will help us (a) reduce and ameliorate risks (of course, identifying a risk is one thing; preventing it is quite another); (b) better equip individuals (in advance) with strategies for coping with stress and adversity, with the hope of promoting resilience; (c) better intervene (on demand) when individuals experience stress and adversity; and (d) better understand how risks are (unevenly) distributed in the population (Rutter, Champion, Quinton, Maughan, & Pickles, 1995). This information is also crucial for the development and reform of social policies and programs that might be directed at these missions.

OTHER STRATEGIES FOR ANALYZING LIVES

Several statistical and methodological developments in the past couple decades have allowed—or have created the potential to allow—more dynamic quantitative analyses of lives. These include event-history and survival analysis, structural equation and LISREL-type models, growth-curve analysis, and multi-level models (see Campbell & Alwin, 1996, for a overview of these approaches). Proponents of these methods have insisted that trajectories and the richness of individual biographies can, in fact, be modeled well. They suggest that typological approaches, especially those meant to represent sequences alone, make inadequate use of the temporal character of data and are insufficient for covering the entire range of possible pathways in most empirical applications (Mayer, 1986; Mayer & Tuma, 1990).

Advances brought about by LISREL-type models are important in that they force us to think more critically about measurement, and they allow us to examine bi-directionality, and both direct and indirect effects. However, several aspects of these models, at least as they are generally used, remain problematic for developmental research. As Bronfenbrenner (1988) points out, in these models, developmental pathways are both conceptualized and analyzed "as if they were invariant across both person and situation. No matter how many pathways through life are found, or how convoluted each course may be, once travelers embark on a particular route, they are seen as proceeding at the same pace to the same place, irrespective of who they are, whence they came, or the nature of the terrain they may be traversing" (p. 43).

Recent developments in multi-level models have also greatly improved our ability to analyze the effects of "nested" social contexts on the individuals in them (e.g., children in families, families in neighborhoods), as well as the multi-point data that are "nested" within individuals (see Bryk & Raudenbush, 1992; DiPrete & Forristal, 1994; Hox, 1994).

Besides classical approaches to sociometry and psychometry, recent advances in social network analysis may also permit more sophisticated analyses of the interdependence of lives (e.g., Freeman, White, & Romney, 1989; Scott, 1991; Wasserman & Faust, 1994; Wasserman & Galaskiewicz, 1994). These methods are an important means through which developmental scientists might better grasp individual development as it is shaped by relational ties, whether through relationships with one or two other people (dyads or triads), small groups (or subgroups), or large groups. However, network analysis and network models can be criticized for being too static; there are few longitudinal applications of these methods. This chasm is driven partly by the fact that network models become extremely complicated when they are placed within a temporal framework, and partly by the fact that temporal data on networks are difficult to collect and handle empirically (though these challenges are obviously not restricted to network analyses). In addition, these methods and their applications are often oriented toward the *structural characteristics* of networks and their relationships. While the structural characteristics of relationships and networks are important to understand, developmental scientists must explore the *social processes* occurring within them, the *substance* of those interactions, and the *meanings* of those relationships. Either way, "good, easy-to-use methods" for gathering and analyzing longitudinal network data are desperately needed and remain an important area for methodological advances (Wasserman & Faust, 1994, p. 731).

Readers interested in learning more about quantitative techniques for collecting and analyzing longitudinal data might also consult Magnusson and Bergman (1990), Magnusson, Bergman, Rudinger, and Törestad (1991), Rovine and von Eye (1991), von Eye (1990).

As discussed earlier in this chapter, there is a significant need for developmental scientists to more adequately bring context and meaning to the study of human lives. This can be promoted through greater use and *acceptance* of qualitative research methods and analytic approaches. There have been important methodological developments and applications in these areas, particularly with respect to new technologies (e.g., via video-tapes, computers, cellular phones, pagers) and software programs for the analysis of qualitative data (e.g., NUDIST or ATLAS, which are among the best of these programs). For an overview of recent developments in qualitative methods, see Denzin and Lincoln (1994); for reviews of recent contributions of qualitative research to social gerontology, and to the field of human development more broadly, see Hendricks (1996) and Jessor, Colby, and Shweder (1996), respectively. As with quantitative research on the life course, qualitative research must also take time more seriously. As we attempt to better understand context and meaning in human lives, we must understand how and why those contexts and meanings change over time. Many of the concerns presented in this book apply to quantitative and qualitative strategies alike.

Variable- versus Person-Oriented Approaches

Approaches to studying human development are themselves varied. This variability is especially driven by differences in the theoretical orientations, baseline assumptions, and methods that developmental scholars bring with them as they approach their research (Asendorpf & Valsiner, 1992). One dimension on which to classify an approach to studying lives is whether it takes a variable- versus person-oriented view. Rather than focus on discrete, uni-dimensional variables, or even a handful of variables combined together as first- or second-order constructs, some scholars have advocated more holistic strategies. For example, if we use Magnusson's (1988, 1995; Magnusson & Cairns, 1996) framework (described earlier) to guide our work, we should not (and cannot) examine *single* variables and the relationships between them. A variable approach allows only a "peephole perspective" on development (Magnusson, Andersson, & Torestad, 1993) and is insufficient for studying individuals and their functioning within "total integrated systems." Instead, Magnusson and his colleagues argue that we must use a "person approach," in which the individual, rather than the variable, is the unit of observation. To do so, we need to examine the larger *patterning of multiple variables* that relate to an individual's functioning within a system (or subsystem). This requires the researcher to first identify the system (or subsystem) to be studied and the "possible operating factors" at the level of analysis at which patterning will be examined, and to then apply a method for analyzing those patterns.

While this approach does capture more information about the person simultaneously, it nonetheless has many of the same problems of variable approaches. It ultimately relies on variables, and particularly on a set "hypothetical" and "abstracted" variables, that summarize the individual's profile. The procedure involves a select set of variables and an investigator's specific interest in the relationships among them. The relationships between those variables stand at the heart of the profile and are often used as a means with which to classify individuals. Ironically, when we classify individuals into a typology, we lose sight of the uniqueness of the "whole" person that we originally intended to capture. Proponents of person-oriented approaches counter such criticisms, saying that not all aspects of an individual's functioning can (or should) be investigated in a single study, and that the "variables included in [profile] analyses have no meaning in themselves. They are only considered components of the pattern under analysis and are interpreted in relation to all the other variables considered simultaneously" (Bergman & Magnusson, 1997, p. 293). Oddly, this view seems to presume and even advocate the absence of theory to guide the selection of variables, and it ignores the important theoretical and empirical connections between specific subsets of variables in the name of the larger pattern. How can, and why should, variables be meaningfully related to all other variables simultaneously, whether theoretically or empirically? Is this either practical or possible?

Despite these concerns, these approaches are important in that they encourage us to bring the person—as an indivisible whole—back into our research. As these scholars note, this mission is by no means new: It relates back to nineteenth-century debates about the dangers of "atomism" (as reflected in the writings of William James, James Dewey, and others). Contemporary developmental (especially empirical) research can certainly be criticized for being too atomistic (see Chapter 6).

There are several methods for pattern analysis, including the multivariate P-technique factor analysis; the Q-sort technique; latent profile analysis; configural frequency analysis; cluster-analytic techniques; higher-order contingency-table techniques; and other methods that have developed for analyzing longitudinal and cross-sectional patterns. (See Magnusson [1995] and Bergman and Magnusson [1997] for further discussion of these procedures and other important measurement issues, including concerns related to linear transformations, multivariate scaling, measuring profile dissimilarity between individuals, and handling missing data.) These procedures are all quantitative in nature (though several are appropriate for categorical data), and they may assist researchers in producing point-in-time pattern descriptions and classifications.

While there are inevitable problems associated with classification procedures, much can also be learned from the fact that "you can't classify all of the people all of the time" (Bergman, 1988; Bergman & Magnusson, 1997). In particular, an examination of the "residue" (that is, those individuals who cannot be well classified or classified at all), and of detectable "white spots" (that is, of the things that do *not* go together and the developmental paths that do *not* occur) can be very informative.

However, little is known about how to handle pattern descriptions, and their links to individual functioning, systematically over time.[7] We must do so if we hope to use these procedures as a means for studying developmental change. The assumptions of person-oriented approaches are also rarely compatible with the assumptions about linearity in most variable-oriented procedures (Bergman & Magnusson, 1997; for illustrations, see Bergman, 1988). At present, these methods are largely descriptive and not model based (they do not have the ability to test comprehensive models or handle measurement error). Proponents of person-oriented methods claim that, at least under current standards, these methods place greater demands on sample size and require greater attention to the quality of measurement than what is typical for variable-oriented approaches. Despite their problems, person-oriented approaches are useful and show great promise for understanding, and even predicting, developmental phenomena. While there have been important advances in person-oriented profile methods in recent years (see Bergman & Magnusson, 1997), these are an important area for which methodological advances are needed.

General versus Differential Approaches

Another dimension on which to classify an approach is whether it takes a *general* (or universal) versus *differential* (or individual) view (Asendorpf & Valsiner, 1992). At one extreme, an approach may emphasize the general experiences of most people or even search for universally shared experiences that transcend time and place (e.g., what I earlier described as the traditional conception of development). At the other extreme, an approach may emphasize the uniqueness of individual experience or even take the perspective that the development of no two people can ever be alike.

Those who take a general view are likely to consider any differences found to be the result of "error variance" or of idiosyncratic "spurts or delays" of a developmental pattern that is (or should be) common to everyone. In contrast, those who take a differential view take for granted the fact that developmental courses vary as a function of individual or group differences, and that these differences result in different types and rates of development. As Asendorpf and Valsiner (1992) note, most research that takes a differential approach examines the stability of individual differences across age groups in a sample. To do so, these researchers generally correlate individual-difference variables across two time points. The more the mean

---

[7] These approaches become even more complicated as we attempt to capture and compare profiles over time, whether intra-individually (viewed over time for the same person) or inter-individually (viewed for different individuals at the same time or over time).

stability approaches 1.0, the more the general perspective would seem to be sufficient for understanding a set of data. (That is, a value of 1.0 is taken to mean that no differential change has occurred—that all individuals have changed in the same way.) The further the mean stability is from 1.0, the more a differential perspective would be required to understand a set of data. Moderate values of mean stability would indicate that either the rank-ordered position of most individuals has shifted somewhat or that the rank-ordered position of most individuals has remained fairly stable but that a few individuals have shifted in rank dramatically, pulling the stability score downward (moderate correlations are almost always interpreted in the former rather than the latter way). These types of analyses pay little to no attention to how much, and in what direction, an individual deviates from an average, both of which are very important for our understanding of development. In addition, these types of analyses, because they focus only on information at two time points, on simple within or between group comparisons, and on exclusive increases or decreases, tell us nothing about longer-ranging developmental functions, which are characterized by both growth and decline, gain and loss.

Outcome- versus Process-Oriented Approaches

We might also classify a methodological approach in terms of whether it focuses on *"intermediate outcomes* of development or on the [processes or] *mechanisms* that generate these outcomes" (Asendorpf & Valsiner, 1992, p. xv). Asendorpf and Valsiner's choice to state this as an either/or proposition, and to focus on intermediate outcomes, seems peculiar. Instead, it would seem more helpful to characterize approaches in terms of the degree to which they emphasize (a) developmental *outcomes* (and whether they are more *proximal and relatively immediate* or whether they are *distal and longer-ranging*), (b) developmental *processes and mechanisms* that bring about these outcomes, or (c) both.

Outcome-focused approaches are generally descriptive, and are concerned with "which functions . . . come into being at particular age levels, and in what ontogenetic sequence these functions appear" (Asendorpf & Valsiner, 1992, p. xv). Outcome approaches generally overlook the processes and mechanisms through which they emerge, and the emergence of novel developmental functions.

In contrast, process- and mechanism-oriented approaches are, by definition, more concerned with explaining how developmental functions emerge. Most of this research is also focused on general developmental functions rather than novel ones. Outcome-oriented research must turn its attention to the processes and mechanisms that determine outcomes and produce differential change, as well as to novel outcomes and processes. Novel outcomes and processes are especially interesting in that they may "either reorganize existing patterns or create entirely new ones," and our "standard theoretical constructs and statistical models are poorly equipped to address either type of novelty" (Magnusson & Cairns, 1996, p. 16; see also Gottlieb, 1992). As we begin to study novelties, we must ask ourselves critical questions about how novelties are to be defined, the circumstances under which and the processes through which they come about, and the methods appropriate for understanding them (see also Winegar, 1997).

Approaches that Emphasize the Person, the Environment, or the Person-Environment Link

Strategies for studying lives also differ in terms of whether they emphasize the *person*, aspects of the *environment*, or the *link between* the person and the environment (Asendorpf & Valsiner, 1992). I would argue that these approaches might also be classified in terms of the degree to which they emphasize *changes* in the person, changes in the environment, or changes in the person-environment link. At present, however, most research examines only the first of these. The person-centered approach has been, and remains, most typical throughout the history of developmental research; it largely neglects environmental contexts. These are followed by environment-centered approaches, of which we have experienced a surge in recent years, but which largely lose sight of the person. Still rarer are those approaches that emphasize the person-environment link and attempt to "bring the person back in" and understand development as a complicated set of interactions, dynamic and reciprocal, between individuals, other people, and social contexts. While most researchers acknowledge the importance of person-environmental linkages, few study them in practice. And still fewer study the dynamic nature of these relationships in a temporal framework. As discussed earlier, neither our theory nor our methods are adequate for understanding the person-environment link, and especially for studying the connection between changing individuals and changing environments.

Formalistic versus Naturalistic Approaches

At a more basic level, there are at least two "fundamentally different" approaches to the study of human development: formalistic and naturalistic (Thorngate, 1992, p. 64). *Formalistic* approaches tend to stress "quantitative research methods, rigorous statistical controls, laboratory settings, sophisticated designs, large numbers of subjects, short observation periods, and omnivariate statistical analyses." *Naturalistic* approaches, on the other hand, tend to stress "intensive observation, qualitative description, non-laboratory settings, long observation periods, small numbers of subjects, and simple data analyses." While there are variations along these lines, this dichotomy nonetheless captures the key epistemological and ontological debates among social scientists, particularly chasms between quantitative versus qualitative, "objective" versus "subjective," and "insider" versus "outsider" orientations. These chasms persist (and plague) developmental research, despite repeated calls for multi-method and interdisciplinary research (see Chapter 6).

On Comparisons

The comparative method is basic to all sciences, natural and social alike, and is the primary tool with which we generate knowledge; its success hinges on whether the units and features of the comparison are explicitly selected and defined on sound scientific bases (Fry, 1990b; Tudge, Shanahan, & Valsiner, 1997). Within-person comparisons over time stand at the foundation of the study of developmental phenomena. It is also common for developmental scientists to routinely make other group comparisons in their analyses. Besides age and cohort comparisons, which were discussed in Chapters 2 and 3, comparisons across sex and race groups are also commonplace (e.g., Mekos & Clubb, 1997). Because individual lives are embedded in historical time, cross-historical comparisons are also essential (e.g., Shanahan & Elder, 1997). Important comparisons can also be made, and are needed, across generations within families (e.g., Attias-Donfut, 1992), across nations, cultures, and subcultures (e.g., Hantrais & Mangen, 1996; van de Vijver & Leung, 1997), and across species (e.g., Sameroff & Suomi, 1996).[8] More coordinated efforts along these lines will allow us to better examine the degree to which aspects of development can be generalized. As discussed earlier, the sharing of data within the larger scientific community would seemingly encourage more, and more explicit, comparisons across studies with similar types of data, across disciplinary boundaries, and across cultures and nations.

When we make comparisons between people, especially in cross-sectional analyses, we must ask ourselves what we expect to learn about development when we make these comparisons and how we might make sense of any similarities or differences that result. Several criticisms have been raised against group-level comparisons in particular. First, these approaches assume that individuals can be classified into discrete categories, which is often not the case. Second, they assume that those categories, and an individual's membership in them, are stable, which also is not always the case. Third, they typically involve comparisons of group means (with which we lose sight of significant within-group variability brought about by the uniqueness of individual experiences), and they tell us nothing about developmental processes. As a result, some have argued that group-level approaches are wholly inappropriate for studying individual development (e.g., Valsiner, 1984).

Proponents of group-level comparisons instead argue that their critics overlook the fact that developmental processes may be tied to group attributes, and that group comparisons may provide important insights into the possible processes and mechanisms that bring about differential patterns in developmental outcomes (e.g., Mekos & Clubb, 1997, p. 139). That is, group comparisons may "serve an important

---

[8] Some investigators make a distinction between cross-national and cross-cultural comparisons. For example, Fry (1990b) argues that *cross-national* comparisons tend to focus on entire nation-states, and describe quantitatively the ways in which nation-states vary along social, economic, political, and demographic indicators. In contrast, *cross-cultural* comparisons tend to focus on less developed societies, smaller-scale societies, or on specific communities within larger societies, and rely on small samples and qualitative methods. Sokolovsky (1997, p. xxiii) argues that cross-cultural approaches are particularly helpful in suggesting hypotheses that might be more fully examined with other methods, larger samples, or in longitudinal studies (especially in that "it is possible to retain a picture of the qualitative nature of socio-cultural variables and thereby avoid overly simple theoretical models"). Both cross-cultural and cross-national comparisons help us understand life-course experiences in diverse environments. It is important to widen our scientific lens by moving the study of the life course beyond contemporary North American and European industrialized societies (Fry, 1990b).

heuristic function for summarizing particular configurations of components—biological, psychological, social, cultural, historical—that accompany group membership." (Mekos & Clubb, 1997, p. 142). But do they? While group comparisons, and any differences that result, may prompt us to think more about relevant processes, membership in a group *per se* tells us nothing about how or why the attribute that defines the group is tied to a developmental outcome. In addition, besides creating groups on the basis of a single category (and holding all else constant), we often create more refined groups based on various combinations of individual characteristics (e.g., young African-American males; elderly White women). How and why are a particular combination of attributes linked to a developmental outcome?

Within-person comparisons are the most fruitful way of studying developmental change, whether via "single-subject longitudinal" methods or "single-subject microgenetic" methods (which are nonetheless longitudinal). While both approaches allow us to examine the rate, direction, and form of change, the basic difference is the span of time studied and the interval of time between measurement points (Mekos & Clubb, 1997, p. 152). *Single-subject microgenetic* methods cover a short span of time, and the sampling of observations is very frequent and continuous in an attempt to better capture ongoing developmental processes (e.g., Catan, 1986; Siegler & Crowley, 1991). Relative to microgenetic methods, *single-subject longitudinal methods* (traditionally called P-techniques) cover a wider span of time and generally have longer intervals between observation points, making the sampling of developmental processes more sporadic or fragmented. However, relative to traditional longitudinal methods, single-subject longitudinal methods are often characterized by a much narrower span of time and much shorter distances between observation points (Mekos & Clubb, 1997; see also Nesselroade, 1991).

If we are to take seriously the challenges of studying lives through time, we must move away from the study of age differences and of specific life stages and instead begin to study the larger life course. The life course itself must become a comparative unit, and we must search for variation in its structure and nature (Fry, 1990b). When we compare the life course across nation-states, it is particularly important to explicate how the state and institutional structures specific to each country shape the life course. When we make these frameworks explicit, and take them into account in our analyses and comparisons, cross-national similarities and differences in the structure and experience of the life course will be better revealed.

OTHER EMERGING ISSUES RELATED TO STUDYING LIVES

Social Structure and Human Agency

As noted in Chapter 1, the concept of social structure is elusive. As Alwin (1995) points out, there is "little theoretical consensus on what [exactly] structure [is], but virtually everyone [agrees] that the conceptual apparatus conveyed by the concept of social structure [is] what [makes] a sociological contribution to the study of individual lives a possibility" (p. 217). Similarly, Sewell (1992) notes that just as "sociologists find it difficult to do without the concept of structure, they also find it nearly impossible to define it in any adequate way . . . [at times] finding it embarrassingly difficult to define the term without using the word 'structure' or one of its variants in the definition" (p. 2). For example, this is a problematic aspect of the framework of Riley and her colleagues, which, as described in Chapter 1, emphasizes the dynamic between "changing structures" and "changing lives." However, while their terms are elusive, their framework deviates in important ways from conventional approaches to structure, which treat structure as "unalterable and given," to use Rytina's (1992, p. 1970) phrase, and as a set of stable, powerful, unidirectional (top-down) forces that sets parameters on individuals' lives. Instead, Riley and her colleagues emphasize the fact that people have the ability to *change* structures (that is, that the relationship between people and structures is reciprocal) and that both structures and lives, and the connection between them, are *dynamic*. However, does the idea of a "dynamic" structure negate the very concept of structure, which would inherently seem to involve *stability?* As an example, consider Alwin's (1995) definition of social structure as a set of "opportunities and constraints within networks of roles, relationships, and communication patterns, which are relatively *patterned and persisting* (p. 218, emphasis added). Alwin's definition may, on the one extreme, refer to "large, organic institutional structures, such as bureaucracies, which structure and orient human activities; or it may refer, at the other extreme, to a set of dyadic norms negotiated between two individuals for the purposes of social exchange" (p. 218). This definition illustrates the point that the traditional concept of structure has *persistence* at its heart. (However, Alwin's definition of structure is atypical in the sense that it emphasizes both constraints *and* opportunities, whereas traditional uses of the term "structure" often emphasize only its constraining aspects.) Our emphasis on the stable nature of social structures has led us to neglect their dynamic aspects. For it is not the stability of structures, but instead the *changes* in them, and their impact on human lives, that represent the most interesting lines of inquiry for life-course scholarship. The importance of these changes—and of social change more generally[9]—has been emphasized throughout this book.

Sociologists of "social stratification" have emphasized the fact that the larger structure of a society can be described with respect to its composition along many dimensions. Age (or cohort), race (or ethnicity), sex (or gender), and social class (education, occupation, income, or some combination thereof) are among the most commonly examined. Some of these characteristics are "ascribed" (that is, they are largely statuses into which an individual is born or over which an individual has little control), while other characteristics are "achieved" (that is, these statuses are largely the result of performance or effort, or of things over which an individual presumably has some control) (for a review, see Foner, 1979). In reality, the boundaries between these two types of status are not always clear. Ultimately, most thought related to

---

[9] The concept of "social change" (see Calhoun, 1992), like the concept of "social structure," is elusive and both imprecisely and overly used.

social stratification has been tied to the question of who gets what in society. In most complex societies, resources are not distributed equally; some individuals or *groups* of individuals hold a disproportionate share of social resources (e.g., property, power, prestige). Sociologists of stratification have traditionally been interested in how and why this allocation varies as a function of the dimensions noted above (for a review, see Grusky & Takata, 1992).

Similarly, the field of human development has been dominated by "personal attribute," "social address," and "social niche" models (Bronfenbrenner, 1988). *Personal attribute models* group individuals based on biological or physical features (e.g., age, sex, physical make-up or status) and then compare these groups. *Social address models* group individuals by geographical or social group (e.g., by social class, by race or ethnic group, by urban or rural) and compare them. (While social address models focus on geographical or social groupings, they nonetheless often rely on individual characteristics as a means for grouping individuals.) *Social niche models* consider the simultaneous intersection of several of these statuses (e.g., Black underclass males).

For all of these models, Bronfenbrenner (1988, p. 27) uses Lewin's (1931) label "Aristotelian" or *class-theoretical models,* because the phenomena under study are somehow "explained" by the categories themselves. (These models stand in direct contrast to "Galileian" or *field-theoretical models,* which instead explicate the specific processes that bring about the phenomena under study.) Class-theoretical models assume that these characteristics of individuals serve as important proxies for "social structure" and an individual's experiences within it. However, these variables tell us little about the characteristics of social structure themselves, the processes occurring within them, or individuals' experiences therein. When we find significant differences between classes, we are then faced with the problem of having to explain these differences. And it is with respect to *explanation* that research based on class-theoretical models does an insufficient job. What is it about structure, and the individual's place within it, that produces these differences? Because these models are ultimately based on the characteristics of individuals, they do not tap what most of us have in mind when we think about social structure. These characteristics tell us little, if anything, about an individual's place within social structures, whether large or small; about what these environments are like; about the processes operating between individuals and these environments; or about whether the experiences of individuals who simply share the same characteristics are, in fact, similar, or whether they might instead vary.

While developmental scientists are beginning to pay more attention to these issues, class-theoretical models remain dominant in the field. Bronfenbrenner notes that the "continued widespread use of class-theoretical models yields results that are not only likely to be redundant but also highly susceptible to misleading interpretations" (p. 28). This is particularly true when class-theoretical models are used to explore field-theoretical questions (that is, when we want to know something about processes).

Given that "social structure" is an elusive concept to begin with, it is not surprising that its measurement and modeling are so difficult. Even characteristics which seem, at first sight, simple proxies for social location become quickly complicated. In fact, the measurement of race and ethnicity, of social class and each of its components (income, education, and occupation, as well as measures of occupational "status" and "prestige"), and of sex and gender are all highly debated practices in the social sciences. Even age, which seems the most straightforward of all the dimensions commonly used, becomes very complicated (see Chapter 2).

We must better understand social structures and their impact the life course. But we must also take the developing person to be active, even *proactive,* in constructing her or his life, and *interactive* with her or his environments. In this sense, we must bridge psychology and sociology, micro and macro. Sociological research on the life course has too often stressed the role that social structures play in shaping human lives, and has downplayed the fact that individuals are, to some degree, "architects" of their own lives, to use George's (1996a, p. 252) term. In the process, sociologists have often lost sight of the person and overlooked the roles of personality traits and characteristics, motivations, desires, aspirations, and expectations. At the same time, psychological research has largely neglected powerful social and historical forces that shape the life course and serve to promote or constrain development. We must now better link these levels in our theoretical and empirical work.

For example, Clausen (1995) states that "the life course is to a considerable degree a personal construction, but it entails *selective processes* and a *sifting and sorting of persons into and out of various contexts*" (p. 367, emphasis added). The contexts in which people find themselves are not entirely their own doing, and the "sifting and sorting" that Clausen mentions is not random but is often driven by social processes that systematically allocate contexts (and opportunities therein) as a function of factors such as race, sex, age, or socioeconomic standing (income, educational attainment, occupational position, or class status of one's family of origin). Despite these processes, Clausen nonetheless envisions the life course as a result of personal choice, and positive trajectories being largely the result of *planful competence* (see also Chapter 1). Similar to what Langer (1989) calls "mindfulness," Clausen argues that planful competence is characterized by three things: *dependability, intellectual involvement,* and *self-confidence.* Of course, the measurement of each of these components is likely a matter of great debate. As a concept, planful competence means knowing your strengths, limitations, and interests; and knowing what options are available and how to take advantage of them. It means being able to assess the actions and feelings of others, and to take these into account when interacting with others. Most importantly, it means having goals and the self-confidence to carry them out, coupled with a high degree of flexibility and openness to new experiences.

Clausen suggests that this characteristic can be discerned by the adolescent years (but that it naturally comes with maturity through the adult years), and that it is this trait (or profile of traits) that best predicts later development. Planfully competent adolescents make good decisions (and have successes) early in life, and these, in turn, cumulate as they move through life, leading to further good decisions (and successes). (This is in line with the "Matthew effect," discussed in Chapter 3 and later in this chapter.) Clausen's argument seems simple, yet intuitive. Planful competence would also seem to be a skill that can be learned, at least in part. If so, researchers and educators must find ways to effectively teach children these skills and incorporate them into standard curricula. Clausen's depiction of the individual as active and self-aware seems part of an emerging "constructivist" view of human lives, emphasizing that individuals at least partially construct their own lives, create their own opportunities, serve as their own developmental "agents," and generate their own meanings. Examples of other recent work along these lines stresses the importance of self-efficacy (Bandura, 1992), personal control (Brandtstädter & Baltes-Götz, 1990; Brandtstädter, 1998), primary and secondary control processes (Heckhausen & Schulz, 1995a), and proactive adaptation (Kahana & Kahana, 1996); and conceptualizes humans as "interactive" and "self-constructing living systems" (Ford, 1987; Ford & Ford, 1987; Magnusson, 1988, 1996).

However, little systematic effort has been aimed at integrating action into perspectives on human development, and to examine the reciprocal interaction between personal action and development. Why has this been so? Brandtstädter (1998) argues that this may be the result of the fact that developmental research has traditionally focused on early childhood to adolescence (see also Birren & Birren, 1990). In Brandtstädter's words, "activities of self-regulation and intentional self-development are related to personal goals, plans, and identity projects; such orientations typically become more differentiated and concrete in the transition to adulthood, when developmental tasks of independence and autonomy gain importance" (p. 808). In addition, there may be "deeper epistemological and methodological reservations" between an action perspective and causal explanatory schemes, and between an action perspective and a search for "deterministic laws and universal principles of development" (p. 808).

The idea that individuals produce of their own development is not new. This notion has been emphasized in interactionist, contextualist, and organismic-structuralist approaches, all of which have stressed the fact that individuals are not simply the passive products of larger environmental forces. The difference is that these approaches have "primarily conceived of development as the result of person-environment *transaction,* rather than as a target area of *intentional action;* in other words, the relation between action and development has been conceptualized primarily as a functional rather than intentional one" (Brandtstädter, 1998, p. 826). While this assumption may be appropriate for early development, it is surely less appropriate during adolescence and throughout adulthood, as conceptions of the self and of the future guide intentional behavior (and vice versa). Personal developmental "projects" and goals, and a larger life plan, become clearer at this time. These plans are not only guided by the input of important others, but they are increasingly dependent on the plans of other intimates (e.g., spouse or partner, children) to whom one's life is bound as one moves through adulthood (that is, lives must be jointly negotiated and coordinated). Throughout adulthood, plans are also shaped by a larger system of cultural norms, as representations of the normal and expectable life are incorporated into, and presumably guide, personal plans (see Chapter 2).

The nature and degree to which these cultural scripts exist in modern societies seems unclear, and whether these cultural scripts affect personal plans seems even less so. In fact, Brandtstädter (1998) suggests that "it becomes a developmental task of its own to interpret and implement the cultural script of the life course in ways that are compatible with personal goals and identity projects" (p. 842). Personal goals and identity projects are hardly constant; instead, they undergo a process of continual revision and readjustment throughout life. An individual's positions or circumstances at a specific point in time may alter these goals and projects. One's life period may also shape the content of these goals and projects. For example, young adults generally construct a large part of their identity in terms of the possible selves they envision in the future, while older adults instead construct identities that are largely tied to past accomplishments (Brandtstädter, 1998, p. 842; Wong & Watt, 1991).

To summarize, one can find perspectives in the literature that place a strong, and even exclusive, emphasis on the role of agency in determining development; let me call these models of *agency without structure* (again, these models are more common in psychology and in North American scholarship). What is dangerous about agency-oriented arguments, at least if carried to an extreme, is that they blame people for negative outcomes and suggest that we need not assist individuals (through state-supported social policies and programs) because their problems and circumstances are of their own doing. One can also find perspectives in the literature that place a strong, and even exclusive, emphasis on the role of social structures in determining or constraining development; let me call these models of *structure without agency* (again, these models are more common in sociology and in European scholarship). Of course, structure-oriented arguments, at least if carried to an extreme, can be equally dangerous because they "externalize" blame and leave little or no room for personal responsibility.

Instead, we must re-conceptualize lives as having some elements of each, and consider the ways in which people actively create their own lives within the confines of the social structures in which they exist; let me call these models of *agency within structure*. Elder (1998, p. 978) makes a similar point, noting that "the constructivist role of the individual in making a life course should be coupled with recognition that all choices and initiatives are constrained, more or less," as does Levy (1996, p. 83), who argues that "life courses are actively constructed *and* passively endured." Along these lines, Heinz (1998) even parallels the life course to a self-service cafeteria, in which individuals make selections from a menu of possible options available to them. If the new life course is partly (or largely) conceived as one of *biographical choices*, the range of which seems to be opening (Heinz, 1998), we must face the fact that greater choices also bring greater responsibility for individuals and families. In addition, while social structures are normally assumed to constrain the lives of individuals, they need not be conceptualized in this way. Social structures also serve to enable individuals, and much remains to be learned about both their enabling *and* constraining aspects.

Heterogeneity and the Matthew Effect

Research on the life course has largely focused on the average experiences of cohorts as a whole rather than on the differentiation of experiences within cohorts.

This is typical not only of approaches to the analysis of cohorts, but to the analysis of group differences more generally. However, recent gerontological research has emphasized the need to better explicate the heterogeneity that exists among older adults (Calasanti, 1996; Light, Grigsby, & Bligh, 1996; Nelson & Dannefer, 1992), and perhaps those studying other age periods will follow their lead. Neugarten has long pushed scholars and policy-makers to account for heterogeneity within age groups. Heterogeneity among older people, in particular, is a function of the fact that "the longer people live, the more different they become . . . Lives fan out with time as people develop their own patterns of interests and commitments, their own sequences of life choices, their own psychological turning points, and their own patterns of relations with the few significant other people whose development impinges most directly on their own" (Neugarten, 1979/1996, p. 48).

Sociologists now use a similar concept—the "Matthew effect"—to explain "aged heterogeneity" (Dannefer, 1987, 1991; Dannefer & Sell, 1988). This principle is based on a passage in the Gospel of Matthew: "For unto every one that hath shall be given and he shall have abundance, but from him that hath not, shall be taken away even that which he hath." Sociologist Merton (1968) first described the "Matthew effect" as a general principle of social life: Advantage breeds further advantage, and disadvantage breeds further disadvantage. (However, neither Merton's nor Dannefer's applications are as extreme as the passage from Matthew, nor are their intentions the same.)

Following this principle, the pathways of cohort members diverge over time, as early experiences set the stage for later ones, either limiting or promoting future life chances along the way. As a cohort grows up and older its members therefore become increasingly different from each other. (In addition to the divergence trajectory, one might consider several other trajectory patterns, including *constancy, u-shaped, trigger-event,* and *convergence* patterns.)[10] In the divergence scenario, early inequalities are exacerbated over time, and much of this is *socially* produced and reproduced. To use Dannefer's (1987) phrase, these patterns of inequity are linked to "socially structured mechanisms of differential allocation." Some scholars have suggested that these social processes continue to generate inequality even into advanced old age, while others have suggested that the power of these processes begins to diminish in later life (e.g., Dowd & Bengtson, 1978). Either way, this supports a dominant generalization in the field of gerontology: that older people are more heterogeneous as a group than are members of younger age groups.

There seems to be evidence for this assertion on several dimensions, including examples that relate to macro-level patterns and processes (e.g., inter-cohort inequality in income; race and sex differences in occupational attainment), organizational processes (e.g., "tracking" in work organizations and schools; allocation and mobility systems in organizations, particularly through "open" and "closed" positions), and interpersonal relations and processes (e.g., the formal and informal labeling of individuals in work organizations and schools which, for better or for worse,

---

[10]These were described in Chapter 3.

may lead to self-fulfilling prophecies) (see the work of Dannefer and his colleagues noted above; see also O'Rand, 1996b).

When we acknowledge heterogeneity, it becomes nearly impossible to discuss any age group as a clear social category, or to discuss general or universal patterns of development, without stereotyping and oversimplifying (Fry, 1990b). Serious attention to heterogeneity requires us to abandon "*a priori* assumptions about the existence of generic developmental laws or of the primacy of such laws" (Lerner, 1995, p. 28). At the same time, some might argue that doing the reverse—making *a priori* assumptions about the *non-existence* of larger developmental laws—may be equally dangerous. From this standpoint, greater attention to heterogeneity should not lead us to cease our examination of the commonalties in developmental experiences within or between groups, or of the ways in which developmental experiences are patterned by the characteristics of, and processes occurring within, social settings. Similarly, the difficulties posed by heterogeneity, and the challenges it brings for developmental theory and research, should not prevent us from attempting to understand and actively incorporate heterogeneity into our "scientific imagination" (Fry, 1990b, p. 129). Because the "world around us is inherently variable, [our] knowledge cannot capture the centrally relevant aspect of the phenomena under investigation, as long as [we continue to] dismiss such variability as scientifically uninteresting or as error variance" (Valsiner, 1984, p. 450). This charge has particularly been leveled against psychological orientations toward the study of human development. As discussed earlier, the terrain of psychology has historically been concerned with phenomena inside individuals (and therefore on phenomena *separated* from the external world). When psychologists have turned their attention to the environment, the environment is generally viewed as the *cause* of a psychological phenomenon rather than a set of contexts *in* which the individual acts and *with* which the individual is interdependent. However, even sociological research, much of which inherently seeks to understand how individuals are shaped by forces outside of the individual, often ignores the important variability concealed within the average.

While recent literature has emphasized the need to recognize the degree of heterogeneity that exists among people within an age bracket, few empirical studies have actually used analytic strategies that tap dispersion or have made questions of heterogeneity their central focus. In fact, references to heterogeneity seem more often to be taken as statements of fact than as empirical questions. The tension between "two competing goals of inquiry—identifying and explaining central tendencies or commonalties versus identifying and explaining systematic variations—seems to end more often than not with the researchers focusing on means or averages and giving short shrift to the range of responses or outcomes" (Grigsby, 1996, p. 145; for similar points, see Light, Grigsby, & Bligh, 1996; Nelson & Dannefer, 1992).

The widespread use of "typological" approaches, discussed earlier, may also have led us to neglect variability and the processes that underlie it (Valsiner, 1984). Typological approaches focus on developing static categories (which are often freed from temporal and spatial contexts), just as the factors used to explain them are also assumed to be constant rather than variable. Two common means of studying development along these lines compound this problem: *averaging,* in which the individuality of particular cases is overlooked, and in which the average is reified and treated as the ideal or typical (Mishler, 1996); and *prototyping,* in which specific cases are put forward as typical or ideal examples of a category (and, ironically, in which averages are often used as a basis for choosing or constructing a prototype). These approaches end up homogenizing biological, psychological, and social phenomena. In contrast, *variational* approaches emphasize the need to examine and explain the *full range* of variation within a class of phenomena.

Attention to individual differences and to empirical patterns of variability is improving. However, attention to these issues remains more common in the gerontological literature than in the broader developmental literature, and especially compared to the literature on child development. In fact, Nelson and Dannefer (1992), in their limited sampling of these literatures, found attention to individual differences and empirical patterns of variability in 43 percent of gerontological studies and 24 percent of studies on child development. (This pattern is not surprising given the strong focus on normative patterns in the literature on child development.) In addition, variability is more likely to be discussed within the context of longitudinal studies than cross-sectional ones (Marshall, 1995a).

We must therefore better document the degree of heterogeneity in life-course experiences. But if we are to take the call to examine heterogeneity seriously, we must do more than simply document it. We must also be prepared to fully *understand* it: to consider explanatory *factors,* the causal *processes* that produce it (whether biological, psychological, social, or otherwise), and its full range of *consequences.* Theories related to the "Matthew effect" are an important development along these lines, as is the recent "synthesized" (though somewhat premature) model developed by Light, Grigsby, and Bligh (1996), which attempts to bring together interactions between genetic, social structural, and personality factors in producing intra-cohort (inter-individual) heterogeneity (see Dannefer, 1996, for an excellent critique of that model). We might also extend these concerns not only to other age groups, but to groups of *any* type. In fact, Caspi (1998) suggests that, "individual differences within a group are generally greater than differences between groups, and regardless of the group in which they are observed, individual differences have real-world consequences. Individual differences thus demand scientific scrutiny" (p. 311). Once documented, what factors and processes might we propose to explain them? What are their consequences, and what factors and processes bring these consequences about?

Finally, we often use the terms "heterogeneity," "variability," "dispersion," and "diversity" interchangeably. Are they the same? Calasanti (1996), for example, argues that we must distinguish between diversity and heterogeneity: While each of these terms are concerned with the same phenomenon, they are aimed at different levels of analysis. Heterogeneity, she argues, refers to individual-level variation (individual differences), while diversity refers to "*groups* in relation to interlocking structural positions within a society" (p. 148). Heterogeneity may stem from the "social location" of individuals within a society, and social location often serves as the basis on which groups are defined (that is, some of the characteristics that individuals share, such as gender or race, define their social position within society, which, in turn, may create heterogeneity). In addition, because diversity refers to groups and their structural position in society, it is ultimately linked to power and power differentials between groups; heterogeneity, in contrast, need not be. Regardless of whether one finds Calasanti's distinctions convincing, we should nonetheless respond to her call for clarification: What do we mean by these concepts? Why they are important? And how we might better incorporate them into our work?

"Successful" Development

The belief that the process of growing older, and that old age in particular, is an "inevitably bleak and unrelieved landscape characterized by irretrievable loss" has only recently been challenged by gerontologists, researchers, and health care professionals (Maddox, 1994, p. 767). With these challenges, we have come to speak of "successful" aging (e.g., Baltes & Baltes, 1990; Kahana & Kahana, 1996; Neugarten, 1996; Rowe & Kahn, 1987, 1997), "robust" aging (Garfein & Herzog, 1995), and "productive" aging (Bond, Cutler, & Grams, 1995; Butler & Gleason, 1985; Glass, Seeman, Herzog, Kahn, & Berkman, 1995). In fact, the number of publications on this topic has increased nearly tenfold during the period from 1970 to the early 1990s (Johnson, 1995). However, despite the proliferation of the literature on "successful" aging, there is little agreement about how to define and measure this concept.

Since the 1950s, there have been numerous attempts to formulate and test models of successful aging. The Kansas City Study of Adult Life was one of the first projects to put forward the proposition of *successful* aging as a possible, and even expected, outcome, rather than an exception to the rule (Maddox, 1994). Prior to the 1950s, research on aging focused primarily on the diseases and problems associated with later life (Rowe & Kahn, 1987, 1997; Wetle, 1991). In addition, that research typically assumed that the process of growing older is experienced uniformly across individuals. As a result, researchers neglected variability in the statuses and experiences of older adults. The movement away from conceptualizing aging as a process of increasing and unavoidable decline has resulted in the exploration of variability within the older population and the intra-individual "plasticity" of older people.

First generated within the Kansas City Study of Adult Life, disengagement theory dominated gerontological thought for nearly two decades. According to this theory, the process of aging is accompanied by the mutual and gradual withdrawal of the older person from society, and of society from the older person. This disengagement is viewed as beneficial for both the aging individual and the society, thereby achieving social equilibrium. Most notably discussed in Cumming and Henry's *Growing Old* (1961), disengagement theory equates successful aging with the ability of an older individual to recognize and accept her or his declining involvement and power in society, and to disengage as a result.

Other research based on the Kansas City Study of Adult Life reached different conclusions. In Williams and Wirth's (1965) *Lives Through the Years*, successful aging is not dependent upon a "single inevitable strategy or outcome," but rather on "the location of individuals in different social milieus . . . [this leads] to the differential interaction between persons and context which, in turn, leads to differential successful lifestyles" (Maddox, 1994, p. 765). Thus, Williams and Wirth expanded the concept of successful aging to encompass the notion that success may be achieved through, and constituted by, any number of pathways.

Neugarten, one of the primary investigators in the Kansas City Study of Adult Life, broadened the concept of "success" still further during the early 1970s. In "Successful Aging in 1970 and 1990," Neugarten (1974b/1996) illustrates some of the complexities involved in capturing the multi-dimensional nature of successful aging. Neugarten considers several different frames of reference from which to define and measure success, including the vantage points of clinician, social psychologist, theologian, and family member. Ultimately, Neugarten sides with the person her or himself, suggesting that successful aging is in the "eye of the beholder." Rather than rely only on performance-based measures of success (as both Cumming and Henry [1961] and Williams and Wirth [1965] had done), Neugarten promoted "life satisfaction" as a viable measure of success, arguing that it anchors success in the subjective experiences of the individual and takes into account differing cultural interpretations of success.

More than a decade later came Rowe and Kahn's (1987) landmark article, "Human Aging: Usual and Successful." Rowe and Kahn argue that when we dichotomize the aging process into *pathological* versus *normal* (or non-pathological) states, we do not fully capture the nature of, and variations found within, aging processes. Instead, they suggest that "normal" aging be further differentiated into two subcategories: *usual* aging, in which individuals experience typical, non-pathological age-related changes, but are at high risk for disease; and *successful* aging, in which non-diseased individuals experience high functioning and are at low risk for disease. As a result, their conceptualization focuses almost exclusively on (objective) physical functioning, and especially disease and disease-related disability. Rowe and Kahn argue that when we fail to differentiate between usual and successful aging, we overlook critical roles that risk factors play in predicting successful or unsuccessful aging, and we miss the opportunity to help "usual" agers become "successful" agers. Like Rowe and Kahn (1987), Kruse, Lindenberger, and Baltes (1993) also make a distinction between "normal" and "pathological" aging, though they emphasize mental functioning as well. These investigators define normal aging as "growing old without a manifest illness, be it physical or mental"; in contrast, pathological aging refers to "aging with clear signs of physical or mental pathology" (p. 172). But is it realistic to assume that normal aging is equivalent to the *complete* absence of physical or mental illness? Likewise, it is realistic to assume that pathological aging is equivalent to exhibiting "clear signs" of physical or mental illness, however small? (Hence, Rowe and Kahn's emphasis on the "usual.")

A decade after their landmark article, Rowe and Kahn (1997, 1998) put forward a three-dimensional conceptual model of successful aging (in contrast to their earlier uni-dimensional model, which largely conceptualized successful aging as the avoidance of disease and disease-related disability). While their revised model includes (a) "low probability of disease and disease-related disability," as it did before, it now also includes (b) "high cognitive and physical functional capacity" and (c) "active engagement with life." The first two components noted by Rowe and Kahn are present in most models of successful aging. Their third component— "active engagement with life"—is unique. To get at this, Rowe and Kahn suggest that both "interpersonal relations" (contact with others for information, emotional support, or instrumental assistance) and "productive activity" (activity that has "social" value and therefore includes both paid and non-paid activities) be measured.[11] They also suggest that for the latter two components, our conception of successful aging should focus less on what a person is *able* to do, and more on what the individual *actually does*.

Most researchers have focused on successful aging as an *outcome*, whether as a (or set of) performance- or achievement-based outcome(s) (e.g., Berkman, Seeman, Albert, Blazer, & Kahn et al., 1993; Glass, Seeman, Herzog, Kahn, & Berkman, 1995) or as a subjective psychological state (or states) of individuals (e.g., Neugarten, 1974b/1996). These investigators assume that higher performance, achievement, or subjective states are indicative of more successful aging.

Some investigators advocate the use of subjective over objective measures of success (or vice versa), while others advocate a combination of both types of measures. For example, Schulz and Heckhausen (1996) argue that the use of "highly individualized and subjective criteria" as indicators of success is problematic because individually determined approaches allow greater opportunity for any indicator to be defined as successful. As a result, Schulz and Heckhausen recommend that only "externally measurable" criteria be used for various dimensions on which success is to be examined (e.g., physical, cognitive, affective, or social functioning) (p. 705). Similarly, Baltes and Baltes (1990) argue that the use of subjective measures as *sole* indicators of success may be misleading because of the "human mind's power to transform reality and in the extreme, even to ignore it" (p. 6, emphasis added). However, unlike Schulz and Heckhausen, Baltes and Baltes argue that it is necessary to use *both* "multiple objective and subjective criteria" and to "explicitly recognize individual and cultural variations" (p. 7).

In later work, Baltes and his colleagues (Kruse, Lindenberger, & Baltes, 1993) cite examples of objective and subjective variables with which to define successful aging. (Their list also well-represents many of the variables commonly examined in this literature.) On the "objective" side, they suggest that we consider length of life, biological health, functional health, mental health, reserve capacity/adaptivity (in mental, physical, social, economic realms), autonomy, social productivity, and social

---

[11]Rowe and Kahn argue that any conception of "productivity" must be sensitive to the activities in which older people are most likely engaged, and must therefore extend beyond paid work. Yet Glass, Seeman, Herzog, Kahn, and Berkman (1995) contend that economic productivity is nonetheless a crucial aspect of successful aging because it is one of the "most cherished values" in modern societies and because individuals derive self-worth based in part on their productive contributions to society. In this sense, Glass and colleagues state that the potential for successful aging may be enhanced for those who are economically productive throughout their lives, and especially during their later years.

integration. On the "subjective" side, they suggest that we consider life satisfaction, optimism, personal control, and self-efficacy/agency. However, it is unclear how, or even whether, these indicators tap the relevant components of the conceptual model of successful aging that Baltes and his colleagues have outlined, including processes and outcomes related to "selective optimization with compensation," and the maintenance of a positive balance between gains and losses; "potentiality" and "optimal aging processes," which are also linked to environmental contexts; and goal-setting and achievement.[12] In addition, because the measurement of these concepts is itself difficult (and highly debated), the task of also determining what constitutes "success" along these lines seems formidable.

Although evidence points to the predictive power of single dimensions such as health (Brooks, 1996), financial status (DeViney, 1995), religious commitment (Johnson, 1995), social networks (Adams & Blieszner, 1995), cognitive status (Baltes & Lang, 1997; Blanchard-Fields & Chen, 1996), exercise (Fontane, 1996; Kahana, Kahana, Kercher, Stange, & Brown, 1996), and humor (Solomon, 1996), most investigators suggest that successful aging is best captured as a multidimensional construct. However, there is no consensus about the dimensions and indicators to be examined, their relative importance, and how they interrelate.

Others have also conceptualized successful aging as a *process*, or as a *moderator* of the aging process. (However, where successful aging is conceptualized as a process, it is seldom *studied* as such. That is, most investigators have examined outcomes rather than processes and mechanisms, and they have analyzed static rather than dynamic data and models.) The broad conceptual model of successful aging proposed by the Kahanas (Kahana & Kahana, 1996) is a good example of a model that emphasizes the importance of *proactivity* and *adaptation* in successful aging. Their model builds upon the stress paradigm and parallels Neugarten's emphasis on human beings as active and adaptive organisms.

Underlying the Kahanas' model of "preventive and corrective adaptivity" is the belief that older people face unique stressors (e.g., illness, losses, "person-environment incongruence") that act as barriers to the processes of successful aging. In order to overcome these barriers, and therefore to achieve successful aging, older individuals must engage in behaviors that not only "delay" or "minimize" stressors before they occur ("preventive" behaviors), but that are adaptive once stressors do

---

[12] Their model of "selective optimization with compensation" and their conception of gain and loss were discussed in Chapter 1. The need for the individual to effectively coordinate these components, and especially compensation, presumably increases in later life due to the diminishing choices available to the aging individual (Baltes, 1997; Baltes & Smith, 1999). Baltes and his colleagues suggest that we explore individual potential, and the "optimal aging" processes that occur within "development-enhancing and age-friendly environmental conditions" (though successful aging may nonetheless occur within less than ideal environments) (Baltes & Baltes, 1990, p. 8). Elsewhere, Baltes and his colleagues (Marsiske, Lang, Baltes, & Baltes, 1995) instead link successful aging to goal setting and attainment. Here, their perspective is that successful development occurs "for a particular individual within a particular [life] domain" when there are "goals to guide development," and when those goals can be achieved (just as unsuccessful development occurs when there are no goals to guide development or when goals cannot be achieved) (p. 64).

occur ("corrective" behaviors). *Preventive* behaviors include "health promotion" (such as regular exercise and healthy diets), "planning for the future" (such as exploring options and resources that are available), and "helping others." Each of these are believed to reduce or postpone disease and impairment as well as enhance social and financial resources. *Corrective* behaviors, on the other hand, include the "marshalling of support," "role substitution," and "environmental modifications." Both internal and external resources serve to promote preventive and corrective behaviors and successful aging outcomes (and presumably, low resources serve as barriers to these). *Internal* resources include "hopefulness" or "optimism," "altruism," "self-esteem," "cognitive coping" (especially accommodative strategies, such as acceptance or reframing), and "cognitive life satisfaction." *External* resources include "financial resources" and the "availability of social supports."

The Kahanas, like Neugarten, also consider "life satisfaction" a primary outcome of successful aging. However, unlike Neugarten, they separate "life satisfaction" into two distinct subcomponents, one of which represents the internal resources that buffer individuals from stressors, and the other of which represents an outcome of successful aging. The Kahanas argue that because the constructs of "optimism," "self-esteem," and "cognitive life satisfaction" are more reflective of internal dispositions, and are therefore more trait- than state-like, they should enter the "armament" of resources upon which aging individuals may draw in an effort to age successfully. As a result, they suggest that successful aging *outcomes* are best captured by the constructs of "positive affect," "meaning in life," and "maintenance of valued activities and relationships" because each of these constructs reflect states that can be modified by environmental factors.

Notably absent from most models of successful aging is a conception of the *structural* opportunities for successful aging that exist in "schools, offices, nursing homes, families, communities, social networks, and society at large" (Riley, 1998, p. 151). Future conceptual and empirical work in this area must incorporate social contexts and institutional environments, and specify how these settings serve to promote or constrain successful development in later life.

In contrast, attention to social context has been an important part of a parallel discussion of successful development at the other end of the life course: adolescence.[13] Conceptions of successful adolescent development have included indicators such as doing well in school; being involved in activities that require self-discipline; cultivating special talents and interactions with others; feeling good about oneself and one's future; avoiding or adapting to mental health problems, especially those related to depression and anger; and avoiding involvement in problem behaviors of various kinds (e.g., Cook, Degirmencloglu, Phillips,

---

[13]It is important to note that the MacArthur Foundation has led both of these initiatives. It has established and supported research networks focused on development during several different life periods, including one devoted to "Successful Aging" (chaired by Rowe; see Rowe and Kahn, 1998), and one devoted to "Successful Adolescent Development in High-Risk Settings" (chaired by Jessor; see Jessor, 1993).

Settersten, & Shagle, forthcoming; Furstenberg, Eccles, Elder, Cook, & Sameroff, 1999; Jessor, 1993; Simmons & Blyth, 1987). And these conceptions of successful development have often focused on the roles that social contexts play in determining success (especially family, school, neighborhood, and peer group environments).

Where *cultural* definitions of successful aging are concerned, Project A.G.E. investigators have found "consistency in the factors that can produce either a good or a difficult old age" as defined by people living in seven separate international sites (Fry, Dickerson-Putnam, Draper, Ikels, Keith, Glascock, & Harpending, 1997, p. 102) (Project A.G.E. was described in Chapter 2.) Those factors, clustered into four broad sets, relate to (1) physical health and functioning, (2) material security, (3) family, and (4) "sociality." While these factors consistently emerge across cultures, they are not necessarily uniform in their importance nor do they manifest themselves in the same ways.

Good physical health and functioning are consistently viewed as promoting a good old age, while physical decline and loss of mobility are consistently viewed as promoting a difficult old age. Poor physical health and functioning are viewed as the most important cause of a *difficult* old age in most sites, while good physical health and functioning are only "modestly" part of definitions of a good old age, especially in many modern and technologically advanced societies in which individuals can find ways to manage their lives even in the face of physical decline and illness.

Material security (as opposed to a more restrictive concept of wealth, which is an inappropriate indicator of access to resources and commodities in many cultures) is consistently viewed as the most important fact promoting a *good* old age, especially when combined with good health.

Family factors also consistently relate to cross-cultural definitions of a good or bad old age, though their importance depends on the varying roles and expectations of family in different cultures (especially those related to the provision of economic, emotional, and physical support, and to cultural ideas about dependence and independence). And just as family factors can contribute to a good old age, they can also promote a difficult old age; the absence or abandonment of children, in particular, causes difficulty.

While physical health, material security, and family relationships factor into definitions of a good or difficult old age across all Project A.G.E. sites, "sociality," a final factor, emerges in Ireland, the United States, and Hong Kong. The concept of "sociality" taps "qualities which facilitate interaction between an ego and an alter," especially affective qualities like one's sentiments, emotions, and mood. In definitions of a good old age, these qualities include references to things such as "contentment, peace, relaxation, toleration, and freedom to do what you want to do" (p. 114)

The strategy of Project A.G.E. is important because these investigators ask natives in a culture to themselves provide definitions of what constitutes a good or a difficult old age, rather than impose a set of culture-specific criteria on them. Their findings also illustrate that some elements of these definitions are, in fact, constant across diverse cultures, and unearth what seem to be a core set of universal ideas about the aging experience. At the same time, their findings call attention to important differences in these definitions between cultures, many of which seem to be related to the social, economic, and political contexts of each community.

In conclusion, while scholarship on successful development, and especially successful aging, has grown dramatically in the last decade, the most challenging conceptual and analytic questions have yet to be resolved. For example, at a *conceptual* level, what exactly constitutes successful development? What are its primary domains? Are some domains more important than others? How do they work together? Is the concept universally applicable or is it restricted in its applicability? Is it a process or an outcome? Is it static or dynamic? What produces it? With what consequences, positive or negative, does it come? Which aspects of an individual's past and present experiences or conditions may promote or constrain successful development? What is its relationship to society (e.g., does successful aging create the potential for a successful society, and vice versa)? Many of these questions also require us to create and analyze conceptual and empirical models that are *dynamic* (and therefore temporal).

At an *analytic* level, what are the essential indicators of success in each of these domains, and are the indicators of equal importance? Should we rely on objective or subjective indicators, or both? Where do we draw the line between "successful" and "unsuccessful" for each indicator and for a larger domain (and what lies between the "successful" and the "unsuccessful," if anything)? Is the form of each indicator linear? Should we use minimal standards (e.g., the simple absence of problems) or should we set higher standards? Are these empirical definitions constant or variable across or time and place? Should domains be analyzed separately or in combination? If in combination, should domains be weighted equally? Need an individual meet "successful" criteria in every domain to achieve success overall? Regardless of how success is measured, how might it and its predictors be analyzed in a dynamic and temporal framework? These are only a few of the pressing questions that must be handled explicitly in future research.

In addition, gerontologists seem particularly committed to promoting positive images of older people, and emphases on "successful," "robust," and "productive" aging are no exception to this trend. These emphases are likely tied to desires to combat negative "stereotypes, myths, and distortions concerning aging and the aged in society," and what Butler (1969) first labeled as ageism: those "negative attitudes and practices that lead to discrimination against the aged" (Butler, 1994, p. 137). While dispelling ageism and eliminating bigotry in society are clearly admirable missions, our portrayals of aging may no longer reflect reality. Ought our portrayals be more balanced? At what costs does our emphasis on the positive come? Do we do ourselves, and especially older people, a disservice when we downplay (and even deny) the significant challenges and hardships that come with aging?

Ultimately, we must also ask ourselves whether research on successful development will improve our understanding of developmental processes and promote successful (or at least non-pathological) development for a majority of individuals (especially through prevention, early diagnosis and treatment of pathology, and the development of social policies and practices that improve the opportunity for individuals to do so). Regardless of whether this area of inquiry will remain a lively topic of interest in scientific research, there is no doubt that it has served as an heuristic tool in developmental, and especially gerontological, research (Baltes & Baltes, 1990).

CHAPTER
6

An Agenda for Developmental Science

As we usher in a new era of developmental science, we must confront many important theoretical and methodological challenges. Drawing largely on discussion from previous chapters, this chapter outlines the most pressing of the challenges facing developmental science. As such, this chapter stands as synthesis of the book and becomes an agenda for the future. These challenges include the need to (1) achieve multi-level, multi-dimensional, temporal understandings of lives; (2) overcome barriers to interdisciplinary scholarship; (3) clarify personal biases; (4) move beyond the study of specific life periods; (5) find greater meaning and significance in research; (6) make multiple, and more systematic, comparisons; (7) understand age and forms of age structuring; (8) gather and share life-course data; (9) analyze trajectories; (10) understand continuity and discontinuity, and (11) adequately measure change; (12) explicitly incorporate social contexts into our theory and research; better understand (13) socialization processes, (14) cohort, (15) variability, (16) the interdependence of lives, and (17) "successful" development; (18) link social structure and human agency; and (19) further emerging debates on the chronologization, institutionalization, and standardization of lives. Each of these will be briefly highlighted in turn.

THE CHALLENGES FACING DEVELOPMENTAL SCIENCE

Achieving Multi-Level, Multi-Dimensional, Temporal Understandings of Lives

One of our most significant challenges is to develop theory and conduct research that bridges multiple levels of analysis (e.g., micro, meso, and macro), multiple domains (e.g., family, work, education, health), and the interaction between them. Time and change must also be incorporated at each level of analysis and in each domain of functioning. This draws our attention to the dynamic nature of human lives, as individuals and groups move through their lives, through age strata of the population, through generations within their families, through organizations and social institutions, and through the course of history; and as they take on the roles and behaviors that are expected of them across these points. We also have much to learn about the experiences, interaction, and synchronization of different types of time. As we take a dynamic view of lives, we must turn our attention to the processes and mechanisms through which these changes are produced, considering not only the proximal forces and processes that shape lives, but also successively more distal ones that are not well understood.

These points emphasize the need for researchers to make the nature of the phenomena they study, and the levels of analysis at which they seek to understand them, more explicit. We must specify the structures and processes involved, collect data in line with these, and analyze them in ways that promote their understanding (Bronfenbrenner & Morris, 1998). As we do, we must also avoid methodological "monism" and be cautious of the methodological "fetishism" that dominates the scientific scene at any given moment (Magnusson & Stattin, 1998).

As we attempt to assemble and track the ways in which the entire system of biological, psychological, and social structures and processes changes across time, we become aware of the fact that we cannot study specific aspects of the person isolated from the whole. What makes this extremely complicated is that both the degree of functioning and the pace of change likely differ across subsystems and across specific aspects of functioning. In addition, micro-level processes may operate according to shorter or finer time schedules than processes operating at higher levels in the system. As a result, the appropriate research design, and especially its time span, hinge on the aspects of functioning being examined. From a practical standpoint, neither our theories nor our methods are able to simultaneously account for an unlimited number of multi-level factors, each of which may vary in degree and pace.

While these and similar frameworks are excellent as broad heuristic devices or "metatheoretical frameworks" (Winegar, 1997), they are nearly impossible to handle theoretically and empirically because they are so global and interactive. Advocates of holistic, interactionist approaches defend themselves against such charges, arguing that the intention of these models is not, and has never been, that the entire universe ought to be examined in a single study. Instead, their intention is to provide a general theoretical framework within which developmental scientists are able to plan and implement their research, granting that individual investigators will attend to different levels of the system and to specific topics and questions. (As we consider the central vantage points from which to study lives, we realize that there is no single "optimum point of entry" for doing so, but that there are instead multiple points of entry [Elder, 1998, p. 944].) A common theoretical framework should also promote more effective communication with other scientists, improve the interpretation of research, and facilitate the accumulation and integration of knowledge (Bergman & Magnusson, 1997; Magnusson, 1995).

An integrative theoretical or empirical framework must fuse together a minimum of four basic assumptions (Lerner, 1998). First, it must be aimed at understanding systematic developmental change and the relative plasticity of development across life. Second, it must be aimed at understanding the ways in which change and plasticity in development are anchored in the relations between the "multiple levels of organization that comprise the substance of human life"—

biological, psychological, and social (relational, institutional, or cultural) (p. 7). Third, it must approach these levels as being embedded in, and changing through, historical time, and with individual and collective mapped out onto that time. Fourth, as a result of these prior points, it must recognize the diversity "of people, of relations, of settings, and of times of measurement," and the resulting limits of generalizability (p. 13).

As we strive to build a more integrated developmental science, we should take a fresh look at traditional developmental concepts, and at approaches to methods, measurement, and analysis, both within and between disciplines. To move forward, we must begin a dialogue about the conception of science that is to lie at the heart of a more unified developmental science. What are our starting points, our limits, and our ultimate goals? For example, are we ultimately interested in discovery or verification? In description or explanation? Are we interested in universal claims or contingent ones? In general principles or specific and complex ones? At present, there is significant variability across developmental research with respect to basic epistemological-ontological assumptions and their associated methodological implications (for a review, see Overton, 1998). These differences create significant barriers to the conduct of interdisciplinary theory and research, which are discussed next.

Overcoming Barriers to Interdisciplinary Scholarship

While we increasingly recognize that the study of lives is necessarily an interdisciplinary enterprise (and not simply a multidisciplinary one), truly interdisciplinary theory and research are rare. Despite frequent references to the importance of interdisciplinary training and inquiry, many forces have prevented developmental scholarship from moving in these directions. One of these barriers is the "inertia" of disciplines and the "rigidity" of their boundaries (Carolina Consortium on Human Development, 1996, p. 2):

> Discipline and institutional barriers are deeply rooted, and the gap between biological-health training and behavioral-social training has proved difficult to bridge . . . To support the concept of interdisciplinary research is one thing; to expect that individuals will embrace and teach the concepts in areas beyond those in which they themselves were trained is another. Not only must opportunities and facilities for such training be provided, but the candidates and faculty must be highly motivated to attain skills that go beyond a single discipline.

These problems are exacerbated by the fact that investigators firmly rooted in particular disciplines often neither value nor take an interest in scholarship outside of their disciplines (Winegar, 1997). Interdisciplinary communication and collaboration will not improve until we better, and more consistently, define common concepts across disciplines, and until we welcome and understand the concepts of other disciplines and how they offer important expansions of our views (Lawrence & Dodds, 1997; Magnusson & Stattin, 1998). Unfortunately, the trend in contemporary scientific research seems to be one of increased specialization rather than integration.

We must also welcome different epistemological-ontological assumptions and their associated methodological implications. While there is significant rhetoric about the importance of conducting "multi-method" research, some methods continue to be valued more than others, and few scholars are adequately trained to use multiple methods. Even within disciplines, insurmountable chasms seem to exist between scholars whose basic methods are different, with each discounting the contributions of others. The chasms between those who use quantitative versus qualitative methods seem particularly difficult to bridge. Funding initiatives also tend to promote specific areas of inquiry (rather than broader, integrative efforts) and certain methods and analytic strategies. In the process, the contributions of some disciplines are valued over others.

In some disciplines, there are also few incentives for interdisciplinary and collaborative work, especially for junior scholars. Single-authored publications are more highly regarded than collaborative ones, even though collaborative publications may take equivalent or even greater time to prepare; and the presence of multiple co-authors automatically reduces the value of a publication in decisions related to tenure and promotion. Faculty are also encouraged to publish in top-tier disciplinary journals, which are held in higher esteem than interdisciplinary journals. In addition, many of these journals tend to publish short, quantitative articles related to longstanding disciplinary concerns.

Publishing norms also discourage theory- and review-oriented contributions. George (1995) has argued that there has been insufficient attention to "Theory (with a capital T)," as opposed to "theory with a lower-case t," in the published literature on aging. I would argue that this is true of literature on the life course more generally. While most published research has some amount of "theory" in it, at least in the terms of "testable hypotheses or conceptual models," it rarely has Theory in it (that is, "broad views of the fundamental processes underlying social structure and social life") (George, 1995, p. S1). The neglect of theory takes its toll on the field: Our knowledge is often fragmented, and our work often trivial. We must bring theory back into our research, and begin to promote and value important theoretical contributions in our journals. The deficiency of theory serves as a barrier to interdisciplinary inquiry. Not only is there little disciplinary theory to guide questions about specific developmental processes and outcomes over time, but there is especially little interdisciplinary theory to guide questions about the connections between multiple levels of analysis and variables from different domains over time.

While interdisciplinary graduate programs have proliferated in recent years, graduates from interdisciplinary programs have trouble landing positions in traditional departments, which have clear preferences for, or are even required to hire, candidates with specific credentials in those disciplines. (This also seems a byproduct of the common perception that graduates of interdisciplinary programs are altogether *un*disciplined.) The options of these graduates are therefore more restricted upon completion of their degrees, and many students forgo the risks associated with pursuing new forms of training in favor of traditional ones.

While representatives from multiple disciplines are also recruited for the planning of longitudinal projects, these projects seldom pose research questions and analyses that are genuinely interdisciplinary in nature. Instead, investigators from different disciplines typically negotiate for a core set of their own variables to be represented in the research instrument. This is especially true of projects that are designed to eventually become secondary data sets in the public domain. It is difficult for the coverage of such a project to be both broad and deep, and to do both well. In addition, many barriers prevent the collection and analysis of longitudinal data, which require substantial investments of time and energy, as well as long-term career commitments.

New developmental models, then, if they are to reflect breadth of disciplines and of people themselves, must bring new attention to multiple spheres of functioning, the interactions between these spheres, the conditions that give rise to them, and their changes over time. This new attention must also be reflected in the development of both interdisciplinary theory and research.

Clarifying Personal Biases

In addition to clarifying our disciplinary biases, we must also clarify our personal biases. What brings us to study human development? If we look around us and within ourselves, we will probably find that we are not attracted to our subject matter randomly. Something in our own biographies or personalities likely draws us to study a specific life period and area of inquiry within it. Hendricks (1996) makes a similar point, noting that our "training, experience . . . [and personal characteristics], all the factors that influence how actors see the world, are present in scholarly interpretation" (pp. 55-56). This point runs counter to frequent claims of "value-free objectivity" and raises our awareness that "explanation of any type is inevitably discretionary" (Hendricks, 1996, p. 56).

For example, putting into words what many of us have likely felt, Gutmann (1997) comments on what he sees as two groups of gerontologists drawn to gerontology for quite different reasons: *gerophiles* and *gerophobes*. Most recruits to the field of gerontology, Gutmann says, are gerophiles who "were once rescued by their grandparents and now they want to repay the favor" (p. xviii). Gerophiles want to do good by old people. However, a smaller "underground community of gerophobes" exists (Gutmann says he is among them, and I, too, am a likely member of this group). Gerophobes are attracted to the field of gerontology, consciously or unconsciously, because they fear, and want to be protected from, growing old.

We will all benefit from asking ourselves difficult questions about what led us to pursue academic or applied careers related to human development. What are our personal assumptions—and those implicit in our questions and methods—about the nature, shape, and meaning of development? Once we know the answers to these questions, and are aware of these biases, our work will not only be better for it, but more honest as well.

Extending the Study of Specific Life Periods

Besides the significant need to value and synthesize research within and across disciplines, there is also a significant need to value and synthesize research within and across life periods. Developmental scientists claiming to take either a "life-course" or "life-span" perspective must better incorporate the whole of life into their thought. While there is a great deal of talk about "life-course" and "life-span" theory and research, few scholars actually *do* it. It is my contention that if scientists who focus on specific age groups were to seriously incorporate (and not just pay lip service to) life-course and life-span concepts, principles, and methods, the face of developmental scholarship would be revolutionized—it would largely change the theory we develop, the questions we ask, the data we collect, and the ways in which we analyze, make sense of, and apply our data. At present, the terms "life course" and "life span" are most often evoked as general references to temporality, and not as references to a central set of concepts, principles, and methods. When used in the former way, these terms are largely meaningless. Another problem is that these terms are flippantly used in conjunction with the term "theory." I would argue that we will never manage (and should not try) to create a larger "theory" of the life course or life span. But we *must* make it our mission to transform substantive areas of disciplinary and interdisciplinary scholarship by infusing them with the concepts, principles, and methods that comprise these frameworks.

Some scholars have expressed the hope that the study of specific life periods will vanish altogether. For example, Neugarten recently made what became a controversial statement among gerontologists: "When I am asked about the future of gerontology, I am greatly tempted to predict that the field of gerontology is going to disappear over the next couple of decades" (Neugarten, 1994/1996, p. 402). Why? From an intellectual or academic standpoint, aging is a lifelong process that begins at birth, not at an arbitrary point in the latter third of life. Age-based academic specialties belittle the idea of lifelong development; an individual cannot be understood at a particular point in time by ignoring her or his past. From a policy standpoint, age-related entitlements are being called into question. And on the "front lines," service providers are also recognizing that it is hard to design and provide services for clients based on age alone. However, age-based specialties continue to "justify professional specialization and the preoccupations of professionals with particular ages, as well as the organization of professionalized services around the age of the population served" (Schroots, 1995, p. 48).

The fragmentation of developmental theory, concepts, and methods related to different life phases, and to subareas of inquiry within each, remain heavy obstacles to building a more integrative developmental science (Magnusson & Stattin, 1998). It is not enough to simply note the importance of placing age-specific research within a lifelong framework. We must actually generate substantive theory, ask questions, collect data, and choose methods with the whole of life in mind.

Finding Meaning and Significance in Research

The last few decades have brought dramatic, and even "revolutionary" (Campbell & Alwin, 1996), technological and methodological developments. Some of these developments seem undeniably positive. For example, we now have large-scale, representative data sets, even longitudinal ones, available for public use; these developments also offer exciting opportunities to test theoretical propositions, whether longstanding or recent, that have not yet been tested. We have also begun to pay more attention to measurement and design issues; and we have furthered our ability to test multivariate models. Many technological changes have also improved our ability to share and analyze data, including advances in computer storage, memory, networks, retrieval programs, and statistical packages (and corresponding reductions in cost). With these developments, our "methodological rigor and statistical sophistication" may also have increased (George, 1995, p. S2)—or at least the possibilities for achieving these have increased.

At the same time, some of these developments have promoted "crass" or "gross and unreflective" empiricism (Lawrence, 1997, pp. 286-287). Have these advances encouraged the development and testing of quick, thoughtless models with whatever methodological and statistical tools are popular at any particular moment? In our rush to "seek the holy grail of the .05 level" (Gutmann, 1997), are we unable to distinguish significant from trivial findings? Being methodologically competent is not the same as knowing statistics (Block, 1993) and, unfortunately, many researchers equate the two. For this reason, Cutler (1995) warns us to "take care to ensure that our ever more sophisticated analytic methods are viewed [and used] as a means to an end—as a way of addressing significant theoretical and substantive questions . . .—and not as a vehicle for demonstrating technical virtuosity at the expense of reader accessibility" (p. S64). We should feel discomforted by the degree to which scholarship is "shackled by the methodology of the day" (Bergman, 1992, p. 147), as the proverbial "wings" flap the "bird" rather than vice versa (Wohlwill, 1991, p. 127). That is, our research methods and statistical procedures too often seem to drive the questions we ask and the theory we develop. This danger is exacerbated when we limit our definition of research to empirical study, and when the "possibilities for grubbing through data seem endless" (Lawrence, 1997, p. 286). Quantification, and advances in quantitative methods, are not necessarily the answers: insight is (Marshall, 1995a, p. 28).

Paraphrasing Carlson's (1971) famous question, where is the person in developmental research? The time has come to "study people in the large, as they exist in their natural and real world, and the way and the why of their differences" (Block, 1993, p. 13). Scholars have recently begun to advocate more holistic strategies for studying individuals and their functioning as "total integrated systems" (Magnusson, 1995). The time has come to return people—with real lives and real voices—to our research. We too often reduce the voices of our respondents to numbers and lose their lives in our computers. This also means that we must take a more careful look at lives as they are actually lived, not as we wish them to be in order to simplify our research (Rindfuss, Swicegood, & Rosenfeld, 1987).

We might do well to follow Gutmann's (1997) suggestion and spend less time in the library (and less time with our computers) and more time learning from our direct experiences—in the field, from our patients, and from ourselves. We will all benefit by being open to, and actually valuing, a variety of methodological strategies. This includes the need for greater acceptance of, and higher regard for, qualitative and biographical approaches (Gubrium & Holstein, 1997), particularly emic methods aimed at unearthing the meanings and experiences (Keith, 1988). There is an important need to examine the subjective sides of the life course, its dynamics and experiences, how and why subjective experiences differ, and with what consequences they come.

A good example of what I mean here comes from Neugarten, who tells the story of a doctoral student who came to ask for her advice on the methods she was planning to use in a project on middle age. The student was going to follow up a sample of now upper-class, highly-placed men for whom she had data from adolescence. "You don't take that kind of man," she says, "and put him in an interview, hand him a batch of lines divided into spaces, and say 'Put on this line, how satisfied are you with your life, how satisfied was your . . . ?' I said to the woman, 'you're talking to *somebody*. Let him *talk*. Ask him what it's like. Don't hand him lines and ask him, 'Is it a 2 or a 3?' This isn't what you should be up to here . . . You have to deal with your subject matter in terms of the merit of the subject matter." Doing right by our subject matter, and finding ways to capture the richness of human life, are serious challenges confronting developmental scientists.

Making Comparisons

The comparative method lies at the heart of all sciences, natural and social alike, and is the primary tool with which we generate knowledge; its success hinges on whether the units and features of the comparison are explicitly selected and defined on sound scientific bases (Fry, 1990b; Tudge, Shanahan, & Valsiner, 1997). Within-person comparisons over time have traditionally served as the foundation for the study of developmental phenomena. But it is also important for developmental scientists to make other systematic comparisons. Besides age and cohort comparisons, comparisons across sex and race groups are also commonplace. Because individual lives are embedded in historical time, cross-historical comparisons are also essential. Important comparisons must also be made across generations within families; across nations, cultures, and subcultures; and across species. More coordinated efforts along these lines will allow us to better understand the degree to which, and to whom, aspects of development can be generalized. However, we should not make comparisons without first giving serious thought to what we can expect to learn about development when we make them and how we might make sense of any similarities or differences that result.

Understanding Age and Forms of Age Structuring

Regardless of discipline, age lies at the heart of most theory and research on human development. Yet because age is an integral dimension for the study of lives, and because of its simplicity, have we taken its importance for granted? We must explore how members of a culture think about, use, and experience age; the ways in which age is embedded in social and cultural expectations about experiences and roles, and in the organization of family, educational, occupational, or political spheres and policies; how age enters into everyday social interaction and affects the expectations and evaluations of individuals involved in those exchanges; and how age is linked to personality attributes and behavioral dispositions.

Research on the life course depends on the accurate measurement of chronological age, which is more complicated than it seems at first sight. However, chronological age is an "empty" variable: We rarely assume that it is chronological age itself that causes something, but whatever it is that age presumably indexes that does, if this is even made explicit. In addition, most researchers likely do not use age as an index for a single underlying dimension or process, but instead for a host of dimensions and processes. Given that chronological age is often a poor indicator of biological, psychological, and social statuses, we must develop alternative, and more specific, measures of age that are sensitive to individual differences. Still better, we might give more thought to the dimensions and processes for which age serves as an index, and attempt to measure them more directly.

We routinely conduct tests of age differences using arbitrarily-defined age brackets. Ironically, any care taken to measure age accurately is lost when these brackets are constructed. Worse still, we habitually break down our data according to such brackets without compelling rationale. Why are a particular set of age brackets meaningful? Why should we expect to find important differences along these divisions? We must also begin to be more critical of the circumstances under which we "hold age constant" in our analyses rather than automatically control for it.

We must be more cautious in the way we interpret the age differences that are unearthed in cross-sectional studies. Besides the fact that many investigators continue to misinterpret age differences as age changes, we must work harder to specify the causes and consequences of age-related differences, and to identify the mechanisms through which age plays a role in producing these differences. Are age-related differences in fact age-related (that is, do they have age-specific onset, asymptote, or rates of change)? Or are they instead simply time-dependent (duration) effects, irrespective of age? In addition, we might consider whether our knowledge of age differences can inform public policy issues, and whether age-related public policy concerns are justified in light of the size and consistency of these differences (Kimmel & Moody, 1990).

With respect to age norms, the biggest problems we face are to clarify what exactly we mean by "age norms," explicate the levels at which we hope to study them, and specify their form and content. Regardless of whether age-related expectations are really "norms" or simply "frames of reference" or "cognitive maps," we know little about how these expectations are "constructed, transmitted, and learned" (Elder, 1998, p. 947). We also know little about the subjective sides of age expectations and timetables: how they are actively negotiated and experienced, their effects on the perceptions and evaluations of self and others, and how they play a role in decision-making processes, particularly in determining the developmental goals that individuals set and pursue at different points in life. We must explore multiple types of timetables (e.g., general, specialized, personal, and interdependent), the synchrony or asynchrony between them, and the costs and benefits of synchrony or asynchrony to individuals and others. There is also inconclusive evidence about whether and how strategies of coping and control change with age.

Much remains to be learned about how members of a society divide the span of time from birth to death into distinct phases, and what age boundaries and markers they use to define these categories and designate movement from one phase to another. We also have much to learn about both the positive and negative images of different age groups (e.g., physically, psychologically, socially), and of "common sense" or "folk" ideas about how different life phases will be experienced and about constancy and change in lives over time.

Finally, the state plays a significant role in structuring opportunities and allocating resources in education, work, family, health care, and other spheres. Systematic, cross-national comparisons are needed to provide important insights into the ways in which states and their policies structure the life course. In addition, questions related to whether age or need should serve as the basis for benefits and entitlements, and whether age-based policies bring the potential for age divisiveness in society, are complicated and have no clear solutions. Our research must fully explore the potential impact of social policies on individuals, families, age and other groups, social institutions, and society at large.

Gathering and Sharing Life-Course Data

Regardless of whether data being analyzed were gathered prospectively or retrospectively, life experiences must be dated if they are to be used optimally with multivariate methods and adequately placed within a life-course framework. Investigators must do everything possible to ensure that the timing, sequencing, duration, density, and spacing of experiences can later be arrayed completely and accurately. Life- history matrices, which plot an individual's experiences within specific life domains over time, are particularly helpful in this regard.

Data collection in most retrospective studies is cross-sectional in character: A sample is interviewed only once, and retrospective questions gather information on most of the respondent's life. The information that results, at least in principle, approaches that obtained in a long-ranging longitudinal study. Single-shot retrospective studies offer an excellent alternative to prospective longitudinal designs, given that the gathering of life-history data requires respondents to offer a detailed account of the past. And because respondents are interviewed only once, an investigator does not face an ongoing struggle with attrition. It is also possible to use this strategy with large, multi-cohort samples, if desired. However, this approach, like any, comes with its own set of concerns. The most common problems associated with retrospective data relate to the accuracy and precision of recall.

Given the importance of understanding lives through time, we must take seriously the need to conduct longitudinal research. Longitudinal strategies are essential for advancing developmental scholarship, but they are accompanied by many serious barriers. As a result of these barriers, research on human lives seldom covers significantly long stretches of time. Most primary "longitudinal" research tends to be anchored in only two data points close to one another in time. (Ironically, the assumption that two observations comprise a longitudinal study has been described as the biggest *myth* about longitudinal research [Rogosa, 1988].) However, even the analysis of two time points is significantly more complicated than it seems at first sight, and the analysis of more than two time points even more so. Opportunities to study lives "the long way" (Block, 1993) are beginning to improve as new investments are made in the gathering of longitudinal data, as new methods for analyzing longitudinal data are developed, and as we recognize that the most pressing and intriguing questions about human development require "a corpus of data" on individual lives over many decades of life (Tomlinson-Keasey, 1993). Some of the secondary data sets now available or in progress allow us to ask long-ranging questions, though the use of secondary data sets inevitably comes with intellectual compromises and practical costs. In addition, because the life-course framework was not well developed when many early studies were designed and conducted, these studies did not gather extensive information on life experiences, preparation for them, and adaptation to them. These studies are also largely focused on cohorts born before 1930 and who are now in later life. As a result, we must have reservations about the degree to which we can generalize what we have learned about the life course from these subjects to current cohorts of young people whose adult lives will span the next century. New longitudinal projects are therefore needed to cover earlier phases of the life course, beginning with those who are now young. For longitudinal studies to be effective, they must not only cover many periods and functions, but observations must be made continuously during these periods and on these functions so that important changes are not missed.

The availability of secondary or archival data sets also poses many unresolved practical and ethical questions about the sharing of data across the scientific community (Sieber, 1991a, 1991b; Weil & Hollander, 1991). Should scientific institutions and gatekeepers (e.g., funding agencies, journals, professional associations) reward investigators for preparing and sharing data files? If so, how? Who should pay the costs associated with documenting and duplicating data files? Who "owns" the set of data? Who should have access to them? Should funded data be controlled by the investigator, the institution, or the funding agency? For what purposes should the use of secondary data be approved? How should we deal with the matter of informed consent, especially when data were not originally intended to be shared? How might confidentiality be breached in the process of sharing data? Do secondary users have obligations to their donors? At what point must data be released? In large-scale collaborative efforts, who controls the set of data and is ultimately responsible and accountable for it? These challenges suggest that scientific research, especially funded research, is likely to be regulated by new rules in the future.

Understanding Trajectories

Because we are interested in studying lives over time, and the antecedents and consequences of various experiences, we must generate theories and use methods that allow a more complete examination of long-ranging trajectories. Research on the life course must better explore how an individual's present has been shaped by the past, and how an individual's anticipated future is shaped by both the past and the present. This involves examining the critical points at which trajectories branch out and lead, through specific sequences of events, to various outcomes.

To advance our ability to handle entire trajectories, we must first develop methods that allow us to generate and describe whole trajectories; these methods must simultaneously incorporate data on timing, sequencing, spacing, density, and duration. We are then faced with the formidable challenges associated with not only analyzing single trajectories within individuals, but also multiple trajectories and the connections between them; and of finding ways to aggregate and compare trajectories across individuals.

As the span of time to be analyzed increases, the number of relevant variables to consider, and the ways in which they may be plotted over time, seem nearly endless. (As the span of time to be analyzed increases, it also becomes increasingly difficult to describe "typical" courses.) This process is made more difficult by the fact that there is little temporal theory to guide the selection process. Significant theoretical advances, whether through the development of new theories or through the revision and extension of existing ones, are necessary for us to answer the following questions in analyzing trajectories: Which is the most important set of variables, when is each variable from that set most important (given that the same variable may be available at multiple data points), how might those variables then be arrayed in some sequence of relationships over time, and what processes and mechanisms drive these relationships? In the absence of temporal theory, these linkages become major "leaps of faith," especially when the time interval between them is dramatic and when extremely distal experiences are included; yet these leaps of faith are often made in the analysis and interpretation of longitudinal data (see also Cairns, Costello, & Elder, 1996). In addition, we must consider the ways in which our variables might be multiply confounded, not only at a single time point but especially across multiple time points. Much also remains to be learned about the bridges between earlier and later development, and especially between the first and second halves of life.

Understanding Continuity and Discontinuity

The theme of continuity and discontinuity, and of stability and change, throughout life is one of the great themes of developmental scholarship. However, seldom are explicit theoretical or empirical models for understanding these offered in the literature. The meanings and uses of these concepts must be clarified. Are continuity and stability and discontinuity and change the same? How do we know these phenomena when we see them? How might they be defined, measured, and validated?

Twenty years ago, the aleatory template, which takes the view that there is little about development that is "preprogrammed," was significantly less developed than the stability or ordered change templates. Twenty years later, most contemporary developmental research now seems to advocate a position in line with the aleatory template, though much more in principle than in practice. Because human lives are considered to be neither stable nor orderly, nor valid beyond specific groups of people in specific environments in specific periods of historical time, theory becomes significantly more difficult, if not impossible, to develop. Similarly, because individuals and the worlds in which they live are taken to be ever-changing, our empirical work becomes increasingly difficult, and the task of prediction becomes nearly impossible. As developmental science becomes increasingly aleatoric, is it destined to become a science of simple description? Will our research do little else but contribute to the historical record?

Because our conception of the developing person is multi-dimensional, that conception must include the possibility of both continuity and stability on the one hand, and of discontinuity and change on the other. Along these lines, we know little about whether the processes and conditions that foster continuity or stability are merely the opposite of those that foster discontinuity or change (Caspi, 1998).

Measuring Change

Many questions related to the measurement of change remain unanswered (or are kept implicit in our work). How shall change be conceptualized? What is it that changes? How much change occurs, and in what forms? Why does it occur? How shall change be represented, measured, analyzed, and interpreted? How much change is meaningful change? How much is "true" change, and how much is measurement error, random, or idiosyncratic? How much change is needed for "development" to occur? From what influences does development arise and where does development lead? Why do some individuals develop in certain ways and others not? Why do individuals change in different directions, and still others not at all? Why do individuals develop at difference paces? What specific conditions facilitate or prohibit these pathways? Is development a property of individuals, collectives, or both?

We have much to learn about analyzing both quantitative and, especially, qualitative change. Most thought on the challenges posed by change relates to change in dependent variables. There has been little discussion of change in relation to independent variables, and of conducting analyses that use change in independent variables to model change in dependent variables (change-on-change analyses).

Because time and change must become a central focus of our measures, we must be sensitive to whether our measures are reliable and valid for individuals of different ages, in different life periods, and at different points in historical time. Do the validity and reliability of a construct and its measures change as individuals grow older? Do they change across different historical periods? Should we expect this? How might these changes affect our measurement and interpretation of these constructs? Concerns about the reliability and validity of dynamic variables pose pressing new questions, given that the available procedures for examining reliability and validity are meant for static variables and are inappropriate for dynamic variables. We must also be sensitive to age biases and stereotypes inherent in our constructs and measures.

The tension between statistical significance and substantive significance also deserves greater attention. Change that is statistically significant may not be substantively significant, just as change that is statistically insignificant may not be substantively significant. The over-reliance on testing for statistical significance is not a very useful means for determining meaningful significance.

Incorporating Social Contexts

Despite the basic premise of "contextualized development," most theory and research does not specify well how social contexts shape individual development. The fact that context-related questions have remained at the periphery of developmental research is a serious problem. We take the "life" out of the "life course" when we neglect or control context. While there have been recent attempts to more systematically bring context into developmental research, these attempts have not advanced a view of context as an explicitly structured and interactive set of relationships and processes. The lack of attention to these issues is largely due to the fact that environments are difficult to measure—not only in terms of their structural characteristics, but especially in terms of the processes occurring within them. The neglect of context is also partially due to the fact that we have neither a comprehensive system of concepts nor a "scientific language" for dealing with the environment (Magnusson, 1985). Ultimately, these problems have prevented us from answering critical questions about how and why variations in environments produce different outcomes.

Contexts, like individuals, are changing, multidimensional, interactive, and interdependent. They must be studied as such. In addition, if the proposition of reciprocity is taken seriously, then changes in context may bring about changes in the individual, just as changes in the individual may bring about changes in the context. Therefore, the very problems encountered in studying individual lives within a temporal framework can be extended to the environments in which lives are lived. As we attempt to map changing individual lives onto a changing context (or, still harder, onto multiple contexts), and attempt to examine interactions across these levels, our theoretical and analytic work becomes immensely complicated. It is also important to note that while individuals may be systematically sorted into, or excluded from, specific contexts through processes of social allocation, they may also self-select themselves into specific contexts.

In addition, the ways in which contexts are conceptualized and believed to have an effect on development will hinge on the aspects of development being examined. It is inadequate to simply explicate which aspects of context are important; we must also specify how and why these aspects of context have a significant connection to the phenomenon under study. This is true not only of spatially proximal environments, and of temporally proximal influences, but especially of environments and influences that are more distal in space and time. We should not assume that distal environments and processes are less significant than proximal ones (though distal environments and processes surely pose bigger theoretical and analytic challenges). It is also important to consider whether the "target phenomenon" of interest is especially open to the influence of the environment at particular points in life, whether (and how) certain contexts are particularly influential at these points, and whether (and how) the strength of their effects on target phenomena change for individuals over time. In terms of life periods, most research on the effects of social context has focused on development during childhood and adolescence. Relatively little research has systematically explored the effects of social contexts, past or present, on development during periods of adult life.

We must better explore the link between individuals, contexts, and developmental "risk." While the field of epidemiology has increased our inventory of risk factors, it has most often examined variables we generally classify as "background" or "demographic" characteristics (especially race, sex, age, socioeconomic status, or some combination thereof). As a result, most risk factors are anchored purely in individual characteristics (and often ascriptive characteristics) and seldom tap aspects of the environment that may also serve to place individuals at risk. Risk-related research faces many significant challenges. Among the most important of these challenges is the need to better understand the processes and mechanisms through which risk factors bring about negative outcomes, and the full range of outcomes they bring about.

Understanding Socialization

While the concept of socialization is an integral part of developmental thought, references to socialization are generally vague and unspecified. Socialization processes and their sources are treated as large, external, and abstract forces that loom above, and impose themselves on, individuals. Little is known about the precise sources of socialization and their relative importance, how their messages are transmitted, the content of those messages, and their successes and failures. Most importantly, little is known about socialization processes as they extend beyond childhood and across the life course, particularly through the many decades of adult life and into old age.

Understanding Cohort

Cohort is also one of the most central but least understood concepts of developmental science. Its uses and measurement must be clarified. What exactly do we mean by cohort, and why? How exactly should cohort be measured and its effects analyzed? The definition of cohorts according to birth year is simultaneously the most common and problematic use of cohort. If we choose to define cohorts this way, what is our rationale for using a particular span of years? Similarly, a common analytic strategy is to subdivide a cohort into finer birth year-brackets or according to social location variables such as sex, race, income, educational attainment, or occupational status. If we subdivide a cohort in these ways, what is our rationale for choosing those dimensions? Most importantly, how might any differences that result be explained?

The measurement of cohort is plagued by three problems—the problems of cohort boundaries, distinctive experiences, and differential effects—each of which bring significant challenges for theory and research. How might we better take history into account when studying lives? How might we build history into our research designs and analyses? In order to fully understand human development, it is important for us to better grasp history, biography, and the relations between the two in a society. Much remains to be learned about how history leaves its imprint on human lives; precisely how, and through what mechanisms, historical events and periods of social change, large or small, play themselves out in the lives of individuals; their proximal and distal effects on individuals; and their unique and differential effects within and between cohorts. It is one thing to acknowledge that cohort and cohort differences are important for understanding lives. It is another thing to demonstrate their effects, and to know how, why, for whom, and with what consequences they come.

In addition, little attention has been paid to the subjective aspects of cohort membership. What is the meaning of a cohort experience to its members? What is shared? Who shares it? Which cohorts perceive themselves as such?

We might also better explore the societal significance of cohort. This might include an examination of the contributions that cohorts make in, and the demands they place upon, various spheres as they move through life—such as relationships, work organizations, voluntary organizations, educational institutions, the housing market, health care systems, or the government and its resources. This line of inquiry offers an exciting avenue for advancing theory and research on cohort.

Developmental science will benefit significantly from greater attention to these challenges. Greater sensitivity to cohort will also force us to temper our desire to generalize what we have learned about specific cohorts to other cohorts, and it may be particularly helpful in explaining results that run counter to our expectations or conflict in the research literature (Uhlenberg & Miner, 1996).

For some developmental scientists, especially sociologists, cohort effects are of central interest and even the primary phenomena for which they search. These scientists are interested in examining the ways in which historical time marks the trajectories of cohorts in unique ways. For others, especially life-span psychologists and those searching for universal laws of development, cohort is instead the very thing they seek to control. From the standpoint of these scientists, cohort is a nuisance; it is something that confounds the pure age changes they hope to uncover. Recent methodological developments have provided a means for better dealing with the age-period-cohort problem. Some of these developments attempt to disentangle age, period, and cohort effects *a priori* through research designs, while others attempt to disentangle these *post hoc* through statistical procedures. However, like age, measures of historical time are "empty" variables. Rather than invest more effort in finding statistical and design solutions to these problems, we might instead specify what it is that we think historical time serves to index and attempt to measure those dimensions and processes more directly.

Finally, a limitation of most developmental research is that it is historically specific. Yet our theory and data are discussed as if they are valid across historical periods. The problem of historical specificity has been largely disregarded, and it is a serious issue to which we must respond.

Understanding Variability

Recent sociological research has emphasized potential variability in life-course definitions and experiences. That is, the life course is not assumed to be uniform, but is instead assumed to be the product of a multi-faceted set of factors and experiences that interact to uniquely shape the pathways of individuals and groups. We must continue to describe and explain these multiple definitions and experiences, and our theory and research must allow for these complexities.

Similarly, recent literature in gerontology has emphasized the need to recognize the degree of heterogeneity that exists among individuals within an age bracket, and especially the degree of heterogeneity that exists among older people, which is taken to be significantly greater than that for other age groups. However, few empirical studies have actually used analytic strategies that tap dispersion or have made questions of heterogeneity their central focus. In fact, references to heterogeneity seem more often to be taken as statements of fact than as empirical questions. Besides the hypothesis that members of a cohort become increasingly different from one another as they grow older (a divergent variance trajectory), we might also consider other possible variance trajectories, depending on the characteristic under study.

We must therefore better document the degree of variability within and between individuals, and within and between cohorts. But if we are to take the call to examine variability seriously, we must do more than simply document it. We must also be prepared to fully understand it: to consider the explanatory factors and causal processes that produce it (whether biological, psychological, social, or otherwise), and to consider its full range of consequences. Theories related to the "Matthew effect," led by the work of Dannefer, are an important development along these lines. Following Baltes' lead, we must strive to understand the range and limits of plasticity, and how to maximize the potential for developmental adaptation. And following Magnusson's lead, we must strive to understand the emergence of "novel" patterns of individual functioning.

Finally, we often use the terms "heterogeneity," "variability," "dispersion," and "diversity" interchangeably. Are they the same? What do we mean by these concepts? Why they are important? And how we might better incorporate them into our work?

Understanding Interdependence

While we recognize that lives, in actuality, are intimately interwoven, we generally study lives as if they exist in isolation of others. Much remains to be learned about interdependence and its effects on the way lives are lived and experienced. We must begin to ask questions of our respondents meant to tap the interdependence of lives. At present, few methods permit us to analyze the nature, meanings, and consequences of interdependence over time. Besides interdependence between spouses or partners, and between parents and young children or young adult children, we must explore interdependence in later periods of life and the impact of multi-generational linkages and dynamics on the lives of family members. We must also explore both the enabling and constraining aspects of interdependence. The assumption in the literature is that these linkages are enabling and provide important resources to individuals. Yet these linkages may also serve to constrain and foreclose the options open to individuals.

Understanding "Successful" Development

While scholarship on successful development, and especially successful aging, has grown dramatically in the last decade, the most challenging conceptual and analytic issues have yet to be resolved. At a conceptual level, what exactly constitutes successful development? What are its primary domains? Are some domains more important than others? How do they work together? Is the concept universally applicable or is it restricted in its applicability? Is it a process or an outcome? Is it static or dynamic? What produces it? With what consequences, positive or negative, does it come? Which aspects of an individual's past and present experiences or conditions may promote or constrain successful development? What is its relationship to society (e.g., does successful aging create the potential for a successful society, and vice versa)? Many of these questions also require us to create and analyze conceptual and empirical models that are dynamic.

At an analytic level, what are the essential indicators of success in each of these domains, and are all indicators equally important? Should we rely on objective or subjective indicators, or both? Where do we draw the line between "successful" and "unsuccessful" for each indicator and for a larger domain (and what lies between the "successful" and the "unsuccessful," if anything)? Is the form of each indicator linear? Should we use minimal standards (e.g., the simple absence of problems) or should set higher standards? Are these empirical definitions constant or variable across time and place? Should domains be analyzed separately or in combination? If in combination, should domains be weighted equally? Need an individual meet "successful" criteria in every domain to achieve success overall? Regardless of how success is measured, how might it and its predictors be analyzed in a dynamic and temporal framework? These are only a few of the pressing questions that must be explicitly handled in future research.

Ultimately, we must ask ourselves whether research on successful development will improve our understanding of developmental processes and promote successful (or at least non-pathological) development for a majority of individuals (especially through prevention, early diagnosis and treatment of pathology, and the development of social policies and practices that improve the opportunity for individuals to do so).

Linking Social Structure and Human Agency

We must better understand social structures and their impact on the life course. But we must also take the developing person to be active, even proactive, in constructing her or his life, and interactive with her or his environments. In this sense, we must bridge psychology and sociology, and micro and macro levels of analysis. Sociological research on the life course has too often stressed the role that social structures play in shaping human lives, and has downplayed the fact that individuals actively create their own lives. In the process, sociologists have often lost sight of the person, and overlooked the roles of personality traits and characteristics, motivations, desires, aspirations, and expectations. We might describe their models as models of *structure without agency*. At the same time, psychological research has largely neglected powerful social and historical forces that shape lives. We might describe their models as models of *agency without structure*. Instead, we must re-conceptualize lives as having some elements of each, as individuals actively create their own lives within the confines of the social structures in which they exist. These models, which we must begin to build, are models of *agency within structure*.

We must also clarify the concept of social structure. A good example of the elusiveness of this term comes from the provocative Program on Age and Structural Change (PASC) of Riley and her colleagues, which emphasizes the link between "human lives" and "social structures." Human lives are shaped by, and themselves shape, social structures, and both are constantly changing. These concepts, and the dynamics between them, are difficult to handle in both theory and practice. How might we conceptualize and measure "structures," and changing structures? Which aspects of "lives," and of changing lives, should we study? How might we illustrate the link between them and their reciprocal relations? What processes or mechanisms drive these changes and relations?

In addition, Riley and her colleagues argue that while lives change rapidly (and have, in fact, changed dramatically in this century), social structures fail to keep pace with these changes, thereby creating "structural lag." But how and why does this lag occur? Can anything be done to control it? From where do pressures for structural change come and how do they come about? What are the effects of structural lag? The asynchrony between structures and lives presumably creates strain for everyone, from individuals to the larger society. Yet is it also possible that asynchrony might serve positive functions? For whom does lag carry negative or positive effects, and in what forms?

Furthering Debates on the Chronologization, Institutionalization, and Standardization of Lives

Several exciting debates emerging in developmental scholarship relate time, age, and the structure of the life course in modern societies. One set of debates concerns the degree to which the lives of successive cohorts are (or have become) *chronologized* (bound to age, and in which *lifetime* is of central concern), *institutionalized* (structured by social institutions and the state and its policies), and *standardized* (the degree to which their life patterns exhibit regularity, especially with respect to the timing of major life experiences). Another debate concerns the degree to which trajectories though specific life spheres are (or have become) chronologized, institutionalized, and standardized. Still another debate relates to differences in the degree to which men's and women's lives are (or have become) chronologized, institutionalized, and standardized. Much more empirical evidence is needed to shed light on each of these debates, even at a descriptive level. Once these patterns (or lack thereof) have been more fully documented, how might we explain them? Most importantly, what are the consequences of these changes for individual lives, for families and other groups, and for social, political, and economic institutions and policies?

The "de-" sides of the chronologization, institutionalization, and standardization continua all point to new hope that the lives are now, or at least have the potential to become, more flexibly structured and experienced. What factors might serve as new opportunities for life-course flexibility? What factors might serve as barriers to flexibility, and how might they be overcome?

While the degree of age segregation varies across cultures, an age-differentiated life course is common in most modern societies. A primary challenge facing developmental scientists and policymakers is how to modify existing "age-differentiated" structures and instead build "age-integrated" structures, in which opportunities for roles and activities in education, work, and leisure are open to all people, regardless of age. How might we do so? With what costs and benefits might this come?

Besides age integration, other forms of integration seem equally important to promote. As a society, we must work harder to provide meaningful opportunities in education, work, family, and leisure for both sexes, all social classes, and all races. And as both kin and kin-like relationships become more complex, we must face difficult questions about—and hopefully enlarge—our social and legal definitions of "family": questions about which types of unions and families are "legitimate" in society and worthy of the support and protection of the state.

TOWARD A NEW ERA OF DEVELOPMENTAL SCIENCE

We have seen that in contemporary and ever-changing societies, the effective analysis and explanation of lives becomes increasingly important *and* complicated. The study of lives is, of necessity, an interdisciplinary and multi-method enterprise. However, as our scientific treatments become more elaborate, they become increasingly fragmented both within and between academic disciplines, within and between the study of specific life periods, and across methods. The ultimate challenge now lies in moving away from this fragmentation toward a more integrated study of lives. However, the many promises of developmental science are contingent upon whether we are able to bridge disparate disciplinary orientations and intellectual concerns and further the debates outlined here. Most importantly, the promises of developmental science depend upon whether we are able to overcome many theoretical and methodological problems, most of which involve time or place in some form. Time and space are not mere variables, but are instead multidimensional processes that are both changeable and relative. Most of the challenges discussed in this book ultimately reflect the difficulties of studying lives through time and in place. These challenges should not prevent us from moving forward. On the contrary, these challenges indicate where important advances must be made so that we are able to usher in an exciting new era of developmental science.

References

Abbott, A. (1983). Sequences of social events. *Historical Methods, 17,* 192-204.
Abbott, A., & Forrest, J. (1986). Optimal matching for historical sequences. *Journal of Interdisciplinary History, 16,* 471-494.
Abbott, A., & Hrycak, A. (1990). Measuring resemblance in sequence data: An optimal matching analysis of musicians' careers. *American Journal of Sociology, 96*(1), 144-185.
Adams, R., & Blieszner, R. (1995). Aging well with family and friends. *American Behavioral Scientist, 39*(2), 209-224.
Aldwin, C. M. (1992). The Elders Life Stress Inventory: Egocentric and nonegocentric stress. In M. A. Stephens, J. H. Crowther, S. E. Hobfoll, & D. L. Tennenbaum (Eds.), *Stress and coping in later-life families* (pp. 49-69). New York: Hemisphere Publishing Corporation.
Aldwin, C. M. (1994). *Stress, coping, and development.* New York: Guilford Publications, Inc.
Alexander, K. L., Entwistle, D. R., & Dauber, S. L. (1994). *On the success of failure: A reassessment of the effects of retention in the primary grades.* New York: Cambridge University Press.
Allison, P. (1984). *Event history analysis.* Beverly Hills, CA: Sage Publications.
Allison, P. D. (1990). Change scores as dependent variables in regression analysis. In C. Clogg (Ed.), *Sociological methodology* (Vol. 20, pp. 93-114). London: Basil Blackwell, Ltd.
Alsaker, F. D. (1992). Modeling quantitative developmental change. In J. B. Asendorpf & J. Valsiner (Eds.), *Stability and change in development: A study of methodological reasoning* (pp. 88-109). Newbury Park, CA: Sage Publications.
Alwin, D. (1995). Taking time seriously: Studying social change, social structure, and human lives. In P. Moen, G. H. Elder, Jr., & K. Lüscher (Eds.), *Examining lives in context: Perspectives on the ecology of human development* (pp. 211-262). Washington, DC: American Psychological Association.
Amin, A. (1994). *Post-Fordism: A reader.* Oxford, UK: Blackwell Publishers.
Amster, L. E., & Krauss, H. H. (1974). The relationship between life crises and mental deterioration in old age. *International Journal of Aging and Human Development, 5*(1), 51-55.
Anderson, N. N. (1967). The significance of age categories for older persons. *The Gerontologist, 7,* 164-168.
Aneshensel, C. S. (1992). Social stress: Theory and research. *Annual Review of Sociology, 18,* 15-38.
Aneshensel, C. S., Pearlin, L. I., Mullan, J. T., Zarit, S. H., & Whitlatch, C. J. (1995). *Profiles in caregiving: The unexpected career.* San Diego, CA: Academic Press.

Angus, D., Mirel, J., & Vinovskis, M. A. (1988). Historical development of age-stratification in schooling. *Teacher College Record, 90,* 33-58.

Ariès, P. (1962). *Centuries of childhood: A social history of family life.* New York: Alfred A. Knopf.

Asendorpf, J. B., & Valsiner, J. (1992). Editor's introduction: Three dimensions of developmental perspectives. In J. B. Asendorpf & J. Valsiner (Eds.), *Stability and change in development: A study of methodological reasoning* (pp. ix-xxii). Newbury Park, CA: Sage Publications.

Atchley, R. C. (1994). *Social forces and aging* (7th ed.). Belmont, CA: Wadsworth.

Attias-Donfut, C. (1992). Transmissions between generations and the life course. In W. J. A. van den Heuvel, R. Illsley, A. Jamieson, & C. P. M. Knipscheer (Eds.), *Opportunities and challenges in an ageing society* (pp. 53-60). Amsterdam: Koninklijke Nederlandse Akademie van Wetenschappen.

Avery, R. J., Bryant, W. K., Douthitt, R. A., & McCullough, J. (1996). Lessons from the past, directions for the future. *Journal of Family and Economic Issues, 17(3/4),* 409-418.

Bachman, J. G., Johnston, L. D., & O'Malley, P. M. (1994). *Monitoring the Future: Questionnaire responses from the nation's high school seniors, 1992.* Ann Arbor, MI: Institute for Social Research.

Back, K., & Averett, C. (1985). Stability and change in life graph types. In E. Palmore, W. Busse, G. Maddox, J. Nowlin, & I. Siegler (Eds.), *Normal aging, v. III: Reports from the Duke Longitudinal Studies, 1975-1984* (pp. 290-305). Durham, NC: Duke University Press.

Back, K., & Bourque, L. B. (1970). Life graphs: Aging and cohort effect. *Journal of Gerontology, 25*(3), 249-255.

Balan, J., Browning, H. L., Jelin, E., & Litzler, L. (1969). A computerized approach to the processing and analysis of life histories obtained in sample surveys. *Behavioral Science, 14,* 105-120.

Balin, A. K. (1994). *Practical handbook of human biologic age determination.* Boca Raton, FL: CRC Press.

Baltes, P. B. (1968). Longitudinal and cross-sectional sequences in the study of age and generation effects. *Human Development, 11,* 145-171.

Baltes, P. B. (1984). Foreward. In R. M. Lerner (Ed.), *On the nature of human plasticity* (pp. ix-x). Cambridge: Cambridge University Press.

Baltes, P. B. (1987). Theoretical propositions of life-span developmental psychology: On the dynamics between growth and decline. *Developmental Psychology, 23,* 611-626.

Baltes, P. B. (1997). On the incomplete architecture of human ontogeny: Selection, optimization, and compensation as foundation of developmental theory. *American Psychologist, 52*(4), 366-380.

Baltes, P. B., & Baltes, M. M. (1990). Psychological perspectives on successful aging: The model of selective optimization with compensation. In P. B. Baltes & M. M. Baltes (Eds.), *Successful aging: Perspectives from the behavioral sciences* (pp. 1-34). New York: Cambridge University Press.

Baltes, P. B., Cornelius, S. W., & Nesselroade, J. R. (1979). Cohort effects in developmental psychology. In J. R. Nesselroade & P. B. Baltes (Eds.), *Longitudinal research in the study of behavior and development* (pp. 61-87). New York: Academic Press.

Baltes, M., & Lang, F. (1997). Everyday functioning and successful aging: The impact of resources. *Psychology and Aging, 12*(3), 433-443.

Baltes, P. B., Lindenberger, U., & Staudinger, U. (1998). Life-span theory in developmental psychology. In R. M. Lerner (Ed.), *Handbook of child psychology: Vol. 1. Theoretical models of human development* (5th ed., pp. 1029-1143). New York: John Wiley & Sons.

Baltes, P. B., Mayer, K. U., Helmchen, H., & Steinhagen-Thiessen, E. (1993). The Berlin Aging Study (BASE): Overview and design. *Ageing and Society, 13*(4), 483-515.

Baltes, P. B., Reese, H. W., & Lipsitt, L. P. (1980). Life-span developmental psychology. *Annual Review of Psychology, 31,* 65-110.

Baltes, P. B., Reese, H. W., & Nesselroade, J. R. (1977). *Life-span developmental psychology: An introduction to research methods.* Monterey, CA: Brooks/Cole Publishing Company.

Baltes, P. B., & Smith, J. (1999). Multilevel and systemic analyses of old age: Theoretical and empirical evidence for a fourth age. In V. L. Bengtson & K. W. Schaie (Eds.), *Handbook of theories of aging.* New York: Springer Publishing Company.

Bandura, A. (1992). Exercise of personal agency through the self-efficacy mechanism. In R. Schwarzer (Ed.), *Self-efficacy: Thought control of action* (pp. 3-38). Washington, DC: Hemisphere.

Barak, B. (1987). Cognitive age: A new multidimensional approach to measuring age identity. *International Journal of Aging and Human Development, 25*(2), 109-128.

Barak, B., & Gould, S. (1985). Alternative age measures: A research agenda. In E. C. Hirschman & M. B. Holbrook (Eds.), *Advances in consumer research* (Vol. 12, pp. 53-58). Provo, UT: Association for Consumer Research.

Barak, B., & Stern, B. (1986). Subjective age correlates: A research note. *The Gerontologist, 26*(5), 571-578.

Baum, S. K., & Boxley, R. L. (1983). Age identification in the elderly. *The Gerontologist, 23,* 532-537.

Bell, T. (1967). The relationship between social involvement and feeling old among residents in homes for the aged. *Journal of Gerontology, 22,* 17-22.

Benedict, R. (1938). Continuities and discontinuities in cultural conditioning. *Psychiatry, 1,* 161-167.

Bengtson, V. L., Rosenthal, C., & Burton, L. (1990). Families and aging. In R. Binstock & L. George (Eds.), *Handbook on aging and the social sciences* (pp. 263-287). San Diego, CA: Academic Press.

Bengtson, V., Rosenthal, C., & Burton, L. (1996). Paradoxes of families and aging. In R. Binstock & L. George (Eds.), *Handbook of aging and the social sciences* (4th edition) (pp. 253-282). San Diego, CA: Academic Press.

Benjamin, H. (1947). Biologic versus chronological age. *Journal of Gerontology, 2,* 217-222.

Berger, B. (1960). How long is a generation? *British Journal of Sociology, 11*(1), 10-23.

Berger, B. (1984). The resonance of the generation concept. In V. Garms-Homolova, E. M. Hoerning, & D. Schaeffer (Eds.), *Intergenerational Relationships* (pp. 219-227). Lewiston, NY: C. J. Hogrefe, Inc.

Berger, P. (1963). *Invitation to sociology: A humanistic perspective.* Garden City, NY: Doubleday Books.

Bergman, L. R. (1988). You can't classify all of the people all of the time. *Multivariate Behavioral Research, 23,* 425-441.

Bergman, L. R. (1992). Studying change in variables and profiles: Some methodological considerations. In J. B. Asendorpf & J. Valsiner (Eds.), *Stability and change in development: A study of methodological reasoning* (pp. 143-149). Newbury Park, CA: Sage Publications.

Bergman, L. R. (1993). Some methodological issues in longitudinal research: Looking ahead. In D. Magnusson & P. Casaer (Eds.), *Longitudinal research on individual development* (pp. 217-241). Cambridge, UK: Cambridge University Press.

Bergman, L. R., & Magnusson, D. (1997). A person-oriented approach in research on developmental psychopathology. *Development and Psychopathology, 9,* 291-319.

Berkman, L. F., Seeman, T. E., Albert, M., Blazer, D., Kahn, R., Mohs, R., Finch, C., Schneider, E., Cotman, C., McClearn, G., Nesselroade, J., Featherman, D., Garmezy, N., McKhann, G., Brim, G., Prager, D., & Rowe, J. (1993). Successful, usual, and impaired functioning in community-dwelling elderly: Findings from the MacArthur Foundation Network on Successful Aging. *Journal of Clinical Epidemiology, 46,* 1129-1140.

Best, F. (1980). *Flexible life scheduling.* New York: Praeger.

Best, F. (1990). Does flexible life scheduling have a future? In J. Habib & C. Nusberg (Eds.), *Rethinking worklife options for older persons* (pp. 217-241). Washington, DC: International Federation on Ageing.

Binstock, R. (1996). Continuities and discontinuities in public policy on aging. In V. Bengtson (Ed.), *Adulthood and aging: Research on continuities and discontinuities* (pp. 308-324). New York: Springer Publishing Company.

Binstock, R., & Day, C. (1996). Aging and politics. In R. Binstock & L. George (Eds.), *Handbook of aging and the social sciences* (4th edition) (pp. 362-387). San Diego, CA: Academic Press.

Birren, J. E. (1959). Principles of research on aging. In J. Birren (Ed.), *Handbook of aging and the individual* (pp. 3-42). Chicago, IL: University of Chicago Press.

Birren, J. E. (1969). The concept of functional age, theoretical background. *Human Development, 12,* 214-215.

Birren, J. E., & Birren, B. A. (1990). The concepts, models, and history of the psychology of aging. In J. E. Birren & K. W. Schaie (Eds.), *Handbook of the psychology of aging* (3rd. ed., pp. 3-20). San Diego, CA: Academic Press.

Birren, J. E., & Cunningham, W. R. (1985). Research on the psychology of aging: Principles, concepts and theory. In J. E. Birren & K. W. Schaie (Eds.), *Handbook of aging and psychology* (pp. 3-34). New York: Van Nostrand Reinhold Company, Inc.

Birren, J. E., & Deutchman, D. E. (1991). *Guiding the autobiography group for older adults: Exploring the fabric of life.* Baltimore: Johns Hopkins University Press.

Birren, J., & Fisher, L. (1992). Speed of behavior and aging: Consequences for cognition and survival. In T. B. Sonderegger (Ed.), *Nebraska symposium on motivation, Volume 39: Psychology and aging* (pp. 2-37). Lincoln, NE: University of Nebraska Press.

Birren, J., & Schroots, J. F. (1996). History, concepts, and theory in the psychology of aging. In J. Birren & K. W. Schaie (Eds.), *Handbook of the psychology of aging* (pp. 3-23). SanDiego, CA: Academic Press.

Blake, J., & Davis, K. (1964). Norms, values, and sanctions. In R. E. Faris (Ed.), *Handbook of modern sociology* (pp. 456-484). Chicago, Illinois: Rand McNally.

Blanchard-Fields, F., & Chen, Y. (1996). Adaptive cognition and aging. *American Behavioral Scientist, 39*(3), 231-248.

Blau, P. M. & Duncan, O. D. (1967). *The American occupational structure.* New York: John Wiley & Sons.

Block, J. (1993). Studying personality the long way. In D. C. Funder, R. D. Parke, C. Tomlinson-Keasey, & K. Widaman (Eds.), *Studying lives through time: Personality and development* (pp. 9-41). Washington, DC: American Psychological Association.

Bloom, B. S. (1964). *Stability and change in human characteristics.* New York: John Wiley & Sons.

Bloom, K. L. (1961). Age and the self concept. *American Journal of Psychiatry, 118,* 534-538.

Blossfeld, H. P., Hamerle, A., & Mayer, K. U. (1989). *Event history analysis: Statistical theory and application in the social sciences.* Hillsdale, NJ: Lawrence Erlbaum Associates.

Blossfeld, H.-P., & Rohwer, G. (1997). Causal inference, time, and observation plans in the social sciences. *Quality and Quantity, 31,* 361-384.

Blum, Z., Karweit, N., & Sørensen, A. B. (1969). *A method for the collection and analysis of retrospective life histories.* Baltimore, MD: Johns Hopkins University Press.

Bohrnstedt, G. W. (1969). Observations on the measurement of change. In E. F. Borgatta (Ed.), *Sociological methodology* (pp. 113-133). San Francisco, CA: Jossey-Bass.

Bollen, K. A. (1989). *Structural equations with latent variables.* New York: John Wiley & Sons.

Bond, L., Cutler, S., & Grams, A. (Eds.). (1995). *Promoting successful and productive aging.* Thousand Oaks, CA: Sage Publications.

Borg, I., & Groenen, P. J. (1997). *Modern multidimensional scaling: Theory and applications.* New York: Springer.

Borscheid, P. (1992). Der alte Mensch in der Vergangenheit. In P.B. Baltes & J. Mittelstrass (Eds.), *Zukunft des Alterns und gesellschaftliche Entwicklung* (pp. 35-61). Berlin, Germany: Walter de Gruyter.

Boruch, R. F., Reiss, A., Jr., Garner, J., Larntz, K., & Freels, S. (1991). Sharing confidential and sensitive data. In J. E. Sieber (Ed.), *Sharing social science data: Advantages and challenges* (pp. 61-86). Newbury Park, CA: Sage Publications.

Botella, L., & Guillem, F. (1993). The autobiographical group: A tool for the reconstruction of past life experience with the aged. *International Journal of Aging and Human Development, 36*(4), 303-319.

Bouffard, L., & Bastin, E. (1996). Future time perspective according to women's age and social role during adulthood. *Sex Roles, 24*(3/4), 253-285.

Bourque, L. B., & Back, K. (1977). Life graphs and life events. *Journal of Gerontology, 32,* 669-674.

Boyd, J. W., & Dowd, J. J. (1988). The diffusiveness of age. *Social Behaviour, 3,* 85-103.

Braithwaite, V., Lynd-Stevenson, R., & Pigram, D. (1993). An empirical study of ageism: From polemics to scientific utility. *Australian Psychologist, 28*(1), 9-15.

Brandtstädter, J. (1989). Personal self-regulation of development: Cross-sequential analyses of development-related control beliefs and emotions. *Developmental Psychology, 25,* 96-108.

Brandtstädter, J. (1990). Development as a personal and cultural construction. In G. Semin & K. Gergen (Eds.), *Everyday understanding: Social and scientific implications* (pp. 83-107). Newbury Park, CA: Sage Publications.

Brandtstädter, J. (1993). Development, aging, and control: Empirical and theoretical issues. In D. Magnusson & P. Casaer (Eds.), *Longitudinal research on individual development* (pp. 194-216). Cambridge, UK: Cambridge University Press.

Brandtstädter, J. (1998). Action perspectives on human development. In R. M. Lerner (Ed.), *Handbook of child psychology: Vol. 1. Theoretical models of human development* (5th ed., pp. 807-863). New York: John Wiley & Sons.

Brandtstädter, J., & Baltes-Götz, B. (1990). Personal control over development and quality of life perspectives in adulthood. In P. B. Baltes & M. M. Baltes (Eds.), *Successful aging: Perspectives from the behavioral sciences* (pp. 197-224). New York: Cambridge University Press.

Brandtstädter, J., & Greve, W. (1994). The aging self: Stabilizing and protective processes. *Developmental Review, 14,* 52-80.

Brandtstädter, J., & Renner, G. (1990). Tenacious goal pursuit and flexible goal adjustment: Explication and age-related analysis of assimilative and accommodative strategies of coping. *Psychology and Aging, 5,* 58-67.

Braungart, R. G., & Braungart, M. M. (1986). Life-course and generational politics. *Annual Review of Sociology, 12,* 205-231.

Brewin, C. R., Andrews, B., & Gotlib, I. H. (1993). Psychopathology and early experience: A reappraisal of retrospective reports. *Psychological Bulletin, 113,* 82-98.

Brim, O. G., Jr. (1966). Socialization through the life cycle. In O. G. Brim, Jr. & S. Wheeler (Eds.), *Socialization after childhood: Two essays* (pp. 1-49). New York: John Wiley & Sons.

Brim, O. G., Jr. (1968). Adult socialization. In J. Clausen (Ed.), *Socialization and society* (pp. 182-226). Boston, MA: Little, Brown and Company.

Brim, O. G., Jr., & Ryff, C. D. (1980). On the properties of life events. In P. B. Baltes & O. G. Brim (Eds.), *Life-span development and behavior* (pp. 367-388). New York: Academic Press.

Brody, E. M. (1981). Women in the middle. *The Gerontologist, 21*, 471-480.

Bronfenbrenner, U. (1963). Developmental theory in transition. In H. W. Stevenson (Ed.), *Child psychology: Sixty-second yearbook of the National Society for the Study of Education* (pp. 517-542). Chicago, IL: University of Chicago Press.

Bronfenbrenner, U. (1979). *The ecology of human development: Experiments by nature and design*. Cambridge, MA: Harvard University Press.

Bronfenbrenner, U. (1988). Interacting systems in human development: Research paradigms, present and future. In N. Bolger, A. Caspi, G. Downey, & M. Moorehouse (Eds.), *Persons in context: Developmental processes* (pp. 25-49). New York: Cambridge University Press.

Bronfenbrenner, U. (1995). Developmental ecology through space and time: A future perspective. In P. Moen, G. H. Elder, Jr., & K. Lüscher (Eds.), *Examining lives in context: Perspectives on the ecology of human development* (pp. 619-647). New York: American Psychological Association.

Bronfenbrenner, U., & Ceci, S. J. (1994). Nature-nurture reconceptualized in developmental perspective: A bioecological model. *Psychological Review, 101*, 568-586.

Bronfenbrenner, U., & Morris, P. A. (1998). The ecology of developmental process. In R. M. Lerner (Ed.), *Handbook of child psychology: Vol. 1. Theoretical models of human development* (5th ed., pp. 993-1028). New York: John Wiley & Sons.

Brooks, J. (1996). Living longer and improving health: An obtainable goal in promoting aging well? *American Behavioral Scientist, 39*(3), 272-287.

Brooks-Gunn, J., Phelps, E., & Elder, G. H., Jr. (1991). Studying lives through time: Secondary data analyses in developmental psychology. *Developmental Psychology, 27*(6), 899-910.

Brose, H.-G. (1989). Coping with instability: The emergence of new biographical patterns. *Life Stories, 5*, 3-25.

Brown, C. (1990). Empirical evidence on private training. *Research in Labor Economics, 111*, 97-113.

Brown, G., & Harris, T. (1978). *The social origins of depression*. New York: The Free Press.

Brückner, E. (1990). Die retrospective Erhebung von Lebensverlaeufen. In K. U. Mayer (Ed.), *Lebensverlaeufe und sozialer Wandel* (pp. 374-403). Opladen: Westdautscher Verlag.

Brückner, E. (1994). *Lebensverlaeufe und gesellschaftlicher Wandel. Konzept, Design and Methodik der Erhebung von Lebensverlaeufen der Gerburtsjahrgaenge 1919-1921*. Berlin: Max Planck Institute for Human Development and Education.

Brunstein, J. (1993). Personal goals and subjective well-being: A longitudinal study. *Journal of Personality and Social Psychology, 65*, 1061-1070.

Bryk, A. S., & Raudenbush, S. W. (1987). Application of hierarchical linear models to assessing change. *Psychological Bulletin, 101*, 147-158.

Bryk, A. S., & Raudenbush, S. W. (1992). *Hierarchical linear models: Applications and data analysis methods*. Beverly Hills, CA: Sage Publications.

Bryman, A., Bytheway, B., Allatt, P., & Keil, T. (1987). Introduction. In A. Bryman, B. Bytheway, P. Allatt, & T. Keil (Eds.), *Rethinking the life cycle* (pp. 1-13). London: Macmillan.

Buchmann, M. (1989). *The script of life in modern society: Entry into adulthood in a changing world.* Chicago, Illinois: University of Chicago Press.

Bultena, G., & Wood, V. (1969). Normative attitudes toward the aged role among migrant and non-migrant retirees. *The Gerontologist, 9*(3), 204-208.

Burkhauser, R., & Quinn, J. (1994). Changing policy signals. In M. W. Riley, R. L. Kahn, & A. Foner (Eds.), *Age and structural lag: Society's failure to provide meaningful opportunities in work, family, and leisure* (pp. 237-262). New York: John Wiley & Sons.

Burton, L. (1996). Age norms, the timing of family role transitions, and intergenerational caregiving among aging African-American women. *The Gerontologist, 36*(2), 199-208.

Bush, D. M., & Simmons, R. G. (1981). Socialization processes over the life course. In M. Rosenberg & R. H. Turner (Eds.), *Social psychology: Sociological perspectives* (pp. 133-164). New York: Basic Books.

Butler, R. N. (1963). The life review: An interpretation of reminiscence in the aged. *Psychiatry, 26,* 65-76.

Butler, R. N. (1969). Ageism: Another form of bigotry. *The Gerontologist, 9,* 243-246.

Butler, R. N. (1994). Dispelling ageism: The cross-cutting intervention. In D. Shenk & W. A. Achenbaum (Eds.), *Changing perceptions of aging and the aged* (pp. 137-143). New York: Springer Publishing Company.

Butler, R. N., & Gleason, H. P. (1985). *Productive aging: Enhancing vitality in later life.* New York: Springer Publishing Company.

Butler, R. N., & Lewis, M. (1982). *Aging and mental health: Positive Psychosocial and biomedical approaches.* St.Louis: Mosby.

Bytheway, B. (1990). Age. In S. M. Peace (Ed.), *Researching social gerontology: Concepts, methods, and issues* (pp. 9-18). Newbury Park, CA: Sage Publications.

Cain, L. D., Jr. (1964). Life course and social structure. In R. E. L. Faris (Ed.), *Handbook of Modern Sociology* (pp. 272-309). Chicago, IL: Rand-McNally.

Cain, L. D., Jr. (1976). Aging and the law. In R. H. Binstock & E. Shanas (Eds.), *Handbook of aging and the social sciences* (pp. 342-368). New York: Van Nostrand Reinhold Company.

Cain, L. D., Jr. (1987). Alternative perspectives on the phenomena of human aging: Age stratification and age status. *The Journal of Applied Behavioral Science, 23*(2), 277-294.

Cairns, R. B., Costello, E. J., & Elder, G. H., Jr. (1996). The making of developmental science. In R. B. Cairns, G. H. Elder, Jr., & E. J. Costello (Eds.), *Developmental science* (pp. 223-234). New York: Cambridge University Press.

Cairns, R. B., Neckerman, H. J., & Cairns, B. D. (1989). Social networks and shadows of synchrony. In G. R. Adams, T. P. Gullota, & R. Montemayor (Eds.), *Advances in adolescent development* (pp. 275-305). Newbury Park, CA: Sage Publications.

Calasanti, T. M. (1996). Incorporating diversity: Meaning, levels of research, and implications for theory. *The Gerontologist, 36*(2), 147-156.

Calhoun, C. (1992). Social change. In E. F. Borgatta & M. L. Borgatta (Eds.), *Encyclopedia of sociology* (Vol. 4, pp. 1907-1912). New York: Macmillan Publishing Company.

Calloway, M. D., & Jorgensen, L. B. (1994). A model program for returning women in higher education. *College Student Journal, 28*(3), 281-286.

Cameron, P. (1969). Age parameters of young adult, middle aged, old, and aged. *Journal of Gerontology, 24*(2), 201-202.

Cameron, P. (1972). Stereotypes about generational fun and happiness versus self-appraised fun and happiness. *The Gerontologist, 12*(2), 120-123.

Cameron, P. (1976). Masculinity/femininity of the generations: As self-reported and as stereotypically appraised. *International Journal of Aging and Human Development, 7,* 143-151.

Campbell, R. T., & Alwin, D. F. (1996). Quantitative approaches: Toward an integrated science of aging and human development. In R. Binstock & L. George (Eds.), *Handbook of aging and the social sciences* (pp. 31-51). San Diego, CA: Academic Press.

Campbell, R. T., & Hudson, C. M. (1985). Synthetic cohorts from panel surveys: An approach to studying rare events. *Research on Aging, 7*(1), 81-93.

Campbell, R. T., Mutran, E., & Parker, R. N. (1991). Longitudinal design and longitudinal analysis: A comparison of three approaches. *Research on Aging, 8*(4), 480-504.

Cantor, N., & Fleeson, W. (1991). Life tasks and self-regulatory processes. In M. L. Maehr & P. R. Pintrich (Eds.), *Advances in motivation and achievement* (Vol. 7, pp. 327-369). Greenwich, CT: JAI Press.

Carden, M. (1978). The proliferation of a social movement: Ideology and individual incentives in the contemporary feminist movement. In L. Kriesberg (Ed.), *Research in social movements, conflicts, and change* (Vol. 1, pp. 179-196). Greenwich, CT: JAI Press.

Carlson, R. (1971). Where is the person in personality research? *Psychological Bulletin, 75,* 203-219.

Carolina Consortium on Human Development. (1996). Developmental science: A collaborative statement. In R. B. Cairns, G. H. Elder, Jr., & E. J. Costello (Eds.), *Developmental science* (pp. 1-6). New York: Cambridge University Press.

Caspi, A. (1998). Personality development across the life course. In N. Eisenberg (Ed.), *Handbook of child psychology: Vol. 3. Social, emotional, and personality development* (5th ed.). New York: John Wiley & Sons.

Caspi, A., & Moffitt, T. E. (1993). When do individual differences matter? A paradoxical theory of personality coherence. *Psychological Inquiry, 4*(4), 247-271.

Caspi, A., Moffitt, T. E., Thornton, A., Freedman, D., Amell, J. W., Harrington, H., Smeijers, J., & Silva, P. A. (1996). The life history calendar: A research and clinical assessment method for collecting retrospective event-history data. *International Journal of Methods in Psychiatric Research, 6,* 101-114.

Catan, L. (1986). The dynamic display of process: Historical development and contemporary uses of the microgenetic method. *Human Development, 29,* 252-263.

Centre for Educational Research and Innovation (CERI). (1987). *Adults in higher education.* Paris, France: Organization for Economic Co-Operation and Development (OECD).

Chan, T. W. (1995). Optimal matching analysis. *Work and Occupations, 22*(4), 467-490.

Chelimsky, E., & Shadish, W. R. (1997). *Evaluation for the 21st century: A handbook.* Thousand Oaks, CA: Sage Publications.

Chiriboga, D. A. (1984). Social stressors as antecedents of change. *Journal of Gerontology, 39*(4), 468-477.

Chiriboga, D. A. (1996). In search of continuities and discontinuities across time and culture. In V. Bengtson (Ed.), *Adulthood and aging: Research on continuities and discontinuities* (pp. 173-199). New York: Springer Publishing Company.

Chiriboga, D. A., & Dean, H. (1978). Dimensions of stress: Perspectives from a longitudinal study. *Journal of Psychosomatic Research, 22,* 47-55.

Christensen, K. (1990). Bridge over troubled waters: How older workers view the labor market. In P. B. Doeringer (Ed.), *Bridges to retirement: Older workers in a changing labor market* (pp. 175-207). Ithaca, NY: ILP.

Christopherson, S. (1991). Trading time for consumption: The failure of working hours reduction in the United States. In K. Hinrichs, W. Roche, & C. Sirianni (Eds.), *Working time in transition: The political economy of working hours in industrial nations* (pp. 171-188). Philadelphia, PA: Temple University Press.

Chudacoff, H. P. (1989). *How old are you? Age consciousness in American culture.* Princeton, NJ: Princeton University Press.

Clausen, J. A. (1972). The life course of individuals. In M. Riley, M. Johnson & A. Foner (Eds.), *Aging and society: A sociology of age stratification* (Vol. 3, pp. 457-515). New York: Russell Sage Foundation.

Clausen, J. A. (1986). *The life course: A sociological perspective.* Englewood Cliffs, NJ: Prentice-Hall.

Clausen, J. S. (1991). Adolescent competence and the shaping of the life course. *American Journal of Sociology, 96*(4), 805-842.

Clausen, J. A. (1993). *American lives: Looking back at the children of the Great Depression.* Berkeley, CA: University of California Press.

Clausen, J. A. (1995). Gender, contexts, and turning points in adults' lives. In P. Moen, G. H. Elder, Jr., & K. Lüscher (Eds.), *Examining lives in context: Perspectives on the ecology of human development* (pp. 365-389). New York: American Psychological Association.

Clipp, E., & Elder, G. H., Jr. (1995). The aging veteran of World War II: Psychiatric and life course insights. In P. E. Ruskin & J. A. Talbott (Eds.), *Aging and post-traumatic stress disorder* (pp. 19-51). Washington, DC: American Psychiatric Press, Inc.

Clipp, E., Pavalko, E., & Elder, G. H., Jr. (1992). Trajectories of health: In concept and empirical pattern. *Behavior, Health, and Aging, 2,* 159-179.

Cochrane, R., & Robertson, A. (1973). The life events inventory: A measure of the relative severity of psycho-social stressors. *Journal of Psychosomatic Research, 17,* 135-139.

Cohen, L. (1988). *Life events and psychological functioning: Theoretical and methodological issues.* Newbury Park, CA: Sage Publications.

Cohen, P. (1991). A source of bias in longitudinal investigations of change. In L. M. Collins & J. L. Horn (Eds.), *Best methods for the analysis of change: Recent advances, unanswered questions, future directions* (pp. 18-25). Washington, DC: American Psychological Association.

Cohler, B., Pickett, S. A., & Cook, J. A. (1996). Life course and persistent psychiatric illness: Social timing, cohort, and intervention. In V. Bengtson (Ed.), *Adulthood and aging: Research on continuities and discontinuities* (pp. 69-95). New York: Springer Publishing Company.

Colby, A., & Phelps, E. (1990). Archiving longitudinal data. In D. Magnusson & L. R. Bergman (Eds.), *Data quality in longitudinal research* (pp. 249-262). Cambridge, England: Cambridge University Press.

Cole, T. R. (1995). What have we "made" of aging? *Journal of Gerontology: Social Sciences, 50B*(6), S341-343.

Coleman, P. (1986). Issues in the therapeutic use of reminiscence with elderly people. In I. Hanley & M. Gilhooly (Eds.), *Psychological therapies for the elderly.* London: Crome Hall.

Collins, L. M. (1991). Measurement in longitudinal research. In L. M. Collins & J. L. Horn (Eds.), *Best methods for the analysis of change: Recent advances, unanswered questions, future directions* (pp. 137-148). Washington, DC: American Psychological Association.

Collins, L. M. (1996). Measurement of change in research on aging: Old and new issues from an individual growth perspective. In J. Birren & K. W. Schaie (Eds.), *Handbook of the psychology of aging* (pp. 38-56). San Diego, CA: Academic Press.

Collins, L. M., & Horn, J. L. (Eds.). (1991). *Best methods for the analysis of change: Recent advances, unanswered questions, future directions.* Washington, DC: American Psychological Association.

Collins, L. M., & Wugalter, S. E. (1992). Latent class models for stage-sequential dynamic latent variables. *Multivariate Behavioral Research, 27,* 131-157.

Compas, B. E. (1987). Stress and life events during childhood and adolescence. *Clinical Psychology Review, 7,* 275-302.

Compas, B. E., Davis, G. E., Forsythe, C. J., & Wagner, B. M. (1987). Assessment of major and daily life events during adolescence: The Adolescent Perceived Events Scale. *Journal of Consulting and Clinical Psychology, 55,* 534-541.

Comte, A. (1839). *The positive philosophy of Auguste Comte* (H. Martineau, Trans.). London, England: Bell.

Conger, R., & Elder, G. H., Jr. (1994). *Families in troubled times: Adaptation to change in rural America.* New York: Aldine de Gruyter.

Connidis, I. (1989). The subjective experience of aging: Correlates of divergent views. *Canadian Journal on Aging, 8*(1), 7-18.

Cook, F. L. (1996). Public support for programs for older Americans: Continuities amidst threats of discontinuities. In V. Bengtson (Ed.), *Adulthood and aging: Research on continuities and discontinuities* (pp. 327-346). New York: Springer Publishing Company.

Cook, F. L., Marshall, V. W., Marshall, J., & Kaufman, J. (1994). The salience of intergenerational equity in Canada and the United States. In T. Marmor, T. Smeeding, & V. Greene (Eds.), *Economic security and intergenerational justice: A look at North America* (pp. 91-129). Washington, DC: Urban Institute Press.

Cook, T. D., Degirmencloglu, S., Phillips, M., Settersten, R., & Shagle, S. (forthcoming). *The contexts of early adolescent development.* Chicago, IL: University of Chicago Press.

Costa, P. T., & McCrae, R. R. (1980). Functional age: A conceptual and empirical critique. In S. S. Haynes & M. Feinleib (Eds.), *Epidemiology of aging* (NIH Pub. No. 80-969, pp. 23-46). Washington, DC: U.S. Government Printing Office.

Costa, P. T., & McCrae, R. R. (1985). Concepts of functional or biological age. In R. Andres, E. L. Bierman, & W. R. Hazzard (Eds.), *Principles of geriatric medicine* (pp. 30-37). New York: McGraw-Hill.

Costa, P. T., & McCrae, R. R. (1994). Set like plaster? Evidence for the stability of adult personality. In T. F. Heatherton & J. L. Weinberger (Eds.), *Can personality change?* (pp. 21-40). Washington, DC: APA Press.

Courgeau, D., & Lelievre, E. (1992). *Event history analysis in demography.* Oxford: Clarendon Press.

Cremin, M. C. (1992). Feeling old versus being old: Views of troubled aging. *Social Science Medicine, 12,* 1305-1315.

Crockett, L. J., & Crouter, A. C. (Eds.). (1995). *Pathways through adolescence: Individual development in relation to social contexts.* Hillsdale, NJ: Lawrence Erlbaum Associates.

Cronbach, L. J., & Furby, L. (1970). How we should measure "change"—or should we? *Psychological Bulletin, 74*(1), 68-80.

Cross, S., & Markus, H. (1991). Possible selves across the life span. *Human Development, 34,* 230-255.

Cumming, E. & Henry, W. (1961). *Growing old: The process of disengagement.* New York: Basic Books.

Cutler, S. (1982). Subjective age identification. In D. Mangen & W. Peterson (Eds.), *Research instruments in social gerontology* (pp. 437-462). Minneapolis, MN: University of Minnesota Press.

Cutler, S. J. (1995). The methodology of social scientific research in gerontology: Progress and issues. *Journal of Gerontology: Social Sciences, 50B*(2), S63-S64.

Dannefer, D. (1984). The role of the social in life-span developmental psychology, past and future: Rejoinder to Baltes and Nesselroade. *American Sociological Review, 49,* 847-850.

Dannefer, D. (1987). Aging as intracohort differentiation: Accentuation, the Matthew effect, and the life course. *Sociological Forum, 2,* 211-236.

Dannefer, D. (1991). The race is to the swift: Images of collective aging. In G. M. Kenyon, J. E. Birren, & J. J. F. Schroots (Eds.), *Metaphors of aging in science and the humanities* (pp. 155-172). New York: Springer.

Dannefer, D. (1992). On the conceptualization of context in developmental discourse: Four meanings of context and their implications. In D. L. Featherman, R. M. Lerner, & M. Perlmutter (Eds.), *Life-span development and behavior* (Vol. 11, pp. 83-110). Hillsdale, NJ: Lawrence Erlbaum Associates.

Dannefer, D. (1993). When does society matter for individual differences? Implications of a counterpart paradox. *Psychological Inquiry, 4,* 281-284.

Dannefer, D. (1996). The social organization of diversity, and the normative organization of age. *The Gerontologist, 36*(2), 174-177.

Dannefer, D., & Perlmutter, M. (1990). Development as a multidimensional process: Individual and social constituents. *Human Development, 33,* 108-137.

Dannefer, D., & Sell, R. (1988). Age structure, the life course, and "aged heterogeneity": Prospects for research and theory. *Comprehensive Gerontology, 2,* 1-10.

David, D. (1990). Reminiscence, adaptation, and social context in old age. *International Journal of Aging and Human Development, 30*(3), 175-188.

David, M. (1991). The science of data sharing: Documentation. In J. E. Sieber (Ed.), *Sharing social science data: Advantages and challenges* (pp. 91-115). Newbury Park, CA: Sage Publications.

Davies, P. (1995). *Adults in higher education: International perspectives on access and participation.* Bristol, PA: Jessica Kingsley Publishers.

Davis, K. (1948). *Human society.* New York: Macmillan.

Dean, W. (1988). *Biological aging measurement: Clinical applications.* Thousand Oaks, CA: The Center for Bio-Gerontology.

Dean, W. (1994). Biological aging measurement: Its rationale, history, and current status. In A. K. Balin (Ed.), *Practical handbook of human biologic age determination* (pp. 3-14). Boca Raton, FL: CRC Press.

Dean, W., & Morgan, R. F. (1988). In defense of the concept of biological aging measurement: Current status. *Archives of Gerontology and Geriatrics, 7,* 191-210.

DeGenova, M. K. (1992). If you had your life to do over again: What would you do differently? *International Journal of Aging and Human Development, 34*(2), 135-143.

Denzin, N. K., & Lincoln, Y. S. (Eds.). (1994). *Handbook of qualitative research.* Thousand Oaks, CA: Sage Publications.

DeViney, S. (1995). Life course, private pension, and financial well-being. *American Behavioral Scientist, 39*(2), 172-185.

deVries, B. Birren, J. E., & Deutchman, D. E. (1990). Adult development through guided autobiography: The family context. *Family Relations, 39,* 3-7.

Dex, S. (1991). *The reliability of recall data: A literature review.* Working papers of the ESRC Research Center on Micro-social change (Paper 11). Colchester: University of Essex.

Dilthey, W. (1875). Uber das Studium der Geschichte der Wissenschaften vom Menschen, der Gesellschaft und dem Staat. In W. Dilthey, *Gesammelte Schriften, Volume 5: Die geistige Welt.* Berlin: Teubner.

DiPrete, T. A., & Forristal, J. D. (1994). Multi-level models: Methods and substance. *Annual Review of Sociology, 20,* 331-357.

Dirken, J. M. (1972). *Functional age of industrial workers.* Gronigan: Wolters-Noordhoff.

Dirken, J. M. & Van Zonneveld, R. J. (1969). International symposium on the assessment of functional age: Psychological and social aspects. *Human Development, 12,* 214-220.

Dittman-Kohli, F. (1991). Meaning and personality change from early to late adulthood. *European Journal of Gerontology, 1,* 98-103.

Dixon, A. R., & Bäckman, L. (Eds.). (1995). *Psychological compensation: Managing losses and promoting gains.* Hillsdale, NJ: Lawrence Erlbaum Associates.

Dodge, K. A. (1993). New wrinkles in the person-versus-situation debate. *Psychological Inquiry, 4*(4), 284-286.

Doeringer, P. B., & Piore, M. J. (1971). *Internal labor markets and manpower analysis.* Lexington, MA: D. C. Heath & Company.

Dohrenwend, B. S., Krasnoff, L., Askenasy, A. R., & Dohrenwend, B. P. (1978). Exemplification of a method for scaling life events: The PERI life events scale. *Journal of Health and Social Behavior, 19,* 205-229.

Donaldson, G., & Horn, J. L. (1992). Age, cohort, and time developmental muddles: Easy in practice, hard in theory. *Experimental Aging Research, 18*(4), 213-222.

Dowd, J., & Bengtson, V. L. (1978). Aging in minority populations: An examination of the double jeopardy hypothesis. *Journal of Gerontology, 33,* 427-436.

Downs, A. (1995). Cruelest cut: Laying off older workers. In A. Downs (Ed.), *Corporate executions: The ugly truth about layoffs: How corporate greed is shattering lives, companies, and communities* (pp. 127-138). New York, NY: AMACOM.

Drevenstedt, J. (1976). Perceptions of onsets of young adulthood, middle age, and old age. *Journal of Gerontology, 31*(1), 53-57.

Easterlin, R. (1987). *Birth and fortune: The impact of numbers on personal welfare* (2nd ed.). Chicago, IL: University of Chicago Press.

Easterlin, R. (1996). Economic and social implications of demographic patterns. In R. Binstock & L. George (Eds.), *Handbook of aging and the social sciences* (4th ed., pp. 73-93). San Diego: Academic Press.

Eccles, J. (1993). *Youth Face-to-Face Interview Schedule.* Middle School Family Survey Study, Institute of Behavioral Sciences. Boulder, Colorado: University of Colorado.

Eglit, H. (1985). Age and the law. In R. H. Binstock & E. Shanas (Eds.), *Handbook of aging and the social sciences* (pp. 528-553). New York: Van Nostrand Reinhold.

Ehmer, J. (1990). *Sozialgeschichte des Alters.* Frankfurt/Main: Suhrkamp.

Eisenstadt, S. N. (1956). *From generation to generation: Age groups and social structure.* Glencoe, Illinois: Free Press.

Elder, G. H., Jr. (1974). *Children of the Great Depression: Social change and life experience.* Chicago, IL: University of Chicago Press.

Elder, G. H., Jr. (1985). Perspectives on the life course. In G. H. Elder (Ed.), *Life course dynamics: Trajectories and transitions, 1968-1980* (pp. 23-49). Ithaca, NY: Cornell University Press.

Elder, G. H., Jr. (1986). Military time and turning points in men's lives. *Developmental Psychology, 22*(2), 233-245.

Elder, G. H., Jr. (1987). War mobilization and the life course: A cohort of World War II veterans. *Sociological Forum, 2*(3), 449-472.

Elder, G. H., Jr. (1992). Life course. In E. G. Borgata & M. L. Borgatta (Eds.), *Encyclopedia of sociology* (Vol. 3, pp. 1120-1130). New York: Macmillan Publishing Company.

Elder, G. H., Jr. (1995). The life course paradigm: Social change and individual development. In P. Moen, G. H. Elder, Jr., & K. Lüscher (Eds.), *Examining lives in context:*

Perspectives on the ecology of human development (pp. 101-139). Washington, DC: American Psychological Association.

Elder, G. H., Jr. (1998). The life course and human development. In R. M. Lerner (Ed.), *Handbook of child psychology: Vol. 1. Theoretical models of human development* (5th ed., pp. 939-991). New York: John Wiley & Sons.

Elder, G. H., Jr. & Bailey, S. L. (1988). The timing of military service in men's lives. In D. M. Klein & J. Aldous (Eds.), *Social Stress and Family Development* (pp. 157-174). New York: The Guilford Press.

Elder, G. H., Jr., & Caspi, A. (1990). Studying lives in a changing society: Sociological and personological explorations. In A. I. Rabin (Ed.), *Studying persons and lives: The Henry A. Murray lectures in personality* (pp. 201-247). New York: Springer.

Elder, G. H., Jr., George, L. K., & Shanahan, M. (1996). Psychosocial stress over the life course. In H. Kaplan (Ed.), *Perspectives on psychosocial stress* (pp. 245-290). San Diego, CA: Academic Press.

Elder, G. H., Jr., & Meguro, Y. (1987). Wartime in men's lives: A comparative study of American and Japanese cohorts. *International Journal of Behavioral Development, 10,* 439-466.

Elder, G. H., Jr., & Pavalko, E. (1993). Work careers in men's later years: Transitions, trajectories, and historical change. *Journal of Gerontology: Social Sciences, 48,* S180-191.

Elder, G. H., Jr., Pavalko, E., & Clipp, E. (1993). *Working with archival data.* Newbury Park, CA: Sage Publications.

Elder, G. H., Jr., Shanahan, M. J., & Clipp, E. C. (1994). When war comes to men's lives: Life course patterns in family, work, and health. *Psychology and Aging, 9*(1), 5-16.

Elias, N. (1969). *The civilizing process* (E. Jephcott, Trans.). New York: Urizen Books. (First American edition published 1978)

Emmons, R. A. (1989). The personal striving approach to personality. In L. A. Pervin (Ed.), *Good concepts in personality and social psychology* (pp. 87-126). Hillsdale, NJ: Lawrence Erlbaum Associates.

Engel, U., & Reinecke, J. (Eds.). (1996). *Analysis of change: Advanced techniques in panel data analysis.* New York: Walter de Gruyter.

Erikson, E. (1980). *Identity and the life cycle.* New York: W. W. Norton Press.

Esler, A. (1984). "The truest community": Social generations as collective mentalities. *Journal of Political and Military Sociology, 12,* 99-112.

Everitt, B. S. (1993). *Cluster analysis* (3rd ed.). New York: Halsted Press.

Fallo-Mitchell, L., & Ryff, C. D. (1982). Preferred timing of female life events: Cohort differences. *Research on Aging, 4,* 249-267.

Featherman, D. (1980). Retrospective longitudinal research: Methodological consideration. *Journal of Economics and Business, 32,* 152-169.

Featherman, D. L. (1986). Biography, society, and history: Individual development as population process. In A. Sørensen, F. Weinert & L. Sherrod (Eds.), *Human development and the life course: Multidisciplinary perspectives* (pp. 99-149). Hillsdale, NJ: Lawrence Erlbaum Associates.

Featherman, D. L., & Lerner, R. M. (1985). Ontogenesis and sociogenesis: Problematics for theory and research about development and socialization across the life span. *American Sociological Review, 50,* 659-676.

Featherstone, M., & Wernick, A. (Eds.). (1995). *Images of aging: Cultural representations of later life.* London: Routledge.

Feibleman, J. K. (1956). *The institutions of society.* London: Allen.

Ferrari, G. (1874). *Teoria dei periodi politici.* Milan, Italy: Hoepli.

Fillenbaum, G. G. (1995). Activities of daily living. In G. L. Maddox (Ed.), *The encyclopedia of aging: A comprehensive resource in gerontology and geriatrics* (2nd ed.) (pp. 7-9). New York: Springer Publishing Company.

Flacks, R. (1988). *Making history.* New York: Columbia University Press.

Flinn, C. J., & Heckman, J. J. (1982). New methods for analyzing individual event histories. In S. Leinhardt (Ed.), *Sociological methodology* (pp. 99-140). San Francisco, CA: Jossey-Bass Publishers.

Foner, A. (1979). Ascribed and achieved bases of stratification. *Annual Review of Sociology, 5,* 219-242.

Fontane, P. (1996). Exercise, fitness, and feeling well. *American Behavioral Scientist, 39*(3), 299-305.

Ford, D. H. (1987). *Humans as self-constructing living systems: A developmental perspective on behavior and personality.* Hillsdale, NJ: Lawrence Erlbaum Associates.

Ford, D. H., & Lerner, R. M. (1992). *Developmental systems theory: An integrative approach.* Newbury Park, CA: Sage Publications.

Ford, M. E., & Ford, D. H. (1987). *Humans as self-constructing living systems: Putting the framework to work.* Hillsdale, NJ: Lawrence Erlbaum Associates.

Fortes, M. (1949). Time and social structure: An Ashanti case study. In M. Fortes (Ed.), *Social structure: Studies presented to A. R. Radcliffe-Brown* (pp. 54-84). Oxford: Clarendon Press.

Fortes, M. (1984). Age, generation, and social structure. In D. I. Kertzer & J. Keith (Eds.), *Age and anthropological theory* (pp. 99-122). Ithaca, New York: Cornell University Press.

Frank, G., & van der Burgh, R. M. (1986). Cross-cultural use of life history methods in gerontology. In C. L. Fry & J. Keith (Eds.), *New methods for old-age research: Strategies for studying diversity* (pp. 185-207). Boston, MA: Bergin and Garvey Publishers, Inc.

Frank, L. K. (1939). Time perspectives. *Journal of Social Philosophy, 4,* 293-312.

Freedman, D., Thornton, A., Camburn, D., Alwin, D., & Young-DeMarco, L. (1988). The life history calendar: A technique for collecting retrospective data. In C. Clogg (Ed.), *Sociological methodology* (pp. 37-68). Washington, DC: American Sociological Association.

Freeman, L. C., White, D. R., & Romney, A. K. (Eds.). (1989). *Research method in social network analysis.* Fairfax, VA: George Mason University Press.

Freud, S. (1923/1974). *The ego and the id.* London: Hogarth.

Fry, C. L. (1986). Emics and age: Age differentiation and cognitive anthropological strategies. In C. L. Fry & J. Keith (Eds.), *New methods for old age research: Strategies for studying diversity* (pp. 105-131). Massachusetts: Bergin and Garvey Publishers, Inc.

Fry, C. L. (1990a). Changing age structures and the mediating effects of culture. In K. Knipscheer (Ed.), *Opportunities and challenges in an aging society.* Amsterdam: Elsevier.

Fry, C. L. (1990b). Comparative research in aging. In K. Ferraro (Ed.), *Gerontology: Perspectives and issues* (129-146). New York: Springer Publishing Company.

Fry, C. L. (1994). Age and the life course. In J. Keith, C. Fry, A. Glascock, C. Ikels, J. Dickerson-Putman, H. Harpending, & P. Draper (Eds.), *The aging experience: Diversity and commonality across cultures* (pp. 144-197). Thousand Oaks, CA: Sage Publications.

Fry, C. L. (1996). Age, aging, and culture. In R. Binstock & L. George (Eds.), *Handbook of aging and the social sciences* (4th ed., pp. 117-136). San Diego: Academic Press.

Fry, C. L., Dickerson-Putnam, J., Draper, P., Ikels, C., Keith, J., Glascock, A. P., & Harpending, H. (1997). Culture and the meaning of a good old age. In J. Sokolovsky (Ed.), *The cultural context of aging: Worldwide perspectives* (pp. 99-123). Westport, CT: Gergin & Garvey.

REFERENCES / 271

Furstenberg, F. F., Jr., Eccles, J., Elder, G. H., Jr., Cook, T. D., & Sameroff, A., & Associates (1999). *Managing to make it: Urban families and adolescent stress.* Chicago, IL: University of Chicago Press.

Garfein, A. J., & Herzog, A. R. (1995). Robust aging among the young-old, old-old, and oldest-old. *Journal of Gerontology: Social Sciences, 50B*(2), S77-S87.

Garmenzy, N. (1993a). Developmental psychopathology: Some historical and current perspectives. In D. Magnusson & P. Casaer (Eds.), *Longitudinal research on individual development* (pp. 95-126). Cambridge, UK: Cambridge University Press.

Garmenzy, N. (1993b). Vulnerability and resilience. In D. C. Funder, R. D. Parke, C. Tomlinson-Keasey, & K. Widaman (Eds.), *Studying lives through time: Personality and development* (pp. 377-398). Washington, DC: American Psychological Association.

Gee, E. M. (1987). Historical change in the family life course of Canadian men and women. In V. Marshall (Ed.), *Aging in Canada* (2nd ed., pp. 265-287). Markham, Ontario: Fitzhenry & Whiteside.

Gee, E. M. (1990). Preferred timing of womens' life events: A Canadian study. *International Journal of Aging and Human Development, 31*(4), 279-294.

George, L. K. (1995). The last half-century of aging research – and thoughts for the future. *Journal of Gerontology: Social Sciences, 50B*, S1-S3.

George, L. K. (1996a). Missing links: The case for a social psychology of the life course. *The Gerontologist, 36*(2), 248-255.

George, L. (1996b). Social factors and illness. In R. Binstock & L. George (Eds.), *Handbook of aging and the social sciences* (4th ed., pp. 229-253). San Diego: Academic Press.

George, L. K., Mutran, E. J., & Pennybacker, M. R. (1980). The meaning and measurement of age identity. *Experimental Aging Research, 6*, 283-298.

George, L. K., Siegler, I. C., & Okun, M. A. (1981). Separating age, cohort, and time of measurement: Analysis of vaiance and multiple regression. *Experimental Aging Research, 7*(3), 297-314.

Gergen, K. (1977). Stability, change, and chance in human development. In N. Datan & H. Reese (Eds.), *Life-span developmental psychology: Dialectical perspectives on experimental research* (pp. 136-158). New York: Academic Press.

Germain, C. (1994). Emerging conceptions of family development over the life course. *Journal of Contemporary Human Services, 75*(5), 259-267.

Gerth, H., & Mills, C. (1953). *Character and social structure: The psychology of institutions.* New York: Harcourt Brace Jovanovich, Publishers.

Gibbs, J. (1965). Norms: The problem of definition and classification. *American Journal of Sociology, 70*, 586-594.

Gibbs, J. (1981). The sociology of deviance and social control. In M Rosenberg & R. H. Turner (Eds.), *Social psychology: Sociological perspectives* (pp. 483-522). New York: Basic Books.

Giddens, A. (1979). *Central problems in social theory.* London: Macmillan.

Giddens, A. (1984). *The constitution of society: Outline of the theory of structuration.* Oxford: Polity Press.

Gilligan, C. (1982). *In a different voice: Psychological theory and women's development.* Cambridge, MA: Harvard University Press.

Glaser, B. G., & Strauss, A. L. (1971). *Status passage.* New York: Aldine.

Glass, T. A., Seeman, T. E., Herzog, A. R., Kahn, R. L., & Berkman, L. F. (1995). Change in productive activity in late adulthood: MacArthur Studies of Successful Aging. *Journal of Gerontology: Social Sciences, 50B*, S65-S76.

Glenn, N., Mason, W. M., Mason, K., Winsborough, H., Knoke, D., & Hout, M. (1976). Cohort analysts' futile quest. *American Sociological Review, 41*(5), 900-904.

Goffman, E. (1959). *The presentation of self in everyday life.* Garden City, NY: Anchor Books.

Goldsmith, R. E. & Heiens, R. A. (1992). Subjective age: A test of five hypotheses. *The Gerontologist, 32,* 312-317.

Gollwitzer, P. M. (1986). The implementation of identity intentions: A motivational-volitional perspective on symbolic self-completion. In F. Halisch & J. Kuhl (Eds.), *Motivation, intention, and volition* (pp. 349-369). New York: Springer-Verlag.

Gottlieb, G. (1970). Conceptions of prenatal behavior. In L. R. Aronson, E. Tobach, D. S. Lehrman, & J. S. Rosenblatt (Eds.), *Development and evolution of behavior: Essays in memory of T. C. Schneirla* (pp. 111-137). San Francisco, CA: W. H. Freeman & Company.

Gottlieb, G. (1992). *Individual development and evolution: The genesis of novel behavior.* New York: Oxford University Press.

Gottman, J. M. (Ed.). (1995). *The analysis of change.* Mahwah, NJ: Lawrence Erlbaum Associates.

Graff, H. (1995). *Conflicting paths: Growing up in America.* Cambridge, MA: Harvard University Press.

Green, B. S. (1993). *Gerontology and the construction of old age: A study in discourse analysis.* New York: Aldine de Gruyter.

Greene, A. L., & Wheatley, S. M. (1992). "I've got a lot to do and I don't think I'll have the time": Gender differences in late adolescents' narratives of the future. *Journal of Youth and Adolescence, 21*(6), 667-686.

Griffin, L. J. (1993). Narrative, event-structure analysis, and causal interpretation in historical sociology. *American Journal of Sociology, 98*(5), 1094-1133.

Grigsby, J. S. (1996). The meaning of heterogeneity: An introduction. *The Gerontologist, 36*(2), 145-146.

Grusky, D. B., & Takata, A. A. (1992). Social stratification. In E. F. Borgatta & M. L. Borgatta (Eds.), *Encyclopedia of sociology* (Vol. 4, pp. 1955-1970). New York: Macmillan Publishing Company.

Gubrium, J. F., & Holstein, J. A. (1995). Life course malleability: Biographical work and deprivatization. *Sociological Inquiry, 65*(2), 207-223.

Gubrium, J. F., & Holstein, J. A. (1997). *The new language of qualitative method.* New York: Oxford University Press.

Gubrium, J. F., Holstein, J. A., & Buckholdt, D. R. (1994). *Constructing the life course.* Dix Hills, NY: General Hall, Inc.

Guillemard, A.-M. & Rein, M. (1993). Comparative patterns of retirement: Recent trends in developed societies. *Annual Review of Sociology, 19,* 469-503.

Guptill, C. S. (1969). A measure of age identification. *The Gerontologist, 9,* 96-102.

Gutmann, D. (1987). *Reclaimed powers: Toward a new psychology of men and women in later life.* New York: Basic Books.

Gutmann, D. (1997). *The human elder in nature, culture, and society.* Boulder, CO: Westview Press.

Habib, J., & Nusberg, C. (1990). The reorganization of work, leisure, and education over the life cycle. In J. Habib & C. Nusberg (Eds.), *Rethinking worklife options for older persons* (pp. 195-198). Washington, DC: International Federation on Aging.

Hagestad, G. O. (1981). Problems and promises in the social psychology of intergenerational relations. In R. W. Fogel, E. Hattfield, S. B. Kiesler, & E. Shanas (Eds.), *Aging, stability, and change in the family* (pp. 11-47). New York: Academic Press.

Hagestad, G. O. (1982a). Life-phase analysis. In D. Mangen & W. Peterson (Eds.), *Research instruments in social gerontology* (pp. 463-532). Minneapolis, MN: University of Minnesota Press.

Hagestad, G. O. (1982b). Parent and child: Generations in the family. In T. M. Field, A. Huston, H. C. Quay, L. Troll, & G. E. Finley (Eds.), *Review of human development* (pp. 485-499). New York: John Wiley & Sons.

Hagestad, G. O. (1987). Parent-child relations in later life: Trends and gaps in past research. In J. B. Lancaster, J. Altmann, A. S. Rossi, & Lonnie R. Sherrod (Eds.), *Parenting across the life span: Biosocial dimensions* (pp. 405-433). New York: Aldine de Gruyter.

Hagestad, G. O. (1988). Demographic change and the life course: Some emerging trends in the family realm. *Family Relations, 37,* 405-410.

Hagestad, G. O. (1990). Social perspectives on the life course. In R. Binstock & L. George (Eds.), *Handbook of aging and the social sciences* (3rd ed., pp. 151-168). New York: Academic Press.

Hagestad, G. O. (1991). Trends and dilemmas in life course research: An international perspective. In W. R. Heinz (Ed.), *Theoretical advances in life course research* (pp. 23-57). Weinheim, Germany: Deutscher Studien Verlag.

Hagestad, G. O. (1996). On-time, off-time, out of time? Reflections on continuity and discontinuity from an illness process. In V. Bengtson (Ed.), *Adulthood and aging: Research on continuities and discontinuities* (pp. 204-222). New York: Springer Publishing Company.

Hagestad, G. O., & Neugarten, B. L. (1985). Age and the life course. In E. Shanas & R. Binstock (Eds.), *Handbook of aging and the social sciences* (2nd ed., pp. 35-61). New York: Van Nostrand and Reinhold Company.

Hagestad, G. O., & Settersten, R. A., Jr. (1994, August). *The problem of age norms: I. A critical look at conceptual and empirical issues.* Paper presented at the Annual Meeting of the American Sociological Association, Los Angeles, California.

Haight, B. (1991). Reminiscing: The state of the art as a basis for practice. *International Journal of Aging and Human Development, 33*(1), 1-32.

Haight, B., & Webster, J. (Eds.). (1995). *The art and science of reminiscing: Theory, research, methods, and applications.* Washington, DC: Taylor & Francis.

Hantrais, L., & Mangen, S. (Eds.). (1996). *Cross-national research methods in the social sciences.* New York: Pinter.

Hareven, T. (1991). Synchronizing individual time, family time, and historical time. In J. Bender & D. E. Wellbery (Eds.), *Chronotypes: The construction of time* (pp. 167-182). Stanford, CA: Stanford University Press.

Hareven, T. K. (1994). Family change and historical change: An uneasy relationship. In M. W. Riley, R. L. Kahn, & A. Foner (Eds.), *Age and structural lag* (pp. 130-150). New York: John Wiley & Sons.

Harris, C. W. (1963). *Problems in measuring change.* Madison, WI: University of Wisconsin Press.

Harris, D. K., & Changas, P. S. (1994). Revision of Palmore's Second Facts on Aging Quiz from a true-false to a multiple-choice format. *Educational Gerontology, 20,* 741-754.

Harris, D. K., Changas, P. S., & Palmore, E. B. (1996). Palmore's First Facts on Aging Quiz in a multiple-choice format. *Educational Gerontology 22*(6), 575-589

Havighurst, R., & Glasser, R. (1972). And exploratory study of reminiscence. *Journal of Gerontology, 27,* 243-253.

Hawkes, R. K. (1975). Norms, deviance, and social control: A mathematical elaboration of concepts. *American Journal of Sociology, 70,* 586-594.

Hays, S. (1996). *The cultural contradictions of motherhood.* New Haven, CT: Yale University Press.

Heckhausen, J. (1991). *CAMAQ: Control Agency Means-Ends in Adulthood Questionnaire.* Berlin, Germany: Max Planck Institute for Human Development and Education, Berlin, Germany.

Heckhausen, J. (1999). *Developmental regulation in adulthood: Age-normative and sociostructural constraints as adaptive challenges.* New York: Cambridge University Press.

Heckhausen, J., & Baltes, P. B. (1991). Perceived controllability of expected psychological change across adulthood and old age. *Journal of Gerontology: Psychological Sciences, 46*(4), P165-173.

Heckhausen, J., Diewald, M., & Huinink, J. (1994). *Control agency means-ends in adulthood questionnaire—short version.* Unpublished questionnaire, Max Planck Institute for Human Development and Education, Berlin, Germany.

Heckhausen, J., Dixon, R., & Baltes, P. B. (1989). Gains and losses in development throughout adulthood as perceived by different age groups. *Developmental Psychology, 25*(1), 109-121.

Heckhausen, J., & Krüger, J. (1993). Developmental expectations for the self and most other people: Age grading in three functions of social comparisons. *Developmental Psychology, 29,* 539-548.

Heckhausen, J., & Lang, F. (1996). Social construction and old age: Normative conceptions and interpersonal processes. In G. R. Semin & K. Fiedler (Ed.), *Applied social psychology* (pp. 374-382). London: Sage Publications.

Heckhausen, J., & Schulz, R. (1995a). A life-span theory of control. *Psychological Review, 102,* 284-304.

Heckhausen, J., & Schulz, R. (1995b). *Conceptualization and assessment of optimization in primary and secondary control.* Unpublished manuscript, Max Planck Institute for Human Development and Education, Berlin, Germany.

Heinz, W. R. (1991a). *Theoretical advances in life course research.* Weinheim, Germany: Deutscher Studien Verlag.

Heinz, W. R. (1991b). *The life course and social change: Comparative perspectives.* Weinheim, Germany: Deutscher Studien Verlag.

Heinz, W. R. (1992). *Institutions and gatekeeping in the life course.* Weinheim, Germany: Deutscher Studien Verlag.

Heinz, W. R. (1998, May). *Work and the life course: Cross-cultural research perspectives.* Paper presented at "Restructuring Work and the Life Course: An International Symposium," University of Toronto, Toronto, Ontario.

Held, T. (1986). Institutionalization and deinstitutionalization of the life course. *Human Development, 29,* 157-162.

Hendricks, J. (1992). Learning to act old: Heroes, villains, or old fools. *Journal of Aging Studies, 6*(1), 1-11.

Hendricks, J. (1994). Revisiting the Kansas City Study of Adult Life: Roots of the disengagement model in social gerontology. *The Gerontologist, 34*(6), 753-755.

Hendricks, J. (Ed.). (1995). *The meaning of reminiscence and life review.* Amityville, NY: Baywood.

Hendricks, J. (1996). Qualitative research: Contributions and advances. In R. Binstock & L. George (Eds.), *Handbook of aging and the social sciences* (pp. 52-72). San Diego, CA: Academic Press.

Hendricks, J., & Cutler, S. J. (1990). Leisure and the structure of our life worlds. In J. Habib & C. Nusberg (Eds.), *Rethinking worklife options for older persons* (pp. 255-268). Washington, DC: International Federation on Ageing.

Hendricks, J., & Peters, C. B. (1986). The times of our lives. *American Behavioral Scientist, 29*(6), 662-678.

Henretta, J. (1992). Uniformity and diversity: Life course institutionalization and late-life work exit. *Sociological Quarterly, 33*(2), 265-279.

Henretta, J. (1994). Social structure and age-based careers. In M. W. Riley, R. L. Kahn, & A. Foner (Eds.), *Age and structural lag* (pp. 57-79). New York: John Wiley & Sons.

Henretta, J., O'Rand, A., & Chan, C. G. (1993). Joint role investments and synchronization of retirement: A sequential approach to couples' retirement timing. *Social Forces, 71,* 981-1000.

Henry, B., Moffitt, T. E., Caspi, A., Langley, J., & Silva, P. A. (1994). On the "remembrance of things past": A longitudinal evaluation of the retrospective method. *Psychological Assessment, 6,* 92-101.

Hernes, H. M. (1987). *Welfare state and woman power: Essays in state feminism.* Oslo, Norway: The Norwegian University Press.

Hickey, T., & Kalish, R. (1968). Young people's perceptions of adults. *Journal of Gerontology, 23*(2), 215-219.

Hill, M. (1993). *Archival strategies and techniques.* Newbury Park, CA: Sage Publications.

Hinde, R. A. (1988). Continuities and discontinuities: Conceptual issues and methodological considerations. In M. Rutter (Ed.), *Studies of psychosocial risk: The power of longitudinal data* (pp. 367-383). New York: Cambridge University Press.

Hinrichs, K., Roche, W., & Sirianni, C. (Eds.). (1991). *Working time in transition: The political economy of working hours in industrial nations.* Philadelphia, PA: Temple University Press.

Hogan, D. P. (1980). The transition to adulthood as a career contingency. *American Sociological Review, 45,* 261-276.

Hogan, D. P. (1981). *Transitions and social change: The early lives of American men.* New York: Academic Press.

Hogan, D. P. (1985). The demography of life-span transitions: Temporal and gender comparisons. In A. Rossi (Ed.), *Gender and the life course* (pp. 65-78). New York: Aldine Publishing Company.

Holahan, C. K., Holahan, C. J., & Belk, S. S. (1984). Adjustment in aging: The roles of life stress, hassles, and self-efficacy. *Health Psychology, 3,* 315-328.

Holmes, T. H., & Rahe, R. H. (1967). The social readjustment rating scale. *Journal of Psychosomatic Research, 11,* 213-218.

House, J. S. (1981). Social structure and personality. In M. Rosenberg & R. H. Turner (Eds.), *Social psychology: Sociological perspectives* (pp. 525-561). New York: Basic Books.

House, J. S. & Mortimer, J. (1990). Social structure and the individual: Emerging themes and new directions. *Social Psychology Quarterly, 53*(2), 71-80.

Hox, J. J. (1994). *Applied multilevel analysis.* Amsterdam: TT-Publikates.

Hughes, C. E. (1950/1984). Cycles, turning points, and careers. In C. Everett Hughes, *The sociological eye: Selected papers* (pp. 124-131). New Brunswick, NJ: Transaction Publishers, Inc.

Imhof, A. E. (1986). Life-course patterns of women and their husbands: 16th to 20th Century. In A. B. Sørensen, F. E. Weinert, & L. R. Sherrod (Eds.), *Human development and the life course: Multidisciplinary perspectives* (pp. 247-270). Hillsdale, NJ: Lawrence Erlbaum Associates.

Inglehart, M. R. (1991). *Reactions to critical life events: A social psychological analysis.* New York: Praeger.

Ingram, D. K., & Stoll, S. (1995). Is attempting to assess biological age worth the effort? *The Gerontologist, 35*(5), 707-710.

Inkeles, A. (1959). Personality and social structure. In R. K. Merton, L. Broom, & L. S. Cottrell, Jr. (Eds.), *Sociology today: Problems and promises* (pp. 249-276). New York: Basic Books.

Jackson, J. (1975). Normative power and conflict potential. *Sociological Methods and Research, 4,* 237-263.

Jackson, S., & Rodriguez-Tomé, H. (Eds.). (1994). *Adolescence and its social worlds.* Hillsdale, NJ: Lawrence Erlbaum Associates.

Jacobs, J. A. (Ed.) (1995). *Gender inequality at work.* Thousand Oaks, CA: Sage.

James, J. B., & Paul, E. L. (1993). The value of archival data for new perspectives on personality. In D. C. Funder, R. D. Parke, C. Tomlinson-Keasey, & K. Widaman (Eds.), *Studying lives through time: Personality and development* (pp. 45-63). Washington, DC: American Psychological Association.

Jeffers, F.C., Eisdorfer, C., & Busse, E.W. (1962). Measurement of age identification: A methodological note. *Journal of Gerontology, 17,* 437-439.

Jencks, C., Bartlett, S., Corcoran, M., Crouse, J., Eaglesfield, D., Jackson, G., McClelland, K., Mueser, P., Olneck, M., Schwartz, J., Ward, S., & Williams, J. (1979). *Who gets ahead? The determinants of economic success in America.* New York: Basic Books.

Jencks, C., Smith, M., Acland, H., Bane, M. J., Cohen, D., Gintis, H., Heyns, B., & Michelson, S. (1972). *Inequality: A reassessment of the effect of family and schooling in America.* New York: Basic Books.

Jessor, R. (1993). Successful adolescent development among youth in high-risk settings. *American Psychologist, 48*(2), 117-126.

Jessor, R., Colby, A., & Shweder, R. A. (Eds.). (1996). *Ethnography and human development: Context and meaning in social inquiry.* Chicago, IL: University of Chicago Press.

Jette, A. M. (1996). Disability trends and transitions. In R. Binstock & L. George (Eds.), *Handbook of aging and the social sciences* (4th ed., pp. 94-117). San Diego: Academic Press.

Johnson, J., & McCutcheon, S. (1980). Assessing life stress in older children and adolescents: Preliminary findings with the life events checklist. In L. G. Sarason & C. D. Spielberger (Eds.), *Stress and anxiety* (Vol. 7, pp. 111-125). Washington, DC: Hemisphere.

Johnson, T. R. (1995). The significance of religion for aging well. *American Behavioral Scientist, 39*(2), 186-208.

Johnston, L. D., O'Malley, P. M., Bachman, J. G., & Schulenberg, J. (1993). *Aims and objectives of the Monitoring the Future study.* (Monitoring the Future, Occasional Paper No. 34). Ann Arbor, MI: Institute for Social Research.

Jolicoeur, P., Pontier, J., Pernin, M.-O., & Sempé, M. (1988). A lifetime asymptotic growth curve for human height. *Biometrics, 44,* 995-1003.

Kahana, B., & Kahana, E. (1999). Toward a temporal-spatial model of cumulative life stress: Placing late life stress effects in a life course perspective. In J. Lomranz (Ed.), *Handbook of aging and mental health: An integrative approach* (pp. 158-178). New York: Plenum Press.

Kahana, E., Fairchild, T., & Kahana, B. (1982). Adaptation. In D. Mangen & W. Peterson (Eds.), *Research instruments in social gerontology* (pp. 145-190). Minneapolis, MN: University of Minnesota Press.

Kahana, E., & Kahana, B. (1996). Conceptual and empirical advances in understanding aging well through proactive adaptation. In V. Bengtson (Ed.), *Adulthood and aging: Research on continuities and discontinuities* (pp. 18-40). New York: Springer Publishing Company.

Kahana, E., Kahana, B., Kercher, K., Stange, K., & Brown, J. (1996, August). *Exercise and well-being in old-old retirement community residents.* Paper presented at the annual meeting of the American Sociological Association, Washington, DC.

Kahn, R. L., & Antonucci, T. C. (1980). Convoys of social support: A life-course approach. In S. Kiesler, J. Morgan, & V. Oppenheimer (Eds.), *Aging: Social change* (pp. 383-405). New York: Academic Press.

Kalicki, B. (1995). *Die Normalbiographie als psychologisches Regulativ. Zum subjektiven Bedeutungsgehalt von Lebensereignissen, die vom normalbiographischen Zeitmuster abweichen.* Unpublished doctoral dissertation, University of Trier, Trier, Germany.

Kanner, A. D., Coyne, J. C., Schaefer, C., & Lazarus, R. S. (1981). Comparison of two modes of stress measurement: Daily hassles and uplifts versus major life events. *Journal of Behavioral Medicine, 4*(1), 1-39.

Kardiner, A. & Linton, R. (1945). *The psychological frontiers of society.* New York: Columbia University Press.

Kastenbaum, R. (1961). The dimensions of future time perspective and experimental analysis. *Journal of General Psychology, 65,* 203-218.

Kastenbaum, R., Derbin, V., Sabatini, P., & Arrt, S. (1972). "The ages of me": Toward personal and interpersonal definitions of functional aging. *Aging and Human Development, 3,* 197-211.

Kaufman, R., & Spilerman, S. (1982). The age structures of occupations and jobs. *American Journal of Sociology, 87*(4), 827-851.

Keith, J. (1988). Participant observation: A modest little method whose presumption may amuse you. In K. W. Schaie, R. T. Campbell, W. Meredith, & S. C. Rawlings (Eds.), *Methodological issues in aging research* (pp. 211-230). New York: Springer Publishing Company.

Keith, J., Fry, C. L., Glascock, A. P., Ikels, C., Dickerson-Putnam, J., Harpending, H. C., & Draper, P. (1994). *The aging experience: Diversity and commonality across cultures.* Newbury Park, CA: Sage Publications.

Keith, J., & Kertzer, D. I. (1984). Introduction to age and anthropological theory. In D. I. Kertzer & J. Keith (Eds.), *Age and anthropological theory* (pp. 19-61). Ithaca, NY: Cornell University Press.

Kenyon, G. M., Birren, J. E., & Schroots, J. J. F. (Eds.). (1991). *Metaphors of aging in science and the humanities.* New York: Springer Publishing Company.

Kerckhoff, A. C. (1990). *Getting started: Transition to adulthood in Great Britain.* Boulder, CO: Westview Press.

Kerckhoff, A. C. (1993). *Diverging pathways: Social structure and career deflections.* New York: Cambridge University Press.

Kertzer, D. (1983). Generation as a sociological problem. *Annual Review of Sociology, 9,* 125-149.

Kertzer, D. I. (1989). Age structuring in comparative and historical perspective. In D. I. Kertzer & K. Warner Schaie (Eds.), *Age structuring in comparative and historical perspective* (pp. 3-21). Hillsdale, New Jersey: Lawrence Erlbaum Associates.

Kessler, R., & Wethington, E. (1992). *Interview schedule for the "Life Experiences Study.* Institute for Social Research, Survey Research Center, Ann Arbor: University of Michigan, 1992-1993.

Kimmel, D. C., & Moody, H. R. (1990). Ethical issues in gerontological research and services. In J. Birren & K. W. Schaie (Eds.), *Handbook of the psychology of aging* (pp. 3-20). San Diego, CA: Academic Press.

Kindermann, T. A., & Skinner, E. A. (1992). Modeling environmental development: Individual and contextual trajectories. In J. B. Asendorpf & J. Valsiner (Eds.), *Stability and change in development: A study of methodological reasoning* (pp. 155-190). Newbury Park, CA: Sage Publications.

Kleigl, R., & Baltes, P. B. (1987). Theory-guided analysis of development and aging mechanisms through testing-the-limits and research on expertise. In C. Schooler & K. W. Schaie (Eds.), *Cognitive functioning and social structure over the life course* (pp. 95-119). Norwood, NJ: Ablex.

Klein, D. M., Jorgensen, S. R., & Miller, B. (1979). Research methods and developmental reciprocity in families. In R. M. Lerner & G. B. Spanier (Eds.), *Child influences on marital and family interaction: A life-span perspective.* New York: Academic Press.

Kling, K. C., Ryff, C. D., & Essex, M. J. (1997). Adaptive changes in the self-concept during a life transition. *Personality and Social Psychology Bulletin, 23*(9), 981-990.

Kluckhohn, C., & Murray, H. A. (1948/1965). Personality formation: The determinants. In C. Kluckhohn, H. A. Murray, & D. M. Schneider (Eds.), *Personality in nature, society, and culture* (2nd ed., pp. 53-67). New York: Alfred P. Knopf.

Knoke, D. (1984). Conceptual and measurement strategies in the study of political generations. *Journal of Political and Military Sociology, 12,* 191-201.

Knoke, D., & Kalleberg, A. (1994). Job training in U.S. organizations. *American Sociological Review, 59,* 537-546.

Knox, V. J., Gekoski, W. L., Kelly, L. E. (1995). The Age Group Evaluation and Description (AGED) Inventory: A new instrument for assessing stereotypes of and attitudes toward age groups. *International Journal of Aging and Human Development, 40*(1), 31-55.

Kohli, M. (1986a). The world we forgot: A historical review of the life course. In V. Marshall (Ed.), *Later life* (pp. 271-303). Beverly Hills, CA: Sage Publications.

Kohli, M. (1986b). Social organization and subjective construction of the life course. In A. B. Sørensen, F. E. Weinert & L. R. Sherrod (Eds.), *Human development and the life course: Multidisciplinary perspectives* (pp. 271-292). Hillsdale, NJ: Lawrence Erlbaum Associates.

Kohli, M. (1994). Work and retirement: A comparative perspective. In M. W. Riley, R. L. Kahn, & A. Foner (Eds.), *Age and structural lag* (pp. 80-106). New York: John Wiley & Sons.

Kohli, M., & Meyer, J. W. (1986). Social structure and the social construction of life stages. *Human Development, 29,* 145-149.

Krain, M. A. (1995). Policy implications for a society aging well. *American Behavioral Scientist, 39*(2), 131-151.

Kreppner, K., & Lerner, R. M. (1989). *Family systems and life-span development.* Hillsdale, NJ: Lawrence Erlbaum Associates.

Krüger, J., Heckhausen, J., & Hundertmark, J. (1995). Perceiving middle-aged adults: Effects of stereotype-congruent and incongruent information. *Journal of Gerontology: Psychological Sciences, 50,* P82-P93.

Krüger, H. (1996). Normative interpretations of biographical processes. In A. Weymann & W. Heinz (Eds.), *Society and biography: Interrelationships between social structure, institutions, and the life course* (pp. 129-146). Weinheim, Germany: Deutscher Studien Verlag.

Krüger, H. (1998, May). *Social change in two generations: Employment patterns and their costs for family life.* Paper presented at "Restructuring Work and the Life Course: An International Symposium," University of Toronto, Toronto, Ontario.

Kruglanski, A. W. (1996). Goals as knowledge structures. In P. M. Gollwitzer & J. A. Bargh (Eds.), *The psychology of action: Linking cognition and motivation to behavior* (pp. 599-618). New York: Guilford.

Kruse, A., Lindenberger, U., & Baltes, P. B. (1993). Longitudinal research on human aging: The power of combining real-time, microgeneity, and simulation approaches. In D. Magnusson & P. Casaer (Eds.), *Longitudinal research on individual development* (pp. 153-193). Cambridge, UK: Cambridge University Press.

Kruskal, J. B. (1983). An overview of sequence comparisons. In D. Sankoff & J. B. Kruskal (Eds.), *Time warps, string edits, and macromolecules: The theory and practice of sequence comparison* (pp. 1-44). Reading, MA: Addison-Wesley.

Kuhn, D. (1995). Microgenetic study of change: What has it told us? *Psychological Science, 6*, 133-139.

Kulka, R., Schlenger, W. E., Fairbank, J. A., Hough, R. L., Jordan, B. K., Marmar, C. R., & Weiss, D. S. (1990). *Trauma and the Vietnam War generation.* New York: Bruner/Mazel.

Labouvie, E. W., & Nesselroade, J. R. (1985). Age, period, and cohort analysis and the study of individual development and social change. In J. R. Nesselroade & A. von Eye (Eds.), *Individual development and social change: Explanatory analysis* (pp. 189-212). San Diego, CA: Academic Press.

LaFontaine, J. S. (1978). *Sex and age as principles of social differentiation.* New York: Academic Press.

Langer, E. J. (1989). *Mindfulness.* Reading, MA: Addison-Wesley.

Lashbrook, J. (1996). Promotional timetables: An exploratory investigation of age norms for promotional expectations and their association with job well-being. *The Gerontologist, 36*(2), 189-198.

Laslett, P. (1991). *A fresh map of life: The emergence of the third age.* Cambridge, MA: Harvard University Press.

Lawrence, B. S. (1996a). Interest and indifference: The role of age in the organizational sciences. *Research in Personnel and Human Resources Management, 14*, 1-59.

Lawrence, B. S. (1996b). Organizational age norms: Why is it so important to know one when you see one? *The Gerontologist, 36*, 209-220.

Lawrence, J. A. (1974). The effects of perceived age on initial impressions and normative role expectations. *International Journal of Aging and Human Development, 5*, 369-391.

Lawrence, J. A. (1997). Developmental science: A case of the bird flapping its wings or the wings flapping the bird? In J. Tudge, M. J. Shanahan, & J. Valsiner (Eds.), *Comparisons in human development: Understanding time and context* (pp. 285-292). New York: Cambridge University Press.

Lawrence, J. A., & Dodds, A. E. (1997). Conceptual transposition, parallelism, and interdisciplinary communication. In J. Tudge, M. J. Shanahan, & J. Valsiner (Eds.), *Comparisons in human development: Understanding time and context* (pp. 293-303). New York: Cambridge University Press.

Leibfried, S. (1998, May). *Policy challenges.* Paper presented at "Restructuring Work and the Life Course: An International Symposium," University of Toronto, Toronto, Ontario.

Lerner, R. M. (1984). *On the nature of human plasticity.* Cambridge: Cambridge University Press.

Lerner, R. M. (1985). Individual and context in developmental psychology: Conceptual and theoretical issues. In J. R. Nesselroade & A. von Eye (Eds.), *Individual development and social change: Explanatory analysis* (pp. 155-187). San Diego, CA: Academic Press.

Lerner, R. M. (1991). Changing organism-context relations as the basic process of development: A developmental contextual perspective. *Developmental Psychology, 27*, 27-32.

Lerner, R. M. (1995). Developing individuals within changing contexts: Implications of developmental contextualism for human development research, policy, and programs. In T. A. Kindermann & J. Valsiner (Eds.), *Development of person-context relations* (pp. 13-37). Hillsdale, NJ: Lawrence Erlbaum Associates.

Lerner, R. M. (1998). Theories of human development: Contemporary perspectives. In R. M. Lerner (Ed.), *Handbook of child psychology: Vol. 1. Theoretical models of human development* (5th ed., pp. 1-24). New York: John Wiley & Sons.

Lessing, E. E. (1968). Demographic, developmental, and personality correlates of length of future time perspective (FTP). *Journal of Personality, 36*, 183-201.

Levin, J., & Levin, W. C. (1991). Sociology of educational late blooming. *Sociological Forum, 6*(4), 661-679.

Levinson, D. J. (1986). A conception of adult development. *American Psychologist, 1,* 3-13.
Levy, R. (1991). Status passages as critical life-course transitions. In W. R. Heinz (Ed.), *Theoretical advances in life-course research* (pp. 87-114). Weinheim, Germany: Deutscher Studien Verlag.
Levy, R. (1996). Toward a theory of life course institutionalization. In A. Weymann & W. Heinz (Eds.), *Society and biography: Interrelationships between social structure, institutions, and the life course* (pp. 83-108). Weinheim, Germany: Deutscher Studien Verlag.
Lewin, K. (1931). The conflict between Aristotelian and Galileian modes of thought in contemporary psychology. *Journal of Genetic Psychology, 5,* 141-177.
Lewin, K. (1935). *A dynamic theory of personality.* New York: McGraw-Hill.
Lewinsohn, P. M., Mermelstein, R. M., Alexander, C., & MacPhillamy, D. J. (1985). The Unpleasant Events Schedule: A scale for the measurement of aversive events. *Journal of Clinical Psychology, 41*(4), 483-498.
Lewis, C. N. (1971). Reminiscing and self-concept in old age. *Journal of Gerontology, 26,* 240-243.
Lieberman, M. A. (1996). Perspective on Adult Life Crises. In V. Bengtson (Ed.), *Adulthood and aging: Research on continuities and discontinuities* (pp. 146-168). New York: Springer Publishing Company.
Lieblich, A. (1989). *Transition to adulthood during military service: The Israeli case.* Albany, NY: State University of New York Press.
Light, J. M., Grigsby, J. S., & Bligh, M. C. (1996). Aging and heterogeneity: Genetics, social structure, and personality. *The Gerontologist, 36*(2), 165-173.
Link, B.G., & Phelan, J. (1995). Social conditions as fundamental causes of disease. *Journal of Health and Social Behavior, Special Issue,* 80-94.
Linn, M. W., & Hunter, K. (1979). Perception of age in the elderly. *Journal of Gerontology, 34,* 46-52.
Linton, R. A. (1942). Age and sex categories. *American Sociological Review, 7,* 589-603.
Little, B. R. (1983). Personal projects: A rationale and method for investigation. *Environment and Behavior, 15,* 273-309.
Little, R. J., & Rubin, D. B. (1987). *Statistical analysis with missing data.* New York: John Wiley & Sons.
Loessi-Miller, K. (1997, August). *Life-course position, work characteristics, and school-work orientation and success: A study of university undergraduates.* Paper presented at the annual meeting of the American Sociological Association, Toronto, Ontario, Canada.
Looft, W. R. (1972). The evolution of developmental psychology: A comparison of handbooks. *Human Development, 15,* 187-201.
Lord, F. M. (1956). The measurement of growth. *Educational and Psychological Measurement, 16,* 421-437.
Lord, F. M. (1958). Further problems in the measurement of growth. *Educational and Psychological Measurement, 18,* 437-454.
Luckmann, T. (1991). The constitution of human life in time. In J. Bender & D. E. Wellbery (Eds.), *Chronotypes: The construction of time* (pp. 151-166). Stanford, CA: Stanford University Press.
Ludwig, F. C., & Masoro, E. J. (Eds.). (1983). The measurement of biological age [Special issue]. *Experimental Aging Research, 9.*
Lynott, R. J., & Lynott, P. (1996). Tracing the course of theoretical development in the sociology of aging. *The Gerontologist, 36*(6), 728-733.
Maas, I., & Settersten, R. A., Jr. (1999). Military service during wartime: Its effects on men's occupational trajectories and later economic well-being. *European Sociological Review, 15*(2), 81-100.

Maddox, G. (1994). "Lives Through the Years" revisited. *The Gerontologist, 34*(6), 764-767.

Maddox, G. L., & Campbell, R. T. (1985). Scope, concepts, and methods in the study of aging. In R. Binstock & E. Shanas (Eds.), *Handbook of aging and the social sciences* (pp. 3-31). New York: Van Nostrand.

Magnusson, D. (1985). Implications of an interactional paradigm for research on human development. *International Journal of Behavioral Development, 8,* 115-137.

Magnusson, D. (1988). *Individual development from an interactionist perspective: A longitudinal study.* Hillsdale, NJ: Lawrence Erlbaum Associates.

Magnusson, D. (1993). Human ontogeny: A longitudinal perspective. In D. Magnusson & P. Casaer (Eds.), *Longitudinal research on individual development* (pp. 1-25). Cambridge, UK: Cambridge University Press.

Magnusson, D. (1995). Individual development: A holistic integrated model. In P. Moen, G. H. Elder, Jr., & K. Lüscher (Eds.), *Examining lives in context: Perspectives on the ecology of human development* (pp. 19-60). Washington, DC: American Psychological Association.

Magnusson, D. (Ed.). (1996). *The life-span development of individuals: Behavioural, neurobiological, and psychosocial perspectives.* New York: Cambridge University Press.

Magnusson, D., Andersson, T., & Torestad, B. (1993). Methodological implications of a peephole perspective on personality. In D. C. Funder, R. D. Parke, C. Tomlinson-Keasey, & K. Widaman (Eds.), *Studying lives through time: Personality and development* (pp. 207-220). Washington, DC: American Psychological Association.

Magnusson, D., & Bergman, L. R. (1990). *Data quality in longitudinal research.* New York: Cambridge University Press.

Magnusson, D., Bergman, L. R., Rudinger, G., & Törestad, B. (1991). *Problems and methods in longitudinal research: Stability and change.* New York: Cambridge University Press.

Magnusson, D., & Cairns, R. B. (1996). Developmental science: Toward a unified framework. In R. B. Cairns, G. H. Elder, Jr., & E. J. Costello (Eds.), *Developmental science* (pp. 7-30). New York: Cambridge University Press.

Magnusson, D., & Stattin, H. (1998). Person-context interaction theories. In R. M. Lerner (Ed.), *Handbook of child psychology: Vol. 1. Theoretical models of human development* (5th ed., pp. 685-759). New York: John Wiley & Sons.

Mannheim, K. (1928/1952). The problem of generations. In K. Mannheim, *Essays on the sociology of knowledge* (pp. 276-322). London: Routledge & Kaegan Paul.

Marini, M. M. (1984). Age and sequencing norms in the transition to adulthood. *Social Forces, 63*(1), 229-244.

Markides, K. S., & Boldt, J. S. (1983). Change in subjective age among the elderly: A longitudinal analysis. *The Gerontologist, 23,* 422-427.

Markides, K. S., & Black, S. A. (1996). Race, ethnicity, and aging: The impact of inequality. In R. Binstock & L. George (Eds.), *Handbook of aging and the social sciences* (4th ed., pp. 153-170). San Diego: Academic Press.

Markus, H., & Herzog, A. R. (1991). The role of the self-concept in aging. *Annual Review of Gerontology and Geriatrics, 11,* 111-143.

Markus, H., Mullally, P. R., & Kitayama, S. (1997). Selfways: Diversity in modes of cultural participation. In U. Neisser & D. A. Jopling (Eds.), *The conceptual self in context: Culture, experience, self-understanding* (pp. 13-61). New York: Cambridge University Press.

Marshall, V. (1984). Tendencies in generational research: From the generation to the cohort and back to the generation. In V. Garms-Homolova, E. M. Hoerning, & D. Schaeffer (Eds.), *Intergenerational Relationships* (pp. 207-218). Lewiston, NY: C. J. Hogrefe, Inc.

Marshall, V. W. (1995a). Social models of aging. *Canadian Journal on Aging, 14*(1), 12-34.

Marshall, V. W. (1995b). The next half-century of aging research—and thoughts for the past. *Journal of Gerontology: Social Sciences, 50B*(3), S131-133.

Marshall, W., Cook, F., & Marshall, J. (1993). Conflict over intergenerational equity: Rhetoric and reality in a comparative context. In V. Bengtson & W. Achenbaum (Eds.), *The changing contract across generations* (pp. 119-140). New York: Aldine de Gruyter.

Marsiske, M., Lang, F. R., Baltes, P. B., & Baltes, M. M. (1995). Selective optimization with compensation: Life-span perspectives on human development. In A. R. Dixon & L. Bäckman (Eds.), *Psychological compensation: Managing losses and promoting gains* (pp. 35-79). Hillsdale, NJ: Erlbaum.

Mason, K. G., Mason, W. H., Winsborough, H. H., & Poole, W. K. (1973). Some methodological problems in cohort analyses of archival data. *American Sociological Review, 38*, 242-258.

Mayer, K.U. (1986). Structural constraints in the life course. *Human Development, 29*, 163-170.

Mayer, K. U. (1988). German survivors of World War II: The impact on the life course of the collective experience of birth cohorts. In M. W. Riley (Ed.), *Social structures and human lives* (pp. 229-246). Newbury Park, CA: Sage Publications.

Mayer, K. U., & Brückner, E. (1989). *Lebensverlaeufe und Wohlfahrtsentwicklung. Konzeption, Design and Methodik der Erhebung von Lebensverlaeufen der Geburtsjahrgaenge 1929-1931, 1939-1941, 1949-1951*. Berlin, Germany: Max Planck Institute for Human Development and Education.

Mayer, K. U., & Huinink, J. (1990). Age, period, and cohort in the study of the life course: A comparison of classical A-P-C-analysis with event history analysis, or Farewell to Lexis? In D. Magnusson, L. R. Bergman (Eds.), *Data quality in longitudinal research* (pp. 211-232). Cambridge: Cambridge University Press.

Mayer, K. U., & Müller, W. (1986). The state and the structure of the life course. In A. B. Sørensen, F. E. Weinert, & L. R. Sherrod (Eds.), *Human development and the life course: Multidisciplinary perspectives* (pp. 217-245). Hillsdale, NJ: Lawrence Erlbaum Associates.

Mayer, K. U., & Schöpflin, U. (1989). The state and the life course. *Annual Review of Sociology, 15*, 187-209.

Mayer, K. U., & Tuma, N. B. (1990). Life course research and event history analysis: An overview. In K. U. Mayer & N. B. Tuma (Eds.), *Event history analysis in life course research* (pp. 3-20). Madison, WI: University of Wisconsin Press.

McAdam, D. (1988). *Freedom summer*. New York: Oxford University Press.

McCall, R. B., & Applebaum, M. I. (1991). Some issues of conducting secondary analyses. *Developmental Psychology, 27*(6), 911-917.

McNaught, W., Barth, M. C., & Henderson, P. H. (1991). Older Americans: Willing and able to work. In A. H. Munnell (Ed.), *Retirement and public policy* (pp. 101-114). Dubuque, IA: Kendall/Hunt Publishing Company.

McNemar, Q. (1958). On growth measurement. *Educational and Psychological Measurement, 18*, 47-55.

McTavish, D. G. (1982). Perceptions of old people. In D. J. Mangen & W. A. Peterson (Eds.), *Research instruments in social gerontology: Vol. 2. Social roles and social participation* (pp. 533-621). Minneapolis, MN: University of Minnesota Press.

Mekos, D., & Clubb, P. A. (1997). The value of comparisons in developmental psychology. In J. Tudge, M. J. Shanahan, & J. Valsiner (Eds.), *Comparisons in human development: Understanding time and context* (pp. 137-161). New York: Cambridge University Press.

Mensh, I. N. (1983). A study of a stress questionnaire: The later years. *International Journal of Aging and Human Development, 16*(3), 201-207.

Merton, R. (1968). The Matthew effect in science: The reward and communications systems of science. *Science, 199,* 55-63.

Meyer, J. W. (1986a). The self and the life course: Institutionalization and its effects. In A. B. Sørensen, F. E. Weinert, & L. R. Sherrod (Eds.), *Human development and the life course: Multidisciplinary perspectives* (pp. 199-216). Hillsdale, NJ: Lawrence Erlbaum Associates.

Meyer, J. W. (1986b). Myths of socialization and personality. In T. C. Heller, M. Sosna, & D. E. Wellberg (Eds.), *Reconstructing individualism: Autonomy, individuality, and the self in Western thought* (pp. 209-221). Stanford, CA: Stanford University Press.

Migdal, S., Abeles, R., & Sherrod, L. R. (1981). *An inventory of longitudinal studies of middle and old age.* New York: Social Sciences Research Council.

Mills, C. W. (1959). *The sociological imagination.* New York: Oxford University Press.

Mishler, E. G. (1995). Models of narrative analysis: A typology. *Journal of Narrative and Life History, 5*(2), 87-123.

Mishler, E. G. (1996). Missing persons: Recovering develomental stories/histories. In R. Jessor, A. Colby, & R. A. Shweder (Eds.), *Ethnography and human development: Context and meaning in social inquiry* (pp. 73-100). Chicago, IL: University of Chicago Press.

Modell, J. (1980). Normative aspects of American marriage timing since World War II. *Journal of Family History, 5,* 210-234.

Modell, J. (1989). *Into one's own: From youth to adulthood in the United States, 1920-1975.* Berkely, CA: University of California Press.

Modell, J. (1996). The uneasy engagement of human development and ethnography. In R. Jessor, A. Colby, & R. A. Shweder (Eds.), *Ethnography and human development: Context and meaning in social inquiry* (pp. 73-100). Chicago, IL: University of Chicago Press.

Modell, J., Furstenberg, F., Jr., & Hershberg, T. (1976). Social change and transitions to adulthood in historical perspective. *Journal of Family History, 1,* 7-31.

Modell, J., Furstenberg, F., Jr., & Strong, D. (1978). The timing of marriage in the transition to adulthood: Continuity and change, 1860-1975. In J. Demos & S. Boocok (Eds.), *Turning Points: Historical and Sociological Essays on the Family.* Chicago, IL: University of Chicago Press.

Moen, P. (1996). Gender and the life course. In R. Binstock & L. George (Eds.), *Handbook of aging and the social sciences* (4th ed., pp. 171-187). San Diego: Academic Press.

Moen, P., Elder, G. H., Jr., & Lüscher, K. (Eds.). (1995). *Examining lives in context: Perspectives on the ecology of human development.* Washington, DC: American Psychological Association.

Montepare, J. M. (1991). Characteristics and psychological correlates of young adult men's and women's subjective age. *Sex Roles, 24,* 323-333.

Montepare, J. M., & Lachman, M.E. (1989). "You're only as old as you feel": Self-perceptions of age, fears of aging, and life satisfaction from adolescence to old age. *Psychology and Aging, 4,* 73-78.

Morris, R. (1956). A typology of norms. *American Sociological Review, 21,* 610-613.

Mortimer, J., & Simmons, R. (1978). Adult socialization. *Annual Review of Sociology, 4,* 421-454.

Murray, I. M. (1951). Assessment of physiologic age by combination of several criteria—vision, hearing, blood pressure, and muscle force. *Journal of Gerontology, 6,* 120-126.

Murrell, S. A., & Norris, F. H. (1984). Resources, life events, and changes in positive effect and depression in older adults. *American Journal of Community Psychology, 12*(4), 445-464.

Mutchler, J. E., Burr, J. A., Pienta, A. M., & Massagli, M. P. (1997). Pathways to labor force exit: Work transitions and work instability. *Journal of Gerontology: Social Sciences, 52B*(1), S4-S12.

National Council on Aging. (1975). *The myth and reality of aging in America.* Washington, DC: National Council on Aging.

Nelson, E. A., & Dannefer, D. (1992). Aged heterogeneity: Fact or fiction? The fate of diversity in gerontological research. *The Gerontologist, 32,* 17-23.

Nesselroade, J. R. (1988). Sampling and generalizability: Adult development and aging research issues examined within the general methodological framework of selection. In K. W. Schaie, R. T. Campbell, W. Meredith, & S. C. Rawlings (Eds.), *Methodological issues in aging research* (pp. 13-42). New York: Springer Publishing Company.

Nesselroade, J. R. (1991). Interindividual differences in intraindividual change. In L. M. Collins & J. L. Horn (Eds.), *Best methods for the analysis of change: Recent advances, unanswered questions, future directions* (pp. 92-105). Washington, DC: American Psychological Association.

Neugarten, B. L. (Ed.) (1968a). *Middle age and aging: A reader in social psychology.* Chicago: University of Chicago Press.

Neugarten, B. L. (1968b). Adult personality. In B. L. Neugarten (Ed.), *Middle age and aging* (pp. 137-147). Chicago, IL: University of Chicago Press.

Neugarten, B. L. (1969). Continuities and discontinuities of psychological issues into adult life. *Human Development, 12,* 121-130.

Neugarten, B. L. (1974a/1996). Age groups in American society and the rise of the young-old. In D. Neugarten (Ed.), *The meanings of age: Selected papers of Bernice L. Neugarten* (pp. 34-46). Chicago, IL: University of Chicago Press.

Neugarten, B. L. (1974b/1996). Successful aging in 1970 and 1990. In D. Neugarten (Ed.), *The meanings of age: Selected papers of Bernice L. Neugarten* (pp. 324-331). Chicago, IL: University of Chicago Press.

Neugarten, B. L. (1979/1996). The young-old and the age-irrelevant society. In D. Neugarten (Ed.), *The meanings of age: Selected papers of Bernice L. Neugarten* (pp. 47-55). Chicago, IL: University of Chicago Press.

Neugarten, B. L. (1982). *Age or need? Public policies for older people.* Beverly Hills, CA: Sage Publications.

Neugarten, B. L. (1994/1996). The end of gerontology? In D. Neugarten (Ed.), *The meanings of age: Selected papers of Bernice L. Neugarten* (pp. 402-403). Chicago, IL: University of Chicago Press.

Neugarten, B. L., & Datan, N. (1973). Sociological perspectives on the life cycle. In P. B. Baltes & K. W. Schaie (Eds.), *Life-span developmental psychology: Personality and socialization* (pp. 53-69). New York: Academic Press.

Neugarten, B. L., & Gutmann, D. (1958/1996). Age-sex roles and personality in middle age: A thematic apperception study. In D. Neugarten (Ed.), *The meanings of age: Selected papers of Bernice L. Neugarten* (pp. 238-255). Chicago, IL: University of Chicago Press.

Neugarten, B. L., & Hagestad, G. O. (1976). Age and the life course. In R. Binstock & E. Shanas (Eds.), *Handbook of aging and the social sciences* (pp. 35-55). New York: Van Nostrand Reinhold Company.

Neugarten, B. L., & Neugarten, D. (1986). Changing meanings of age in the aging society. In A. Pifer & L. Bronte (Eds.), *Our aging society* (pp. 33-52). New York: W. W. Norton.

Neugarten, B. L., Moore, J. W., & Lowe, J. C. (1965). Age norms, age constraints, and adult socialization. *American Journal of Sociology, 70,* 710-717.

Neugarten, B. L., & Peterson, W. A. (1957). A study of the American age-grade system. *Proceedings of the 4th Congress of the International Association of Gerontology, 3,* 497-502.

Neugarten, D. A. (Ed.) (1996). *The meanings of age: Selected papers of Bernice L. Neugarten.* Chicago, IL: University of Chicago Press.

Newcomb, M. D., Huba, G. J., & Bentler, P. M. (1986). Life change events among adolescents: An empirical consideration of some methodological issues. *Journal of Nervous and Mental Disease, 174,* 280-289.

Newman, K. (1996). Ethnography, biography, and cultural history: Generational paradigms in human development. In R. Jessor, A. Colby, & R. A. Shweder (Eds.), *Ethnography and human development: Context and meaning in social inquiry* (pp. 371-393). Chicago, IL: University of Chicago Press.

Nurmi, J.-E. (1991). How do adolescents see their future? A review of the development of future orientation and planning. *Developmental Review, 11,* 1-59.

Nurmi, J.-E. (1992). Age differences in adult life goals, concerns, and their temporal extension: A life-course approach to future-oriented motivation. *International Journal of Behavioral Development, 15,* 487-508.

Nurmi, J.-E., Pulliainen, H., & Salmela-Aro, K. (1992). Age differences in adults' control beliefs related to life goals and concerns. *Psychology and Aging, 7*(2), 194-196.

Nuttall, R. L. (1972). The strategy of functional age research. *International Journal of Aging and Human Development, 3,* 149-152.

Nuttin, J. R., & Lens, W. (1985). *Future time perspective and motivation: Theory and research method.* Hillsdale, NJ: Lawrence Erlbaum Associates.

Nydegger, C. N. (1981). On being caught up in time. *Human Development, 24,* 1-12.

Nydegger, C. N. (1986a). Age and life-course transitions. In C. L. Fry & J. Keith (Eds.), *New methods for old age research: Strategies for studying diversity* (pp. 131-161). South Hadley, MA: Bergin and Garvey.

Nydegger, C. N. (1986b). Timetables and implicit theory. *American Behavioral Scientist, 29*(6), 710-729.

Nydegger, C., Mitteness, L., & O'Neil, J. (1983). Experiencing social generations: Phenomenal dimensions. *Research on Aging, 5,* 527-546.

Oakes, J. (1985). *Keeping track.* New Haven, CT: Yale University Press.

O'Rand, A. (1996a). Stratification and the life course. In R. Binstock & L. George (Eds.), *Handbook of Aging and the Social Sciences* (4th ed., pp. 188-207). San Diego, CA: Academic Press.

O'Rand, A. (1996b). The precious and the precocious: Understanding cumulative advantage and disadvantage over the life course. *The Gerontologist, 36*(2), 230-238.

O'Rand, A., & Ellis, R. A. (1974). Social class and time perspective. *Social Forces, 53*(1), 53-62.

O'Rand, M., & Krecker, M. L. (1990) Concepts of the life cycle: Their history, meanings and issues in the social sciences. *Annual Review of Sociology, 16,* 241-262.

Ortega y Gasset, J. (1933). *The modern theme.* New York: Norton.

Overton, W. F. (1998). Developmental psychology: Philosophy, concepts, and methodology. In R. M. Lerner (Ed.), *Handbook of child psychology: Vol. 1. Theoretical models of human development* (5th ed., pp. 107-188). New York: John Wiley & Sons.

Palmore, E. B. (1977). Facts on aging: A short quiz. *The Gerontologist, 17*(4), 315-320.

Palmore, E. B. (1978). When can age, period, and cohort be separated? *Social Forces, 57,* 282-295.

Palmore, E. B. (1981). Facts on aging: Part Two. *The Gerontologist, 21*(4), 431-437.

Parsons, T. (1942). Age and sex in the social structure of the United States. *American Sociological Review, 7,* 604-616.

Parsons, T. (1964). *Social structure and personality.* New York: The Free Press.

Passuth, P. M., & Maines, D. R. (1981). *Transformations in age norms and age constraints: Evidence bearing on the age-irrelevancy hypothesis.* Paper presented at the meeting of the World Congress of Gerontology, Hamburg, Germany.

Paykel, E. S., Prusoff, B. A., & Uhlenhuth, E. H. (1971) Scaling of life events. *Archives of General Psychiatry, 25,* 340-347.

Pearlin, L. I., Aneshensel, C. S., Mullan, J. T., & Whitlatch, C. J. (1996). Caregiving and its social support. In R. Binstock & L. George (Eds.), *Handbook of aging and the social sciences* (pp. 283-302). San Diego, CA: Academic Press.

Pearlin, L. I., Lieberman, M. A., Menaghan, E. G., & Mullan, J. T. (1981). The stress process. *Journal of Health and Social Behavior, 22,* 337-356.

Pearlin, L. I., Mullan, J. T., Aneshensel, C. S., Wardlaw, L., & Harrington, C. (1994). The structure and functions of AIDS caregiving relationships. *Psychosocial Rehabilitation Journal, 17*(4), 51-67.

Pearlin, L. I., Mullan, J. T., Semple, S. J., & Skaff, M. M. (1990). Caregiving and the stress process: An overview of concepts and their measures. *The Gerontologist, 30,* 583-594.

Pearlin, L. I., & Skaff, M. M. (1995). Stressors and adaptation in late life. In M. Gatz (Ed.), *Emerging issues in mental health and aging* (pp. 97-123). Washington, DC: American Psychological Association.

Pearlin, L., & Skaff, M. M. (1996). Stress and the life course: A paradigmatic alliance. *The Gerontologist, 36*(2), 239-247.

Peters, G. R. (1971). Self-conceptions of the aged, age identification and aging. *The Gerontologist, 11*(2), 69-73.

Petersen, T. (1995). Analysis of event histories. In C. Clogg & M. E. Sobel (Eds.), *Handbook of statistical modeling for the social and behavioral sciences* (pp. 453-517). New York: Plenum Press.

Peterson, C. (1996). The ticking of the social clock: Adult awareness of age norms. *International Journal of Aging and Human Development, 42*(3), 189-203.

Peterson, D. R. (1992). Interpersonal relationships as a link between person and environment. In W. B. Walsh, K. H. Craik, & R. H. Price (Eds.), *Person-environment psychology: Models and perspectives* (pp. 127-156). Hillsdale, NJ: Lawrence Erlbaum Associates.

Pickles A., & Rutter, M. (1989). Statistical and conceptual models of turning points. In D. Magnusson, L. Bergman, G. Rudinger, & B. Törestad (Eds.), *Problems and methods in longitudinal research: Stability and change* (pp. 133-165). Cambridge, UK: Cambridge University Press.

Piore, M. J. (1971). The dual labor market: Theory and implications. In D. M. Gordon (Ed.), *Problems in political economy: An urban perspective* (pp. 90-94). Lexington, MA: D. C. Heath & Company.

Plath, D. W. (1980). Contours of consociation: Lessons from a Japanese narrative. In P. B. Baltes & O. G. Brim, Jr. (Eds.), *Life-Span Development and Behavior, vol. 3* (pp. 287-305). New York: Academic Press.

Plath, D. W. (1982, April). *Arcs, circles, and spheres: Scheduling selfhood.* Paper presented at Midwest Regional Seminar on Japan, Earlham College, Richmond, IN.

Plath, D. W., & Ikeda, K. (1975). After coming of age: Adult awareness of age norms. In T. R. Williams (Ed.), *Socialization and communication in primary groups.* Mouton: The Hague.

Plomin, R. (1994). *Genetics and experience: The interplay between nature and nurture.* Thousand Oaks, CA: Sage Publications.

Plomin, R., & McClearn, G. E. (Eds.). (1993). *Nature, nurture, and psychology.* Washington, DC: American Psychological Association.

Pressey, S., & Kuhlen, R. (1957). *Psychological development through the life span.* New York: Harper and Row.

Preston, S. H. (1984). Children and elderly: Divergent paths for America's dependents. *Demography, 25*(6), 44-49.

Pruchno, R. A., Blow, F. C., & Smyer, M. A. (1984). Life events and interdependent lives. *Human Development, 27,* 31-41.

Quadagno, J., & Hardy, M. (1996). Work and retirement. In R. Binstock & L. George (Eds.), *Handbook of aging and the social sciences* (4th ed., pp. 325-345). San Diego, CA: Academic Press.

Quinn, J. F., & Burkhauser, R. V. (1994). Public policy and the plans and preferences of older Americans. *Journal of Aging and Social Policy, 6*(3), 5-20.

Rapkin, B. D., & Fischer, K. (1992). Personal goals of older adults: Issues in assessment and prediction. *Psychology and Aging, 7,* 138-149.

Ravanera, A. R., Rajulton, F., & Burch, T. K. (1994). Tracing the life courses of Canadians. *Canadian Studies in Population, 21*(1), 21-34.

Reese, H. W., & McCluskey, K. A. (1984). Dimensions of historical constancy and change. In K. A. McCluskey & H. W. Reese (Eds.), *Life-span developmental psychology: Historical and generational effects* (pp. 17-45). San Diego, CA: Academic Press.

Reese, H. W., & Overton, W. F. (1970). Models of development and theories of development. In L. R. Goulet & P. B. Baltes (Eds.), *Life-span developmental psychology: Research and theory* (pp. 115-145). New York: Academic Press.

Reff, M. E., & Schneider, E. L. (1982). Biological markers of aging (NIH Pub. No. 82-2221). Washington, D.C.: Government Printing Office.

Rehn, G. (1977). Towards a society of free choice. In J. Wiatr & R. Rose (Eds.), *Comparing public policies* (pp. 121-157). Wroclaw, Poland: Ossolineum/Polish Academy of Sciences.

Rehn, G. (1990). Flexibility and free choice in working life. In J. Habib & C. Nusberg (Eds.), *Rethinking worklife options for older persons* (pp. 199-215). Washington, DC: International Federation on Ageing.

Reinharz, S. (1987). The embeddedness of age: Toward a social control perspective. *Journal of Aging Studies, 1*(1), 77-93.

Reskin, B., & Padavic, I. (1994). *Women and men at work.* Thousand Oaks, CA: Pine Forge Press.

Riegel, K. F. (1976). The dialectics of human development. *American Psychologist, 16,* 346-370.

Riegel, K. F. (1979). *Foundations of dialectical psychology.* New York: Academic Press.

Riley, M. W. (1973). Aging and cohort succession: Interpretations and misinterpretations. *Public Opinion Quarterly, 37,* 35-49.

Riley, M. W. (1985). Men, women, and the lengthening of the life course. In A. Rossi (Ed.), *Gender and the life course* (pp. 333-347). New York: Aldine.

Riley, M. W. (1987). On the significance of age in sociology. *American Sociological Review, 52*(1), 1-14.

Riley, M. W. (1998). Letter to the editor: Response to "successful aging." *The Gerontologist, 38*(2), 151.

Riley, M. W., Foner, A., Moore, M. E., Hess, B. B., & Roth, B. K. (1968). *Aging and society, volume 1: An inventory of research findings.* New York: Russell Sage.

Riley, M. W., Foner, A., & Waring, J. (1988). Sociology of age. In N. Smelser (Ed.), *Handbook of sociology* (pp. 243-290). Newbury Park, CA: Sage Publications.

Riley, M. W., Johnson, M., & Foner, A. (1972). *Aging and society, Volume 3: A sociology of age stratification.* New York: Russell Sage Foundation.

Riley, M. W., Kahn, R. L., & Foner, A. (Eds.). (1994). *Age and structural lag: Society's failure to provide meaningful opportunities in work, family, and leisure.* New York: John Wiley & Sons.

Riley, M. W., & Riley, J. W., Jr. (1994). Structural lag: Past and future. In M. W. Riley, R. L. Kahn, & A. Foner (Eds.), *Age and structural lag: Society's failure to provide meaningful opportunities in work, family, and leisure* (pp. 15-36). New York: John Wiley & Sons.

Riley, M. W., & Uhlenberg, P. (1996). Cohort studies. In J. Birren (Ed.), *Encyclopedia of gerontology: Age, aging, and the aged,* Volume I (pp. 299-309). San Diego, CA: Academic Press.

Rindfuss, R., Swicegood, C., & Rosenfeld, R. (1987). Disorder in the life course: How common and does it matter? *American Sociological Review, 52,* 785-801.

Rix, S. (1998, May). *Policy challenges.* Paper presented at "Restructuring Work and the Life Course: An International Symposium," University of Toronto, Toronto, Ontario.

Robbins, L., & Hall, J. H. (1970). *How to practice prospective medicine.* Indianapolis, IN: Methodist Hospital of Indiana.

Robins, L. N. (1988). Data gathering and data analysis for prospective and retrospective longitudinal studies. In M. Rutter (Ed.), *Studies of psychosocial risk: The power of longitudinal data* (pp. 315-324). New York: Cambridge University Press.

Rodgers, W. L. (1982). Estimable functions of age, period, and cohort effects. *American Sociological Review, 47,* 774-787.

Rogoff-Ramsoy, N. (1973). *The Norwegian Occupational Life History Study: Design, purpose, and a few preliminary results.* Unpublished manuscript, Institute for Applied Social Research. Oslo, Norway.

Rogosa, D. R. (1988). Myths about longitudinal research. In K. W. Schaie, R. T. Campbell, W. Meredith, & S. C. Rawlings (Eds.), *Methodological issues in aging research* (pp. 171-209). New York: Springer Publishing Company.

Rogosa, D. R. (1995). Myths and methods: "Myths about longitudinal research" plus supplemental questions. In J. M. Gottman (Ed.), *The analysis of change* (pp. 3-66). Mahwah, NJ: Lawrence Erlbaum Associates.

Rogosa, D. R., Brandt, D., & Zimowski, M. (1982). A growth curve approach to the measurement of change. *Psychological Bulletin, 90,* 726-748.

Rogosa, D. R., & Willett, J. B. (1985). Understanding correlates of change by modeling individual differences in growth. *Psychometrika, 50,* 203-228.

Romesburg, H. C. (1990). *Cluster analysis for researchers.* Malabar, FL: Robert E. Krieger Publishing Company.

Rose, C. L. (1972). The measurement of social age. *Aging and Human Development, 2,* 153-168.

Rosenbaum, J. E. (1976). *Making inequality: The hidden curriculum of high school tracking.* New York: John Wiley & Sons.

Rosenbaum, J. E. (1984). *Career mobility in a corporate hierarchy.* New York: Academic Press.

Rosenbaum, J.E. (1987). Structural models of organizational careers: A critical review and new directions. In R. L. Breiger (Ed.), *Social mobility and social structure* (pp. 272-307). New York: Cambridge University Press.

Rosenbaum, J. E., Kariya, T., Settersten, R. A., Jr., & Maier, T. (1990). Market and network theories of the high school-to-work transition: Their application to industrialized societies. *Annual Review of Sociology, 16,* 263-299.

Rosencranz, H. A., & McNevin, T. E. (1969). A factor analysis of attitudes toward the aged. *The Gerontologist, 9,* 55-59.

Rosow, I. (1978). What is a cohort and why? *Human Development, 21,* 65-75.

Rossetti-Ferreira, M. C., & de Oliveira, Z. M. R. (1992). Modeling environmental development: The necessity of discussing some other basic assumptions. In J. B. Asendorpf & J. Valsiner (Eds.), *Stability and change in development: A study of methodological reasoning* (pp. 198-206). Newbury Park, CA: Sage Publications.

Rossi, A. (1986). Sex and gender in an aging society. In A. Pifer & L. Bronte (Eds.), *Our aging society: Paradox and promise* (pp. 111-139). New York: W. W. Norton & Company.

Roth, J. A. (1963). *Timetables: Structuring the passage of time in hospital treatment and other careers.* Indianapolis, IN: Bobbs-Merrill.

Rothbaum, F., Weisz, J. R., & Snyder, S. S. (1982). Changing the world and changing the self: A two-process model of perceived control. *Journal of Personality and Social Psychology, 42,* 5-37.

Rothman, J., & Thomas, E. J. (1994). *Intervention research: Design and development for the human services.* New York: Haworth Press.

Rovine, M. J., & von Eye, A. (1991). *Applied computational statistics in longitudinal research.* New York: Academic Press.

Rowe, J., & Kahn, R. L. (1987). Human aging: Usual and successful. *Science, 237*(4811), 143-149.

Rowe, J., & Kahn, R. L. (1997). Successful aging. *The Gerontologist, 37*(4), 433-440.

Rowe, J., & Kahn, R. L. (1998). *Successful aging: The MacArthur Foundation Study.* New York: Pantheon Books.

Runyan, W. M. (1980). The life satisfaction chart: Perceptions of the course of subjective experience. *International Journal of Aging and Human Development, 11*(1), 45-64.

Rutter, M. (1988). Longitudinal data in the study of causal processes: Some uses and pitfalls. In M. Rutter (Ed.), *Studies of psychosocial risk: The power of longitudinal data* (pp. 1-28). New York: Cambridge University Press.

Rutter, M. (1993). Developmental psychopathology as a research perspective. In D. Magnusson & P. Casaer (Eds.), *Longitudinal research on individual development* (pp. 127-152). Cambridge, UK: Cambridge University Press.

Rutter, M., Champion, L., Quinton, D., Maughan, B., & Pickles, A. (1995). Understanding individual differences in environmental risk exposure. In P. Moen, G. H. Elder, Jr., & K. Lüscher (Eds.), *Examining lives in context: Perspectives on the ecology of human development* (pp. 61-93). Washington, DC: American Psychological Association.

Rutter, M., & Garmezy, N. (1983). Developmental psychopathology. In E. M. Hetherington (Ed.), *Handbook of child psychology: Vol 4. Socialization, personality, and social development* (4th ed., pp. 775-911). New York: John Wiley & Sons.

Ryder, N. (1964). Notes on the concept of a population. *American Journal of Sociology, 69,* 447-463.

Ryder, N. (1965). The cohort as a concept in the study of social change. *American Sociological Review, 30,* 843-861.

Rytina, S. L. (1992). Social structure. In E. F. Borgatta & M. L. Borgatta (Eds.), *Encyclopedia of sociology* (Vol. 4, pp. 1970-1976). New York: Macmillan Publishing Company.

Sackmann, R., & Weymann, A. (1989). Generations, social time, and "conjunctive" experience. In H. A. Becker (Ed.), *Life histories and generations* (pp. 247-274). Wassenaar: Netherlands Institute for Advanced Study in the Humanities and Social Sciences.

Salthouse, T.A. (1986). Functional age, examination of a concept. In J. E. Birren, P. K. Robinson, & J. E. Livingston (Eds.) *Age, health and employment* (pp. 78-92). Englewood Cliffs, NJ: Prentice Hall.

Sameroff, A. J., Suomi, S. J. (1996). Primates and persons: A comparative developmental understanding of social organization. In R. B. Cairns, G. H. Elder, Jr., &

E. J. Costello (Eds.), *Developmental science* (pp. 97-120). New York: Cambridge University Press.

Sampson, R. J., & Laub, J. H. (1993). *Crime in the making: Pathways and turning points through life.* Cambridge, MA: Harvard University Press.

Sarason, I. G., Johnson, J. H., & Siegel, J. M. (1978). Assessing the impact of life changes: Development of the Life Experiences Survey. *Journal of Consulting and Clinical Psychology, 46,* 932-946.

Scarr, S. (1982). Development is internally guided, not determined. *Contemporary Psychology, 27,* 852-853.

Scarr, S. (1993). Genes, experience, and development. In D. Magnusson & P. Casaer (Eds.), *Longitudinal research on individual development* (pp. 26-50). Cambridge, UK: Cambridge University Press.

Schaie, K. W. (1965). A general model for the study of developmental problems. *Psychological Bulletin, 64,* 92-107.

Schaie, K. W. (1984). Historical time and cohort effects. In K. A. McCluskey & H. W. Reese (Eds.), *Life-span developmental psychology: Historical and generational effects* (pp. 1-15). New York: Academic Press.

Schaie, K. W. (1986). Beyond calendar definitions of age, time, and cohort: The general developmental model revisited. *Developmental Review, 6,* 252-277.

Schaie, K. W. (1992). The impact of methodological changes in gerontology. *International Journal of Aging and Human Development, 35*(1), 19-29.

Schaie, K. W., & Baltes, P. B. (1975). On sequential strategies in developmental research: Description or explanation? *Human Development, 18,* 384-390.

Schroeder, E. (1992). Modeling qualitative change in individual development. In J. B. Asendorpf & J. Valsiner (Eds.), *Stability and change in development: A study of methodological reasoning* (pp. 1-20). Newbury Park, CA: Sage Publications.

Schroots, J. J. F. (1992). Aging as hypothetical construct. *European Journal of Gerontology, 1,* 457-479.

Schroots, J. J. F. (1995). Psychological models of aging. *Canadian Journal on Aging, 14*(1), 44-66.

Schroots, J. J. F. (1996). Theoretical developments in the psychology of aging. *The Gerontologist, 36*(6), 742-748.

Schroots, J. J. F., & Birren, J. E. (1988). The nature of time: Implications for research on aging. *Contemporary Gerontology, 2,* 1-29.

Schroots, J. J. F., & Birren, J. E. (1990). Concepts of time and aging in science. In J. E. Birren & K. W. Schaie (Eds.), *Handbook of psychology and aging* (4th ed., pp. 45-64). San Diego: Academic Press.

Schroots, J. J. F., & Birren, J. E. (1993). Theoretical issues and basic questions in the planning of longitudinal studies of health and aging. In J. J. F. Schroots (Ed.), *Aging, health, and competence: The next generation of longitudinal research* (pp. 3-34). Amsterdam: Elsevier.

Schultz, J. H. (1995). *The economics of aging* (6th ed.). Westport, CT: Auburn House.

Schulz, R., & Heckhausen, J. (1996). A life span model of successful aging. *American Psychologist, 51*(7), 702-714.

Schuman, H., & Scott, J. (1989). Generations and collective memories. *American Sociological Review, 54,* 359-381.

Schütze, H. G. (1987). *Adults in higher education: Policies and practice in Great Britain and North America.* Stockholm, Sweden: Almquist & Wiskell International.

Scott, J. (1991). *Social network analysis: A handbook.* Newbury Park, CA: Sage Publications.

Scott, J., & Zac, L. (1993). Collective memories in Britain and the United States. *Public Opinion Quarterly, 57*(3), 315-331.

Settersten, R. A., Jr. (1997a). The salience of age in the life course. *Human Development, 40*(5), 257-281.

Settersten, R. A., Jr. (1997b). Crafting the study of lives: The legacy of Bernice Neugarten and the future of gerontology. *The Gerontologist, 37*(5), 693-698.

Settersten, R. A., Jr., & Hagestad, G. O. (1996a). What's the latest? Cultural age deadlines for family transitions. *The Gerontologist, 36*(2), 178-188.

Settersten, R. A., Jr., & Hagestad, G. O. (1996b). What's the latest? II. Cultural age deadlines for educational and work transitions. *The Gerontologist, 36*(5), 602-613.

Settersten, R. A., Jr., & Lovegreen, L. D. (1998). Educational experiences throughout adult life. *Research on Aging, 20*(4), 506-538.

Settersten, R. A., Jr., & Mayer, K. U. (1997). The measurement of age, age structuring, and the life course. *Annual Review of Sociology, 23*, 233-261.

Sewell, W. H., Jr. (1992). A theory of structure: Duality, agency, and transformation. *American Journal of Sociology, 98*, 1-29.

Shanahan, M. J., & Elder, G. H., Jr. (1997). Nested comparisons in the study of historical change and individual adaptation. In J. Tudge, M. J. Shanahan, & J. Valsiner (Eds.), *Comparisons in human development: Understanding time and context* (pp. 109-136). New York: Cambridge University Press.

Shanan, J. (1991). Who and how: Some unanswered questions in adult development. *Journal of Gerontology: Psychological Sciences, 46*(6), P309-316.

Shenk, D., & Achenbaum, W. A. (Eds.). (1994). *Changing perceptions of aging and the aged*. New York: Springer Publishing Company.

Sherman, E. (1991) *Reminiscence and the self in old age*. New York: Springer Publishing Company.

Sherman, S. R. (1994). Changes in age identity: Self perceptions in middle and later life. *Journal of Aging Studies, 8*(4), 397-412.

Sherrod, L. R., & Brim, O. (1986). Retrospective and prospective views of life course research on development. In A. B. Sørensen, F. E. Weinert & L. R. Sherrod (Eds.), *Human development and the life course: Multidisciplinary perspectives* (pp. 557-580). Hillsdale, NJ: Lawrence Erlbaum and Associates.

Sieber, J. E. (1991a). Introduction: Sharing social science data. In J. E. Sieber (Ed.), *Sharing social science data: Advantages and challenges* (pp. 1-18). Newbury Park, CA: Sage Publications.

Sieber, J. E. (1991b). Social scientists' concerns about sharing data. In J. E. Sieber (Ed.), *Sharing social science data: Advantages and challenges* (pp. 141-150). Newbury Park, CA: Sage Publications.

Siegler, R. S., & Crowley, K. (1991). The microgenetic method: A direct means for studying cognitive development. *American Psychologist, 46*, 606-620.

Silbereisen, R. K., & Todt, E. (Eds.) (1993). *Adolescence in context: The interplay of family, school, peers, and work in adjustment*. New York: Springer-Verlag.

Simmons, R. G., & Blyth, D. A. (1987). *Moving into adolescence: The impact of pubertal change and school context*. New York: Aldine de Gruyter.

Singer, J. D., & Willett, J. B. (1991). Modeling the days of our lives: Using survival analysis when designing and analyzing longitudinal studies of duration and the timing of events. *Psychological Bulletin, 110*(2), 268-290.

Sirianni, C. (1991). The self-management of time in postindustrial society. In K. Hinrichs, W. Roche, & C. Sirianni (Eds.), *Working time in transition: The political economy of working hours in industrial nations* (pp. 231-274). Philadelphia, PA: Temple University Press.

Smelser, N. J., & Halpern, S. (1978) Historical triangulation of family, economy, and education. *American Journal of Sociology, 84(Supplement),* 288-315.

Smith, T. W. (1992). A life events approach to developing an index of societal well-being. *Social Science Research, 21,* 353-379.

Sokolovsky, J. (1997). Starting points: A global, cross-cultural view of aging. In J. Sokolovsky (Ed.), *The cultural context of aging: Worldwide perspectives* (pp. xiii-xxxi). Westport, CT: Gergin & Garvey.

Solomon, J. (1996). Humor and aging well: A laughing matter or a matter of laughing? *American Behavioral Scientist, 39*(3), 249-271.

Sørensen, A. (1991). The restructuring of gender relations in an aging society. *Acta Sociologica, 34,* 45-55.

Sørensen, A. B. (1986). Social structure and mechanisms of life-course processes. In A. B. Sørensen, F. E. Weinert, & L. R. Sherrod (Eds.), *Human development and the life course: Multidisciplinary perspectives* (pp. 177-197). Hillsdale, NJ: Lawrence Erlbaum Associates.

Spenner, K. I., Otto, L. B., & Call, V. R. (1982). *Career lines and careers: Entry into career series.* Lexington, MA: Lexington Books.

Spilerman, S. (1977). Careers, labor market structure, and socioeconomic achievement. *American Journal of Sociology, 83*(3), 551-593.

Sprott, R. L., & Baker, G. T. (Eds.) (1988). Biomarkers of aging. *Experimental Gerontology, 23(Special Issue).*

Staats, S., Romine, N., Atha, G., & Isham, J. (1994). Hoping for the best: The future time perspective. *Time & Society, 3*(3), 365-376.

Staudinger, U. M. (1989). *The study of life review: An approach to the investigation of intellectual development across life span.* Berlin, Germany: Max Planck Institute for Human Development and Education.

Strauss, A. L. (1959). *Mirrors and masks: The search for identity.* Glencoe, IL: The Free Press.

Super, C. M., & Harkness, S. (1997). The cultural structuring of child development. In J. W. Berry, P. R. Dasen, & T. S. Saraswathi (Eds.), *Handbook of cross-cultural psychology: Vol. 2. Basic processes and human development* (pp. 1-39). Boston, MA: Allyn & Bacon.

Suzman, R. M., Willis, D. P., & Manton, K. G. (Eds.) (1992). *The oldest old.* New York: Oxford University Press.

Swadener, B. B. (1995). Children and families "at promise": Deconstructing the discourse of risk. In B. B. Swadener & S. Lubeck (Eds.), *Children and families "at promise": Deconstructing the discourse of risk* (pp. 17-49). Albany, NY: State University of New York Press.

Swadener, B. B., & Lubeck, S. (1995). The social construction of children and families at risk: An introduction. In B. B. Swadener & S. Lubeck (Eds.), *Children and families "at promise": Deconstructing the discourse of risk* (pp. 1-14). Albany, NY: State University of New York Press.

Sweeting, H., & West, P. (1994). The patterning of life events in mid- to late adolescence: Markers for the future? *Journal of Adolescence, 17,* 283-304.

Teri, L., & Lewinsohn, P. (1982). Modification of the Pleasant and Unpleasant Events Schedules for use with the elderly. *Journal of Consulting and Clinical Psychology, 50*(3), 444-445.

Thelen, E. (1992). Development as a dynamic system. *Current Directions in Psychological Science, 1,* 189-193.

Thelen, E., & Smith, L. B. (1994). *A dynamic systems approach to the development of cognition and action.* Cambridge, MA: MIT Press.

Theorell, T. (1992). Critical life changes: A review of research. *Psychotherapy and Psychosomatics, 57,* 108-117.

Thomae, H. (1993). Foreword. In J. J. F. Schroots (Ed.), *Aging, health, and competence: The next generation of longitudinal research* (pp. xi-xiii). Amsterdam: Elsevier.

Thomas, G., Meyer, J., Ramirez, F., & Boli-Bennett, J. (1987). *Institutional structure: Constituting state, society, and the individual.* Newbury Park, CA: Sage Publications.

Thomas, W. I., & Znaniecki, F. (1918-1920). *The Polish peasant in Europe and America, vols. 1-5.* New York: Alfred Knopf.

Thompson, P. (1992). "I don't feel old": Subjective ageing and the search for meaning in later life. *Ageing and Society, 12,* 23-47.

Thorngate, W. (1992). Evidential statistics and the analysis of developmental patterns. In J. B. Asendorpf & J. Valsiner (Eds.), *Stability and change in development: A study of methodological reasoning* (pp. 63-83). Newbury Park, CA: Sage Publications.

Thorngate, W. (1995). Accounting for person-context relations and their development. In T. A. Kindermann & J. Valsiner (Eds.), *Development of person-context relations* (pp. 39-54). Hillsdale, NJ: Lawrence Erlbaum Associates.

Tismer, K. G. (1971). Vergangenheitsbezug im hoeheren Alter. *Zeitschrift fur Entwicklungspsychologie und Paedagogische Psychologische Psychologie, 3,* 14-24.

Tobin, S. (1996). A non-normative old age contrast: Elderly parents caring for offspring with mental retardation. In V. Bengtson (Ed.), *Adulthood and aging: Research on continuities and discontinuities* (pp. 124-142). New York: Springer Publishing Company.

Tomlinson-Keasey, C. (1993). Opportunities and challenges posed by archival data sets. In D. C. Funder, R. D. Parke, C. Tomlinson-Keasey, & K. Widaman (Eds.), *Studying lives through time: Personality and development* (pp. 65-92). Washington, DC: American Psychological Association.

Treiman, D. (1985). The work histories of men and women: What we need to know and what we need to find out. In A. Rossi (Ed.), *Gender and the life course* (pp. 213-231). New York: Aldine Publishing Company.

Tuckman, J., & Lorge, I. (1953). Attitudes toward old people. *Journal of Social Psychology, 37,* 249-260.

Tudge, J., Shanahan, M. J., & Valsiner, J. (1997). *Comparisons in human development: Understanding time and context.* New York: Cambridge University Press.

Turner, J. H. (1991). *The structure of sociological theory.* Belmont, CA: Wadsworth Publishing Company.

Turner, R. (1960). Modes of social ascent through education: Sponsored and contest mobility. *American Sociological Review, 25,* 855-867.

Turner, V. (1969). *The ritual process.* Chicago, IL: Aldine Publishing Company.

Tyack, D. (1989, March). *The mismatch between schools and students who don't fit them.* Paper presented at the annual meeting of the American Educational Research Association, San Francisco, CA. (Cited in Swadener, 1995)

Uhlenberg, P. (1980). Death and the family. *Journal of Family History, 5,* 313-320.

Uhlenberg, P. (1988). Aging and the societal significance of cohorts. In V. Bengtson & J. Birren (Eds.), *Emergent theories of aging* (pp. 405-425). New York: Springer Publishing Company.

Uhlenberg, P., & Miner, S. (1996). Life course and aging: A cohort perspective. In R. Binstock & L. George (Eds.), *Handbook of aging and the social sciences* (4th ed., pp. 208-228). San Diego, CA: Academic Press.

Uhlenberg, P., & Riley, M. W. (1996). Cohort studies. In J. Birren (Ed.), *Encyclopedia of Gerontology: Age, aging, and the aged* (Vol. 1, pp. 299-309). San Diego, CA: Academic Press.

Underhill, L., & Cadwell, F. (1983). "What age do you feel" age perception study. *Journal of Consumer Marketing, 1,* 18-27.

Uttal, D. H., & Perlmutter, M. (1989). Toward a broader conceptualization of development: The role of gains and losses across the life span. *Developmental Review, 9,* 101-132.

Uttley, M., & Crawford, M. H. (1994). Efficacy of a composite biological age score to predict ten-year survival among Kansas and Nebraska Mennonites. *Human Biology, 66*(1), 121-144.

Valsiner, J. (1984). Two espistemological frameworks in psychology: The typological and variational modes of thinking. *Journal of Mind and Behavior, 5,* 449-470.

Valsiner, J. (1989). *Human development and culture.* Lexington, MA: D. C. Heath.

Valsiner, J. (1994). Culture and human development: A co-constructivist perspective. In P. van Geert & L. Mos (Eds.), *Annals of theoretical psychology* (Vol. 10, pp. 247-298). New York: Plenum Publishing.

Valsiner, J. (1998). The development of the concept of development: Historical and epistemological perspectives. In R. M. Lerner (Ed.), *Handbook of child psychology: Vol. 1. Theoretical models of human development* (5th ed., pp. 189-232). New York: John Wiley & Sons.

Valsiner, J., & Lawrence, J. A. (1997). Human development in culture across the life span. In J. W. Berry, P. R. Dasen, & T. S. Saraswathi (Eds.), *Handbook of cross-cultural psychology: Vol. 2. Basic processes and human development* (pp. 69-106). Boston, MA: Allyn & Bacon.

van Aken, M. A. G. (1992). Modeling environmental development: Some comments from a developmental task perspective. In J. B. Asendorpf & J. Valsiner (Eds.), *Stability and change in development: A study of methodological reasoning* (pp. 191-197). Newbury Park, CA: Sage Publications.

van de Vijver, F., & Leung, K. (1997). *Methods and data analysis for cross-cultural research.* Thousand Oaks, CA: Sage Publications.

van Gennep, A. (1908/1960). *The rites of passage* (M. B. Vizedom & S. T. Kimball, Trans.). Chicago, IL: University of Chicago Press.

Veevers, J. E., Gee, E. M., & Wister, A. V. (1996). Homeleaving age norms: Conflict or consensus? *International Journal of Aging and Human Development, 43*(4), 277-295.

Verdonik, F., & Sherrod, L. R. (1984). *An inventory of longitudinal research on childhood and adolescence.* New York: Social Sciences Research Council.

von Eye, A. (Ed.). (1990). *Statistical methods in longitudinal research.* New York: Academic Press.

von Eye, A., Kreppner, K., & Wessels, H. (1992). Differential change in systems of categorical variables. In J. B. Asendorpf & J. Valsiner (Eds.), *Stability and change in development: A study of methodological reasoning* (pp. 21-53). Newbury Park, CA: Sage Publications.

Wadsworth, M. (1991). *The imprint of time: Childhood, history, and adult life.* Oxford: Clarendon Press.

Wagner, B. M., Compas, B. E., & Howell, D. C. (1988). Daily and major life events: A test of an integrative model of psychosocial stress. *American Journal of Community Psychology, 16*(2), 189-205.

Wallace, M. (1956). Future time perspective and schizophrenia. *Journal of Abnormal and Social Psychology, 52,* 240-245.

Ward, R. A. (1977). The impact of subjective age and stigma on older persons. *Journal of Gerontology, 32,* 227-332.

Ward, R.A. (1984). The marginality and salience of being old: When is age relevant? *The Gerontologist, 24,* 227- 232.

Waring, J. M. (1975). Social replenishment and social change: The problem of disordered cohort flow. *American Behavioral Scientist, 19*(2), 237-256.

Wasserman, S., & Faust, K. (1994). *Social network analysis: Methods and applications.* New York: Cambridge University Press.

Wasserman, S., & Galaskiewicz, J. (Eds.). (1994). *Advances in social network analysis: Research in the social and behavioral sciences.* Thousand Oaks, CA: Sage Publications.

Waterman, A. S., & Archer, S. L. (1990). A life-span perspective on identity formation: Developments in form, function, and process. In P. B. Baltes, D. L. Featherman, & R. M. Lerner (Eds.), *Life-span development and behavior* (Vol. 10, pp. 29-57). Hillsdale, NJ: Erlbaum.

Weber, M. (1904-5/1994). *The Protestant Ethic and the spirit of capitalism.* London: Routledge.

Watkins, S. C., Bongarts, J., & Menken, J. A. (1987). Demographic foundations of family change. *Annual Sociological Review, 52,* 346-358.

Weil, V. & Hollander, R. (1991). Normative issues in data sharing. In J. E. Sieber (Ed.), *Sharing social science data: Advantages and challenges* (pp. 151-156). Newbury Park, CA: Sage Publications.

Werner, E. E., & Smith, R. S. (1992). *Overcoming the odds: High-risk children from birth to adulthood.* Ithaca, NY: Cornell University Press.

Wetle, T. (1991). Successful aging: New hope for optimizing mental and physical wellbeing. *Journal of Geriatric Psychiatry, 24*(1), 3-12.

Weymann, A. (1994). Technological innovation and technology-generations: East and West German inequalities. In R. Blackman (Ed.), *Social inequality in a changing world* (pp. 28-49). Cambridge, Great Britain: Sociological Research Group.

Weymann, A. (1996a). Interrelating society and biography: Discourse, markets, and the welfare state's life course policy. In A. Weymann & W. Heinz (Eds.), *Society and biography: Interrelationships between social structure, institutions, and the life course* (pp. 241-258). Weinheim, Germany: Deutscher Studien Verlag.

Weymann, A. (1996b). Modernization, generational relations, and the economy of life time. *International Journal of Sociology and Social Policy, 16*(4), 37-57.

Weymann, A., & Heinz, W. R. (1996). *Society and biography: Interrelationships between social structure, institutions, and the life course.* Weinheim, Germany: Deutscher Studien Verlag.

Whalen, J., & Flacks, R. (1989). *Beyond the barricades: The 60s generation grows up.* Philadelphia, PA: Temple University Press.

Wheeler, S. (1966). The structure of formally organized socialization settings. In O. G. Brim, Jr. & S. Wheeler (Eds.), *Socialization after childhood: Two essays* (pp. 51-116). New York: John Wiley & Sons.

Whitbourne, S. K. (1996). *The aging individual: Physical and psychological perspectives.* New York: Springer Publishing Company.

White, D. R. (1991). Sharing anthropological data with peers and Third World hosts. In J. E. Sieber (Ed.), *Sharing social science data: Advantages and challenges* (pp. 42-60). Newbury Park, CA: Sage Publications.

White, L. (1994). Coresidence and leaving home: Young adults and their parents. *Annual Review of Sociology, 20,* 81-102.

Whiting, B. B., & Whiting, J. W. M. (1975). *The children of six cultures: A psychocultural analysis.* Cambridge, MA: Harvard University Press.

Widaman, K. F. (1991). Qualitative transitions amid quantitative development: A challenge for measuring and representing change. In L. M. Collins & J. L. Horn (Eds.), *Best methods for the analysis of change: Recent advances, unanswered questions, future directions* (pp. 204-217). Washington, DC: American Psychological Association.

Willett, J. B. (1989). Questions and answers in the measurement of change. In E. Rothkopf (Ed.), *Review of research in education* (Vol. 15, pp. 345-422). Washington, DC: American Educational Research Association.

Willett, J. B., & Sayer, A. G. (1994). Using covariance structure analysis to detect correlates and predictors of individual change over time. *Psychological Bulletin, 116*(2), 363-381.

Williams, C. L., & Uchiyama, C. (1989). Assessment of life events during adolescence: The use of self-report inventories. *Adolescence, 24,* 95-118.

Williams, R., & Wirth, C. (1965). *Lives through the years: Styles of life and successful aging.* New York: Atherton Press.

Wilson, R. W. (1985). Assessing the impact of life change events. In E. B. Palmore, E. W. Busse, G. L. Maddox, J. B. Nowlin, & I. C. Siegler (Eds.), *Normal Aging III* (pp. 356-372). Durham, NC: Duke University Press.

Winegar, L. T. (1997). Developmental research and comparative perspectives: Applications to developmental science. In J. Tudge, M. J. Shanahan, & J. Valsiner (Eds.), *Comparisons in human development* (pp. 13-33). New York: Cambridge University Press.

Winegar, L. T., & Valsiner, J. (Eds.). (1992). *Children's development within social context: Vol. 1. Metatheory and theory.* Hillsdale, NJ: Lawrence Erlbaum Associates.

Winsborough, H. H. (1980). A demographic approach to the life cycle. In K. W. Back (Ed.), *Life course: Integrative theories and exemplary populations* (pp. 65-75). Boulder, CO: Westview Press.

Wohlwill, J. F. (1983). Physical and social environment as factors in development. In D. Magnusson & V. L. Allen (Eds.), *Human development: An interactional perspective* (pp. 111-129). New York: Academic Press.

Wohlwill, J. F. (1991). Relations between method and theory in developmental research: A partial-isomorphism view. In P. van Geert & L. P. Mos (Eds.), *Annals of theoretical psychology* (Vol. 7, pp. 91-138). New York: Plenum Publishing.

Wong, P. T. P., & Watt, L. M. (1991) What types of reminiscence are associated with successful aging? *Psychology and Aging, 6,* 272-279.

Wood, V. (1972, November). *Role allocation as a function of age.* Paper presented at the annual meeting of the Gerontological Society, Miami Beach, Florida.

Wrosch, C., & Heckhausen, J. (forthcoming). Being on-time or off-time: Developmental deadlines for regulating one's own development. In A. N. Perret-Clermont, J. M. Barrelet, A. Flammer, D. Miéville, J. F. Perret, & W. Perrig (Eds.), *Mind and time.* Göttingen, Sweden: Hogrefe & Huber Publishers.

Yamaguchi, K. (1991). *Event history analysis.* Newbury Park, CA: Sage Publications.

Young, C. H., Savola, K., & Phelps, E. (1991). *Inventory of longitudinal studies in the social sciences.* Newbury Park, CA: Sage Publications.

Young, M. (1988). *The metronomic society: Natural rhythms and human timetables.* Cambridge, MA: Harvard University Press.

Youniss, J. (1995). The still useful classic concept of development. *Human Development, 38,* 373-379.

Zautra, A. J., Guarnaccia, C. A., & Dohrenwend, B. P. (1986). The measurement of small life events. *American Journal of Community Psychology, 14,* 629-655.

Zepelin, H., Sills, R., & Heath, M. (1987). Is age becoming irrelevant? An exploratory study of perceived age norms. *International Journal of Aging and Human Development, 24*(4), 241-255.

Zola, I. K. (1962). Feelings about age among older people. *Journal of Gerontology, 17,* 65-68.

Author Index

Abbott, A., 150, 176
Abeles, R., 171
Achenbaum, W. A., 74
Acland, H., 172
Adams, R., 230
Albert, M., 105, 229
Aldwin, C. M., 142-144, 155-157
Alexander, C., 142
Alexander, K. L., 174
Allatt, P., 6
Allison, P., 149, 187
Alsaker, F. D., 188, 195
Alwin, D., 13, 17, 125, 150, 180, 211, 218, 219, 241
Amell, J. W., 150
Amin, A., 41
Amster, L. E., 142
Anderson, N. N., 84
Andersson, T., 212
Andrews, B., 152
Aneshensel, C. S., 147, 148, 174
Angus, D., 68
Antonucci, T. C., 15
Applebaum, M. I., 169, 170
Archer, S. L., 66
Ariès, P. , 104
Arrt, S., 84
Asendorpf, J. B., 201-203, 212, 214-216
Askenasy, A. R., 142
Atchley, R. C., 51
Atha, G., 167
Attias-Donfut, C., 217
Averett, C., 164
Avery, R. J., 76

Bachman, J. G., 165
Back, K., 164
Bäckman, L., 28
Bailey, S. L., 126
Baker, G. T., 79
Balan, J., 149, 150
Balin, A. K., 79
Baltes, M., 28, 29, 227, 229, 230, 234
Baltes, P. B., 6, 25-33, 100, 101, 105, 123, 124, 154, 206, 210, 227, 229, 230, 234, 251
Baltes-Götz, B., 222
Bandura, A., 222
Bane, M. J., 172
Barak, B., 84, 85
Barth, M. C., 55
Bartlett, S., 172
Bastin, E., 167
Baum, S. K., 84, 85
Belk, S. S., 142
Bell, T., 84
Benedict, R., 7
Bengtson, V. L., 42, 43, 224
Benjamin, H., 79, 80
Bentler, P. M., 143
Berger, B., 114, 121
Berger, P., 87
Bergman, L. R., 37, 156, 191, 212-214, 236, 241
Berkman, L. F., 105, 227, 229
Best, F., 44, 61, 62
Binstock, R., 106, 108
Birren, B. A., 222
Birren, J. E., 74, 77-79, 81, 82, 163, 222
Black, S. A., 69

Blake, J., 87
Blanchard-Fields, F., 230
Blau, P. M., 130
Blazer, D., 105, 229
Blieszner, R., 230
Bligh, M. C., 184, 224-226
Block, J., 66, 137, 156-159, 241, 245
Bloom, B. S., 185
Bloom, K. L., 84
Blossfeld, H. P., 149, 151, 162, 163
Blow, F. C., 15
Blum, Z., 84, 149
Blyth, D. A., 232
Bohrnstedt, G. W., 185
Boldt, J. S., 84
Boli-Bennett, J., 23
Bollen, K. A., 183
Bond., L., 227
Bongarts, J., 76
Borg, I., 72
Borscheid, P., 104
Boruch, R. F., 170
Botella, L., 163
Bouffard, L., 167
Bourque, L. B., 164
Boxley, R. L., 84, 85
Boyd, J. W., 65, 66, 82
Braithwaite, V., 103
Brandt, D., 157, 187
Brandtstädter, J., 25, 26, 66, 88, 98-101, 124, 155, 173, 222, 223
Braungart, M. M., 110, 120, 122
Braungart, R. G., 110, 120, 122
Brewin, C. R., 152
Brim, O. G., Jr., 13, 86, 146
Brody, E. M., 16
Bronfenbrenner, U., 33-35, 37, 193, 195, 211, 220
Brooks, J., 230
Brooks-Gunn, J., 146, 156, 168, 169
Brose, H.-G., 40, 76
Brown, C., 61
Brown, G., 147
Brown, J., 230
Browning, H. L., 149, 150
Brückner, E., 151, 152
Brunstein, J. C., 99
Bryant, W. K., 76
Bryk, A. S., 187, 211
Bryman, A., 6

Buchmann, M., 40, 66, 68, 149
Buckholdt, D. R., 173
Bühler, C., 26
Burkhauser, R., 48, 52, 55, 62
Busse, E.W., 84
Bultena, G., 90, 91
Burch, T. K., 176, 178
Burr, J. A., 174, 175
Burton, L., 42, 43
Bush, D. M., 13
Butler, R. N., 162, 227, 233
Bytheway, B., 6, 77

Cadwell, F., 84
Cain, L. D., Jr., 7, 11, 74
Cairns, B. D., 15
Cairns, R. B., 15, 156, 173, 212, 215, 246
Calasanti, T. M., 224, 226, 227
Calhoun, C., 219
Call, V. R., 172
Calloway, M. D., 60
Camburn, D., 150
Cameron, P., 101, 105
Campbell, R. T., 123, 125, 145, 155-157, 211, 241
Cantor, N., 98, 99
Carden, M., 126
Carlson, R., 241
Carolina Consortium on Human Development, 1, 237
Caspi, A., 13, 14, 117, 134, 135, 150-153, 160, 182-184, 204-206, 226
Catan, L., 218
Ceci, S. J., 35
Centre for Educational Research and Innovation, 46, 57, 58, 60
Champion, L., 211
Chan, C. G., 174
Chan, T. W., 150, 176
Changas, P. S., 103
Chelimsky, E., 207
Chen, Y., 230
Chiriboga, D. A., 142, 179
Christensen, K., 55
Christopherson, S., 57
Chudacoff, H. P., 39, 40, 66, 77
Clausen, J. A., 24, 58, 59, 139-142, 153, 164, 181, 200, 221, 222

Clipp, E., 17, 126, 145, 158, 169, 170, 174, 175
Clubb, P. A., 217, 218
Cochrane, R., 142
Cohen, D., 172
Cohen, L., 142
Cohen, P., 189
Cohler, B., 96
Colby, A., 171, 212
Cole, T. R., 74
Coleman, P., 162
Collins, L. M., 184-188, 190
Compas, B. E., 142, 143
Comte, A., 114
Conger, R., 17, 126
Connidis, I., 85
Cook, F. L., 107, 108
Cook, J. A., 96
Cook, T. D., 196, 231, 232
Corcoran, M., 172
Cornelius, S. W., 33, 123
Costa, P. T., 66, 79, 80
Costello, E. J., 156, 173, 246
Courgeau, D., 149
Coyne, J. C., 142
Crawford, M. H., 80
Cremin, M. C., 84
Crockett, L. J., 196
Crouse, J., 172
Crouter, A. C., 196
Cronbach, L. J., 185, 186
Cross, S., 101
Crowley, K., 154, 218
Cumming, E., 227, 228
Cunningham, W. R., 78, 82
Cutler, S. J., 45, 84, 227, 241

Dannefer, D., 32, 33, 50, 78, 81, 82, 93, 94, 96, 108, 124, 130-132, 134, 194-196, 206, 224-226, 251
Datan, N., 82, 87
Dauber, S. L., 174
David, D., 164
David, M., 169, 171
Davies, P., 51, 57, 58
Davis, G. E., 143
Davis, K., 7, 87
Day, C., 108
Dean, H., 142

Dean, W., 79, 80
DeGenova, M. K., 164
Degirmencloglu, S., 196, 231
Denzin, N. K., 212
de Oliveira, Z. M. R., 202
Derbin, V., 84
Deutchman, D. E., 163
deViney, S., 230
DeVries, B., 163, 164
Dex, S., 152
Dickerson-Putnam, J., 42, 69, 94, 232
Diewald, M., 99
Dilthey, W., 114
DiPrete, T. A., 211
Dirken, J. M., 79
Dittman-Kohli, F., 101
Dixon, A. R., 28, 101
Dodds, A. E., 237
Dodge, K. A., 146, 206
Doeringer, P. B., 56
Dohrenwend, B. P., 142, 143
Dohrenwend, B. S., 142
Donaldson, G., 125
Douthitt, R. A., 76
Dowd, J., 65, 66, 82, 224
Downs, A., 51
Draper, P., 42, 69, 94, 232
Drevenstedt, J., 105
Duncan, O. D., 130

Eaglesfield, D., 172
Easterlin, R., 113
Eccles, J., 46, 166, 196, 232
Eglit, H., 74
Ehmer, J., 104
Eisdorfer, C., 84
Eisenstadt, S. N., 7, 104
Elder, G. H., Jr., 6, 10, 12-17, 19, 20, 29, 31, 32, 34, 35, 65, 93, 116, 117, 125, 126, 137, 138, 145-148, 156, 158, 168-170, 173-175, 196, 205, 217, 223, 232, 236, 243, 246
Elias, N., 93
Ellis, R. A., 168
Emmons, R. A., 99
Engel, U., 184, 185
Entwistle, D. R., 174
Erikson, E., 6, 26, 104, 162
Esler, A., 129

Essex, M. J., 173
Everitt, B. S., 72

Fairbank, J. A., 126
Fairchild, T., 142
Fallo-Mitchell, L., 86, 89
Faust, K., 211, 212
Featherman, D., 9, 32, 153, 180
Featherstone, M., 74
Feibleman, J. K., 21
Ferrari, G., 114
Fillenbaum, G. G., 105
Fischer, K., 101
Fisher, L., 81
Flacks, R., 126
Fleeson, W., 98, 99
Flinn, C. J., 149
Foner, A., 7-9, 12, 13, 15, 42, 43, 54, 83, 87, 109, 219
Fontane, P., 230
Ford, D. H., 35, 222
Ford, M. E., 35, 222
Forrest, J., 150
Forristal, J. D., 211
Forsythe, C. J., 143
Fortes, M., 7, 115
Frank, G., 150
Frank, L. K., 1, 69
Freedman, D., 150
Freels, S., 170
Freeman, L. C., 211
Freud, S., 6, 18
Fry, C. L., 42, 65, 68-70, 72, 77, 94, 217, 218, 225, 232, 242
Furby, L., 185, 186
Furstenberg, F. F., Jr., 40, 196, 232

Galaskiewicz, J., 211
Garfein, A. J., 227
Garmenzy, N., 160, 208, 209
Garner, J., 170
Gee, E. M., 76, 86, 88, 89
Gekoski, W. L., 103
George, L. K., 69, 84, 125, 128, 147, 148, 197, 198, 221, 238, 241
Gergen, K., 179-181
Germain, C., 6
Gerth, H., 13

Gibbs, J., 87
Giddens, A., 10
Gilligan, C., 41, 67
Glascock, A. P., 42, 69, 94, 232
Glaser, B. G., 21
Glass, T. A., 227, 229
Glasser, R., 164
Gleason, H. P., 227
Glenn, N., 125
Goffman, E., 198
Goldsmith, R. E., 84
Gollwitzer, P. M., 99
Gotlib, I. H., 152
Gottlieb, G., 25, 215
Gottman, J. M., 184, 185
Gould, S., 84, 85
Graff, H., 39
Grams, A., 227
Green, B. S., 74
Greene, A. L., 167
Greve, W., 66
Griffin, L. J., 149
Grigsby, J. S., 184, 224-226
Groenen, P. J. F., 72
Grusky, D. B., 220
Guarnaccia, C. A., 143
Gubrium, J. F, 25, 173, 242
Guillem, F., 163
Guillemard, A.-M., 52, 62
Guptill, C. S., 84
Gutmann, D., 26, 27, 38, 39, 179, 239, 241, 242

Habib, J., 63, 64
Hagestad, G. O., 6, 15, 34, 40, 41, 54, 58, 65, 67, 68, 76, 81-83, 86-89, 91, 92, 95-97, 101, 104, 117, 122, 153
Haight, B., 163, 165
Hall, J. H., 80, 169
Halpern, S., 44
Hamerle, A., 149, 151
Hantrais, L., 217
Hardy, M., 48
Hareven, T., 34, 82, 83
Harkness, S., 69
Harpending, H., 42, 69, 94, 232
Harrington, C., 148, 150
Harris, C. W., 185
Harris, D. K., 102, 103

Harris, T., 147
Havighurst, R. 164
Hawkes, R. K., 87
Hays, S., 67
Heath, M., 86, 89
Heckhausen, J., 66, 84, 87, 93, 96-103, 222, 229
Heckman, J. J., 149
Heiens, R. A., 84
Heinz, W. R., 21, 223
Held, T., 23, 40
Helmchen, H., 105
Henderson, P. H., 55
Hendricks, J., 11, 45, 83, 89, 165, 212, 239
Henretta, J., 39, 40, 55, 56, 68, 174
Henry, B., 152
Henry, W., 227, 228
Hernes, H. M., 41, 67
Hershberg, T., 40
Herzog, A. R., 66, 227, 229
Hess, B. B., 7
Hickey, T., 101
Hill, M., 170
Hinde, R. A., 181, 184
Hinrichs, K., 47, 57
Hogan, D. P., 40, 65, 88, 149, 176
Holahan, C. J., 142
Holahan, C. K., 142
Hollander, R., 171, 245
Holmes, T. H., 142
Holstein, J. A., 25, 173, 242
Horn, J. L., 125, 184, 185
Hough, R. L., 126
House, J. S., 13
Hout, M., 125
Howell, D. C., 142
Hox, J. J., 211
Hrycak, A., 150
Huba, G. J., 143
Hudson, C. M., 145
Hughes, C. E., 12
Huinink, J., 99, 125
Hundertmark, J., 87
Hunter, K., 84

Ikeda, K., 86, 89
Ikels, C., 42, 69, 94, 232
Imhof, A. E., 76
Inglehart, M. R., 142

Ingram, D. K., 79-81
Inkeles, A., 13
Isham, J., 167

Jackson, J., 87
Jackson, S., 196
Jacobs, J. A., 46
James, J. B., 169
Jeffers, F.C., 84
Jelin, E., 149, 150
Jencks, C., 172
Jessor, R., 196, 212, 231
Jette, A. M., 69
Johnson, J., 142
Johnson, M., 7, 87, 109
Johnson, T. R., 227, 230
Johnston, L. D., 165
Jolicoeur, P., 77
Jordan, B. K., 126
Jorgensen, L. B., 60
Jorgensen, S. R., 15

Kahana, B., 142, 147, 222, 227, 230, 231
Kahana, E., 142, 147, 222, 227, 230, 231
Kahn, R. L., 8, 9, 13, 15, 42, 43, 54, 105, 227-229, 231
Kalicki, B., 88
Kalish, R., 101
Kalleberg, A., 61
Kanner, A. D., 142
Kardiner, A., 38
Kariya, T., 49
Karweit, N., 149
Kastenbaum, R., 84, 168
Kaufman, J., 107
Kaufman, R., 172
Keil, T., 6
Keith, J., 42, 69, 71-73, 94, 105, 232, 242
Kelly, L. E., 103
Kenyon, G. M., 74
Kercher, K., 230
Kerckhoff, A. C., 50, 149, 172
Kertzer, D. I., 9, 39, 66, 67
Kessler, R., 147
Kimmel, D. C., 243
Kindermann, T. A., 197, 199, 200-203
Kitayama, S., 173
Kleigl, R., 30

302 / AUTHOR INDEX

Klein, D. M., 15
Kling, K. C., 173
Kluckhohn, C., 38
Knoke, D., 61, 116, 118, 119, 125
Knox, V. J., 103
Kohli, M., 21, 22, 32, 39, 40, 44, 52, 55, 62, 66, 68, 82, 93
Krain, M. A., 51
Krasnoff, L., 142
Krauss, H. H., 142
Krecker, M. L., 5, 6, 109
Kreppner, K., 185, 187, 193
Krüger, H., 47, 48, 67, 162
Krüger, J., 84, 87, 96, 102
Kruglanski, A. W., 29
Kruse, A., 154-156, 228, 229
Kruskal, J. B., 176
Kuhlen, R., 164
Kuhn, D., 154
Kulka, R., 126

Labouvie, E. W., 125
Lachman, M.E., 84, 85
LaFontaine, J. S., 66
Lang, F., 28, 103, 230
Langer, E. J., 221
Langley, J., 152
Larntz, K., 170
Lashbrook, J., 68, 94
Laslett, P., 104
Laub, J. H., 183
Lawrence, B. S., 68, 85, 92-95
Lawrence, J. A., 26, 75, 76, 93, 193, 237, 241
Lazarus, R. S., 142
Leibfried, S., 22
Lelievre, E., 149
Lens, W., 167
Lerner, R. M., 30, 32, 35, 37, 107, 180, 193, 195, 207, 225, 236
Lessing, E. E., 168
Leung, K., 217
Levin, J., 50
Levin, W. C., 50
Levinson, D. J., 162
Levy, R., 21, 193, 223
Lewin, K., 33, 220
Lewinsohn, P. M., 142, 143
Lewis, C. N., 164

Lewis, M., 162
Lieberman, M. A., 144, 147
Lieblich, A., 145
Light, J. M., 184, 224-226
Lincoln, Y. S., 212
Lindenberger, U., 6, 154, 228, 229
Link, B. G., 58
Linn, M. W., 84
Linton, R. A., 7, 38, 66
Lipsitt, L. P., 31, 33
Little, B. R., 99, 155, 170
Litzler, L., 149, 150
Loessi-Miller, K., 61
Looft, W. R., 37
Lord, F. M., 185
Lorge, I., 102
Lovegreen, L. D., 42, 58
Lowe, J. C., 86, 89
Lubeck, S., 207
Luckmann, T., 1
Ludwig, F. C., 79
Lüscher, K., 35
Lynd-Stevenson, R., 103
Lynott, R. J., 115
Lynott, P., 115

Maas, I., 126
MacPhillamy, D. J., 142
Maddox, G., 123, 227, 228
Magnusson, D., 35-38, 154-157, 194, 198, 209, 212-215, 222, 236, 237, 240, 241
Maier, A., 49
Maines, D. R., 86, 89
Mangen, S., 217
Mannheim, K., 110-112, 114, 122
Manton, K. G., 104
Marini, M. M., 88
Markides, K. S., 69, 84
Markus, H., 66, 101, 173
Marshall, J., 107
Marshall, V., 11, 20, 21, 45, 107, 120, 121, 226
Marsiske, M., 28, 29, 230
Mason, K. G., 125
Mason, W., 125
Masoro, E. J., 79
Massagli, M. P., 171, 175
Maughan, B., 211

Mayer, K.U., 20, 21, 23, 24, 40, 74, 105, 125, 126, 149, 151, 211
McAdam, D., 126
McCall, R. B., 169, 170
McClearn, G. E., 31
McCluskey, K. A., 126, 160
McCrae, R. R., 66, 79, 80
McCullough, J., 76
McCutcheon, S., 143
McNaught, W., 55
McNemar, Q., 185
McNevin, T. E., 102
McTavish, D. G., 102
Meguro, Y., 126
Mekos, D., 217, 218
Menaghan, E. G., 147
Menken, J. A., 76
Mensh, I. N., 143
Mermelstein, R. M., 142
Merton, R., 50, 130, 224
Meyer, J. W., 21, 23, 32, 40, 93
Migdal, S., 171
Miller, B., 15
Mills, C. W., 12, 13, 121
Miner, S., 13, 76, 119, 120, 122, 250
Mirel, J., 68
Mishler, E. G., 153, 176, 226
Mitteness, L., 126
Modell, J., 40, 88, 149, 204
Moen, P., 35, 41, 67, 69, 172
Moffitt, T. E., 150, 152, 204-206
Montepare, J. M., 84, 85
Moody, H. R., 243
Moore, J. W., 86, 89
Moore, M. E., 7
Morgan, R. F., 79, 80
Morris, P. A., 236
Morris, R., 35, 87
Mortimer, J., 13
Mullally, P. R., 173
Mullan, J. T., 147, 148, 174
Müller, W., 21, 23, 40
Murray, H. A., 38
Murray, I. M., 80
Murrell, S. A., 142
Mutchler, J. E., 174, 175
Mutran, E., 85, 157

National Council on Aging, 105
Neckerman, H. J., 15

Nelson, E. A., 224-226
Nesselroade, J. R., 33, 123, 125, 218
Neugarten, B. L., 6, 12, 20, 22, 41, 54, 65, 67, 74, 81, 82, 86-89, 95, 101, 104-107, 162, 179, 224, 227-231, 240, 242
Neugarten, D., 54, 65
Newcomb, M. D., 143
Newman, K., 129
Norris, F. H., 143
Nurmi, J.-E., 98, 100, 101
Nusberg, C., 63, 64
Nuttall, R. L., 79
Nuttin, J. R., 167
Nydegger, C. N., 6, 65, 95, 122, 123, 125, 126, 138, 139, 173

Oakes, J., 49
Okun, M. A., 125
O'Malley, P. M., 165
O'Neil, J., 126
O'Rand, A., 5, 6, 50, 55, 109, 130, 168, 174, 225
Ortega y Gasset, J., 114
Otto, L. B., 172
Overton, W. F., 180, 237

Padavic, I., 46
Palmore, E. B., 102, 103, 123
Parker, R. N., 157
Parsons, T., 7, 13, 66
Passuth, P. M., 86, 89
Paul, E. L., 169
Pavalko, E., 145, 158, 169, 170, 174, 175
Paykel, E. S., 142
Pearlin, L. I., 137, 143, 147, 148, 174
Pennybacker, M. R., 84
Perlmutter, M., 28, 81, 82, 196
Pernin, M.-O., 77
Peters, C. B., 83
Peters, G. R., 84
Petersen, T., 149
Peterson, C., 86, 89
Peterson, D. R., 34
Peterson, W. A., 101, 104, 105
Phelan, J., 58
Phelps, E., 146, 156, 168, 169, 171
Phillips, M., 196, 231

Pickett, S. A., 96
Pickles A., 140, 141, 211
Pienta, A. M., 174, 175
Pigram, D., 103
Piore, M. J., 56
Plath, D. W., 15, 16, 86, 89
Plomin, R., 31
Pontier, J., 77
Poole, W. K., 125
Pressey, S., 164
Preston, S. H., 107
Pruchno, R. A., 15
Prusoff, B. A., 142
Pulliainen, H., 100

Quadagno, J., 48
Quinn, J. F., 48, 52, 55, 62
Quinton, D., 211

Rabin, A. I., 13
Rahe, R. H., 142
Rajulton, F., 176, 178
Ramirez, F., 23
Rapkin, B. D., 101
Raudenbush, S. W., 187, 211
Ravanera, A. R., 176, 178
Reese, H. W., 31, 33, 126, 160, 180
Reff, M. E., 79
Rehn, G., 53, 55, 59, 60, 63
Rein, M., 52, 62
Reinecke, J., 184, 185
Reinharz, S., 87, 94
Reiss, A., Jr., 170
Renner, G., 99-101
Reskin, B., 46
Riegel, K. F., 33, 82
Riley, J. W., Jr., 8, 10, 43, 45, 54, 66, 122
Riley, M. W., 7-13, 15, 20, 31, 42, 43, 45, 54, 65, 66, 76, 83, 86, 87, 109, 111, 113, 116, 122, 219, 231, 253
Rindfuss, R., 65, 176-178, 241
Rix, S., 45
Robbins, L., 80
Robertson, A., 142
Robins, L. N., 152, 153
Roche, W., 47, 57
Rodgers, W. L., 125
Rodriguez-Tomé, H., 196

Rogoff-Ramsoy, N., 149, 151
Rogosa, D. R., 157, 187-189, 245
Rohwer, G., 162, 163
Romesburg, H. C., 72
Romine, N., 167
Romney, A. K., 211
Rose, C. L., 79
Rosenbaum, J. E., 49, 50, 68, 172
Rosencranz, H. A., 102
Rosenfeld, R., 65, 176, 177, 241
Rosenthal, C., 42, 43
Rosow, I., 13, 115
Rossetti-Ferreira, M. C., 202
Rossi, A., 46, 54, 66
Roth, B. K., 7
Roth, J. A., 87
Rothbaum, F., 98
Rothman, J., 207
Rovine, M. J., 212
Rowe, J., 227-229, 231
Rubin, D. B., 155, 170
Rudinger, G., 212
Runyan, W. M., 164
Rutter, M., 140, 141, 160, 161, 208-211
Ryder, N., 11, 13, 18, 20, 109, 111, 112, 114, 115, 120, 124
Ryff, C. D., 86, 89, 146, 173
Rytina, S. L., 219

Sabatini, P., 84
Sackmann, R., 118, 119
Salmela-Aro, K., 100
Salthouse, T. A., 79
Sameroff, A. J., 196, 217, 232
Sampson, R. J., 183
Sarason, I. G., 142
Savola, K., 171
Sayer, A. G., 187
Scarr, S., 25, 210
Schaefer, C., 142
Schaie, K. W., 33, 115, 119, 123-126
Schlenger, W. E., 126
Schneider, E. L., 79
Schöpflin, U., 23, 74, 105
Schroeder, E., 188
Schroots, J. J. F., 74, 77-79, 81, 115, 240
Schulenberg, J., 165
Schulz, R., 66, 100, 222, 229
Schultz, J. H., 113

Schuman, H., 116, 126, 128
Schütze, H. G., 50, 58
Scott, J., 116, 126-128, 211
Seeman, T. E., 105, 227, 229
Sell, R., 130-132, 224
Sempé, M., 77
Semple, S. J., 148
Settersten, R. A., Jr., 39, 40, 42, 49, 58, 86-89, 91, 97, 117, 126, 149, 196, 232
Sewell, W. H., Jr., 218
Shadish, W. R., 207
Shagle, S., 196, 232
Shanahan, M. J., 17, 126, 145, 147, 148, 217, 242
Shanan, J., 184
Shenk, D., 74
Sherman, E., 164
Sherman, S. R., 85
Sherrod, L. R., 86, 171
Shweder, R. A., 212
Sieber, J. E., 171, 245
Siegel, J. M., 142
Siegler, I. C., 125, 154, 218
Silbereisen, R. K., 196
Sills, R., 86, 89
Silva, P. A., 150, 152
Simmons, R. G., 13, 232
Singer, J. D., 149
Sirianni, C., 47, 57, 63, 64
Skaff, M. M., 137, 143, 147, 148
Skinner, E. A., 197, 199-203
Smeijers, J., 150
Smelser, N. J., 9, 44
Smith, J., 26, 230
Smith, L. B., 35
Smith, M., 172
Smith, R. S., 209
Smith, T. W., 148, 149
Smyer, M. A., 15
Snyder, S. S., 98
Sokolovsky, J., 217
Solomon, J., 230
Sørensen, A., 45-47, 54, 55, 66
Sørensen, A. B., 22, 149
Spenner, K. I., 172
Spilerman, S., 172
Sprott, R. L., 79
Staats, S., 167
Stange, K., 230

Stattin, H., 199, 236, 237, 240
Staudinger, U. M., 6, 162
Steinhagen-Thiessen, E., 105
Stern, B., 84, 85
Stoll, S., 79-81
Strauss, A. L., 21, 87
Strong, D., 40
Suomi, S. J., 217
Super, C. M., 69
Suzman, R. M., 104
Swadener, B. B., 207
Sweeting, H., 143, 145
Swicegood, C., 65, 176, 177, 241

Takata, A. A., 220
Teri, L., 143
Thelen, E., 35
Theorell, T., 145
Thomae, H., 158
Thomas, E. J., 207
Thomas, G., 23
Thomas, W. I., 20, 91
Thompson, P., 84
Thorngate, W., 29, 203, 204, 216
Thornton, A., 150
Tismer, K. G., 164
Tobin, S. S., 96
Todt, E., 196
Tomlinson-Keasey, C., 157, 170, 171, 245
Torestad, B., 212
Treiman, D., 46
Tuckman, J., 102
Tudge, J., 217, 242
Tuma, N. B., 20, 21, 23, 24, 149, 151, 211
Turner, J. H., 10
Turner, R., 50
Turner, V., 7
Tyack, D., 207

Uchiyama, C., 143
Uhlenberg, P., 13, 69, 76, 116, 119, 120, 122, 132-134, 250
Uhlenhuth, E. H., 142
Underhill, L., 84
Uttal, D. H., 28
Uttley, M., 80

AUTHOR INDEX

Valsiner, J., 26, 75, 76, 172, 193, 196, 201-203, 212, 214-217, 225, 242
van Aken, M. A. G., 202
van de Vijver, F., 217
van der Burgh, R. M., 150
van Gennep, A., 7, 138
van Zonneveld, R. J., 79
Veevers, J. E., 88
Verdonik, F., 171
Vinovskis, M. A., 68
von Eye, A., 185, 187, 212

Wadsworth, M., 149
Wagner, B. M., 142, 143
Wallace, M., 168
Ward, R. A., 81, 84
Wardlaw, L., 148
Waring, J. M., 7, 9, 12, 15, 83, 87, 111
Wasserman, S., 211, 212
Waterman, A. S., 66
Watkins, S. C., 76
Watt, L. M., 163, 164, 223
Weber, M., 8, 68
Webster, J., 165
Weil, V., 171, 245
Weisz, J. R., 98
Werner, E. E., 209
Wernick, A., 74
Wessels, H., 185, 187
West, P., 143, 145
Wethington, E., 147
Wetle, T., 227
Weymann, A., 21, 53, 113, 118, 119
Whalen, J., 126
Wheatley, S. M., 167
Wheeler, S., 13

Whitbourne, S. K., 173
White, D. R., 171, 211
White, L., 90
Whiting, B. B., 69
Whiting, J. W. M., 69
Whitlatch, C. J., 148, 174
Widaman, K. F., 187
Willett, J. B., 149, 157, 184-187
Williams, C. L., 143
Williams, R., 227, 228
Willis, D. P., 104
Wilson, R. W., 143
Winegar, L. T., 37, 196, 216, 236, 237
Winsborough, H. H., 40, 125
Wirth, C., 227, 228
Wister, A. V., 88
Wohlwill, J. F., 198, 241
Wong, P. T. P., 163, 164, 223
Wood, V., 90, 91
Wrosch, C., 96
Wugalter, S. E., 188

Yamaguchi, K., 149
Young, C. H., 171
Young, M., 39
Young-DeMarco, L., 150
Youniss, J., 25

Zac, L., 127
Zarit, S. H., 174
Zautra, A. J., 143
Zepelin, H., 86, 89
Zimowski, M., 157, 187
Znaniecki, F., 20
Zola, I. K., 84

Subject Index

Absolute continuity, 182
Accentuation principle, 16
Accommodative coping strategies, 101
Achieved/ascribed characteristics, 219–220
Activities of Daily Living (ADL), 105
Adaptation, 27–28, 230–231
Adolescence
　person-context linkages, 196–197
　sequence patterns, transitions and analyzing, 177–178
　stressful life events, 143
　successful development, 231
Adulthood, transition to, 149-150, 173-174, 177–178
A.G.E., Project, 69–73, 78, 232–233
Age and age structuring, 66
　ageism, 42
　biases against older students/workers, 50–51
　challenges facing developmental science, 242–244
　cognitive meanings of age, 70–73
　cohort problem/effects, 122–125
　constraints, age-normative, 97
　cultural issues, 69–76
　gender, 66–67
　goal-setting, developmental, 96–101
　images and stereotypes, 101–104
　life periods, 104–106
　life spheres, 42–44, 68–69
　policy, social, 106–108
　social dimensions, 68
　socialization, age-bound life course as an institution of, 22
　standardized life course, 40
　stratification framework, 7–9, 11–12

[Age and age structuring]
　subjective age identification, 84–86
　successful aging, 227–234
　time budgets for the life course, new, 76
　types of age and time, 77–83
　See also Elderly population; Norms and expectations, age
"Age-Appropriate Behavior" (Wood), 90, 91
"Age Association Items" (Neugarten & Peterson), 101
Age Game, 70–72
Age Group Evaluation and Description (AGED) Inventory, 103
"Age Groups in American Society and the Rise of the Young-Old" (Neugarten), 104
Age or Need? Public Policies for Older People (Neugarten), 106
"Age Parameters" (Cameron), 105
Agency, human, 32–33, 218–223, 253
Aggregate change, 185
Aging Semantic Differential (ASD), 102
Aleatory change, 180–181
Ambient strain, 147
Analytic level, successful development at an, 233
Anterograde vs. retrograde methods, 160
Apparent simultaneity, 162
Archival and secondary data, analyzing, 169–172, 245
Assimilative coping strategies, 101
Attributes of the person, 24
Attrition and longitudinal frameworks, 155–156
Attunement model, 201–202
Averaging, 226

Barriers to interdisciplinary scholarship, 237–239 *See also* barriers to a *under* Flexible life course
Bean pole family structures, 42–43
Behavioral
  continuity, 205
  individuality, 17
Benefits, rules related to employer pensions and Social Security, 48
Berkeley Growth Study/Guidance Study, 139
Biases, 50–51, 152, 239
Bi-directionality, 211
Bio-ecological model, 35
Biographical choices, 223
Biographical level and rules/regulations, 22
Biological age, 78, 79–81
Biological constraints, 97
Birth cohort. *See* Cohort
Boundaries, cohort, 115–116

Canadian General Social Survey of 1990, 178
Canalization of development, the cultural, 75–76, 97
Cause and effect, 13-14, 145, 161-162, 200–204
Centre for Educational Research and Innovation, 60
Challenges facing developmental science
  age and age structuring, 242–244
  barriers to interdisciplinary scholarship, overcoming, 237–239
  biases, clarifying personal, 239
  change, measuring, 247–248
  chronologization, 253–254
  cohort, 249–251
  comparative method, 242
  continuity and discontinuity, 246–247
  data, gathering/organizing/analyzing, 244–245
  extending the study of specific life periods, 240
  institutionalization, 253–254
  interdependence, 251–252
  multi-level/multi-dimensional understandings, 235–237
  new era of developmental science, toward a, 254–255

[Challenges facing developmental science]
  research, finding meaning and significance in, 241–242
  social context:
    theoretical/methodological issues, 248–249
  socialization, 249
  social structure and human agency, 253
  standardization, 254
  successful development, 252
  trajectories through different life spheres, 246
  variability, 251
Change, social/individual
  challenges facing developmental science, 247–248
  cohort, 112–115
  conception of, 183–184
  empirically-driven measures and definitions, 184
  life-course sociology, 13–18
  measurement of, 185–191
  models of adult development, 179–181
  pace of, 112–114
  qualitative/quantitative change, 187–188
  social structure and human agency, 218–223
  time and the examination of, 162
  See also Transitions
Characterological continuity, 205-206
Children and stressful life events, 143
Chronological age, 81–82, 85
Chronologization, 22, 39–41, 71, 253–254
Classes of influence on an individual's development, 24–25
Classification of life events, 145–146, 148
Class-theoretical models, 220
Co-adaptation model, 201
Co-constructivist framework, 75
Cohort
  age-period-cohort problem and cohort effects, 122–125
  challenges facing developmental science, 249–251
  change, social/individual, 112–115
  generations, the problem of, 110–112
  history, linking lives and, 126–130, 134–135
  longitudinal frameworks, 157
  measuring and analyzing, 117–134

SUBJECT INDEX / 309

[Cohort]
  metaphors of cohort aging, 134
  societal significance of, 132–134
  trajectories of heterogeneity, 130–132
"*Cohort as a Concept in the Study of Social Change*" (Ryder), 112
Collaborative work, 238
Comparative age identification, 84–85
Comparative method, 216–218, 242
"*Comparisons of Age Groups*" (Cameron), 101
Compensation model, 28
Competence, planful, 58–59, 221–222
Conceptual level, successful development at a, 233
Concurrent criterion validity, 190
Configural Frequency Analysis, 187
Congeneries, context remaining a, 195
Constancy trajectory, 224
Constraints to developmental potential, 75, 97–98 *See also* barriers to a *under* Flexible life course
Constructivist view of human lives, 222
Construct validity, 190
Content validity, 190
Context in life-span developmental psychology, 31–33 *See also* Social context: theoretical/methodological issues
Contextualist approaches, 222
Contingency principle, 29
Contingent models of work, 56–57
Continuity
  challenges facing developmental science, 246–247
  concepts and measures, 179–184
  environmental change creating individual change, 205–206
  status passages, the life course as a series of, 21–22
  See also Change, Stability
Control, social, 22, 87
Control Agency Means-Ends in Adulthood Questionnaire, 99
Control cycles, 16
Control over development, 98–99
Convergent trajectory, 132, 224
Coping skills/strategies, 59, 101, 147
Corrective adaptivity, 230–231
Criterion validity, 190

Critical life events, 142–148
Critical periods, 199-200, 210
Cross-sectional analysis, 123, 217
Cross-sequential design, 124
Cultural scripts, 88, 222–223
Culture and age structuring
  A.G.E., Project, 69–73
  canalization of development, 75–76
  materials, cultural, 74
  states and their policies, 74
  successful development, 232
Cyclical time, 67

Data, gathering/organizing/analyzing, 149
  archival and secondary data, 169–172
  challenges facing developmental science, 244–245
  change, the measurement of, 185–191
  continuity and discontinuity, 179–184
  life-history calendars and matrices, 150–151
  prospective life course questions and future perspectives, 165–168
  retrospective *vs.* prospective strategies, 151–153, 162–165
  sharing data, 171–172, 244–245
  trajectories, analyzing, 172–179 *See also* Longitudinal frameworks; Research
Death in society, aggregate processes of life and, 112
Debates. *See* Propositions/controversies in the study of lives
Deficit-breeds-growth view of development, 28
Defined benefit/contribution plans, 48
Demographers, 88
Density, 138
Density of Future Events, 167–168
Dependability, 221
Dependency, transition to, 105–106
Dependent variables, 189
Developmental attunement model, 201–202
Developmental co-adaptation model, 201
Developmental frames, 199-200, 210

Developmental science, overview of, 1–4
  See also Challenges facing developmental science; Flexible life course; Propositions/controversies in the study of lives; *individual subject headings*
Developmental stability model, 179–180
Developmental transition model, 200
Dialectically articulated experiences, 111
Differences in development, individual, 27
Differential change, 185
Differential continuity, 182
Differential effects, 116
Differential *vs.* general approaches, 214–215
Discontinuity. *See* Continuity
Discrimination, age, 50–51
Distal *vs.* proximal
  contexts, 199
  events and outcomes, 13-15
Distinctive experience, 116
Divergent trajectory, 132, 224
Diversity, 226
Duration, 138
Dynamic latent variables, 190–191

Early crystallization model, 18–19
Ecology of human development, 33–38
Ecology of Human Development: Experiments by Nature and Design (Bronfenbrenner), 33
Economic considerations and age norms and expectations, 90
Economic sphere and flexible life course, 40
Education
  adult enrollment in higher education/education programs, 57–58
  age biases against older students, 50–51
  cognitive meanings of age, 72
  environment, a good school, 196
  gender, 46–47
  graduate programs, interdisciplinary, 238
  life-history calendars and matrices, 150
  longevity, increased, 54–55
  risk-taking, 60
  scholarships/tuition benefits/financial aid, 49

[Education]
  social responses to adult students, 51
  tracking, 49–50
  work and, 48–49
Effort, investment of, 24 *See also* Agency, human; competence, planful
Elderly population
  age biases against older students and workers, 50–51
  change, social/individual, 115
  divisiveness, social policy and age, 107–108
  stressful life events, 142–143 *See also* Age and age structuring
Elders Life Stress Inventory, 142
Employment. *See* Work
Endogenous casual system, 23
Environments, social, 194 *See also* Social context: theoretical/methodological issues
Equifinality, 29
Evaluative meanings of age, 73
Events, life, 19, 137, 142–148
Exosystem, 34
Expected Balance Scale (EBS), 167
Extreme non-normative sequencing, 177

Facts on Aging (FAQ) quizzes, 102
Failure, compensation of, 98
Fallacies in making causal attributions about life events, 146
Family, the
  age and age structuring, 68
  environment, 196–197
  flexible life course, 42–44, 60–61
  life-history calendars and matrices, 150
  perpetual parents, 96
  sequencing, 178–179
  successful development, 232
  time, family, 82
Fertility, 55
Field-theoretical models, 220
Flexible Goal Adjustment Scale, 100
Flexible life course
  barriers to a
    age biases against older students and workers, 50–51
    benefits, rules related to employer pensions and Social Security, 48

[Flexible life course]
  [barriers to a]
    gender, 46–48
    midlife squeeze, 52
    retirement, 51–52
    scholarships/tuition benefits/financial aid, 49
    social responses to adult students, 51
    state and public resistance to flexibility, 52–53
    tracking, educational and occupational, 49–50
    tripartition of the life course, 44–45
  characteristics that affect, individual
    competence, planful, 58–59
    employment status and occupational position, 61
    family responsibilities and support, 60–61
    motivation and coping skills, 59
    resources, time and financial, 60
    risk-taking, 59–60
  economic sphere, 40
  family, the, 42–44
  future, the, 61–64
  opportunities for, 53
    educational programs for adults and higher education, 57–58
    flextime work policies, 57
    lifetime models of work, erosion of, 56–57
    retirement, 55–56
    time budgets for adulthood, new, 54–55
    work in the last third of life, 55
  structural lag, 42 *See also* Propositions/controversies in the study of lives
Flextime work policies, 57
Formalistic *vs.* naturalistic approaches, 216
Fragmentation, scientific treatments and, 1, 237-240
Functional age, 79
Funding issues, 157, 238
Future time perspectives, 167–168

Gains and losses, 27, 28, 101–102
Gender
  age and age structuring, 66–67

[Gender]
  flexible life course, barriers to a, 46–48
  norms and expectations, age, 89–90
  sequencing, 177–179
Generalizability, 14, 156
General Social Survey, 148–149
General timetables, 95
General *vs.* differential approaches, 214–215
Generation concept, 109–110 *See also* Cohort
Geriatric Scale of Recent Life Events, 142
Geriatric Social Readjustment Rating Scale, 142
German Life History Study, 151
Gerophiles, 239
Gerophobes, 239
Goal-setting, age and developmental, 96–101
Graduate programs, interdisciplinary, 238
Group-level comparisons, 217–218
Growing Old (Cumming & Henry), 227
Guidance, individual sources of, 24
"Guide to Resources and Services" (ICPSR), 170
"Guide to the Data Resources" (Murray Research Center), 170

Health, physical, 232
Henry A. Murray Research Center, 170
Herero people, 72
Heterogeneity in life-course experiences. *See* Variability around life experiences
Historical events
  cohort, 126–130
  historical embeddedness, 31
  historical specificity, 134–135
  life-course sociology, 13–18
  longitudinal frameworks, 158
Holistic conceptions of human lives, 5–6, 35, 212–214, 235-237
Hong Kong, 73, 232
Hope Index, 167
Household composition and life-history calendars/matrices, 150
"Human Aging: Usual and Successful" (Rowe & Kahn), 228

312 / SUBJECT INDEX

Identification, subjective age, 84–86
Identity age, 84
Illnesses, life-threatening, 96
Images and stereotypes, age-related, 101–104
Independent variables, 189
Index of social change, 134
"*Index to the Guide*" (Murray Research Center), 170
Individualization, 22
Individuals and society, dynamic interplay between, 9–12, 75 *See also* Social context: theoretical/methodological issues
Informal age norms, 89
Institutionalization of lives, 22–23, 39–41, 71, 253–254
Integrative framework, 236–237
Intentional action, 222
Interactionist approaches, 35, 134, 222
Interdependence of lives, 15–16, 36, 90, 146–147, 251–252
Interdependent timetables, 95–96
Interest age, 84
Intergenerational equity, 107
Inter/intra-cohort differentiation, 116
Intermediate non-normative sequencing, 176–177
Interpersonal sanctions, 90
Inter-university Consortium for Political and Social Research (ICPSR), 170
Interviews, 163–164
Ireland, 232

Journals, interdisciplinary, 238

Kansas City Study of Adult Life, 89, 227–228
Kin and kin-like relationships, 43–44
!Kung people, 72

Labels and life periods, 104–105
Labor, emphasis on the system of, 22
  See also Work
Launch model, 200
Lawful organization of structures, 36–37

Life and death in society, aggregate processes of, 112
Life course principle, 146
Life-course sociology
  age-stratification framework, 7–9, 11–12
  classes of influence on an individual's development, 24–25
  concepts/parameters in the study of the life course, 137–149
  endogenous casual system, 23
  historical events and social change, 13–18
  individuals and society, dynamic interplay between, 9–12
  multiple levels of analysis, 23–24
  nature and rhythm of the life course, 39–41
  reorganizing the life course, 63 *See also* Data, gathering/organizing/analyzing; Flexible life course; Propositions/ controversies in the study of lives; *individual subject headings*
Life course/span/cycle, differences between, 5–6
Life Experiences Survey, 142
Life events, 137, 142–148
Life Events and Difficulties Schedule (LEDS), 147
Life Events Inventory, 142
Life Events Questionnaire, 142
Life-history calendars and matrices, 150–151
Life History Questionnaire, 151
Lifelong development and life-span developmental psychology, 26–27
Life periods, 104–106, 240
Life review, 162–165
Life-span developmental psychology
  adaptive tasks, three major, 27–28
  context in, 31–33
  equifinality, 29
  gains and losses, 28
  lifelong development, 26–27
  long view of individual development, 31
  multidimensional/multidirectional development, 28
  optimization, 29
  plasticity of the human organism, 29–30
  probabilistic epigenesis, 25
  traditional psychological model, 25

Life-span dynamics, 17–18
Life spheres, 68–69
Life-stage principle, 15, 116
Lifetime models of work, erosion of, 56–57
Liminality and cultural meanings, 76
Linear time, 67
Linked lives, the principle of, 15–16
LISREL-type models, 211
Lives Through the Years (Williams & Wirth), 227–228
Longevity, increased, 54–55, 114
Longitudinal frameworks
 advantages of, 159–160
 challenges facing developmental science, 245
 change, challenges to assumptions about the analysis of, 188–189
 data, 123, 157
 disadvantages of, 153–154
 expense of, 154
 exploratory procedures for use with, 190
 funding issues, 157
 new projects needed, 157–158
 real-time, 154
 recommendations for starting/conducting, 158–159
 risk, 209–210
 sampling, 156
 selection and attrition, 155–156
 single-subject methods, 218
 stimulation studies, 155
 time constraints, 156
 trajectories through different life spheres, 160–162
Losses and gains, 27, 28, 101–102
Louisville Older Persons Scale, 142

Macro-sociological perspective, 20–22
Macrosystem, 34
Maintenance and recovery, 27
Material security, 232
Matthew effect, 50, 130-132, 221, 223–227, 251
Mature self, 86
Mechanism oriented approaches, 215
Medicare/Medicaid, 113, 132
Mental maps, age-linked, 65
Mesosystem, 34

Metatheoretical frameworks of developmental science, 37, 135, 236
Methodological level and the problem of historical specificity, 135
Microgenetic intervention, 154–155, 218
Micro-sociological approaches, 21
Microsystem, 34
Middle School Family Survey Study, 166
Midlife squeeze, 52
Mobility, loss of, 232
Modeling, structural equation, 156
Moderating resources, 147–148
Motivation and coping skills, 59
Multidisciplinary research, 23–24, 28, 235–239

National Archive of Computerized Data on Aging (NACDA), 170
National Opinion Research Center (NORC), 148
Naturalistic *vs.* formalistic approaches, 216
Nature-nurture question, 31
Need-based approach to social policies, 106–107
Neighborhood environment, 197
Nested social contexts, 211
Network models, 211–212
"*Normative Attitudes Toward the Aged Role*" (Bultena & Wood), 90–91
Normative sequencing, 176
Norms and expectations, age
 ambiguity, 86
 gender, 89–90
 informal age norms, 89
 Kansas City Study of Adult Life, 89
 proscriptions/prescriptions, 87–88
 psychology, the field of, 87
 research instruments, additional, 90–91
 role differentiation, 87–88
 statistical regularity, 87
 transition patterns/norms, change in, 88
 unresolved issues and new directions for research, 91–96
Norwegian Life History Study, 151
Novel outcomes and processes, 215–216

314 / SUBJECT INDEX

Obstacles in the environment, encountering, 24 See also barriers to a under Flexible life course
"Onset of Adult Phases" (Drevenstedt), 105
Ontogenetic reductionism, 32
Opportunities available to the person, 24, 90 See also opportunities for under Flexible life course
Optimization, 29
Orderly change model, 179–180
Organismic-structuralist approaches, 222
Other-perceived ages, 85
Outcome- vs. process-oriented approaches, 215–216

Parents, perpetual, 96 See also Family, the
Pattern analysis, 213–214
Peer group environment, 197
Pensions, 48
"Perceptions of Adults" (Hickly & Kalish), 101
PERI Life Events Scale, 142
Personal attribute models, 220
Personality attributes and age, 66
Personal timetables, 95
Person-context linkages, 216 See also Social context: theoretical/methodological issues
Person- vs. variable-oriented approaches, 212–214
"Phases of Adulthood" (Neugarten & Peterson), 104
Plasticity of development, 18, 27, 29–30
Pleasant and Unpleasant Events Schedules, 143
Policy, social, 22, 106–108
Popular culture and cohort, 134
Population Association of America, 107
Positive outcomes resulting from life crises, 144–145
Post-fordism, 41
Postnatal age, 77
Predictability, 72–73
Prediction, 37
Predictive criterion validity, 190
Prescriptions/proscriptions, age-linked, 87–88
Preventive adaptivity, 230–231

Prior experiences, 23
Proactivity, 230
Probabilistic epigenesis, 25
Process-person-context (PPC), 34–35
Process-person-context-time approach (PPCT), 35
Process- vs. outcome-oriented approaches, 215–216
Program on Age and Structural Change (PASC), 253
Project A.G.E., 69–73, 78, 232–233
Propositions/controversies in the study of lives
  debates on nature and rhythm of life, 39-41
  early crystallization model, 18–19
  ecology of human development, 33-38
  life-course sociology, 7–25
  life-course flexibility, 42–64
  life-span developmental psychology, 25–33
  overview, 5–6
  regulations/rules ordering key dimensions of life, 22–23
  triaxial view of human lives, 38–39
Proscriptions/prescriptions, age-linked, 87–88
Prospective life course questions, 164–168
Prototyping, 226
Proximal vs. distal
  contexts, 199
  events and outcomes, 13-15
Psychological age, 78
Psychosocial disturbance and stressful life events, 144
Public resistance to flexibility, 52–53
Publishing norms, 238

Qualitative/quantitative research on the life course, 211–212
Quantitative/qualitative change, 187–188
Quotidian strain, 147

Random change model, 179–180
Raw gain score, 186
Real-time longitudinal frameworks, 154

SUBJECT INDEX / 315

Recall, accuracy and precision of, 152
Reciprocity, 17, 35, 195-204
Reference group, 134
Regularity, 27, 87, 88, 139
Regulations/rules ordering key dimensions of life, 22-23
Relative age identification, 84-85
Reliability, 173, 190-191
Reminiscence and the life review, 162-165
Research
  challenges facing developmental science, 237-239, 241-242
  change, social/individual, 185-191
  comparative method, 216-218, 242
  cross-sectional analyses, 123, 217
  cross-sequential design, 124
  dynamic quantitative analyses of lives, 211
  empirically-driven measures and definitions, 184
  formalistic vs. naturalistic approaches, 216
  general vs. differential approaches, 214-215
  LISREL-type models, 211
  multidisciplinary, 23-24, 28, 235-237
  nested social contexts, 211
  network models, 211-212
  norms and expectations, age, 90-96
  outcome- vs. process-oriented approaches, 215-216
  person-context linkages, 216
  social context, 198-199
  typological approaches, widespread use of, 225-226
  variable- vs. person-oriented approaches, 212-214 See also Data, gathering/organizing/analyzing; Longitudinal frameworks
Residence and life-history calendars and matrices, 150
Residualized gain score, 186-187
Resilience, 27
Resources, time and financial, 60
Retirement, 51-52, 55-56, 105
Retraining programs, 61
Retrograde vs. anterograde methods, 160
Retrospective self, 86

Retrospective studies, 151-153, 162-165
  See also Longitudinal frameworks; Research
Revision, life, 164
Risk, developmental
  flexible life course and aversion to risk-taking, 59-60
  individuals and social contexts, 207-211
  longitudinal frameworks, 160-161
Role differentiation, 87-88
Role strain, 147
Role transitions, 138-139
Rules/regulations ordering key dimensions of life, 22-23

Sampling in longitudinal frameworks, 156
Sanctions, interpersonal, 90
Schedule of Recent Events, 142-143
Scholarships, 49
School environment, 49-51, 57-58, 199
Secondary and archival data, analyzing, 169-172, 245
Selection and longitudinal frameworks, 155-156
Selective optimization with compensation (SOC), 29
Selectivity, management of, 98
Self-confidence, 221
Self-efficacy, 222
Self-selection into specific contexts, 145, 197-198, 210
Sensitive periods, 199-200, 210
Sequencing, 90, 138, 176-179
Sharing data, 171-172, 244-245
Significance, tension between statistical and substantive, 188
Simple difference scores, 186, 187
Single-authored publications, 238
Single-subject microgenetic/longitudinal methods, 218
Situational imperatives, 16
Size and composition, cohort, 112-113, 133
Small Life Events Scale, 143
Social address models, 220
Social age, 78
Social context: theoretical/methodological issues
  barriers to studying, 203-204

[Social context: theoretical/methodological issues]
challenges facing developmental science, 248–249
critical period, 199
developmental attunement model, 201–202
developmental co-adaptation model, 201
developmental frame, 199
developmental transition model, 200
dynamically/systematically organized processes, 194–196
environmental change creating individual change, 204–207
functionally unimportant, 194
future research directions, 198–199
lack of attention paid to, 193–194, 199–200, 202–203
launch model, 200
nested social contexts, 211
organized but passive, 194
powerful but unorganized, 194
risk, individuals/contexts and developmental, 207–211
self-selection into specific contexts, 197–198
stressful life events, 148
successful development, 231
weather model of co-development, 200–201
Social control, 22, 87
Social field and cognitive meanings of age, 72–73
Social historical response to the problem of historical specificity, 135
Sociality, 232
Socialization, 22, 24, 249
Social network analysis, 211–212
Social niche models, 220
Social participation, age as a criterion for, 73
Social phenomena, principles of generations as, 111
Social policy, 22, 106–108
Social Readjustment Rating Scale, 142
Social science theory, 134
Social Security, 48, 113, 132
Social stratification, 219–220
Social structure, 32–33, 218–223, 253

Social time, 82
Social Time Perspective (STP), 168
Societal significance of cohort, 132–134
Societal well-being, 148–149
Sociological reductionism, 32
Socio-structural constraints, 97
Spacing, 138
Spatially proximal environments, 199
Specialization, academic/methodological, 1, 237–240
Specialized timetables, 95
Spurious phenomenon model, 28
Stability, 184, 206, 219
Stability model, 179–180
Staged life course, 73
Standardized Life Events and Difficulties Interview, The (SL), 147
Standardized lives, 39–41, 254
Stanford-Terman Study, 174
State, the
 culture and age structuring, 74
 flexibility, resistance to, 52–53
 life course, structuring the, 23
 policy, social, 22, 106–108
Statistical and substantive significance, tension between, 188
Statistical regularity, 87
Statistical strategies and cohort effects, 124
Status passages, life course as a series of, 21–22
Stereotypes and images, age-related, 101–104
Stimulation studies, 155
Stratification, age/social, 7–9, 11–12, 219–220
Stressful life events, 142–148
Structural characteristics of networks and their relationships, 212
Structural continuity, 182
Structural equation modeling, 156
Structural lag, 10, 41–42
Structural level and rules/regulations, 22
Study of lives, overview of, 1–4 *See also*
 Challenges facing developmental science; Flexible life course; Propositions/controversies in the study of lives; *individual subject headings*
Substitutability principle, 29

SUBJECT INDEX / 317

Successful development, 227–234, 252
Support, individual sources of, 24
Suppression model, 28
Survey of Income and Program Participation (SIPP), 175
Synchrony, 90

Technological change, 114, 118–119
Temporary Assistance for Needy Families (TANF), 132
Tenaciousness of Goal Pursuit Scale, 99, 100
Terman Longitudinal Study, 174
Third variable effects, 161
Time
  budgets, new, 54–55, 76
  change, examination of, 162
  describing and analyzing lives, 138
  essential for understanding the life course, 23
  longitudinal frameworks, 156
  social context and temporally proximal influences, 199
  temporality, 17, 22, 147, 162
  timetables, general/specialized/personal/ interdependent, 95–96
  types of, 82-83
Timing, principle of, 15, 24
Total age, 77
Tracking, educational and occupational, 49–50
Traditions, cultural, 74
Traits predicting behavior, 205–206
Trajectories through different life spheres
  challenges facing developmental science, 246
  chronologized/institutionalized/ standardized, 40
  data, gathering/organizing/analyzing, 172–179
  heterogeneity, cohorts and trajectories of, 130–132
  longitudinal frameworks, 160–162
  Matthew effect, 224
  multiple and interdependent trajectories, 19, 137
Transitions
  defining, 19
  to dependency, 105–106

[Transitions]
  ecological, 35
  inequality and, 206
  marriage to divorce, 137–138
  model, developmental transition, 200
  role, 138–139
  sequence patterns, analyzing, 177 *See also* Change, social/individual
Triaxial view of human lives, 38–39
Trigger effect, 132
Trigger-event trajectory, 224
Tripartition of the life course, 42–45
Troublesome Creek (documentary), 16
Tuition benefits, 49
Turning points, 139–142
Typological approaches, widespread use of, 225–226

Universal change, 185
Unrelated phenomenon model, 28
Urbanization, 114
U-shaped trajectory, 224

Validity, 173, 190-191
Variability around life experiences
  challenges facing developmental science, 251
  cohorts, 123–124, 130–132
  Matthew effect, 223–227
  plasticity of development, 18
  Project A.G.E., 72–73
  transitions, 139
Variable- *vs.* person-oriented approaches, 212–214

Waged life course, 72–73
Weather model of co-development, 200–201
"*What is a Cohort and Why*" (Rosow), 115
Within-person comparisons, 218
Work
  age biases against older workers, 51
  benefits, rules related to employer pensions and Social Security, 48

[Work]
  education and, 48–49
  employment status and pursuit of other experiences, 61
  flextime work policies, 57
  gender, 46–47
  labor, emphasis on the system of, 22
  in the last third of life, 55
  life-history calendars and matrices, 150
  lifetime models of work, erosion of, 56–57

[Work]
  retirement, 51–52, 55–56, 105
  tracking, 49–50

Young adulthood, 111, 115, *See also* Adolescence; Adulthood, transition to;
"*Young-Old and the Age-Irrelevant Society*" (Neugarten), 104

Zeitgeist, 110

About the Author

Richard A. Settersten, Jr. is Assistant Professor and Director of Graduate Study in Sociology at Case Western Reserve University. Professor Settersten received his Ph.D. in Human Development and Social Policy from Northwestern University. Before moving to Case Western Reserve University, he held fellowships at the Institute for Policy Research at Northwestern University and the Max Planck Institute for Human Development and Education in Berlin, Germany. One strand of his recent research has been devoted to social timetables, and to the ways in which behaviors and self-perceptions are regulated by age. Another strand of his research has been devoted to the ways in which human lives are structured by social contexts such as schools, neighborhoods, peer groups, families, work organizations, the state and its policies, and even history itself.

Other Titles in the
SOCIETY AND AGING SERIES
Jon Hendricks, Series Editor

Aging Public Policy: Bonding the Generations (2nd Ed.)
Theodore H. Koff and Richard W. Park

Older Adults with Developmental Disabilities
Claire M. Lavin and Kenneth J. Doka

Rural Health and Aging Research:
Theory, Methods and Practical Applications
Wilbert M. Gesler, Donna J. Rabiner, Gordon H. DeFriese, and the North Carolina Rural Aging Program

Health & Economic Status of Older Women:
Research Issues and Data Sources
A. Regula Herzog, Karen C. Holden and Mildred M. Seltzer

Special Research Methods for Gerontology
M. Powell Lawton and A. Regula Herzog

The Old Age Challenge to the Biomedical Model:
Paradigm Strain and Health Policy
Charles F. Longino, Jr. and John W. Murphy

Surviving Dependence: Voices of African American Elders
Mary M. Ball and Frank J. Whittington

Staying Put: Adapting the Places Instead of the People
Susan Lanspery and Joan Hyde

Defining Acts: Aging as Drama, *Robert Kastenbaum*

Dorian Graying: Is Youth the Only Thing Worth Having?
Robert Kastenbaum